'Political leadership is an enduringly fascina
the grasp of normal political science. This b
hensive and highly accessible. Enlivened ar
it provides a valuable introductory text th
anyone interested in leadership.'

– **John Kane**, *Griffith University, Australia*

'This book is an excellent addition to the complex and often disparate field of political leadership. Students and researchers will benefit from the expert way Matthew Laing has synthesised a vast array of theories and approaches into a really accessible and informative book. When political leadership is rightly under great scrutiny, this is a very welcome and timely introductory publication.'

– **Mark Bennister**, *University of Lincoln, UK*

'Laing provides clarity and direction to the study of political leadership. He completes his systematic analysis of the field's most important topics with informative and attention-grabbing case studies. This textbook will be a benefit in the classroom for both students and professors.'

– **Scott Cook**, *Longwood University, USA*

'This is a valuable new contribution to leadership studies. Clearly written and approachable, its great virtue is its synoptic approach, exploring the psychological, moral, and institutional dimensions of political leadership and above all the formidable challenge of good leadership in modern democracies.'

– **Haig Patapan**, *Griffith University, Australia*

'*Political Leadership* is a great and much needed contribution to the field. This comprehensive book discusses the art of political leadership from different disciplinary perspectives and covers the various roles political leaders fulfil, making it a great textbook for introductory and advanced courses on the topic. Sensitive to the current times, it also – and quite uniquely – covers both democratic and autocratic leadership in one book.'

– **Femke van Esch**, *Utrecht University, the Netherlands*

POLITICAL LEADERSHIP

AN INTRODUCTION

MATTHEW LAING

macmillan international HIGHER EDUCATION

RED GLOBE PRESS

First published 2021 by

RED GLOBE PRESS

Red Globe Press in the UK is an imprint of Macmillan Education Limited, registered in England, company number 01755588, of 4 Crinan Street, London, N1 9XW.

Red Globe Press® is a registered trademark in the United States, the United Kingdom, Europe and other countries.

ISBN 978-1-352-01131-9 hardback

ISBN 978-1-352-00772-5 paperback

Printed and bound by CPI Group (UK) Ltd, Croydon, CR0 4YY

A catalogue record for this book is available from the British Library.

A catalog record for this book is available from the Library of Congress.

MIX
Paper from responsible sources
FSC® C013604

For Paul 't Hart, who studies leadership,
and my mother, who practises it.

CONTENTS

List of Figures ix
List of Tables x

1 **Introduction and Key Concepts** **1**
The paradox of leadership 2
Why study political leadership? 5
Defining leadership 8
Defining 'political' leadership 12
Defining 'good' political leadership 15

2 **Power, Authority, Followers and Elites** **21**
Power 21
Authority 27
Followers 38
Elites 42

3 **Philosophy, Legitimacy and Morality** **48**
The legitimacy of leaders 49
The role of leaders 54
The morality of leadership 62

4 **Democrats and Dictators** **76**
Comparing systems 77
The challenges of autocratic rule 87
The challenges of democratic rule 93

5 **Biology, Culture and Gender** **102**
Biology and evolution 103
Anthropology and culture 110
Gender and feminism 119

6 **Biography, Psychology and Personality** **129**
Biography 130
Psychology and personality 133

7 Context, Institutions and Change **155**
Context and circumstance 156
Institutional analysis 170

8 Decisions, Policy and Advice **178**
The governing role 179
Making decisions 182
Decision-making structures 191
Managing the policy process 194
The process in action 202

9 Persuasion, Rhetoric and Negotiation **206**
Rhetoric 206
Negotiation 219

10 Contemporary Trends and Challenges **231**
Presidentialization 232
Populism 234
Polarization 239
Democracy and leadership 240
Symbolism 246
Conclusion 247

References 250
Index 289

LIST OF FIGURES

1.1	Purported depiction of Gilgamesh, circa 700 BCE	2
1.2	Suharto in 1993*	18
2.1	A heuristic model of leaders, followers and the power relationships between them	22
2.2	Margaret Thatcher in 1983*	28
2.3	Juan and Eva Perón around 1948*	36
2.4	Haile Selassie in 1970*	44
3.1	Jeannette Rankin, US Congresswoman and pacifist	69
3.2	Harry Truman in 1945*	72
4.1	Wim Kok in 1994*	84
4.2	Thomas Sankara in 1987*	90
4.3	Lee Kuan Yew in 1968*	98
5.1	Slobodan Milošević in 1994*	106
5.2	Simón Bolívar*	116
5.3	Statue of Hatshepsut	119
5.4	Violetta Chamorro in 1990*	126
6.1	Mustafa Kemal Atatürk*	134
6.2	Richard Nixon in 1973*	142
6.3	Saddam Hussein*	152
7.1	Lech Wałęsa in 1991*	162
7.2	Dowager Cixi in 1900*	168
7.3	János Kádár in 1962*	174
8.1	Golda Meir in 1973*	180
8.2	Anthony Eden*	188
8.3	Guy Mollet*	188
8.4	Julius Nyerere in 1965*	200
9.1	Barbara Jordan in 1976	209
9.2	Gamal Abdel Nasser*	220
9.3	Vallabhbhai Patel in 1939*	228
10.1	Evo Morales in 2006*	236
10.2	Jacinda Ardern in 2019	243
10.3	Benazir Bhutto in 1995*	244

*Also features as a case study.

LIST OF TABLES

1.1 The tasks of leaders and managers 11
2.1 Rating authority types from positional to personal 30
4.1 Classifications of autocratic regimes 78
4.2 Classifications of democratic regimes 80
4.3 Patterns of executive dominance across democracies 82
5.1 Stogdill's 15 'universal' leadership traits 110
6.1 Barber's personality matrix from *The Presidential Character* (1992) 141
6.2 Core leadership personality traits from five studies 145
6.3 The Five Factor Model and its personality implications 146
6.4 Hermann's leadership styles 150
7.1 Robert House's path-goal leadership style matrix 161
7.2 Leader authority in political time 170

1 INTRODUCTION AND KEY CONCEPTS

Chapter Outline

- Why is political leadership interesting and why should we study it? Can it be even be taught?
- How do we define leadership, and what should we include or exclude when discussing it?
- How do *leadership* and *management* differ?
- What makes specifically *political* leadership unique? How closely related is it to leadership in other domains?
- Is there such a thing as *good* leadership? If so, how would we assess it?

Greater than other kings, lofty in stature, a hero born in Uruk, a wild and rampaging bull was he. He leads forth at the front, the leader; he brings up the rear, a trusted companion. He is a great net who protects his men, a thrashing flood-wave capable of devastating even walls of stone.

The Epic of Gilgamesh, c.2100 BCE

He is the very definition of the American success story, setting the standards of excellence in his business endeavors, and now, for the United States of America... he has always dreamed big and pushed the boundaries of what is possible his entire career, devoting his life to building business, jobs and the American Dream.

Donald Trump Campaign Website, 2020 CE

The paradox of leadership

The oldest surviving work of literature known is the *Epic of Gilgamesh.* Written on clay tablets in Akkadian cuneiform, it is the story of Gilgamesh (Figure 1.1), a king of the ancient Sumerian civilization who lived around 2700 BCE, chronicling the exploits of his rule and his search for eternal life. It is a work of mythology, propaganda and history that tells us much about society and belief in ancient Mesopotamia.

It is telling that our oldest known story is about a political leader. And it is telling too, as evidenced in the excerpt above from Donald Trump's 2020 campaign website, that despite the intervening four millennia of human history, the stories of leadership we try to tell have perhaps little changed.

Indeed, a civilization's history has long gone hand-in-hand with the stories of its leadership. For many the Roman Empire is almost synonymous with the biographies of Julius Caesar, Augustus or Nero. Chinese and British history are divided up into periods named for the monarchs who ruled – we speak of the Georgian, Victorian and Edwardian eras in Great Britain, or the Song, Tang and Qing dynasties in China. Political leaders become the foremost symbols of their states, and their actions and personalities often

Figure 1.1 Purported depiction of Gilgamesh, circa 700 BCE

overshadow the complex happenings in the places they ruled over. From the distant echoes of history, nearly all have forgotten the story of the Macedonian Empire and its golden era in the third century BCE. But most people will still know the name and deeds of Alexander the Great, that empire's greatest leader.

Political leaders are thus nothing new. They are a seemingly ubiquitous part of human society. They have been revered and celebrated, loathed and despised, or just tolerated and obeyed, throughout recorded history. We have been discussing, debating and trying to understand political leadership for just as long. In today's world, leaders are seemingly no less central to contemporary political and social life than they were in the times of the ancients. For most people, not a day will go by without some news, thought or discussion of what their political leaders are doing, whether in their own region or elsewhere. Indeed, the rise of mass media has arguably made the melodrama of political leadership even more omnipresent in our daily lives.

Yet despite our abiding love affair with political leadership, it is almost laughable how little we can say we know for sure about it. Go to any bookstore and browse the non-fiction or self-help shelves – there will be innumerable volumes dedicated to leadership and biographies of leaders from all manner of human endeavour. Yet as any practitioner of leadership knows, one can no more read a how-to book on leadership and become a great leader any more than one can learn from a book how to get rich quick, paint a masterpiece or find true love.

It's what prompted leadership scholar James MacGregor Burns to state: "Leadership is one of the most observed and least understood phenomena on earth" (1978: 2). It seems that for all the ink spilled on leadership over the millennia, we no more know the secret of being a great political leader than we do the meaning of life.

I would proffer several reasons for this. The first is because at its core, leadership is about social relationships and interactions between people. It is an emergent property of social relations that inevitably appears in some form when we live and/or work in groups. As such it will always be beholden to the foibles and follies of human beings. Understanding political leadership is thus in large part about understanding human nature – something that routinely defies pure rationality, reliable prediction or deliberate engineering. And whilst we have created more sophisticated political systems and leadership structures over time, and we pass those systems on to our descendants, the occupants of those systems – human beings – do not change quite so readily or permanently. The wisdom and instincts of those who have led well are not automatically passed on to those who come after – they must be learned from scratch, and usually by experience, by each new generation. So while long experience has taught us to create robust political systems with checks on our leaders to prevent them from monopolizing power and becoming tyrants, we have not changed the nature of human ambition and its hunger for power quite so easily, nor eliminated the instinctive desire, apathy, anger or fear amongst people that sometimes allows tyrants to take power.

Secondly, what constitutes 'good' political leadership is always in flux. The demands on a leader change from era to era, even week to week. The evolution of technology, social values, public expectations, policy problems and political systems means that what worked for great leaders a century or even a decade ago may not pass muster today. Because of this, it's often very difficult to establish any hard and fast 'laws' of leadership, despite many popular self-help books that promise otherwise. For each 'rule' or 'principle' of good leadership you might find, there will be leaders who ignore them yet are effective and beloved by followers regardless. Indeed, some of the most successful political leaders of recent decades seemingly owe much of their appeal to a willingness to defy convention and break rules.

Not only this, but our judgment of leaders and their actions may shift over time. Values and morality change, and so too will the estimation of leaders in the past. Moreover, the ramifications of a leader's words or actions may not be fully realized until many years after their departure, if at all. Some leaders once widely admired and emulated by successive generations have fallen from favour and are even considered pariahs today.

Thirdly, context and timing create leaders just as much as leaders create themselves. History is littered with the footnotes of aspirants who tried and failed to achieve the highest office, many of whom were some of the most talented figures of their day. Though an effective leader may recognize the opportunities created by circumstance and turn them to their advantage, usually they cannot create those fortuitous opportunities from thin air. And of those who have reached the political apex, many saw their rule was circumscribed or cut short by external events. Wars, natural disasters, economic crises, and social change have bested and brought down even the most capable of political leaders. Yet by the same token, many unremarkable leadership prospects have been carried aloft by chance developments not of their own making.

Fourthly, as Cronin and Genovese describe, political leadership is fundamentally paradoxical in its nature, making rules for leading hard to establish. We want leaders to be confident and work hard to make our lives better, yet we also want them to be humble, earnest, and selfless. We want our leaders to see the big picture and inspire us with their ideas yet be practical and get things done quickly. We want our leaders to be extraordinary and talented people with charisma and presence, yet at the same time should have the common touch and feel relatable to the average citizen (Cronin & Genovese 2012). There are many more such paradoxes and there is no 'right' way to resolve them. No leader can be all things to all people, and thus all leaders must find a workable balance between these paradoxical demands that best suits their circumstances and style.

And finally, though we have thousands of biographies chronicling good and bad leaders and can theorize endlessly about what makes for effective leadership, experience seems to tell us that you cannot teach a person to be a good leader from history and theory alone. Partly it is because so much of effective leadership is experiential learning. Read a biography of a leader that inspires you – you will quickly see that part of their later greatness rested on skills and relationships developed in their earlier lives, as well as learning from early setbacks or mistakes. Moreover, much of leadership is rooted in intangible qualities. How a person thinks, remembers and understands the world can be hugely consequential for decision-making and judgment, and yet very hard to synthetically emulate or instil in others. Even inborn traits, such as how a person looks, sounds, and gesticulates can have a bearing on how effective they are at persuading and communicating with others. There are many aspects of leadership that seemingly operate on a deeply instinctive level that are almost impossible to clearly elucidate, much less learn.

One doesn't have to look far to find the puzzles of leadership and its seeming determination to avoid predictability. The 2016 match-up between Hillary Clinton and Donald Trump for the United States presidency is one of the clearest-cut contemporary examples of why trying to say anything definite about political leadership can be so frustrating. At the time of her run, Hillary Clinton was one of the most experienced political leaders in the United States with most of her life spent in politics. Her 2016 presidential campaign was one of the most thoroughly organized and resourced in history. Clinton herself had spent many years preparing, studying past examples and refining her technique from previous political campaigns (including a failed run for the Democratic nomination in 2008, and her husband's two presidential campaigns in 1992 and 1996). Donald Trump was by comparison a political novice with a campaign that became notorious for its chaos, disorganization and staff turnover. His speeches were infamous for their unpolished and extemporaneous style, and he consciously broke or ignored most of the accepted conventions of 'good' leadership practice, delighting and outraging the media and public in equal measure.

Trump flummoxed just about every credible pundit and pollster by winning the presidency that year. Yet experts were hardly grievously deluded in their analysis – previous candidates with similar styles to Trump had made runs at politics before and lost, often badly. Trump himself had made tilts at the presidency for decades and had never achieved anything near the cut-through with the public that he did in 2016. Moreover, the rule-breaking leadership style that won him so much support during the election campaign seemed much less effective for governing, as within months of taking office the president was struggling to build support for his policies, pass promised legislation, and keep his party together – indeed, the 'laws' of leadership he'd flouted so successfully in 2016 had seemingly returned with a vengeance by 2017 and ultimately his re-election defeat in 2020.

Why study political leadership?

So, if we seemingly can be sure of so little, and there is so much we cannot teach, why bother reading a book on political leadership?

Although we cannot really teach it, we can still understand and analyse it. Leadership is more art than science, and though you cannot directly teach someone to be a great artist, many great artists went to art school or apprenticed to great artists and learned the techniques and principles that would later underpin their own greatness. Although no great leader I know of got to where they were by simply following a textbook on leadership, many learned principles, spotted opportunities, refined techniques, avoided mistakes and got inspired by learning from leaders in the past and present. And while no leader is taught how to be effective from theory alone, all leadership is made more effective through learning.

Though studying political leadership is subject to significant (and sometimes quite frustrating) methodological constraints, it does not mean that there can be no rigour to our approach. Indeed, throughout the many scholarly fields traversed in this book are innumerable efforts to creatively apply quantitative and qualitative methods to explain leadership phenomena. Subsequently developed models of leadership, even if they are not completely predictive and do not satisfy the most demanding tests of causality, are nevertheless still capable of providing satisfying explanations (Dowding 2016: 45–67). Moreover, they are *heuristically* very valuable, that is to say, they serve as a rule-of-thumb or way of looking at leadership that helps guide our thinking towards areas that promote understanding, even if they have not uncovered all the relevant variables and causal mechanisms that might have a bearing on an outcome.

And though political leadership seemingly rejects immutable rules or consistent prediction, there is much we do know about leadership that is *generally* true, and has been for millennia. Many of the principles of rhetoric, for example, that were familiar and taught by the Greeks and Romans are just as relevant today as they were millennia ago. Because the *practice* of political leadership is so old and so much of it is rooted in the human condition, there is a surprising amount that can be gleaned from history, as leaders of the past had to grapple with much the same dilemmas of leadership as their contemporary counterparts.

Finally, studying leadership is still as essential to understanding politics today as it was in the time of the pharaohs and satraps. Even in modern, mature democracies, it is political leaders who make decisions, shape opinion, build coalitions and set agendas that define our political world more than any other entity. While studying political theory, political philosophy and systems of government is foundational to understanding what we hope politics *should be*, studying political leaders and leadership is key to understanding how politics *actually is*. It is political leaders who breathe life, effect change and create dynamism in politics.

As such, this book is designed to furnish the reader with a toolkit for understanding and perhaps even practicing political leadership. It reaches into the past and into the present day to bring together the essential wisdom and recurring madness of political leadership. It collates the many theories from many disciplines that have tried to explain political leadership, and each in their own way offers glimmers of insight into this most complex and ancient of human endeavours.

To best make sense of this diverse field, my exploration of political leadership is divided across four key areas – *foundations* of political leadership, *philosophy* of political leadership, *understanding* political leadership and *practicing* political leadership.

Foundations of political leadership are the core concepts and mechanisms required to understand leadership generally and political leadership specifically. The remainder of this chapter will look at how to define political leadership and some of the most elementary distinctions we make when discussing it. Chapter 2 explores power, authority, followers and elites – four crucial concepts to understanding the relationship between leaders and the led, and the structures of society that enable and constrain political leadership.

Philosophy of political leadership explores what constitutes the legitimate role and normative expectations of political leadership within our society. Chapter 3 covers a representative sample of projects within political philosophy concerning the legitimacy, morality and proper role of political leadership. Chapter 4 discusses the role and practice of leadership in application, focusing on the differences and similarities between democratic and autocratic systems.

Understanding political leadership looks at the different scholarly disciplines that have attempted to explain the behaviour of leaders and followers. Chapter 5 covers the biological, cultural and gender lenses, and how environmental and evolutionary factors help explain leadership outcomes. Chapter 6 covers the rich fields of psychology, personality and biographical studies that look to unpack leaders as unique individuals and explain what makes them tick. Chapter 7 attends to the external forces that shape a leader's context – temporal, historical and institutional factors – which can greatly shape the prospects of a leader and provide a counterpoint to individual-centric explorations of leadership.

Finally, **practicing political leadership** examines what constitutes the essential skills and core tasks of leadership in practice. Chapter 8 covers political leaders as decision-makers and the formal powers of their role as the managers of a government, political institution or movement. Chapter 9 looks at the softer powers of rhetoric, persuasion, agenda-setting and negotiation, all of which are essential tools of a political leader but constitute the more informal levers of leadership.

In the final chapter, I draw out some of the consistent threads of political leadership that can be gleaned by studying it, whilst offering some of the major challenges political leadership faces in the twenty-first century.

Throughout the book, I attempt to draw out ideas and illustrate concepts through short case studies of political leaders from a variety of cultures, political systems and backgrounds. We have the luxury of studying different dimensions of political leadership in splendid isolation within the confines of a textbook, but they all collide together rather messily in the lived reality. Precisely disentangling each factor and quantifying its contribution to an outcome are rarely possible, yet a "good description is better than bad explanation" (King et al. 1994: 45). Case studies of leaders are invaluable descriptive exercises that, due to issues of access and observation, are often the only empirical building blocks we have for constructing models and theories of political leadership and testing their validity.

Defining leadership

Leadership has many definitions. As Ralph Stogdill opines in his encyclopaedic *Handbook of Leadership*, "there are almost as many different definitions of leadership as there are persons who have attempted to define the concept" (1974: 7). There is no universally accepted or clearly superior definition of leadership despite the innumerable studies that have attempted to create one (Bennis & Nanus 1985: 4). Instinctively though, everyone has a sense of what leadership is and what it looks like, even if people differ greatly on the traits and styles of leadership they find desirable.

At its core, leadership involves at least three components: influence, followers and goals. Leadership at its simplest is about influencing others (i.e., followers) purposively to think, feel or act in some way (i.e., achieve goals). There cannot be leadership in the absence of followers or purpose. Peter Northouse in *Leadership: Theory and Practice* provides a common-sense definition, which is as good as any other and summarizes the above:

> Leadership is a process whereby an individual influences a group of individuals to achieve a common goal. (Northouse 2016: 7)

However, there are a great many complexities, caveats and potential exceptions that plague even this simple definition. For example:

Do only *individuals* lead? Yes and no. Leadership is commonly exercised through groups of leaders (like committees, cabinets, parliaments, juntas) or shared between individuals in various arrangements. And in recent decades there has been an increasing interest in moving away from individualistic models of leadership and focusing more instead on networks or 'plural leadership' in which many individuals are involved (Masciulli & Knight 2009: 102–105; Sergi, Denis & Langley 2016). In doing so, leadership becomes conceptualized as a *process* of governance rather than a relationship between an individual and their followers. Distributed, collective ideals of leadership have been advocated as important for democratic practice and creating political structures that have plenty of *leadership* but not necessarily individual *leaders* (Raelin 2011).

Yet even in collective leadership settings it is usually particular individuals who in practice wield significantly more influence and 'lead' within those structures, even though it may not be obvious from the outside. Historical experiments with 'leaderless' movements and parties have oft proven to be deceptive, the result being the emergence of de facto structures of authority. The idea of 'leaderless' or non-hierarchical rule has been stridently critiqued as a dangerous fantasy by those who have seen it fail within the socialist (Michels 1911), feminist (Freeman 1972), and anarchist (Bufe 1998) movements. Even the oft-romanticized consuls of the Roman Republic – co-leaders who legally shared executive power exactly equally – in practice evolved a system of alternating who acted as the 'lead' consul on a monthly basis.

Must leadership work towards common goals? Some have stipulated that any reasonable definition of leadership must state that it works to achieve the goals of followers and the group. Certainly, most leadership is built on this premise – people generally follow leaders because they believe that it is to their benefit and they can better achieve their own goals by doing so. Leadership helps unlock the potential of groups to coordinate action and resources, the outcomes of which provide returns to group members.

But does all leadership do this? Many potentates have ascended to rule without interest in anything other than their own enrichment or pleasure – yet they continued to command the obedience, even if begrudgingly, of their subjects. Many military commanders have successfully led their troops into hopeless battles in which none of the group are likely to benefit or even survive. Furthermore, when we speak of politicians leading very large groups, it becomes very difficult to say what the common goals of the group are. For a modern pluralistic society with millions of voices it is virtually impossible to define what the public good really is beyond the broadest of generalities. One of the most famous political debates of the twentieth century questioned whether there was any such thing as the 'public interest', and even if there was, whether it could be known and pursued by leaders with any accuracy (Lippmann 1925; Dewey 1927).

Moreover, does a group always know what is in its own interest? Public opinion can be manipulated or hampered by imperfect information, and it is prone to rapid change in the face of new events. Sometimes leaders act in ways that are unpopular and seemingly contrary to stated common goals and yet are proven in the long run to have acted in the long-term public interest.

Despite all of this, there is no doubt that leadership at least aspires to serving common goals, and it is readily observable that any leader who wishes to gain power and enduring popularity must establish that they "serve and stand for something other than themselves, to achieve something beyond merely private ends" (Kane 2001: 10).

Is leadership an active process? Most assume that leadership is an active and interactive process between leaders and followers. Yet many leaders have exerted almost as much influence over followers in death than they did in life. Millions have been inspired by and influenced in their thoughts and actions by George Washington and Che Guevara. Is their influence over future generations still leadership, even if those leaders no longer play an active role in propagating it? Leaders craft and create their image in the public space to inspire people to follow them, but those images can live on far beyond the leader themselves.

Undoubtedly there are many more potential complexities even for simple definitions like ours, but the point here is not to catalogue them all. Rather it is to demonstrate that being precise about what constitutes leadership is fraught with challenges. Certainly, the working definition given at the beginning of this section by Northouse captures what leadership is for the most part, but there will always be exceptions and complex examples that challenge our understanding.

Leadership versus power-wielding

Sometimes it can be harder to say what leadership *isn't* rather than what it *is*. One of the biggest questions that attends to defining leadership is the role that coercion plays within it. A criminal who robs a bank at gunpoint would not be considered a leader in anyone's mind – even though they have influenced a group of people to achieve a goal, few would call this 'leadership'. James MacGregor Burns calls this merely 'power-wielding' (Burns 1978: 9–22) and most people would agree that "leadership is not simply about getting people to do things. It is about getting them to *want* to do things" (Haslam, Reicher & Platow 2011: ix). Hence the importance of 'common' goals as part of the definition here – a bank robber is influencing a group for the purpose of achieving a personal goal only.

Yet sometimes leaders can, and sometimes must, use coercive tools to achieve the public good, even if it is not appreciated as such by followers, and even if it is not the intent of the leader. Often in these situations the line between leadership and power-wielding becomes blurred. A Viking warlord may use little else but fear and violence to maintain his hold over a clan and may do so with the intent only to enrich himself and monopolize power, yet in the process may provide certainty and stability, and create a highly disciplined and effective band whose raids and pillaging enrich all of the group in the end.

Moreover, no leader can coerce an entire community by themselves any more than a lone thief could single-handedly plunder Fort Knox. "Even the most powerful and the most despotic government cannot hold a society together by sheer force" (Sabine 1937: 731). Although a coercive regime may be unseemly, even unethical and tyrannical, it is usually the case that at least some sectors of the population believe it serves common goals – enough to sustain the leader's power. Adolf Hitler and other demagogues from history are the first to be excluded from many analyses of 'legitimate leadership'. Yet Hitler's power did not only come from the barrel of a gun – he was supported by a large section of the German population before the war, he used rhetoric and argument to establish a popular political platform and his political movement attracted significant political support in the elections of the 1930s, which initially allowed his movement to take power, even if it was later sustained by coercion. Hitler's economic and social policies during his early years in power were extremely popular with large sections of the population, as well as businesses, the armed forces and other key social groups – many members of which quite voluntarily supported the Nazi regime and helped it succeed. And his pursuit of expansionism and extremist social engineering was, sadly, in keeping with the common goals of many Germans at the time – restoration of lost German territory, purification of German society and assertion of German superiority. While it is tempting to dismiss a monster like Hitler as not a 'leader' but merely a 'power-wielder', the fact is he did much more than simply wield power – he effectively mobilized millions of Germans to create

Europe's largest war machine in the pursuit of collective goals which, only in hindsight, proved to be tragic mistakes by his followers.

Though Hitler is an extreme and challenging case, ultimately political leaders only differ on the use of coercion by a matter of degree. Even democratic rulers must sometimes turn to coercion as the most effective means to maintain order, defend the community, or contend with a crisis. Abraham Lincoln employed a raft of coercive measures in fighting the American Civil War: forced conscription of fighting-age men and the use of federal troops to suppress subsequent draft riots, the suspension of *habeas corpus* and use of military courts, press censorship and martial law (sometimes politically motivated), were all ultimately coercive and anti-democratic means used by Lincoln throughout his administration in order to save the world's great democratic experiment (Neely 1992). Lincoln knew both how to inspire followers but also coerce them, and neither aspect can be separated out from how we judge his effectiveness as a leader.

Thus, sometimes the coercive tendencies of leadership are mild and used judiciously to protect the public good and maintain order, whilst other times they are abused and used to advance the personal goals of tyrants. Just where the lines lie are moral, rather than definitional, questions.

Leadership versus management

Another important distinction often drawn in leadership studies is between that of leadership and management. Historically, the study of leadership and management have constituted distinct intellectual traditions, but in recent decades there has been more crossover between the two and attempts to find synergy across both (Knight 2009).

Henri Fayol, one of the founders of modern management studies, described the key tasks of a manager in 1916 – planning, organizing, commanding, coordinating and controlling – concepts that have been recurring in business studies and the definitions of management ever since (Kumar & Sharma 2000: 151–152). John Kotter, one of the most popular writers on business leadership and management, sets out the primary differences he sees between the role of leaders and the role of managers in the table below (Table 1.1).

Table 1.1 The tasks of leaders and managers

Leaders	Managers
Produce change and movement	Produce order and consistency
Establish direction, set the vision, and paint the big picture	Make plans, produce budgets, and allocate resources
Communicate and convince, build teams and attract followers	Hire and fire, create rules, maintain order, and provide organization
Motivate, inspire, empower and meet the needs of followers	Solve problems, maintain control, manage risk

Based on Kotter (1990).

Most comparisons tend to describe management as day-to-day, tactical, pragmatic and narrow in focus, whilst leadership is big-picture, strategic, inspirational and broad. Put another way, management is about *déjà vu* (seen before) but leadership is about *vu jàdé* (never seen before). That is to say, management is about applying the right process to a known problem whilst leadership finds new solutions to new problems (Grint, Smolovic Jones & Holt 2017: 3). But the distinction is not always clear cut. The qualities that make good managers and good leaders overlap significantly, and effective rulers are usually both. Indeed, modern government is so vast and complex that significant managerial capacity is required at all levels for its smooth functioning (Pfiffner 1999). There have been many inspiring and charismatic leaders who have crafted compelling visions and attracted great followings, and yet were unable to manage the implementation of their ideas, appoint competent staffs to run their governments, or balance budgets and resources. Australian Prime Minister Kevin Rudd (2007–2010, 2013) was much lauded for his campaigning skill, inspiring rhetoric and popularity as opposition leader. Yet after winning power in a landslide in 2007, his subsequent government became a study in the poor management of people and processes, and his own colleagues deposed him within a few years (Kelly 2014: ch. 10).

Thus, while we might draw a distinction between what we consider the realms of 'management' and 'leadership', to discuss political leadership in practice we have to recognize that management goes hand-in-hand with being an effective political leader.

Defining 'political' leadership

Having tried to establish what is and is not 'leadership', we must also attend to what we mean specifically by 'political' leadership, and if and how political leadership differs from leadership in any other area of human endeavour. Some even might consider 'political leadership' a truism since leadership can be considered an inherently political task (Tucker 1995).

For the purposes of this book I'll adopt an 'arena' definition of politics – political leaders are those involved in the circles of government, party politics or political movements. Even here, though, we can quickly get into trouble. There are many leaders who exert considerable and undeniable influence over political affairs yet don't hold any formal position within a government, party or movement. Religious leaders have traditionally been common examples, with popes, cardinals and bishops possessing political power rivalling kings in medieval Europe. In the modern era, celebrities and superstars may exert great influence over politics without taking explicitly political roles (Marsh, 't Hart & Tindall 2010). Thus, while political leaders are generally those we find in government, parties or movements, undeniably leaders from all sectors may find themselves, wittingly or not, political leaders of a sort.

Political leadership is not solely distinguished from other forms of leadership by its location within society. Though leadership shares many characteristics across sectors of human endeavour, they are also specialized within their discipline to a degree that means effective leaders in one area may not be similarly effective in another. Tihomir Orešković, one of Croatia's richest men and most successful business leaders, soon found out excellent business leadership does not automatically translate into politics. After coming into office as prime minister in 2016 as an outsider candidate, he lasted less than a year in the position before his government collapsed (Milekic 2016). Yet even if there are many unique challenges to political leadership, much can still be learned from other areas. Easily the largest canon of work on leadership is to be found in business studies, and scores of books on the subject in the context of leading corporations are published every year. There are many excellent insights in such works that readily translate to a political context, some of which appear in this book.

What makes political leadership unique?

One of the most distinctive features of political leaders is that they tend to serve many groups and occupy many leadership roles simultaneously, all of which may have different values, tasks and expectations attached to them.

Take, for example, the Prime Minister (PM) of the United Kingdom. She or he is, foremost, the leader of the nation and is expected to lead for the common good of the British public. In this sense all citizens of the United Kingdom are her or his followers, and the leader must set national priorities and move the country forward. Yet the British PM has several other leadership roles and follower groups that require often radically different approaches:

- **Leader of the Government:** The British PM is considered 'first among equals' in their cabinet of ministers. She or he must lead the decision-making process within their government and corral colleagues (and often rivals) to set direction and achieve the government's policy goals.
- **Leader of a Parliamentary Majority:** To sustain a government, the PM must be able to command a majority in the House of Commons and can only enact legislation by parliamentary majority. This may include cross-bench parties, with whom constant negotiation may be required. Yet even when the PM's own party commands a parliamentary majority, the PM will face a diverse party room with hundreds of members from different parts of the country and with different ideas and interests. She or he must use negotiation, tact, incentive and punishment to keep that majority united behind an agenda, while mastering the formal rules of parliamentary procedure.

- **Leader of their Party:** The PM is concurrently the leader of their political party. The party includes not just the elected members of parliament, but also the rank-and-file party members across the country. The PM holds her or his position at the behest of their party and must maintain their party's confidence to keep it. This often means they must uphold the party platform and ideology, reward supporters, build alliances and mollify rival factions to stay in power. And it may mean very different things to maintain the confidence of colleagues in parliament, who know you more intimately and have an inside perspective, and the broader rank-and-file of the party, who do not.
- **Leader of the Administration:** The PM sits atop the apex of a massive civil service that is politically independent and charged with implementing the government's policies and running the country. The bureaucracy cannot be commanded like a military battalion – they have their own agendas, personalities and ideas that must be managed. Moreover, good ideas do not automatically become good policy that can be immediately implemented – effective national policymaking can take years of careful work managing highly complex processes across many government departments at many levels, all of which the PM ultimately takes responsibility for.
- **Leader of the Campaign:** In election years, the PM (if they are running for election) is also the face of her or his party's efforts to win government. In election years the tasks change once more, and the PM must win over public opinion, debate the opposition, develop narratives and platforms, and build their followership amongst the general public as much as possible. In the near-constant campaigning of the twenty-first century in Western democracies, there is less and less difference between election and non-election years, and the PM must continuously work to sell the government's policies to the media and the public.

A political leader must tend to all these roles simultaneously and switch between them seamlessly, yet each requires different skills and tactics. A political leader may have to use persuasion and negotiation one moment to win key votes in parliament, use detailed policy argument and strategy to win over colleagues in cabinet the next and then harangue and excoriate the political opposition to fire up supporters in the electorate afterwards.

Leaders in other sectors may find themselves switching leadership styles and roles too, but few need the sheer breadth of skills and the flexibility to switch between them that political leadership requires.

Furthermore, political leadership is by far the most closely scrutinized and widely talked about form of leadership, and subjected to the most complex and diverse expectations from many different constituencies. Leaders in organizations like businesses have relatively clear goals and narrow audiences – they must maintain and grow the business, produce returns on investment, and maintain the confidence of investors, workers and consumers. Business leaders may take on different agendas and goals from time to time, but these too are usually clearly agreed upon by boards and have clear performance indicators. Political leaders have a much vaguer goal – to advance the public good – which as we established in our earlier consideration of what defines leadership, is notoriously difficult to pin down. They have far less immediacy with their stakeholders and constituents, and do not have precise tools to gather input from or directly communicate with them. Multiple overlapping bodies set the agenda – there are parties, cabinets, public opinion, media, social movements and ordinary citizens who compete to set the issues of the day, only a few of which the political leader can work on at any one time. The efficacy of their work is, on most issues, very hard to assess and subject to dispute, and given the complexity of government and long time-frames over which policy development and implementation occur, it may take years or decades for the impact of what a political leader does to become clear. Shareholders primarily need only look at profits made, and dividends returned, to assess a CEO's performance. Politicians, on the other hand, will be judged by thousands of different metrics, from current account balances and unemployment indices to crime rates and surgery waiting lists, and potentially even before their policies have had a chance to be fully realized.

So, while much can be learned from what other disciplines of leadership have to say, political leadership does have its own unique challenges, and requires skills and approaches that aren't necessarily developed in other realms.

Defining 'good' political leadership

What is a good political leader? A common-sense definition might be a leader who is able to effectively achieve common goals and improve the lives of those they have stewardship over. Yet rarely do we get to assess leaders in such a clear-cut way. Inevitably in politics, where time and resources are limited, leaders make difficult trade-offs about which goals to pursue, which policies to enact and what costs are acceptable in the course of doing both. These are judgment calls for which political leaders ultimately bear responsibility and will be assessed by the public both in their time, and by future generations, possibly in radically different ways. Indeed, so much of what we think of as 'good leadership' is tied in with normative values people hold, differing interpretations of what constitutes the 'common good' and what trade-offs people are willing to accept.

Political leadership is also marked, perhaps more than any other type of leadership, with a central concern as to the motivations of the individuals involved within it. Self-interest and group interests are always a problematic source of conflict in leader–follower relations, but there is far more natural alignment in say a business (it is in the interests of shareholders and CEOs alike to improve performance and increase the value of a company) than there is in politics, where there is a complex interplay between the two.

To implement the policies and ideas they believe are right and will serve the public interest, political aspirants must of course hold political office, and do so in a highly competitive and often merciless environment. Thus politicians surveyed usually see career advancement as critical to achieving their values and implementing their policies, and they see their policy goals and political ideals as tools to win office and further their careers (Wittman 1983; Lewin 1991; Callander 2008). This is logical enough, but such a logic can easily give rise to an environment where any career-advancing action becomes justified and ruthless politicking becomes the norm, the public good served often becoming obscured or unclear in the process.

As we might expect, the public does not want self-interested careerists to rule over them. Surveys of Americans find that large majorities believe their political leaders to be selfish, dishonest, career-focused and uninterested in the public good (Pew Research Center 2015a). Yet this may be a case where the public does not fully appreciate what is in their collective interest. Career politicians generally have more power through seniority and established relationships, and more experience navigating complex political systems. Thus, they are usually better at crafting and negotiating policy, and better able to direct benefits to, and represent the interests of, their constituencies than political novices (Maestas 2000; Padró i Miquel & Snyder 2006). Though it's easy to turn them into self-serving caricatures, career politicians may be more necessary to a functional political system than many realize (Rauch 2016).

Despite a wealth of writing on political leaders, only a relatively small group of leadership scholars have ventured to develop schemas by which we might evaluate whether a political leader is 'good' or not. One developed by 't Hart and Tummers, though, can help structure our thinking as we go through this book. Their schema assesses leaders on three criteria:

- **Prudence:** Is the leader wise and effective? Has the leader made sound decisions? Have they produced outcomes beneficial to their communities and/or organizations?
- **Support:** Is the leader democratic? Has the leader upheld the social contract and maintained public confidence? Does the leader engage, consult and communicate genuinely with followers?
- **Trustworthiness:** Is the leader ethical? Have they followed the institutional and legal norms associated with their role? Have they been accountable for their actions? ('t Hart & Tummers 2019: 143–148)

These three criteria for good leadership are very sound ones, insofar as most people would agree that a good leader should indeed be prudent, supported and trustworthy. Yet these criteria will often come into conflict with each other. And when they do, there is often no obvious 'right' answer as to which principle should take precedence. Ranking exercises of political leaders are fairly common, yet they are rarely uncontroversial. In the United

Kingdom, for example, Clement Attlee and Margaret Thatcher are routinely ranked as the two best prime ministers of the nation since World War II, yet their leadership styles and the balances they struck between our three criteria were very different (Theakston 2013). Prominent leaders like Thatcher are often polarizing, with supporters lionizing her as a great leader, whilst her opponents have denounced her as one of the worst (e.g., see Case 2.1).

Moreover, the context in which leaders are judged, and thus how we judge their prudence, support and trustworthiness, also changes. Andrew Jackson, America's seventh president, has varied greatly in the historical memory, with scholarly rankings rating him progressively worse over time as standards of political ethics have evolved. Even biographers of his own era found it nearly impossible to evaluate a man who was "a democratic autocrat. An urbane savage. An atrocious saint" (Parton 1860: vii).

So, while prudence, support and trustworthiness are worthy yardsticks when evaluating leaders, they are necessarily only a starting point, and context is crucial. Commentators often like to present leaders through simple dichotomies as either heroes or villains, right or wrong. So does the public – 'good' leaders get statues and buildings named for them, and 'bad' leaders receive perpetual scorn. Yet upon close inspection, almost all leaders fall somewhere within uncomfortably grey areas. The most impactful leaders tend to be those who made bold moves, brave decisions and moved an agenda forward, and yet there is always a price to be borne for such, and not everyone will agree whether the cost was justified (see Case 1.1).

This book is not about normative judgment of political leaders – what makes a 'good' leader is highly contextual and dependent on many other factors, and sometimes very difficult ethical trade-offs. I seek to be even-handed as much as possible and explore the complex nature of political leadership without trying to evaluate whether specific examples of such should be considered objectively 'good' or not. For better or worse, dictators and democrats alike are part of our political past and present, and probably our political future, and it behoves us to study both with an open mind (without necessarily endorsing either) if we are to truly understand political leadership.

Case 1.1 What is a 'good' leader?

Suharto

President of Indonesia, 1968–1998

Figure 1.2 Suharto in 1993

Suharto is a prime example of the challenge of evaluating a political leader, and how leaders can fall truly short of some criteria of 'good' leadership whilst excelling in others.

Leading Indonesia for three decades, Suharto ran one of the most authoritarian and corrupt administrations in modern history. He and his family are believed to have embezzled between $15 and $35 billion during their reign – more than any other modern leader (Sandbrook 2016). His regime was responsible for brutal political repression and censorship. And though Suharto's role and culpability have been difficult to assess, more than half a million people died in political massacres and civil strife surrounding Suharto's rise to power in 1965–1966. As offered by 't Hart and Tummers, trustworthiness and support are at the very core of most normative evaluations of leadership. Corruption and censorship are nearly universally abhorred as untrustworthy, whilst the tools of repression are diametrically opposed to modern expectations of a popularly supported leader. By these yardsticks, Suharto is surely one of the worst leaders of the last century.

And yet, Suharto was arguably one Indonesia's most prudent leaders. Over three decades of rule, Suharto presided over an unprecedented era of political stability and economic growth in Indonesia, slashing the rate of poverty by three quarters and increasing GDP per capita fivefold, whilst adding 20 years to the average lifespan of his people and dramatically improving public access to healthcare, education and food (Elson 2001: ch. 11). To some degree, Suharto's prudence even relied upon untrustworthy and undemocratic methods. Corruption and authoritarian rule were essential tools used by Suharto to hold a disparate and fractious emerging nation together, to coerce and incentivize a loyal political structure that could govern the country and to contain the chronic instability that had plagued the nation in the recent past (Mackie 2010). Suharto seemingly embodied the ***support*** element of a good leader as well, even if he did not meet our contemporary standards for achieving it, as Suharto was enormously popular for much of his rule, especially amongst the nation's poorest (Vatikiotis 1998: 2–6). Indeed, many Indonesians today are nostalgic for the Suharto era as a time of unprecedented economic growth, political stability, and improvement in the lives of ordinary Indonesians, in contrast somewhat to what has come under Suharto's successors (Hussain 2014). Yet undeniably Suharto was not a democratic leader, and his New Order implemented an illiberal quasi-democratic regime that suppressed dissent and alternative viewpoints.

Predictably, Suharto's reign is fiercely debated both within Indonesia and abroad. On the one hand, his government lifted millions of his citizens out of a life of poverty, and just about every major metric of Indonesian public life had improved significantly over his term of office. Yet on the other hand, he betrayed both democratic and civic values by abusing his office to maintain power and serve his personal interests. His corrupt system of economic management embezzled millions, rapidly depleted Indonesia's natural resources and proved unsustainable. During the Asian Financial Crisis in 1997, Indonesia was hit particularly hard, in part due to the poor financial management of the Suharto regime (Elson 2001: ch. 11).

Unfortunately, there just is no easy answer to a question such as, 'was Suharto a good leader?' Yet even as people quite rightly dispute whether Suharto was a ***good*** leader, more might feel comfortable conceding he was an ***effective*** one. He enacted an ambitious agenda and created change, and for better or worse, his legacy has defined modern Indonesia. Some might argue the improvements he brought about were possible without systemic corruption and suppression. Others might argue such things were painful but necessary for building a functional state that could govern an unstable, impoverished post-colonial nation. People will naturally differ on whether the trade-offs were acceptable, and how much emphasis prudence, support and trustworthiness should receive when evaluating a complex legacy like Suharto's.

Chapter Summary

- Leadership is a complex and paradoxical phenomenon that has been found in every society in every era.
  - Leadership is a process whereby an individual influences a group of individuals to achieve a common goal.
  - Though it is sometimes distinguished from power-wielding, in practice the boundaries between the two are hard to draw.
- Leadership produces change and movement, while management produces order and consistency. Yet effective leadership and effective management tend to go hand in hand.
- Political leadership is leadership found within the arenas of government and politics.
  - Political leaders serve many constituencies, play many roles and require diverse skill sets concurrently.
  - Political leaders are subjected to higher levels of scrutiny, yet vaguer standards of evaluation, than leaders in other arenas.
- What makes political leadership 'good' is highly subjective and context-specific. Good leaders are generally considered to be prudent, supported, and trustworthy, yet these three principles can easily conflict with each other in the practice of leadership.

2 POWER, AUTHORITY, FOLLOWERS AND ELITES

Chapter Outline

- What are power and authority? How do they differ from each other?
- From where do leaders draw power and authority?
- How do leaders use power and authority to influence others?
- How do followers respond to power and authority, and how do they assess its credibility and legitimacy?
- What power do followers have? Why does it feel like they are less powerful than leaders?
- Who are elites? How do they differ from leaders? Where do they fit in between leaders and followers?

In the previous chapter, we adopted a definition of leadership as "a process whereby an individual influences a group of individuals to achieve a common goal". How leaders achieve that influence requires us to examine four core concepts – *power, authority, followers* and *elites*. These have traditionally been challenging areas of scholarship with many different definitions and approaches that do not always agree. However, even if we cannot always be as precise as we would like in this area, it is still essential to provide a grounding in these core concepts if we want to understand the underlying mechanisms of leadership.

Power

Power, when talked about in a political or social context, is perhaps the most challenging of all the concepts we'll come across in this book to precisely describe. Many volumes have been dedicated exclusively to its study; and, as with leadership, many definitions of power have been offered. Two of the most widely cited are those of British philosopher Bertrand Russell – "Power may be defined as the production of intended effects" (Russell 1938: 18) – and by the American psychologist Rollo May as "the ability to cause or prevent change" (May 1972: 99). There are dozens of others that you might find, but most are fairly close to these two.

A key distinction to make when studying power in the context of leadership is between what Keith Dowding describes as *outcome power* and *social power*. The former refers to the ability of someone to make an outcome happen directly. The latter refers to the ability of someone to change the incentive structures of others to bring about outcomes (Dowding 1996: 4–5). This second sense is what we are interested in and what we mean when we talk about leadership – the *power* over others a leader has that can incentivize them to act or think in ways they wouldn't have otherwise.

To some, the term 'power' holds negative connotations, and as a result some leadership texts will prefer terms like 'influence' or 'persuasion' instead (Cameron & Green 2017: 30–43). Others see influence or persuasion as merely a form of power (Wrong 2004: 21–34). There are often caveats placed on the definition of power as well, especially regarding intentionality and causation (Allison 2009). Such caveats can make the terminology confusing as you move between different works on the same subject.

Power becomes easier to grasp, though, when we break it down and look at the forms it takes when it is used to influence others. Scholars have developed schemas to categorize the types of social power a leader can use – well-known examples are by French and Raven (1959) and Wrong (1979/2004). But for the purposes of this book, I have created my own schema that ties together leaders and followers and the power relationships between them. Other works on power may use concepts I use below somewhat differently, but the goal here is to create a heuristic model to help us think about these concepts and how they relate in the context of leadership (Figure 2.1).

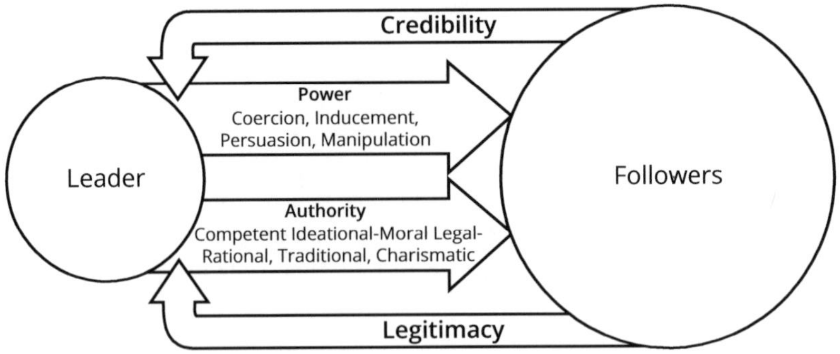

Figure 2.1 A heuristic model of leaders, followers and the power relationships between them

In this model, we see leaders trying to use various forms of both *power* and *authority* to influence what followers do. It is not a one-way relationship though. Followers have the ability assess the credibility of power and the legitimacy of authority, such that they collectively have power over their leaders too. A leader's power is thus socially determined and variable, rather than fixed and quantifiable. This is not always obvious at first glance, and we tend to spend a lot more time discussing the power of leaders rather than the power of followers. However, as any toppled dictator can tell you, this can obscure a more nuanced reality of power relations.

Let's start, though, by looking at the conventional forms of power that leaders use to affect outcomes and influence the behaviour of others.

Coercion

To coerce is to deploy pain, suffering, deprivation or restriction upon others to get them to do something. Coercion is generally defined as someone making a *threat* to another to create negative consequences for them should they choose to take or not take a certain course of action (Nozick 1969: 441–445; c.f. Bayles 1972; Gorr 1986).

Coercive power may be physical or non-physical. It incentivizes followers to behave in certain ways out of fear and self-preservation. Threats of physical force that may result in incarceration, injury or death are well-known tools of the ruthless leader. Yet there are other tools less physical in nature. Control over water, for instance, has long been a basis for regimes of political control, particularly in the ancient world (Solomon 2011: ch. 3; Mithen 2012: 287–291). Those who controlled access to water could command people who relied on it and threaten to withhold it from those who did not obey. The House of Saud, the powerful political dynasty that founded the Kingdom of Saudi Arabia in 1932, drew much of their power from strategic control of water and oil, resources that continue to dominate Saudi politics today (Jones 2011).

Coercion is generally seen, at best, as a necessary evil whose use must be justified, and as wrongful when used indiscriminately (van der Rijt 2011: 110–111). Coercive power is most obviously associated with autocratic regimes, which may use fear and force openly to coerce compliance. Yet democratic regimes too are ultimately reliant upon the power to sanction, punish or imprison those who do not comply with its laws and values. Few people would pay parking fines or income tax without the coercive power of the state as an ever-present threat to punish those who refuse. This is a widely accepted use of coercive power, and the public generally agrees that to have a fair system in which everyone contributes to government expenses, everyone should pay their share. When protecting the common goals of a society, it can be said that all regimes use coercive power, at least in limited ways.

And whilst democratic leaders are generally restricted in their ability to use coercive power in the public sphere, they may have far more access to such power within their government, their party or within the elite. In Canada for example, the prime minister as head of both the government and their party can very credibly threaten their own ministers and party colleagues with demotions, deselection or sometimes even expulsions, potentially ending their careers, and such power is routinely used to ensure party discipline.

Inducement

At the other end of the spectrum is inducement. Leaders use rewards, incentives and other forms of enrichment to influence the behaviour of others and attract followers. Inducement is the opposite of coercion: someone in this case is making an *offer* to another party that if they act in a certain way, positive consequences will result. Most leader-follower relationships are predicated in some way on inducement – we follow because we believe it is in our material interest to do so.

Inducement of large groups of followers necessarily occurs indirectly and on broad promises of rewards to come rather than specific offers. In modern democracies, voters expect their political leaders to create economic growth and prosperity in their own lives. At each election, politicians will compete fiercely with promises of rewards to those who vote for them – better healthcare, better schools, higher wages, cheaper housing and so on. And if they want to keep many of their followers come the next election, they'd have better made good on these promises. There is a well-established relationship between economic performance and government popularity that suggests that when assessing which leaders to support, material factors are highly influential (see Nadeau et al. 2013).

Political leaders will hence spend a great deal of time balancing off the various inducements they can offer within the scope of finite resources. National budgets are a gargantuan negotiation over rewards. Few political leaders have the luxury of unlimited resources, and so hard decisions must be made about who gets what. Though much of the budgeting process is driven by the needs of various sectors, leaders inevitably use their power in the process to reward strategically. Pork-barrelling, the use of state funds to sponsor local projects, is a common and more directed use of inducement by political leaders, usually to improve standing with critical constituencies. In the Philippines, presidents have traditionally relied heavily on local patronage and pork-barrelling to local interests to forge political coalitions to support their agenda (Teehankee 2012; Quimpo 2015). Tax havens and corporate welfare are other forms of inducements. Governments use these to attract businesses and investment, which in turn give political leaders electoral popularity for 'creating jobs' or 'economic development', even though the evidence of the effectiveness of such policies is mixed (Jensen & Malesky 2018). Political leaders also often rely on inducement in their inner circles and within the government, with leaders using promotions, career advancement and perks to reward loyalty and talent.

Persuasion

Persuasion is the use of argument, reason and rhetoric to convince people to follow. It is a cornerstone of leadership – leaders inspire, set goals, make arguments, debate and create visions that will convince followers to get behind them. Essentially, persuasion is the ability of someone to make someone else change how they *understand* their incentive structure or view their options for action.

For example, a political leader might try and persuade the public on the wisdom of a tax cut. They argue that a tax cut will stimulate economic activity and increase employment and warn that failing to pursue tax cuts will leave the nation uncompetitive. They might even argue that the tax cuts are designed to help the poorest in the nation get on their feet – a moral and social argument that may persuade people to support it even if they don't stand to benefit personally. Effective persuasion will shift how others perceive their interests or options and may change their thinking and/or behaviour accordingly.

Traditionally, problems have arisen with defining persuasion as a form of power – after all, persuasion is predicated on the free acceptance of arguments by the follower (Uhr 2011: 478–479). Yet as we know, the power to persuade is not evenly distributed. Some individuals have incredible skills of oratory that allow them to communicate much more persuasively than others. The means of communication – access to mass media, publishing platforms and communications technology – is also unevenly distributed and the ability to speak directly to the masses is generally possessed only by certain political offices and public personas (Wrong 2004: 32–34).

Persuasion is a critical part of what leaders do at all levels and the most common way in which they can get others to do what they otherwise wouldn't. They are constantly engaged in it with their ministers, with the press, with their constituents and even with their families. Coercion and inducement are inherently finite power resources – there are real limits to the rewards leaders can offer, or the force they can use to coerce. Yet persuasion and argument are virtually limitless – a good leader can always argue for future benefits, warn of future harms, and inspire their followers through principle or reason.

Manipulation

"Manipulation, unlike coercion, does not interfere with a person's options. Instead it perverts the way that person reaches decisions, forms preferences, or adopts goals" (Raz 1988: 377). Whilst persuasion is the free acceptance of argument, manipulation attempts to bypass reason or otherwise change how others think or behave without their full consent or consciousness (Easton 1958: 179; Barnhill 2014: 73).

The *faces of power* debate is particularly relevant here and can help us understand how manipulation may manifest. Described by Stephen Lukes, it stipulates that the previous forms of power we've discussed are all best considered part of an overt and fairly obvious 'first face' of power, insofar as it is clear who is deploying power and why (Lukes 2005).

But there are additional faces of power that are often hidden from view. The 'second face' recognizes that power is not just about making decisions, but also controlling the context in which a decision is made (Bachrach & Baratz 1962). Political leaders are oft able to exert great power over not just *what* gets decided, but also *how* we decide it and *what doesn't* get decided. For example, in legislatures the leadership can manipulate the rules to control which bills come to the floor to be debated and how much time is allocated for debate. In cabinet meetings the leader often sets the agenda, dropping issues they don't want discussed and promoting others they do. They might choose who gets to talk on an issue, in what order they get to speak, and set the parameters for debate, all in aid of manipulating the decision-making process to favour a certain outcome (James 1995: 76–87; Bennister 2012: 39–60).

They exert this power by setting the tone for public discourse as well. Consider the example of our political leader pushing their tax cut. They talk about the issue repeatedly in every public forum, tweet about tax reform daily, and make it central to their election campaign. Politicians spend months debating it, but the public remains divided and it is ultimately voted down in the legislature. On one level, the leader has failed to get others to act towards the desired outcome. Yet in another way they may have. Tax reform may have very little real relevance to the interests of a country facing a crisis in its social welfare programs and crumbling infrastructure, but months have been spent discussing tax reform and treating it as the most important political issue. This may have been a deliberate tactic – obsession with tax reform may have prevented the public from focusing on other issues that the leader did not want debated (see also Case 2.1).

The 'third face' of power, as outlined by Lukes, is another form of manipulation and a far more insidious type. It involves "shaping [a person's] perceptions, cognitions, and preferences in such a way that they accept their role in the existing order of things" (Lukes 2005: 28). It involves effectively creating a *false consciousness,* preventing people from understanding what is truly in their own interests, and making them a complicit party in their own domination. This manifestation of power has proven controversial to define and measure (Dowding 2006); however, it is a useful exercise to consider how leaders use their role to influence followers in hard-to-see ways.

Propaganda, for example, is biased rhetoric that uses intense emotion and/or deception to manipulate how people think and feel, particularly in media environments where there are limits on expression or debate. In such circumstances, people may no longer be freely accepting persuasive arguments, but rather experience domination in an environment where there is limited capacity for free thought. The line though between persuasion and manipulation can be difficult to draw and there are techniques common to both (Jenkins 2013). Even in societies of free speech, leaders may have enormous sway in the public discourse and use emotion and ideology in ways that verge on the manipulative. Consider our tax cut debate, and the emotive terms either side might use, like *socialism, government waste* or *corporate welfare,* which rather than encouraging rational assessment of the arguments, may quite deliberately instil emotive or ideological associations that can entirely change the character of the debate.

Asymmetry in access to knowledge, procedure, rules, or information can also be used to achieve this effect (Riker 1986). In 1504, Christopher Columbus's fleet became stranded on Jamaica, and after some months angered the native Taino people, who then stopped supplying them food. Having with him an almanac of astronomical tables, Columbus noticed that a lunar eclipse was soon to arrive. He told the Taino that the gods were angry with them for denying him supplies and would punish them by making the moon "inflamed with wrath". When the scheduled eclipse turned the moon red, the terrified Taino immediately submitted to Columbus and did his bidding until relief ships arrived. Columbus was able to use his superior access to information to create 'fake news' and manipulate the Taino's understanding of their interests, much as contemporary leaders may attempt to use disinformation to likewise distort a discussion.

Authority

Authority is a critical concept in understanding political leadership. Although in some ways it is just another form of power (i.e., something that is used to get someone to do something), unlike previously discussed forms, authority works because it is backed by normative force. It is the agreed-upon *right* to compel someone to do something within a system of social relations, while other forms of power are merely the *means* to do so (Dowding 2011: 36–39; Huemer 2012: 5–8). When a manager asks an employee to do something, so long as it is reasonable, we would expect the employee to do it without question. Usually they would not need persuasive argument to convince them or to coerce by threatening dismissal. The employee complies because they acknowledge the manager's *authority* to ask them to do the task. It is implicit that the manager does have power to fire or reward them, yet it's unlikely the employee would think about this potential explicitly when deciding whether to do the task or not.

What is interesting, however, is that authority can be powerful even without any actual power behind it. For example, if the Queen of the United Kingdom appeared and asked that same employee to do something, even though she has no power to punish or reward that employee and has no jurisdiction in that situation, it's quite likely the employee would still comply with the request if it were reasonable. This is authority – it is willing compliance based on *who* the leader is or what they represent, rather than an evaluation of the *what* or *how* they asked. As such, it operates by different rules and has a markedly different character to other forms of power. It is an especially important concept in politics.

Authority is utterly essential to the practical functioning of leadership. It would be enormously problematic and time-consuming if the manager of a business, or the leader of a community, had to constantly threaten, induce, persuade or manipulate others to do even the most basic tasks. But to unpack the concept of authority further, we must consider how it is obtained and the limits to its usage.

Sources of authority

At the outset, the most important distinction to make in authority is whether it is attached to the *person* themselves or the *position* they occupy. *Personal authority* is attached to a specific leader. It is reputation: it cannot be easily passed onto another and largely disappears when the individual does.

Case 2.1 Power at work

Margaret Thatcher

Prime Minister of the United Kingdom, 1979–1990

Figure 2.2 Margaret Thatcher in 1983

Margaret Thatcher's handling of the 1984–1985 miner's strike is an example that shows all the levers of power in play. Coal mining played a pivotal role in Britain's development as an industrial power in the nineteenth century. Yet by the 1980s most mines were inefficient and unprofitable, and the industry heavily subsidized. However, it still employed nearly 200,000 people, with many small communities dependent on mines for their livelihoods. Thatcher saw the coal industry as a symbol of dilapidated economic policies. In 1984 she proposed a reduction of 20 mines and 20,000 jobs as the first step towards major reform of the industry. Previous reform attempts in the mining sector had failed after immense resistance from unions, so Thatcher used various power strategies to ensure the 1984 attempt would not meet the same fate.

Persuasion: Thatcher had long made the case to both the public and her own cabinet that the mining industry and trade unions were major obstacles to economic recovery. She had made that case to voters at the elections in 1979 and 1983, noting the significant cost to the taxpayers of subsidizing the industry and her beliefs regarding the disproportionate power of 'undemocratic' trade unions in Britain. She personally appointed ideological allies to lead the National Coal Board (NCB) and fill other key posts in the sector, who pressed these arguments within the government and bureaucracy (Phillips 2014). By 1984, most of her government now supported a confrontation with the coal industry, and polling revealed a growing proportion of the public were being convinced of Thatcher's arguments (King & Wybrow 2001: 337).

Coercion: When the closures were announced, there was widespread condemnation from miners. The National Union of Miners (NUM), led by Arthur Scargill, supported local strikes and called for nationwide action in solidarity. It was to become one of the largest industrial actions in British history with nearly 150,000 people striking at its height. They sought to force Thatcher to back down, not only by drawing intense public attention and sympathy to the issue, but also to coerce a settlement by disrupting the supply of coal and thus Britain's predominantly coal-powered electricity supply. Thatcher too had coercive powers. The police were mobilized around the country to breakup problematic strikes, and some violent confrontations resulted. Ultimately though, perhaps Thatcher's most important move was denying the NUM their plan to disrupt the electricity supply. Anticipating the devastating effect this could have, Thatcher ensured that six months' worth of coal was stockpiled before the cuts were announced, as well as recruiting backup truck fleets to transport coal if the railroad unions also struck (Moore 2016: 142–145). The strategy was highly effective, and it deprived the strikers of their most potent leverage.

Inducement: Thatcher sought to divide the union through inducements. Throughout the 1980s redundancy payments were continuously raised, which persuaded many to leave mines voluntarily. Some regions of the country did not join the mass strikes, with the NCB offering favourable conditions and pay to non-strikers, as well as encouraging them to break away from the NUM and form their own union (Winterton & Winterton 1989: 234). Meanwhile, with most strikers going without pay for months, Scargill and the NUM had much more limited means to reward followers, and they were accused of using donations from the public to favourably reward the more militant branches rather than equally support all those striking (Adeney & Lloyd 1988: 228).

Manipulation: Both sides similarly sought to use manipulation to further their cause. In 1984, Thatcher presented her approach as limited, announcing only 20 mines for closure and stating no more were planned. Yet cabinet documents later revealed that almost half of the UK's mines were being earmarked for closure (Higham 2014). Thatcher also directed government and media attention onto the violent actions of some of the strikers, shifting emphasis onto their tactics rather than their cause to undermine public sympathy for the miners. Within the NUM, Scargill also used manipulation to secure his own preference for militant confrontation. When he began organizing resistance, the NUM's constitution required a vote of its members to call a nation-wide strike. Scargill did not do so, instead using technical workarounds to call the strikes at a regional level, thereby preventing an open debate by the membership on the strategy. Polling of NUM members revealed significant internal division on the strikes.

Ultimately Thatcher's strategy worked – the strikes ended in defeat for the unions in 1985, and Thatcher proceeded with the government's plans to dismantle much of the sector. Conversely, Scargill's leadership has often been criticized for its poor tactical use of what power the unions had (Taylor 1993: 292–298). The British economy made a dramatic recovery from recession by the mid-1980s, seemingly justifying Thatcher's economic policies for many voters. The power of the unions and the prevalence of industrial action declined dramatically in the aftermath, proving to be one of Thatcher's most enduring political victories, though leaving bitter divisions in its wake and devastating many coal mining communities.

Positional authority, however, is only attached to the individual so long as they hold a certain job or title.

Most political leaders will have both kinds of authority, but it is quite possible for positional and personal authority to diverge in a political system. Even though positional authority takes legal precedence over personal authority in theory, in practice it is personal authority that is often the most powerful in politics. When Lyndon Johnson assumed the presidency after the assassination of John F. Kennedy in 1963, he inherited the exact same legal authority of the presidency. Yet he had not been elected to the position, and concerned about his personal authority to fill the role in the wake of his much beloved predecessor, Johnson sought to closely associate himself with the image of the former president, stress continuity between the two administrations, shore up support from others in the Kennedy faction, and in doing so try to inherit some of Kennedy's personal authority and the public approval to pursue his ambitious agenda (Caro 2012: 330–364).

Considering personal and positional authority as broad categories, we can now consider the sources from which authority is derived. German sociologist Max Weber, one of the key early thinkers on the subject, distinguished three types of political authority (Weber 1922/1958):

- **Traditional:** Evolving from the long-standing customs and practices of societies and cultures.
- **Legal-Rational:** Created by the legal, constitutional and bureaucratic order of modern societies.
- **Charismatic:** Based on the perceived extraordinary qualities of an individual, or a heroic belief in the leader, by followers.

These are a good starting point, however, in this chapter I'll add two more types to this classification that have been developed elsewhere and make sense to discuss in this context (Kane 2001; Wrong 2004: 52–59).

- **Ideational-Moral:** Generated by leader's association with the moral values and ideological goals of followers.
- **Competent:** Generated by the perception that the leader is competent and has superior knowledge or skill to followers.

These five sources can be arrayed from more position to more personal (Table 2.1).

Table 2.1 Rating authority types from positional to personal

More Positional	←		→	More Personal
Legal-rational	Traditional	Competent	Ideational-moral	Charismatic

Legal-rational authority

Legal-rational authority stems from the rules and structures that a community formally agrees upon and operates their society by. Legal frameworks of authority have evolved over centuries to define how leaders are appointed; what their role, powers and responsibilities are; and how they can be removed. These are premised on widespread belief in, and acceptance of, those laws by followers, such that even if some voters are disappointed or angry with who wins elections or assumes power, so long as it's done legally they will still respect the outcome of the process and accept the authority of the victor.

In Costa Rica, the President derives his prime authority from the Constitution – Article 139 states what the President has the sole authority to do, Article 140 states what the President has the authority to do in consultation with ministers, and Articles 148 and 149 specify the limits of what the President can do and under what circumstances their authority can be revoked. Costa Ricans have both rights and obligations under that Constitution, creating a social contract whereby they vest legal authority in their leader to do certain things and lead them in certain ways, in exchange for the maintenance of "good functioning of the Government and the progress and well-being of the Nation" as well as respecting the rights of the nation and citizens they serve. Of course, the citizens of Costa Rica don't explicitly analyse the actions of the president from a constitutional perspective every day, but in general, when the president leads it is accepted in the first instance because he has a legal-rational authority to do so within the political system to which they belong.

Traditional authority

Weber's explanation of traditional authority starts with the example of a father in a nuclear family (Weber 1922/1958). Family structures in pre-industrial societies were built around a patriarch (or occasionally a matriarch) who commanded loyalty and compliance from the others. Although that authority weakens once children reach the age of majority and leave home, in most cases parents will continue to maintain loyalty and some level of authority over their children long into adulthood. The psychoanalyst Sigmund Freud opined that the patterns of dependence on parents established in childhood become a mental template for a person's concept of political authority in adulthood (Miller 2007).

It is through long-standing customs that many authority structures have evolved and stay with us today. The Emperor of Japan has virtually no formal powers over government, yet commands extraordinary authority in the nation as by tradition he is a semi-divine figure descended from the sun-goddess Amaterasu. Traditional authority need not be logical, and indeed may be upheld by stereotypes and historical inequalities.

Though traditional and legal-rational authority stem from different sources, in most political systems leadership structures incorporate both. If you read the Indian Constitution, for example, you would assume the President of India leads the country. They have the most important powers, including command over the armed forces, power to appoint most positions of importance, and many executive and budgetary powers as well. Yet by convention and Westminster tradition, it is in fact the Prime Minister of India who in practice is the foremost leader of the country. Indian presidents, such as B.D. Jatti, Zail Singh and K.R. Narayanan, have occasionally come into conflict with elected governments and tried to use their enshrined legal powers in more assertive ways or to intervene in government decisions, though in most cases the traditionally accepted authority of the prime minister has politically triumphed (Kochanek & Hardgrave 2008: 74–84). Thus, in most systems, a combination of legal precepts and traditional practice defines what we think of as right and acceptable for our leaders to do.

Competent authority

Competent authority regards the belief that a leader possesses knowledge or skills in a domain such that it is in our best interests to follow them. In a medical emergency, for example, we will likely accept a doctor's judgment without question because we trust them to make decisions better than we could. Competent authority can also bolster the use of power, particularly persuasion. We are likely to be more persuaded by a doctor's arguments on health than an engineer's. But this is an area that sits astride the positional/personal authority divide, or as Keith Dowding describes it, being *in* authority versus being *an* authority (Dowding 2011: 36). A faith healer, for example, may have an enormous personal following and be considered *an* authority on health, perhaps even to a greater degree than doctors formally certified by the state and thus *in* authority.

Modern politicians have only a little competent authority attached to their positions, and public trust in political representatives is generally far lower than that of other experts (Pew Research Center 2015a; Listhaug & Jakobsen 2018). We do not assume a politician is an expert in anything the same way we do a doctor or engineer. More often, political leaders must try to establish themselves as competent authorities personally. One method is to highlight their professional background – in government, business, the military, etc. And elected leaders will constantly seek to reassure the public that their governments are making the right decisions, enacting good policies, and making things better. They will look for on-the-ground successes and positive data to support their claims. Opposition politicians will of course try to undermine that authority by highlighting mistakes, emphasizing inaction or finding data that undercuts those claims. Politicians can also seek endorsement from others who have it. If their healthcare policies are endorsed by prominent doctors and medical associations, they will seem to have greater authority on those grounds, and indeed, public policy often involves complex relationships between politicians and experts around competent authority (see Heazle & Kane 2015).

President Urho Kekkonen of Finland is a good example of how competent authority can be a powerful claim. Sandwiched between the Soviet Union and NATO, Finland faced a precarious situation during the Cold War and the ever-looming threat of Soviet incursion. Kekkonen, first elected as Finnish President in 1956, adopted a strategy of 'active neutrality' in which he maintained strong relations with leaders on either side of the Cold War, successfully trading and working with both. As time passed, whenever Kekkonen's authority was questioned or retirement discussed, he would play the 'Moscow Card', claiming that no other politician could possibly manage Finland's complex foreign policy or keep the Soviet Union at bay as he had. By the late 1970s, Kekkonen had become increasingly autocratic, going beyond the established legal authority of the presidency with an emergency law that extended his term without election, yet he was ultimately successful in convincing both the public and political parties that his expertise in safeguarding Finland's independence superseded all other considerations (Allison 1985: 146–155).

Ideational-moral authority

Leaders also draw authority from their followers when those followers believe the leader shares their values, beliefs and identities. "A loyal constituency is won when the leader is seen as symbolizing their norms, and when their image of the leader (whether or not it corresponds to reality) is congruent with their inner environment of myth and legend" (Gardner 1990: 28–29).

Some values, beliefs and identities might be widely held across an entire society, making it necessary for every national leader to express them. Even the most competent atheist would struggle to get elected in the Comoros, where 98 per cent of the population identify with Islam. Yet inevitably there will also be ideological, social and political divisions within a society that leaders will have to contend with. The Comoros is a deeply divided archipelago where your identity and authority as a political leader are very much tied to the island onto which you were born. Comorian presidents have faced a constant crisis of authority on the islands they didn't originate from, and the use of coercive power to compensate has frequently been the unfortunate result (Hassan 2009).

Like competence, leaders must work to maintain their moral-ideational authority. Their speeches, policies and actions constantly communicate political ideals that are important to maintaining that trust. Leaders perceived to have 'sold out' on their ideals will lose followers who were attracted to those ideals. A politician elected on a platform of family values and social conservatism will rapidly lose their authority with supporters if a string of extra-marital affairs is revealed, often regardless of how competent they might otherwise be. On the other hand, those the public believe to be moral authorities can command immense respect and influence over politics even in the absence of much positional authority like Aung San Suu Kyi and Martin Luther King (Kane 2001: 17–44).

It is commonplace in politics, though, that the ideal and the practical come into conflict, and hence political leaders often face a tough balancing act between ideational-moral and competent authority. For example, Alexis Tsipras was elected Prime Minister of Greece in 2015 at the height of the county's debt crisis amidst immense political pressure from the European Union. Tsipras' party, Syriza, was a coalition of left-wing political forces, with Tsipras and the party winning election due in large part to promises of opposing the severe austerity measures being implemented in response to the crisis.

Tsipras had strong ideational authority in the movement – he had served in the Communist Youth of Greece and had run on anti-neoliberal platforms throughout his career. Yet after taking office, Tsipras was faced with Greece's precarious financial situation, and the very real possibility of sovereign default and collapse of the Greek economy, unless it accepted a European Union bailout. No bailout, however, would be forthcoming unless Greece implemented austerity measures, including deep cuts to public services, pensions and welfare programs. After protracted negotiations and even a national referendum rejecting the proposed terms of the bailout deal, Tsipras nevertheless accepted the austerity conditions. For some of his supporters, Tsipras had abandoned everything he stood for (Lapavitsas 2016). Many left-wing activists abandoned Syriza, and nearly a third of its MPs crossed the floor of parliament against Tsipras's deal, forcing Tsipras to secure passage with support from the conservative parties he had spent his career opposing. Tsipras framed the decision as 'staying alive or suicide' (Adams 2015). Under extraordinarily difficult circumstances he believed he had tried and had made the best choice possible for the country. It was a sentiment that the public seemed to agree with when Tsipras was re-elected shortly after the bailout with only a slightly reduced margin, though popular support fell steeply as austerity measures were implemented the following year (The Economist 2016; Van Esch 2017).

Charismatic authority

Weber defined charisma as "a certain quality of an individual personality, by virtue of which he is set apart from ordinary men and treated as endowed with supernatural, superhuman, or at least specifically exceptional powers or qualities" (Weber 1922/1964: 48). Weber's concept of charismatic authority captures a quintessential part of leadership that has always been difficult to rationally explain – a belief in the greatness of the leader even in the face of contrary evidence. They may even take on supernatural qualities in the eyes of their followers. Charismatic authority is highly emotive and involves an intense degree of attachment and devotion. Emotion is an extremely powerful driver of leader-follower behaviour, and many have followed a leader into hopeless causes on account of it (Willner 1984: 18–41).

Charismatic authority is hard to precisely define. It seems to stem not from manifest competence or ideological purity, but from personal qualities. Personality, energy, strength, honesty, authenticity, self-sacrifice or even attractiveness can all contribute to perceptions of a leader's authority. Hannah Arendt upheld self-confidence as the key to the charismatic appeal: "extraordinary self-confidence and displays of self-confidence therefore inspire confidence in others; pretensions to genius waken the conviction in others that they are indeed dealing with a genius" (Canovan 2004: 246).

Many have seen the 'charismatic bond' as one that emerges particularly in response to psychological and social distress on behalf of a group, with the leader being placed in the position of a 'saviour' (Madsen & Snow 1991). Certainly, many leaders with strong charismatic holds over their followers have emerged in periods of great crisis, or as near mythical figures in social and political movements amongst the oppressed and marginalized (Stutje

2012). Fear is one of the most powerful of all human emotions, and Paschen and Dihsmaier argue that key to understanding charismatic appeal is that certain leaders, through their own confidence and personality, alleviate the fears of others – they fulfil a deep psychological need on behalf of their followers and form an enduring bond in the process. Other psychological needs a charismatic leader might fulfil arise when people are faced with uncertainty and insecurity, when they feel isolated or ignored, or when they feel threatened by outside forces (Paschen & Dihsmaier 2014: 33–45).

Competent, ideational and charismatic authority readily coincide in talented leaders (see Case 2.2). Yet it's not unusual for leaders who are competent and moral to lack the 'x-factor' that makes for a charismatic leader. Bill English, for example, a long-time leader in the National Party of New Zealand, was considered even by opponents as one of the most intelligent and capable policymakers in the parliament. His conservative credentials and track-record of problem-solving won the confidence of his party colleagues, and he became leader of his party twice – as opposition leader in 2002 and as successor to Prime Minister John Key in 2016. Yet despite widespread respect, he was unable to inspire the wider electorate – he was frequently described as 'dull' in the press, and the public never warmed to him (Watkins 2017). Notwithstanding an otherwise highly successful political career, he led his party to disappointing election losses during both his stints as leader.

On the other end of the scale, the charismatic leader can command incredible devotion, sometimes in ways that are hard to explain. Ruhollah Khomeini, the political and spiritual leader of the Islamic Revolution in Iran in 1979, was an intensely beloved figure by a great majority of Iranians. His mystique and charisma were legendary, with crowds spellbound for hours listening to him speak. As one of the many scholars who have tried to explain his leadership states, "he gave the masses a sense of personal integrity, collective identity, historical rootedness, and feelings of pride and superiority" (Ashraf 1994: 102). Millions of his followers felt he had divine and God-given powers. Secularists who ideologically opposed the Revolution and its politics were themselves often personally loyal to Khomeini regardless. One dissident journalist compared the relationship as one of a father, who still loves and is loved by his rebellious children (Molavi 2005; Ashraf 1994). Upon his death in 1989, even his most bitter political opponents were deeply shaken and went into mourning, and his funeral was one of the largest human gatherings in history with over 10 million Iranians in attendance.

Leaders with great charismatic authority are not necessarily any better at achieving the goals of a group, but they are often given far greater latitude by their followers than those without such appeal, and they may be able to inspire much greater commitment to achieving a goal (Willner 1984: 184–194; Paschen & Dihsmaier 2014: 30–33). Because it serves to satisfy deep-seated psychological needs on the part of followers, the charismatic bond, once formed, can be nearly unshakable. It can endure when faced with the immorality, incompetence or even illegality of the leader. Hugo Chávez, President of Venezuela from 1999 until his death in 2013, maintained a strong and emotive loyalty from millions of working-class Venezuelans who saw him as their champion and one of them, even in the face of widespread

Case 2.2 Many roots of authority

Juan Perón

President of Argentina, 1946–1955

Eva Perón

First Lady of Argentina, 1946–1952

Figure 2.3 Juan and Eva Perón around 1948

Juan and Eva 'Evita' Perón were founders of the Peronist political movement in Argentina and two of the most influential political leaders in Argentinian history. Their story offers a case study of how leaders amass sources of authority, and how clashes over authority can lead to their demise.

Ideational-Moral: Juan Perón's early career was as a military officer, and as a member of the United Officers' Group who staged a coup in Argentina in 1943. His long army career and participation in the coup gave him trust and respect within the military, highly valued in a political system where the military played a significant role (Page 1983: 54–62). Yet unlike many of his colleagues, Juan also cultivated ideational authority amongst the working class. After becoming the Minister for Labour in the new military government, Perón worked actively with the trade union movement to raise minimum wages, reduce working hours, and introduce other wide-ranging reforms that dramatically improved working conditions in Argentina. A subscriber to social democratic ideas, in just two years as labour minister Perón commanded significant authority over working-class voters and the powerful trade union movement (Page 1983: 63–72). During his presidency, Perón and his wife Eva would pursue social democratic policies to help the poor, effecting great improvement in employment, social security, housing and health. Eva Perón's tireless work with the most disadvantaged in the country during her life won her the undying loyalty of many traditionally ignored by Argentinian politics. The Peróns became heroes of social democratic ideals for millions of Argentines that served as the foundation for much of their political influence.

Competent: Juan Perón's election to the presidency in 1946 was greatly helped by prominent accomplishments in his political career. As a leading minister in the response to the 1944 San Juan earthquake, Perón very successfully organized massive relief efforts that won him national acclaim and helped make him a popular hero (Page 1983: 3–6). Though not without disappointments and failures, the Perón presidency was also marked by tangible improvements in the lives of many, particularly around wages and working conditions, but also significant economic growth, and great strides in health, education and welfare. Recognition of the competence of the administration drew many more supporters, and a much-increased margin of victory for Perón when he ran for re-election in 1951.

Legal-Rational: Juan Perón was vested with legal-rational authority by his clear electoral victories in 1946 and 1951, and the strong executive powers vested in the president by the constitutional framework, including command over the armed forces, which gave the Peróns (who always campaigned and operated as a political team) great authority to pass major reforms quickly with limited oversight or negotiation with other political institutions. The Peróns further augmented these powers by passing a constitutional amendment in 1949 that removed term limits on the presidency and enshrined into law many of their social democratic ideals such as rights to education and fair working conditions (Page 1983: 200–206).

Traditional: Traditional authority became a key aspect of the story of the Peróns. On the one hand, it accrued to Juan Perón in part due to the culture of the 'caudillo' in Spanish-speaking countries. The caudillo is a long-standing tradition of populist rule by military-political leaders, often associated with romantic ideals of nationalism, masculinity and strength (see Case 5.2). It was consciously channelled by Perón, who sought to project strength and his personal connection to the people and fused his military and political identities in his public appearances (Cuevillas 1992). It was traditional authority too that led to the end of his first presidency in 1955. The previous year Perón had sought to legalize abortion and prostitution, bringing him into conflict with the Catholic church, which commanded enormous traditional authority in heavily Catholic Argentina. It was a battle for political authority that Perón lost, as much of the pro-Catholic military defected from Perón and forced him to relinquish power (Page 1983: 296–315).

Charismatic: Though the Peróns wielded significant authority of all kinds, it was their charismatic hold over many Argentines that continues to captivate today. Eva Perón particularly was a beloved figure in the nation. Her perceived beauty, grace, kindness, strength and devotion to the poor led to her obtaining a semi-divine status amongst millions who thought her a saint or even a manifestation of the Virgin Mary. Though she never held a formal political office, she was nonetheless an intrinsic part of the Perónist movement and appeared constantly, even on ballot papers and official portraits, next to her husband. Eva's early death in 1952 has only intensified her personal cult (Hedges 2017). Both she and Juan commanded intense personal loyalty both in life and death that went far beyond their policy achievements and ideals, and the mystique of the Peróns still casts a long shadow over Argentinian politics.

corruption and economic collapse resulting from Chávez's increasingly disastrous policies (Weyland 2003; Merolla & Zechmeister 2011).

Like power, various forms of authority are at play simultaneously in political leadership (see Case 2.2). Authority often works to modify the potency of other forms of power. A leader who loses their competent authority will find their powers of persuasion greatly reduced. A leader may have a powerful army at their disposal or a vast fortune, but if they use it indiscriminately to oppress the public or exclusively reward themselves and their friends, they may soon lose moral authority and have a revolution on their hands. In this sense, authority is a special form of power, as it has the ability to greatly influence the effectiveness of all other forms of power, as well as having the ability to influence the behaviour of others in the absence of the use of power.

Followers

Thus far, we have talked about power and authority largely as flowing in one direction, from leaders to followers. Yet a leader has no power or authority if followers refuse to recognize it. Both are consensually determined – followers choose to be influenced by leaders on some level.

It is not always a fair choice. A leader who threatens to arrest you and your family if you do not obey has presented you with a dismal set of options. But even the most brutal forms of power, like violence and torture, cannot force someone to do something they refuse to do. The Roman Emperors Decius and Valerian in the third century CE set increasingly severe policies to eradicate the growing influence of Christianity in the Roman Empire. Despite extreme coercion from the authorities, many Christians chose death instead of recanting their beliefs, and ultimately the policy was a failure. Indeed, far from eliminating the followers of Christ, within half a century it would be emperors themselves who began to convert to Christianity.

Political societies are large, dynamic, heterogenous groups of ever-changing individuals, and how a given individual responds to power and authority varies greatly. Some will be more persuaded by ideals and emotions, others by facts and logic. Some followers can be induced through material rewards, others are looking to be inspired. Often, different leaders will draw certain types of followers who might have a predilection towards their specific strengths and claims. Highly charismatic leaders will draw followers with different characteristics than those who stress competence or fidelity to ideals (e.g., Paschen & Dihsmaier 2014: 45–49).

Followers do not just differ in their predispositions though – they are also always engaged in assessing both the *credibility* and *legitimacy* of potential leaders, their power and their authority.

Credibility

Credibility is how believable or convincing something is, and the credibility of power or claims to authority as perceived by potential followers is fundamental to its effectiveness, and the effectiveness of political leadership in general (Kouzes & Posner 2011; Bennister, Worthy & 't Hart 2017: ch. 1).

When a politician makes a promise in an election, we are going to both consider *what* the promise is, and *who* is making that promise, in order to determine credibility. This can be a sophisticated process whereby many different factors are considered. Sabine Van Zuydam breaks down the process of analysing a leader's credibility into three areas – Do they know what's right or best? Are they trustworthy and honest? Do they have my best interests at heart? (Van Zuydam 2018: 21–23).

For example, a party leader facing a vote of no confidence may use the power of their office to offer a colleague an enticement – in exchange for their support in the vote, they'll receive a prominent government position in the future. But how likely is it that the party leader will win the vote and stay on as leader (and thus be able to reward them)? Does the party leader keep their promises? Will they look out for the colleague's interest in the future or toss them aside once they have secured power? These are the questions which help determine how credible the offer, and the offeror, are.

It is the same for claims of authority. A candidate running for office in the Comoros who stresses their religious piety and Islamic adherence to the devout voters of that country is not going to be credible as a moral authority if most of the public know they are an atheist who loves wine and pork. But because we operate in an environment of information disparity, how followers determine credibility is by no means uniform or accurate. Our candidate may only be known to be an apostate by a small group of people who know the candidate personally. They speak publicly about it, but the leader denounces them as bitter personal enemies seeking to destroy his career. With conflicting claims and no proof either way, how do the voters assess the two claims? Especially when a leader has so many tools at their disposal to manage their image with the public, what followers are assessing is the credibility of that public image, which may diverge significantly from reality (Axford et al. 1992; Landtsheer et al. 2008; Case 10.2).

Persuasion are other areas where assessing credibility is rarely straightforward. A leader making a speech on environmental policy may be determined by scientists to be inaccurate and wrong-headed, yet the vast majority of the public, lacking the expertise to analyse the arguments in detail, may be greatly supportive of the speech and consider the leader a credible voice on environmental matters as a result. The credibility of the leader's power is thus a complex determination where there may be significant disagreement amongst followers.

Legitimacy

Legitimacy is the acceptance by followers that a leader has the right to use certain powers or assume certain authority over them. While credibility is about judging if power or authority claims are 'convincing', legitimacy is about judging whether they are 'right'. "The basis of every system of authority, and correspondingly of every kind of willingness to obey, is a belief, a belief by virtue of which persons exercising authority are lent prestige" (Weber 1964: 382). However, legitimacy has become a fiercely debated concept in political philosophy (see Chapter 3). Some argue that legitimacy must rest on normative and objective standards – does the use of power and authority conform with universal ideas of justice? Others see it is a largely subjective matter that is determined only through the peculiar beliefs of a group or society (Netelenbos 2016: 4–26; Coicaud 2002: 10–85).

The process of the legitimation of authority is a crucial one. Authority deemed to be illegitimate will always provoke resistance, and societies create rules and processes to validate the authority of rulers. Such processes have long dominated political life. The Maya, for example, required their rulers to undergo bloodletting to prove their bravery and self-sacrifice to the gods. Elections are the modern bloodletting equivalent, with most of the public engaged at some level, and both campaigns and results are intensively scrutinized. Bitterly fought or very close elections are long remembered by the public, as are those in which electoral irregularities are thought to have played a role, and some leaders who come to office under contested circumstances never quite manage to escape the perception of illegitimacy (e.g. Dundas 2012).

How followers assess a leader's legitimacy will in turn affect how that leader's use of power is received. Leaders who win a resounding electoral victory are often said to have received a 'mandate' to pursue their policies and use the full power of their government to implement them. Leaders with narrow victories, or forming minority governments, will be expected to be more tempered or perhaps share power going forward (see Grossback, Peterson & Stimson 2012). Different kinds of power also have different rules regarding their legitimate use. For example, in most modern societies, using the military to coercively enforce the leader's policies is considered legitimate only in extreme situations.

The credibility and legitimacy of a leader are being constantly assessed and reassessed by the public. With credibility this is often a gradual process of change – over time most political leaders make mistakes, change positions, break promises or even just age and lose their touch, such that their credibility with the public and elites starts to erode, though a major scandal can end a career overnight. Structures of leader legitimacy tend to be more stable, though when change comes it is often dramatic. For instance, it was the December 2010 self-immolation of Mohamed Bouazizi, a Tunisian street vendor protesting his unfair persecution by the authorities, that triggered a chain of events that led to the Arab Spring and brought down four of the Arab world's most powerful and long-running dictatorships. Of course, this event was merely the catalyst – political attitudes had been changing long before, until a breaking point was reached where autocratic rule could no longer be justified as legitimate amongst the populace. As David Beetham argues, a "power relationship is not legitimate because people believe in its legitimacy, but because it can be justified in terms of their beliefs" (Beetham 2013: 11).

Conformity

So, if followers ostensibly have so much capacity to determine both power and authority, why do seemingly illegitimate leaders rule for so long? Why does it seem like leaders have more influence over the course of circumstances than followers do?

The foremost reason is that while *followers* collectively have a lot of power, an individual *follower* does not; this is what Mancur Olson famously describes as the 'collective action' problem (Olson 1965). The problem stipulates that the larger the group, the more difficult it is for that group to collectively mobilize and unite behind a common goal. Smaller, more concentrated interests can act cohesively far more easily. Moreover, they will tend to gain more individually from, and thus be more dedicated to, a particular outcome. While leaders and their governments are relatively small, well-organized and usually disciplined institutions, their constituents are diverse, heterogenous and unorganized. A disciplined military dictatorship's coercive power is thus very credible over individuals or small groups – to overwhelm it requires vast numbers of people working towards a common alternative to resist its coercive powers. To revolt without being sure of widespread public solidarity is to risk everything, while the benefits to you personally of a regime change might be only modest or theoretical (Finer 1962: 6–13).

The same goes for structures of authority in a democratic society. While they have evolved as responses to collective action problems and to give power to leaders and institutions to advance common goals that individuals can't easily achieve (Hampton 1998: 77), what do we do if we no longer accept the legitimacy of the government, our traditions, our institutions? Only mass action on a grand scale can generate enough pressure to have constitutions rewritten, institutions reformed, or traditions overturned. Action on such a scale is in practice very challenging to achieve.

Another aspect is the asymmetry of access to resources, information and communication platforms. Followers generally lack the technical understanding to assess whether a leader has made competent decisions, or the intimacy with the leader to truly know their moral character or the credibility of their power. Yet even if they do, it is usually harder (though still eminently possible) to disseminate that information widely and raise general consciousness sufficiently to mobilize enough opposition to challenge a regime. That said, the digital age is greatly expanding access to information and each other, diminishing the disparity significantly.

Apathy may be the biggest obstacle of all. The authority of leaders is often enabled by the passive, rather than active, acceptance of the majority, "either because they can see or imagine no alternative to it, or because they see it as natural and unchangeable" (Lukes 2005: 28). Low levels of popular engagement in politics have been much studied as modern phenomena, and they pose a problem to the effective functioning of democratic government and as a check on the power of leaders (Neuman 1986; DeLuca 1995), especially amongst younger generations (Zukin et al. 2006). Yet political apathy has been a concern for eons. Plato and Aristotle highly valued public participation as key to a healthy politics but bemoaned its frequent absence. Alexis De Tocqueville, observing American democracy in the 1830s, observed that it faced a danger of descending into soft despotism due to apathy and a lack of public engagement. A fate that Martyn Lyons argues befell the French Revolution, as revolutionary fervour gave way over the years to political exhaustion and indifference that paved the way for despotism to return (Lyons 1994: 29–42).

Social psychologists have provided further clues, and various experiments have suggested that submission to authority may be a basic instinct. Stanley Milgram famously tested this idea in the 1970s. In a series of experiments, participants were instructed by a researcher to administer electric shocks to an unseen but audible test subject behind a screen, under the guise of testing whether painful stimuli would improve memory recall in the test subject. Unknown to the participants, the test subjects were actors who merely imitated receiving painful shocks, and the real experiment was to see how long the participants administering the shocks would continue to obey the researcher. Despite the actors imitating increasingly severe pain, injury or even death, the majority of participants continued to administer shocks and obey instructions to 'turn up the voltage' until an obviously dangerous 'maximum voltage' was reached (Milgram 1974). Several other group experiments, such as those by Solomon Asch (1955) and Philip Zimbardo (1971/2008), found similarly high levels of conformity in response to supposed authority, though late analyses of such experiments have noted significant nuances in individual responses to authority, and arguably reasoned, rather than slavish, compliance (Haslam & Reicher 2012).

Finally, we cannot discount the possibility that many individuals are not merely apathetic towards power and authority, but actually seek to be subordinated by it. Sociologist Georg Simmel commented that "the majority of men not only *cannot* exist without leadership; they also *feel* they cannot; they *seek* higher power which relieves them of responsibility; they seek a restrictive, regulatory rigour which protects them not only against the outside world but also against themselves" (Simmel 1964: 193). Psychologist Erich Fromm concurs in the landmark *Escape From Freedom* (1941), stating that most people do not enjoy pure freedom but rather seek security, certainty, prosperity and identity through the rule of others, even authoritarian rule (see also Lipman-Blumen 2005). Unsettling though it may be, history has demonstrated that followers are often at least partly the creators, and sometimes the fiercest defenders, of their own submission to the authority of leaders.

Elites

When we speak of political leaders, our attention usually turns to just the most prominent leader in a hierarchy – the prime minister or president, the monarch or mayor. Yet such leaders do not hold all the power, or anything like it, and are usually just the most prominent members of what have historically been called the 'elites' of a society. "Elites may be distinguished from the public … by their exertion of substantial power and influence over the public and political outcomes" (Etzioni-Halevy 1997: xxv). Elites occupy a tricky place in our society and the model we've advanced in this chapter, and an even trickier place in leadership studies generally (Blondel 2018). They have significant power, but often complex or weak claims of authority to use it and may encounter significant public resistance when they try (Gilens & Page 2014).

Political leaders must work with, or sometimes engage in, power struggles with other elites in order to preserve their power. Yet at the same time leaders are reliant upon an elite to implement their rule (Case 2.3). The Sultan of the Ottoman Empire officially maintained unquestioned authority over his lands, yet to manage the sprawling and diverse empire required the leadership of vast networks of elites, from the aristocrats and generals who administered far-flung provinces and armies to the viziers and clerics who oversaw the Ottoman bureaucracy and church. Such elites were not just extensions of the ruler's will, but individuals and groups with their own agendas and ambitions. They enabled the Sultan's rule, yet also had the ability to constrain him, and in several cases acted to remove him entirely. Indeed, with far greater access to power than the public, historically it has been more common for elites to remove their rulers than for the public to do so. Even in modern democracies it is not uncommon for legislators, judges or parties, rather than the public at the ballot box, to decide when a leader's time is up. Just who the key elites are varies greatly from country to country. In contemporary Iran, for example, Shia Islam and its hierarchy of jurists, scholars and clergy have influence rivalling that of any elected office (Rakel 2009).

German-Italian sociologist Robert Michels argues that a division of society into 'rulers' and 'ruled' is not an accident or perversion, but rather an inevitability. In *Political Parties* (1911), he argues that all complex societies and organizations, no matter how avowedly egalitarian, must eventually develop elite structures. He offers several reasons for this. Firstly, because as groups expand and governing becomes more complex, it's practically impossible for everyone to maintain an equal share in the decision-making process. A village of 20 can easily meet in one place to debate and decide upon issues affecting them on an equal basis, but it's very hard as a town of 2,000 and impossible as a city of 2 million. Secondly, as communities or organizations get larger, the complexity of the issues they must make decisions on also increases. Specialization naturally follows, which creates elites with specific knowledge, skills, or resources that few others possess. Thirdly, it's practically impossible for everyone in a large polity to make their voice heard to everyone else, and those who control the means of mass communication will inevitably (even if unintentionally) have far more power than those who don't. Michels did not see this process as purely elite-driven – he contended, based on theories of crowd psychology, that the non-ruling class craved the direction, inspiration and certainty that elites provided.

Agreeing upon the inevitability of a ruling elite, Vilfredo Pareto argued that it was ability of the elite to change and circulate its membership that was central to healthy politics. In the ideal society, elites are meritocratic, and the most talented and capable people move into the elite from the non-elite, with free circulation between the followers and leaders. Yet as Pareto argues, this is frequently not the case. Elites tend to become stagnant and conservative over time, and instead of dynamically assimilating new generations of talented leaders and their ideas they often close ranks and attempt to maintain a monopoly on power as long as possible (Pareto 1935). Many have attributed the poor circulation of elites in the Soviet Union as leading to a 'gerontocracy' – rule by the elderly – that stymied innovation and necessary

Case 2.3 Elites make and unmake

Haile Selassie

Regent & Emperor of Ethiopia, 1916–1974

Figure 2.4 Haile Selassie in 1970

Haile Selassie's entire political career is a story inextricably tied with the management, and mismanagement, of elites. Born of royal blood, but not in the direct line of succession, Selassie masterfully courted both church and nobility as an ambitious young noble during the unpopular reign of Lij Iyasu. After a few years, he and his elite allies skilfully manoeuvred to have the Emperor excommunicated by the Ethiopian clergy and then deposed.

His subsequent appointment as regent by the nobility was done in large part because the aristocracy believed he would be weak and easily manipulated. Selassie started with little political capital and was not able to hold much sway over powerful government ministers or regional princes (Marcus 1994: 116–129). Yet slowly he consolidated his power. A reformer who wanted to transform Ethiopia into a modern state, Selassie expanded the coalition of elites for change behind him. Conservatives in the government were gradually replaced by reformist allies, and he applied a 'divide and conquer' strategy – instead of trying to radically transform the nation quickly, he trod carefully, maintaining the support of most of the aristocracy whilst drawing out and defeating isolated nobles who challenged his rule. By 1930, Selassie had manoeuvred himself to succeed as Emperor outright (Asserate 2015: 38–74).

Selassie gradually but systematically implemented centralization that saw regional rulers lose most of their financial, military and legal powers. In doing so, he created a modern government in Addis Ababa and abolished much of the medieval practice that had governed the country previously, like the slave trade, whilst using the new powers of centralized government to foster economic development. By the 1940s his authority was total and unquestioned, underpinned by a now highly loyal military, bureaucratic and aristocratic elite entirely dependent on Selassie for patronage. He continued to use 'divide and conquer' to maintain his absolute grip on power – potential rivals within the elite were transferred to far-flung provinces, whilst ministers and governors were regularly rotated through jobs by the Emperor to prevent them from building a power base or loyal following (Asserate 2015: ch. 6–7).

Though Selassie had united the nation under his person and began to create a modern economy in the large cities, conditions throughout the rest of country remained semi-feudal with the aristocracy and church holding most of the land and power. Reliant on traditional elites to maintain his rule in the provinces, Selassie passed only relatively meagre reforms in this area, which proved a growing problem for a discontented populace. In the capital, Selassie had created a new elite of modern bureaucrats to rule the country and implement his policies. Selassie used the state and his personal wealth to fund thousands of Ethiopians to study overseas and then return home to help modernize Ethiopia, personally meeting with every student before they departed. Although this new generation were initially extremely loyal to Selassie, his paternalistic rule soon jarred with them, as they would learn abroad that their home country was one of the last absolute monarchies on the planet (Kebede 2006). Constant intrigue to limit the power of the bureaucracy meant that government was slow and lacked capacity due to Selassie's attempts to personally rule the entire country.

During the 1960s, Selassie's strengths became his weaknesses. Ethiopia began to stagnate, its economy and agricultural sector increasingly backwards. Without an independent elite to seriously challenge his power or question his decisions, Selassie remained largely oblivious to the growing problems. Eventually, the new generation of Western-educated bureaucrats and military officers was his undoing. Their personal loyalty to the emperor could not blind them to the growing problems, and many began to convert to Marxism and agitate for revolution (Kebede 2006). His traditional allies saw the growing threat, but their undying loyalty to Selassie prevented them from forcing a change of course. By the 1970s, famines had broken out across the nation and became the pretext for widespread uprisings. The very elite that Selassie had created to rule a modern nation loyal to him turned to progressively seize power for themselves. Known as the Derg, they began to take control in early 1974, ironically using the same incremental strategy that Selassie had done decades earlier, progressively arresting the Emperor's loyal ministers and generals in the name of fighting 'corruption' and 'backwardness', whilst continuing to profess loyalty to the Emperor. Yet by the end of the year, the Emperor's entire elite power structure had been subverted, and there was nothing left to do but for the Derg to arrest the Emperor himself, now isolated and alone in his palace (Asserate 2015: ch. 9).

reform, and ultimately led to stagnation and decline (Kort 2019: 349–350). Contemporary studies have found similar problems in modern electoral democracies – governing elites have a tendency to cling on, politicians advance on the basis of seniority rather than talent, new politicians are often 'insiders' who have worked within the political system and have deep connections with the elite rather than representing the most talented aspirants (Verzichelli 2018: 581–586).

The top political leaders are very often drawn and recruited directly from the elite stratum. For eons this was fixed in law and custom – noble houses and aristocrats would ascend to the leadership through the collective assent of other elites. Even in modern democracies, very often political leaders are drawn from the business, intellectual or established political elite of the nation (Mills 1956). In turn they rely heavily on elites to sustain and implement their rule. And yet leaders are *not* synonymous with elites, and this is often thrown into stark contrast when leaders and elites clash (Case 2.3). Leaders like Thaksin Shinawatra in Thailand and Hugo Chávez in Venezuela were previously elites themselves (business and military, respectively) and yet pursued political projects that brought them into immediate conflict with the elite establishment. On the other hand, true outsiders taking power – like the Communist revolutionaries in Eastern Europe – tend to simply become a new elite themselves rather than abolishing elites as intended, replicating the disparities of power they originally revolted against, a point made famously by Yugoslavian Communist leader Milovan Đilas's *The New Class* (1957).

Power and authority, followers and elites make up a complex ecosystem of relationships at the core of leadership. They can only be discussed very briefly in this chapter, but they are central to how leadership works and will be foundational as we go forward in thinking about the more specific dimensions of political leadership.

But the most important takeaway is to understand that leadership is *not a unidirectional process* whereby leaders simply command followers. It's a dynamic process in which *both* leaders *and* followers interact and influence each other. And some in a society, such as elites, may be leading and following *simultaneously*. Power and authority are fluid concepts, with many different manifestations, and thus a leader's 'power' must always be considered within a broader constellation of actors and processes.

Chapter Summary

- Power is the production of intended effects, and *social power*, used in leadership, is the means by which a leader changes the behaviour of others. It can take four forms:
  - Coercion: the threat of pain or deprivation
  - Inducement: the offer of rewards or benefits
  - Persuasion: using argument or emotion to convince
  - Manipulation: using deception or hidden methods

- Authority is like power, but is the socially accepted *right,* rather than the mere *means,* to change the behaviour of others. It can be attached to either a person, or to a position, and takes five forms:
    - Legal-Rational: established by laws and institutions.
    - Traditional: established by customs and traditions.
    - Competent: established through knowledge and skill.
    - Ideational-Moral: established through values and ideas.
    - Charismatic: established through personality and emotion.
- Followers collectively determine both the credibility (believability) of power and authority, as well as its legitimacy (its right to be used). Followers appear less powerful than they are, due to the collective action problem, apathy, resignation and perhaps even a basic psychological disposition towards accepting authority.
- Elites are the echelon of society that hold a disproportionate amount of power. They both lead and follow, and so do not fit into the leader/follower dichotomy as easily. Political leaders rely on other elites to maintain and implement their rule.

3 PHILOSOPHY, LEGITIMACY AND MORALITY

Chapter Outline

- How has political philosophy treated the concept of leadership?
- What is legitimacy? What gives leaders the right to rule over us? What obligations do followers have in return?
- What is the appropriate role of a leader in a political system? How much power should we give leaders?
- How *should* leaders lead? What moral principles should leaders strive to uphold?
- By what moral standards should we judge our leaders? Do special rules of morality apply to leadership?

Though we might use terms like 'power' and 'authority' objectively when trying to define them in Chapters 1 and 2, these are phenomena that are subjectively experienced by all political societies, with ramifications for the lives of everyone. As such, who leads us and how have been central concerns of philosophers throughout the ages. Positions have varied greatly, from extolling leaders as the creative drivers of history and civilization, to cursing their existence as a constant threat to liberty.

In this chapter I try to make sense of this vast ocean of work by considering just three key projects that philosophers have most consequentially engaged with regarding political leadership: the legitimacy of political leadership, its proper role within political society and the moral standards it should follow. In considering each of these three projects, I'll discuss some of the most important thinkers and thought associated with each, and why these areas of inquiry are still relevant to the contemporary political world.

The legitimacy of leaders

Legitimacy speaks to the *right* to rule, and *why*, or perhaps *why should*, followers follow a leader. Establishing the legitimacy of authority is a central aspect of political life. In the previous chapter, various types of authority were described that might be associated with a leader, and we established that followers have final responsibility for assessing the legitimacy of their rulers.

What societies establish as legitimate though will not always be universally agreed upon as 'right'. John Rawls makes the important observation that while the ideas of *justice* and *legitimacy* are related and may even emerge from the same conceptual frameworks, they are not the same thing. It is quite possible for a leader to be both legitimate and unjust, a somewhat uncomfortable conclusion, but one with plenty of examples we might draw from history (Rawls 1993: 225; 1995: 175). Because political legitimacy ultimately finds it roots in the mercurial beliefs of, and interactions between, leaders and followers, it can deviate, sometimes radically, from broader and more stable ideals of the just. David Beetham illustrates this by articulating three dimensions to the determination of legitimacy (2013: 16).

1. Conforming to established rules and norms.
2. Justification in the shared beliefs of leaders and followers.
3. The consent of those being governed or subordinated.

All three components contribute to legitimacy to varying degrees depending on context and culture, yet they also capture potential tensions between *what is* and *what should be* (2013: 19). Rules and norms tend towards normative principles, while popular consent may be entirely malleable and contextual. Shared beliefs might sit somewhere between those two poles.

Even legal-rational authority, which is the most formally constituted type of a leader's authority, can be subject to same dilemma. The Electoral College of the United States, the constitutional body that formally elects the US president, is a good example. The US Constitution proscribes a method of apportioning the electoral college that benefits smaller states. Combined with the 'winner-take-all' method that most states use to appoint their electors, it's technically possible that this design will elect a president who has not won the nationwide popular vote. In fact, this has happened five times in US history. Each occasion has sparked intense controversy which tarnished the perceived legitimacy of the presidents that were elected. Although the process of their accession was in all cases completely valid within the established constitutional rules, it nonetheless came into conflict with shared beliefs over fairness and popular sovereignty, and arguably runs counter to the principle of the 'consent of the governed'.

An added layer of complication comes with the concept of *obligation*. If people could freely opt-in or opt-out of the state and the rules it makes, then the legitimacy of the rules and who made them would be less important. This is not the case however – the state and its rulers have significant powers over the individual that he or she cannot avoid. They can oblige us to obey laws, pay taxes, attend school, seek employment, participate in military or civic service etcetera, and they possess powers to coerce us to do so if we don't comply. The determination of legitimacy is thus not just about establishing right to rule, but also right to rule *over us*.

Whether or not legitimate political rule also entails an obligation for us to obey it has long been a subject of fierce contestation. Some, like John Locke, have argued that properly established political legitimacy automatically entails an obligation to obey it (Locke 1689/1980: s.95–99), whilst others like Robert Paul Wolff reject any obligation to obey the state at all (1998). Still more have argued that the obligation is conditional, and we must consider normative and moral justifications of how power is used, with the obligation to obey applying only to rule that is just (Buchanan 2002; Edmundson 1998).

A comprehensive synthesis of millennia of debate over how to legitimize rulers and obedience to rule is impossible here and is besides better done elsewhere (e.g. Beetham 2013); however, we can gain a good introductory insight into the major contentions by examining some of the most prominent voices in this debate in modern history, and what it has meant for political leadership as it has evolved over time.

Utilitarianism: Jeremy Bentham and John Stuart Mill

Irish philosopher Francis Hutcheson defines the most righteous, and therefore most legitimate, course of action as that which creates "the greatest happiness for the greatest number". This classic position was developed extensively by the English philosopher Jeremy Bentham (1748–1832), who went on to found the utilitarian school of moral philosophy.

The utilitarian position on legitimacy and morality, and the implications for political leadership, are easy to grasp. Leaders should justify their right to rule on actions that maximize the beneficial outcomes for those subjected to that rule. Assessing legitimacy this way only considers the consequences their actions have on others (Schneewind 1990). To put it another way classically formulated over the centuries, 'the ends justify the means'. This doctrine is also known as *consequentialism* and has significant implications for moral theory as well.

Bentham's argument for political action begin with the basic assumption that political leaders face nothing but a series of harmful choices, and the best they can do is minimize the harm they cause in the act of governing:

> Every law is an evil, for every law is an infraction of liberty: And I repeat that government has but a choice of evils: In making this choice, what ought to be the object of the legislator? He ought to assure himself of two things; 1st, that in every case, the incidents which he tries to prevent are really evils; and 2ndly, that if evils, they are greater than those which he employs to prevent them. (Bentham 1830: 259)

John Stuart Mill (1806–1873) augmented many of Bentham's arguments and refined the utilitarian position. Bentham's utilitarianism could freely ignore the rights and liberties of individuals if the greatest number were benefited by doing so. Mill countered this notion however, maintaining "that the only purpose for which power can be rightfully exercised over any member of a civilised community, against his will, is to prevent harm to others" (Mill 1863: 23). In other words, utility legitimizes authority, but cannot justify overriding individual rights unless it is to prevent harm to others.

Yet Mill also contends that the rights of liberty accrue only to peoples capable of free and equal discussion – 'barbarians' can quite legitimately be ruled by despotism if the purpose is to improve their lives (Mill 1863: 24–25). Such thinking was ultimately used by a generation of European rulers, and Mill himself, in justifying their rule over much of the rest of the world through colonial possessions (Harris 1964).

Both Bentham and Mill ultimately favoured representative democracies as a means to constrain the acts of rulers. Bentham's views changed over time and whilst he believed it was possible for absolute rulers to maximize the beneficial outcomes to citizens, in practice rulers sought largely to maximize their own selfish interest. He thus gravitated towards a democratic systems as the best "security against misrule" (see Schofield 2006).

The philosophy of utilitarianism is easy to grasp conceptually but becomes complex when applied in practice. Consider the damage done to the perceived legitimacy of George W. Bush, Tony Blair and other western leaders over the decision to invade Iraq in 2003, an invasion that cost hundreds of billions of dollars and tens of thousands of lives. It was publicly justified on the basis of preventing the use of weapons of mass destruction the Hussein regime was believed to have developed. Such weapons were never found, leading many to conclude it was a costly war that yielded little benefit. But what if such weapons *had* been found? What if the invasion had prevented untold suffering and war by neutralizing such weapons? Would we view the invasion as legitimate, even if those leaders had exaggerated or lied to build support for their actions? And if, hypothetically, those leaders *genuinely believed* the weapons were there, wasn't their decision-making ultimately legitimate on that basis? Moreover, how do we place a value on the outcome of the war? Although far from a utopia, Iraq has emerged from the war as a democratic state with modest improvements in human rights, social institutions and economic development (Zinsmeister 2018). What means does this end justify?

For these and many other reasons, utilitarianism as a basis of political legitimacy has many critics, and tends to raise more questions than it answers. Inevitably, the legitimacy of political action thus ends up being in the eye of the beholder. As Jeremy Waldron contends, utilitarian logic serves to legitimize action only for those who stand to benefit from it but has no argument for those who stand to lose (Waldron 1987: 144).

Consent: John Locke and Jean-Jacques Rousseau

Let us move now to the idea of legitimacy resting on consent of the governed. Though the concept was promulgated by figures as early as Hugo Grotius, it was the English philosopher John Locke (1632–1704) who most influentially developed it in political philosophy. Locke contends that, in our natural prehistoric state, we live in total freedom and independence from each other, and only by our mutual consent and for our collective benefit did we form societies with governments to rule over us. The authority of a leader or government thus finds its legitimacy in the consent of those who are subject to their rule because they have voluntarily delegated their own natural authority. "No one can be put out of this estate and subjected to the political power of another without his own consent" (Locke 1689/1980: 52).

The 'consent of the governed' is a simple but powerful concept that has dominated modern political thought. However, it starts to become complicated when you consider (a) what constitutes 'consent' and (b) whether this essentially gives license to simple majoritarianism.

In terms of the first problem, nearly every person born is born into a political society and immediately subject to the authority of others – parents and political leaders alike. We have little opportunity either to express consent, or to opt out of this system should we object. Locke resolves the issue partially by laying down the concept of *tacit consent*. Every time we use a road, or attend a school, or enjoy a safe society, by enjoying those benefits we are consenting tacitly to abide by the rule of those who provide them (Locke 1689/1821: 291–293). In the modern era, we have furthermore created numerous rituals designed to elicit active consent from the populace – elections, parliaments, citizens forums, public inquiries and so on are all designed to help confer legitimacy through public input into government.

Yet most people scarcely have a choice if they do not recognize the legitimacy of these processes. Surely Locke didn't intend to mean that by walking down the roads or using wells to survive, those living under the tyrannical regime of the Taliban in Afghanistan were consenting to their authority (Pitkin 1965). And does consent as a guide for legitimacy simply mean that majoritarianism should prevail? Should leaders merely do what is popular? Such an idea undermines the role of leaders then as anything other than mouthpieces for the majority, and moreover could be used to justify persecution of minorities and inequitable enrichment of the majority.

French philosopher Jean-Jacques Rousseau (1712–1778) took up many of Locke's core arguments and expanded upon the theme, rejecting the divine right of monarchs to rule and seeing legitimacy as ultimately resting on consent. The public has the right to overthrow governments that lose public confidence. Yet he posits that political leaders should primarily serve not just the day-to-day whims of the majority, but rather their 'general will' – the interests of all people – which is protected by a rule of law. Rousseau's general will though didn't always translate into a direct connection between popular approval and political action (Cawthorn 2017: ch. 7). As he argues:

> Of themselves the people always will the good, but of themselves they do not always see in what it consists. The general will is always right, but the judgment that guides it is not always enlightened. It is therefore necessary to make the people see things as they are, and sometimes as they ought to appear, to

> point out to them the right path which they are seeking. (Rousseau 1762/1947: 35)

Leaders thus should not be mere slaves to the whims of the majority but to work towards serving the higher ideals of the general will. Such a view finds agreement with Locke, who argues indeed that rulers require extra-legal prerogatives in order to protect the public good and prevent harm (Locke 1689/1821: 327–335; Pasquino 1998).

In our modern times, we have echoes of the debate around modern democratic practice. Contemporary sentiment is often derisive of leaders who are slavishly subservient to political polling and wish to see them do 'what is right' rather than 'what is popular'. Ironically, the sentiment is effectively giving public consent for the ruler to ignore public consensus. However, popularity alone is generally considered a poor indicator of whether a course of action will serve the public interest (Weissberg 2001). Thus, consent may be a starting point for legitimacy in any democratic system, but it cannot alone determine what legitimate political action or leadership consists of.

Public reason: *John Rawls*

An important evolution in the concept of the 'consent of the governed' has come from John Rawls (1921–2002), who espoused public reason as a key variation on the idea, and saw legitimate authority requiring a basis in reasoning that all reasonable persons can share. Political action thus cannot be justified on the basis of narrow interests, ideologies, or other areas where people are likely to reasonably disagree – instead it must be rooted in common human values, like freedom and equality.

> Political power is legitimate only when it is exercised in accordance with a constitution (written or unwritten) the essentials of which all citizens, as reasonable and rational, can endorse in the light of their common human reason. (Rawls 2001: 41)

The concept of public reason as a foundation for legitimate political action has been extremely influential in recent decades, but its specific implications can vary. If upheld as meaning *consensus* on *substantive reasoning*, then perhaps there is very little action taken in politics that is truly legitimate, as on most important political issues contentiousness is inevitable, and it would be almost impossible for everyone to agree on the reasoning behind a decision (see Quong 2011).

Others have stipulated that it is the process that is key – as long as the means by which a decision was made are agreed by all to have been fair, transparent and democratic, then there can be legitimacy since everyone consented to the procedure by which the decision was made, even if they don't agree with the outcome (Peter 2008). Some have gone even further, arguing that perhaps only a consensus that a decision must be made is sufficient, even if not everyone accepts the substantive or procedural reasons used to reach that final decision (Gaus 2011).

With the rise of the public reason school of legitimacy, we see that philosophers have run the gamut, from utilitarians who emphasize *ends* as the core justification of political action, and public reasoners who emphasize *means* as the basis of legitimacy. Yet interestingly, different eras and circumstances have often prompted different trends in legitimizing political action. Even within a ruler's lifetime, different standards may apply. Consider again the Iraq War. In the aftermath of the attacks of 9/11 its legitimacy was greatly buttressed by strong shows of public support for decisive action against 'rogue states' or potential sponsors of terrorism, yet within a few years was being increasingly delegitimized in public fora through scrutiny of the procedures used to establish its *casus belli.*

The role of leaders

What is the right and proper role of the leader within a political system? What value do leaders provide to the state and their people? Are leaders necessary to the success of government? Are leaders necessary at all?

Such questions are continually being informed by historical practice as well as philosophical thought. In periods of prolonged political stagnation, weak government or public anarchy, strong leaders are often seen as righteous antidotes. Julius Caesar, who more than anyone was responsible for the replacement of the Roman Republic with an imperial dictatorship, did so as a popular hero. He ended a period of long civil strife, instituted popular policies long obstructed by the wealthy elites, and ended chronic paralysis in Roman politics. Many contemporaries of the era concluded thusly that strong political leaders were a virtue, while democracy tended towards chaos. The influential Greek philosopher Plutarch, who lived just after the time of Caesar, comments in *Parallel Lives:*

> It was plain that the ills of the state required a monarchy, and that Caesar, like a most gentle physician, had been assigned to them by Heaven itself. (Plutarch 1918: 251)

Yet political philosophy has shown itself to turn on a dime when faced with tyrannical self-serving leaders, such as occurred during the eighteenth century, when Europe was dominated by oppressive aristocracies living in unprecedented luxury while the populace lived in poverty and near-constant warfare. A generation of political philosophers decried political power as inherently corrupting and its concentration a road to ruin:

> The fundamental article of my political creed is, that despotism, or unlimited sovereignty, or absolute power, is the same in a majority of a popular assembly, an aristocratical council, an oligarchical junto, and a single emperor; equally arbitrary, cruel, bloody, and in every respect diabolical. (Adams 1815/2003: xxi)

The philosophers highlighted below represent a diverse sample of the various positions that have been taken on the appropriate role of leaders in society throughout the ages.

Plato

The vibrant interaction between diverse systems of political arrangement in Ancient Greece gave rise to a rich tradition of debate in political philosophy. Foremost amongst the debaters was Plato (c.428–347 BCE), whose views on the role of political leaders within society would evolve over a lifetime of observation and study.

Plato's most important work on this subject is the *Republic,* in which he addresses the political structure for a model society. Plato discusses the various forms of government common in his day – democracy, aristocracy and monarchy – and identified strengths and weaknesses within each. Yet Plato ultimately argues that the best society is one which is ruled by a 'philosopher-king':

> Until philosophers are kings, or the kings and princes of this world have the spirit and power of philosophy, and political greatness and wisdom meet in one, and those commoner natures who pursue either to the exclusion of the other are compelled to stand aside, cities will never have rest from their evils. (Plato 1892: III.170–171)

Plato spends much of the *Republic* (Books VI and VIII) defending such a system and elaborates upon the educational, social and economic conditions that would produce a leadership class for the ideal state. The empowerment of philosopher-kings, who have both the power and the foresight to best guide a society towards happiness, was the *Republic*'s answer to an ideal society. This idea was popular for centuries afterwards, not only throughout Europe and the Mediterranean but also the Near East – the Arabic scholars Al-Farabi (872–950) and Ibn Rushd (1126–1198) both expanded and defended Plato's ideal government and found its expression in the Islamic fusion of secular power and religious guidance. And indeed, the popularity of a 'benevolent dictator' in Plato's mould tends to resurface periodically in times of political paralysis or public dissatisfaction with political systems.

Yet there is evidence that Plato began to doubt his ideas towards the end of his life, after becoming involved with the politics of the Greek city-state of Syracuse. Over several periods he spent in the city, he served as an educator and advisor to two of its rulers who sought to become philosopher-kings. Yet the city was beleaguered by political instability and its rulers soon turned to war and tyranny. In his later dialogues, *Laws* and *Statesman,* Plato turns to a so-called 'second-best' form of government, which is more open and meritocratic, and one in which laws play an important role in constraining leaders and guiding society (Plato 1892: IV.493–508). The significance of these works has long been debated in light of his earlier idealism around enlightened personal rule (see Klosko 2006).

Though long lauded as an enlightened ideal, philosopher Karl Popper argues that Plato's conception of political society is a dangerous myth that is at heart tyrannical and antithetical to social, moral and political progress (Popper 1971: 86–168). Marcus Aurelius, Emperor of Rome (161–182 CE) is perhaps the closest exemplar of the philosopher-king concept, and his *Meditations* on Stoicism continue to be influential today. Marcus was noted as an unusually thoughtful emperor, taking great time and care in matters of administration and justice, a fact remarked upon favourably by Roman historians like Cassius Dio. Yet in spite of his Stoic calm, Marcus Aurelius's empire was wracked with wars and conflicts, both internal and external. His rule was enlightened for its day and stepped back from many of the autocratic measures of his forebears, yet persecution was still practiced extensively. And his reign did not prove the antidote Plato had hoped in preventing political systems sliding towards miserable tyranny – indeed, Marcus was the last of the 'good emperors' and Roman political history is largely downhill after his reign (McLynn 2009: 487–494). The philosopher-king may be more of an enticing dream than a realistic guide to political leadership.

Ibn Khaldūn and Thomas Aquinas

The Arabic historian and scholar Ibn Khaldūn (1332–1406) is indicative of a class of scholarship during the Middle Ages which began to break away from Ancient Greek philosophy. Khaldūn's masterwork, the *Muqaddimah,* is a diverse discourse on subjects from chemistry to geography, and its commentary on politics anticipated key discussions on political philosophy that were soon to emerge in Europe.

Khaldūn first questions the basic premise of the 'philosopher-king'. He contends that God has given humanity laws to follow in order to achieve happiness (in Islam, the *sharia*), and rulers should rule in accordance with those laws rather than seek to embody or redefine them. As such, the instrumental purpose of the state – to prevent chaos, provide stability and further the public good – can be fulfilled perfectly well by uninspired secular leaders who simply follow those laws. We should seek leaders thus who are servants to law, rather than law unto themselves, and rule which stands in opposition to law, is rightfully subject to public rejection (Khaldūn 1377/1989: 114–115).

History also informs much of Khaldūn's political theory. Central to his thesis is the concept of *asabiyyah*, or 'collective will'. Khaldūn argues that elites rule based on their ability to be embody the ideas and values, and satisfy the needs and wants, of the general public. Yet ruling dynasties rarely last long, because over time the ability of their leaders to embody the *asabiyyah* wanes. While the first generation of leaders – those who fight for power and establish rule – are drawn from the people themselves, successive generations born into power become increasingly indulgent and out of touch with the public. In time, another movement with a better ability to embody the *asabiyyah* will rise and depose the old system. Khaldūn observes these cycles are ongoing and endless, suggesting a kind of revolutionary fatalism in the study of political leadership and offering a frank assessment of political leaders as all too human (Khaldūn 1377/1989: ch. 3).

In the same period, the thirteenth century Italian theologian St Thomas Aquinas in *Summa Theologica* argues that the secular and religious worlds are separate, and though monarchs may rule with ultimate authority on secular matters, their moral authority is limited and checked by the church (Aquinas I-II.92.1-2). There is a law above that of the ruler and that which they cannot change: "human law does not put forward precepts about anything other than acts of justice" (Aquinas 1273/1920: I-II.100.2).

In *De Regno,* Aquinas goes further, concluding that a monarch with undivided power was the most effective form of political rule for creating a happy society and powerful state. However, he acknowledges that in practice unbridled power can corrupt political leadership, and the expectations of monarchs are not always realized in reality:

> Danger thus lurks on either side. Either men are held by the fear of a tyrant and they miss the opportunity of having that very best government which is kingship; or, they want a king and the kingly power turns into tyrannical wickedness. (Aquinas 1267/1949: I.5.35)

Significantly, Aquinas recommends 'mixed' forms of government, in which a monarch rules but certain institutions are put in place to check their power and protect against tyranny, and the best features of aristocracy, monarchy and democracy are fused together (Aquinas 1485/1920: I-II.105.1).

Thomas Hobbes

Thomas Hobbes (1588–1679) was an English philosopher who lived through some the most important times in his nation's history, particularly the English Civil War, which strongly influenced his views. Hobbes is cynical about human nature, seeing us as fundamentally power-hungry and self-interested. Moreover, he sees government and political leadership as the natural result of human nature, arguing that humans in their primitive state are locked in a war of 'all against all' in a never-ending struggle for survival. Civilization, knowledge, art and pleasure can only come from a political society that subjects itself to a higher authority that can provide stability and order (Hobbes 1651/1996: 86–90).

To create these conditions, Hobbes argues in *Leviathan* for the undivided absolutism of a ruling class, preferably a monarchy. He believes an absolute sovereign, answerable only to God and providence, best provides the conditions for peace and prosperity. He rejected separation of powers or the division of sovereignty, noting that the inherent hunger for power and competition between factions inevitably creates rivalries and conflict which can (as it did in the English Civil War) lead to the collapse of the state and return mankind to its primitive, violent origins (Hobbes 1651/1996: 121–128). Or just as bad, he argues, is the potential for paralysis, as different institutions disagree on policy, or argue over jurisdiction, and good government grinds to halt. Though he believes that absolute authority may be vested in parliaments or oligarchies, he prefers rule by monarchy, arguing its interests will be closer to the people it rules:

> Now in monarchy the private interest is the same with the public. The riches, power, and honour of a monarch arise only from the riches, strength, and reputation of his subjects...whereas in a democracy, or aristocracy, the public prosperity confers not so much to the private fortune of one that is corrupt, or ambitious, as doth many times a perfidious advice, a treacherous action, or a civil war. (Hobbes 1651/1996: 131)

Hobbes's ideas were in keeping with many of his contemporaries, who saw much to recommend in divine absolutism after the chaos of the English Civil War. A strand of political philosophy extolling the virtues of *enlightened absolutism* would flourish in the next century, embodied by leaders like Frederick the Great, who saw limitless potential for rulers who embraced enlightenment ideals to "enlighten minds, cultivate morality, and to make people as happy as it suits human nature" (MacDonogh 2001: 341). Indeed, the concentration of power in absolute monarchies would reach its zenith in this period.

Montesquieu and James Madison

Charles-Louis de Secondat (1689–1755), more usually referred to as the Baron Montesquieu, was a French political philosopher of the Enlightenment. The seventeenth century had given rise to unprecedented centralization of political power in the monarchies of Europe, and with it an era of burgeoning empires, near-constant warfare and tyrannical rule. Locke, Rousseau and other Enlightenment thinkers were influential in shifting intellectual opinion on legitimacy towards a new principle of the 'consent of the governed'. Enlightenment thought began to turn towards a new belief that political systems needed to restrain the tyrannical impulses of the human drive for power.

Montesquieu powerfully makes the argument that the best protection against tyrannical leaders is to set them against themselves. In *The Spirit of the Laws,* Montesquieu sets out a political system of three powers – a legislative power, which makes law, a judicial power, which interprets law, and an executive power, which implements the law. Montesquieu sees the only safeguard against a tyrant to be this 'separation of powers', whereby these three functions act as a check upon each other:

> When the legislative and executive powers are united in the same person... there can be no liberty; because apprehensions may arise, lest the same monarch or senate should enact tyrannical laws, to execute them in a tyrannical manner. Again, there is no liberty if the judiciary power be not separated from the legislative and executive. Were it joined with the legislative, the life and

> liberty of the subject would be exposed to arbitrary control; for the judge would be then the legislator. Were it joined to the executive power, the judge might behave with violence and oppression. (Montesquieu 1748/2011: 151–152)

Montesquieu's thought would significantly influence events across the Atlantic during the American Revolution. Charged with determining a government for the newly independent United States, the Constitutional Convention of 1787 gave rise to debates about how to create a system of rule that could learn from the lessons of history. The role of the presidency was perhaps the most contentious. Various proposals to constrain the power of the presidency, and avoid the emergence of a tyrant, were developed. Separation of powers, election by an electoral college of the states, possibility of impeachment by the legislature, judicial oversight, four year terms, and a Constitution as the highest authority were some of the ideas that were eventually enacted.

This was a new, much more constrained form of political leadership than had been the norm in Europe. The case for its ratification was made most notably in *The Federalist Papers,* co-authored by James Madison (1751–1836), a key drafter of the constitution. In *Federalist Paper No. 51*, Madison famously sets out the proposition that 'if men were angels' there would be no need for government, and that 'ambition must be made to counteract ambition', adopting Montesquieu's separation of powers as an organizing doctrine.

Madison sought balance between the powers of leaders and public interest. In *Federalist No. 10*, Madison also warns against the dangers of 'faction', tyranny by the majority, and mob rule that might result from too much democracy. His remedy here too is a form of republicanism and federalism that can protect local interests and minorities from oppression by the majority. Madison's co-author, Alexander Hamilton, goes on in the later papers, particularly *Federalist No. 70*, to defend a unified executive with strong powers, arguing that 'energy', accountability, unity, competent decision-making and a 'leading character' are all essential qualities provided by the political leader that should be checked, but not critically weakened. Their arguments ultimately won the day, and the United States Presidency was created in that image.

Not all accepted their arguments though. A group opposed to the new Constitution wrote the *Anti-Federalist* papers in response to Madison and Hamilton, arguing for a much more limited national government. One paper argued that even the most rigorous system of checks would prove ineffective against the dominating impulses of rulers:

> Americans are like other men in similar situations, when the manners and opinions of the community are changed by the causes I mentioned before, and your political compact inexplicit, your posterity will find that great power connected with ambition, luxury, and flattery, will as readily produce a Caesar, Caligula, Nero, and Domitian in America, as the same causes did in the Roman empire. (Cato 1787)

Friedrich Nietzsche

The German philosopher Friedrich Nietzsche (1844–1900), one of the most important philosophers of the Western tradition, has had an unusual influence on political philosophy and the leadership question, despite many questioning whether Nietzsche intended to articulate a philosophy of politics at all (Nussbaum 1997).

In *Thus Spoke Zarathustra,* Nietzsche explores the ideal of the *übermensch* (or 'super-human') and praises heroic self-mastery and self-improvement for both ourselves and following generations as a means for humanity to escape the 'human condition' (Nietzsche 1883/2008a: 11–18). He goes on to coin the phrase the *will to power*, describing it as the "unexhausted procreative will of life" and the drive of all things to enjoy the feelings of power, a drive that possibly outranks even the will to survive (Nietzsche 1886/2008b: 151–162). Implicit or explicit in much of Nietzsche's work is the sentiment that the creative force of individuality unleash the potential of humanity:

> Companions the creator seeks, not corpses, nor herds and believers either. Fellow creators the creator seeks, those who write new values on new tablets. Companions the creator seeks, and fellow harvesters: for all that is with him is ripe for the harvest. (Nietzsche 1883/2008a: 21)

Nietzsche is profoundly critical of the 'herd' by contrast: "it is not the ferocity of the beast of prey that requires a moral disguise but the herd animal with its profound mediocrity, timidity, and boredom with itself" (Nietzsche 1887/1974: 295). By way of example, Napoleon Bonaparte, the 'enlightened dictator' of early nineteenth century France, is cited frequently by Nietzsche as an example of an individual who comes close to the ideal of the 'super-human', though far from a perfect one (Glenn 2001).

Nietzsche casts his critique against communitarian structures, or any social order, that suppresses will to power. He calls the state a 'cold beast', rejecting the notion that it can represent the best of humanity (Nietzsche 1883/2008a: 43–45). Moreover, Nietzsche is a fierce critic of universal morality and particularly Judeo-Christian moralism, questioning whether behaviour like domination, destruction and exploitation are universally bad. Indeed, he suggests different kinds of morality are better suited to different social classes or stations in life, with those in subordinate social roles subscribing to different standards than those in leading roles (Nietzsche 1886/2008b: 109–130).

Nietzsche's ideas were appropriated into the militaristic philosophy of the German Empire of the early twentieth century (see Aschheim 1992: ch. 1), but also became a central body of thought within the philosophy of Fascism – German philosophers and politicians used them extensively to legitimize the ideology of the Nazi Party (Whyte 2008). Yet Nietzsche never advocated specifically for a political project that would satisfy his philosophical beliefs, and he was critical of the rising patriotism, anti-Semitism, and German nationalism he saw emerging in his own lifetime (Nietzsche 1887/1974: 338). Post-war philosophers have attempted to rehabilitate Nietzsche's political reputation (e.g. Bataille 2015), drawing a connection between his individual-centric philosophy and political libertarianism. However, as Nietzsche was also critical of egalitarianism, democracy, and liberalism, finding a home for Nietzsche in politics is a complicated business (Warren 1985).

However, Nietzsche's themes of enlightened individualism, the will to power and moral relativism capture some of the core justifications for the empowerment of leaders in society throughout the ages – the idea that it is leaders and elites that most move society forward and unlock human potential. That they are the creative and destructive force necessary for societal advancement found much support amongst contemporaries, including the American philosopher William James (1842–1910), who believed even within a democracy it was leaders and the elite who had the most responsibility to drive forward civilization and steer the 'herd' (James 1912: 317–319).

Rejecting leadership?

Throughout the ages a strand of political philosophy has rejected the contention that leadership is a necessary fixture of society, and that debates over empowering or constraining leadership rest on a faulty assumption. The philosophy of anarchism that thrived in the nineteenth century rejects most structures of political authority and the necessity of rulers. Russian anarchist Mikhail Bakunin was one of the most influential voices in this movement, arguing that even the most dysfunctional democracies were superior to the best autocracies (Bakunin 1867/1972: 102–147). However, this doesn't mean total dismissal of authority:

> Does it follow that I reject all authority? Far from me such a thought. In the matter of boots, I refer to the authority of the bootmaker; concerning houses, canals, or railroads, I consult that of the architect or engineer.... But I allow neither the bootmaker nor the architect to impose his authority upon me. I listen to them freely and with all the respect merited by their intelligence, their character, their knowledge, reserving always my incontestable right of criticism and censure. (Bakunin 1867/1972: 229)

Other philosophers have adopted sceptical attitudes towards authority and leaders without necessarily rejecting these concepts entirely. Michael Foucault and Noam Chomsky have both questioned the legitimacy of political authority, generally placing far higher standards upon the two concepts in order to be accepted as just and useful, rather than merely oppressive. Hannah Arendt, profoundly impacted by her observations of the totalitarian regimes of Nazism and Stalinism, sought to reevaluate the place of power and authority in modern politics in light of the horrors witnessed, explain the terrifying potential for totalitarian leadership that lies within, and articulate a political philosophy that would help guard against it (Arendt 1973).

Modern democratic theory has incorporated some of these ideas into its canon. Yet post-war political philosophy and democratic theory have tended, more than anything, to simply ignore the leadership dimension within politics (Kane & Patapan 2012: ch. 1). Contemporary movements, like deliberative democracy which has been highly influential in recent decades, have relatively little to say about the role or impact of leadership in a society or in decision-making (Kuyper 2012). Whereas the political thought of centuries previous intimately concerned with the place of elites and leaders in politics, contemporary offerings are remarkably unengaged with the subject and often skirt around it.

This silence is perhaps a reflection of the contentious place of political leaders within a modern society that strives for democratic egalitarianism. But although it is hard to theoretically conceptualize where leadership fits into a thriving democracy, it cannot be ignored without missing something essential about politics. As Carnes Lord contends:

> The theory of democracy tells us that the people rule. In practice, we have leaders who rule people in a manner not altogether different from the princes and potentates of times past. This paradox seems for the most part cheerfully accepted by contemporary electorates. That it remains problematic nevertheless is evident. (Lord 2003: xi)

The resurgence of populist leadership across democracies in the twenty-first century has taken many democratic theorists by surprise, and almost by force the debate about the right role of political leaders has come back into the fore.

The morality of leadership

Finally, we come to the question of how *should* leaders lead. Now that we have given leaders power and authority, what constitutes their moral and virtuous use? Many political philosophers, from Plato to Rawls, have written extensively on political ethics, as debates over the nature of political legitimacy also bear significantly on the question of the morality of political rule.

Three foci and three problems have emerged as the thorniest in discussing the morality of political leadership. The three foci regard what aspect of political leadership should be the primary focus of moral philosophy:

1. the character of the ruler
2. the outcomes of their rule, or the 'ends'
3. the processes by which they rule, or the 'means'.

Character, ends and means, and the ethical importance of all three, continue to be debated today by the public. Following on from these are:

1. the problem of dirty hands
2. the problem of many hands
3. the problem of moral disengagement.

These problems set political leaders apart from other types of moral agent, both in terms of their moral duties and culpability, as well as how their morality is policed. As in previous sections these three foci and three problems will be discussed through some of their most prominent historical scholars.

Character: Confucius

Confucius (551BCE–479BCE) was indisputably one of the most influential philosophers in history, and the school of thought he established (along with his successors Mencius and Xunzi) has been central to Eastern philosophy and politics right into the present day (Zhang 2016).

Confucians greatly opposed the simplistic association of mere power with authority, instead believing that *virtue* was the ultimate aspiration for good rulers. Confucius wrote "the rule of virtue can be compared to the Pole Star, which commands the homage of a multitude of stars without leaving its place" (*Analects* 2.1). He explicitly compares moral and legal authority:

> If the people be led by laws, and uniformity among them be sought by punishments, they will try to escape punishment and have no sense of shame. If they are led by virtue, and uniformity sought among them through the practice of ritual propriety, they will possess a sense of shame and come to you of their own accord. (Analects 2.3)

Confucian thought echoes this sentiment throughout the centuries, believing that laws are just words – words that can be ignored, circumvented or twisted – and only good moral character by leaders can truly create an orderly society (Chan & Chan 2014: 59–60). Confucius stipulated a long list of desirable virtues that would underpin a ruler's moral authority, such as humility, generosity, impartiality, honesty and temperance. These virtues were codified in the "Three Li", which became a central part of the Chinese education system for over a thousand years (Confucius 1885: 1–14). It argues that it is necessary and expected that rulers should hold themselves to higher standards of virtue than those they lead (*Liji*: 30.12).

However, virtuous conduct alone does not legitimate political leaders in the Confucian tradition. Mencius touts the reciprocal responsibility of the leader to look after the material and spiritual well-being of their subjects, and to be 'father and mother to the people' (Mencius 1A4). To great debate among scholars, subsequent passages by the Confucians have, in some interpretations, extended this responsibility to mean that the legitimacy of political authority ultimately lies with consent of the people themselves, evidenced perhaps by Mencius' use of the phrase *minben,* meaning 'the people as basis'. Many have concluded that it is at least a 'service conception of authority' (Chan 2007: 188); however, both Confucius and Mencius do not believe the common people can govern themselves effectively. Government should be *for* them, but not *by* them (Elstein 2010; El Amine 2015: 47–51).

The need for 'virtuous' rule, and a focus on the moral character of leaders, has historically been popular amongst philosophers in the West also, and though declining in importance in moral debates since the nineteenth century, continues to find prominent proponents (e.g. Foot 1978; Hursthouse 1999).

Confucius and the virtue proponents are perhaps increasingly justified as to the pragmatic consequences of character in an age of mass media. As Thomas Dumm comments, in the media age being a successful leader increasingly involves "acting *like* a president more than it does acting *as* a president" (Dumm 1999: 144). That is to say, political leaders have an ever greater presence in the public discourse and consciousness, such that what they say and do on the public stage is for many far more noticeable than how they actually make decisions and operate a government. In such circumstances, character matters – what a leader says will be heard by millions, and very directly influences how their supporters and detractors think and act, sometimes to extremes (Kalmoe 2014; Gubler & Kalmoe 2015).

There is no doubt that the public generally expects their political leaders to be virtuous, much as Confucius proscribed. Indeed, we often contend that leaders should have virtues above and beyond what we might expect from others – we look to our leaders for moral authority. Although scandals about a politician's personal life are as old as the Roman politician Clodius, the intensity of media interest in the 'private morality' of politicians has become a hallmark of the information age. Silvio Berlusconi, Prime Minister of Italy periodically between 1994 and 2011, became infamous for his private life and his prejudicial remarks, such that the media tended to focus on little else about his premiership. Yet Berlusconi himself encouraged the extreme personalization of his political image and "enjoyed playing the parts both of a showman and of someone who is 'ordinary' and who has the same reactions, desires and even prejudices of the man in the street" (Mancini 2011: 2). For his supporters, opponents and the general public alike, it became nearly impossible to separate judgement of Berlusconi's leadership from his personal character and image (Mancini 2011).

We might question however whether such debates really touch upon issues of political ethics, and how relevant issues of character, virtue and vice are upon the ultimate morality of what leaders do and how they do it. Although sometimes a leader's private actions have a very direct connection with their public lives, more often they do not. What bearing does a politician's sex life, for example, have on their ability to negotiate a trade deal or enforce environmental protections? Some have contended that, regardless of their specific political position, virtues like integrity are universally desired in leaders, and ultimately the public decides through its own support or derision what virtues are appropriate in their leaders (Hampshire 1978: 23–54; Schauer 2000). But although the 'moral character' of our leaders has been the subject of unceasing popular scrutiny for eons, one would think there is a difference between the public interest and what the public is interested in.

Ends: Niccolò Machiavelli

A key thinker of the Italian renaissance, Niccolò Machiavelli (1469–1527) starts with the observation that discussions about political morality and legitimacy are meaningless in practice – power held illegitimately is just as effective as power obtained justly, and a good and moral character does not make a leader any more powerful:

> This leads to a debate: is it better to be loved than feared, or the reverse? The answer is that is it desirable to be both, but because it is difficult to join them together, it is much safer for a prince to be feared than loved. (Machiavelli 1532/1999: 62)

Machiavelli applies a logic of effectiveness to his philosophy of leadership. He agrees good laws are important to creating a fair society, yet laws are meaningless unless the leader has power to enforce them (Machiavelli 1532/1999: 47). The consequence of this logic is that strong leadership is essential to a functioning state and public justice.

Machiavelli advocates a position that is now generally described as *realpolitik*. It is a pragmatic approach to politics that focuses on outcomes, and sees the world as dominated by individuals who are fundamentally self-interested and in constant rivalry. In such a world, morals, ideas and ethics are secondary considerations at best, and the focus of the leader should instead be on the tactics that will help them maintain or increase their power and defeat their rivals. *The Prince* is his guidebook for leaders who seek to do just that, regardless of their goals or ideologies. Indeed, Machiavelli contends the key virtue of a leader is their ability to do what is necessary to maintain power at all costs. The leader who isn't willing to go to such lengths will simply be pushed aside by those that are, and being a 'good' person alone cannot defeat an invading army, enforce the law, or defeat those who seek to bring them down (Machiavelli 1532/1999: 66). Machiavelli also puts great stock in the importance of *fortuna* – fortune or luck. He sees it as an unpredictable and unstoppable force that creates events like natural disasters and wars that produce chaos and disorder, and that only leaders who are prepared to act boldly, unrestrained by moral qualms in the face of uncertainty, can lead a strong state and protect its people (Machiavelli 1532/1999: 90–92).

Machiavelli's ideas have been discussed endlessly in the history of leadership, and many have found his conclusions disquieting. His *realpolitik* perspective has been used widely in explaining the paucity of morality in international relations (e.g. Korab-Karpowicz 2018), but Machiavelli's ideas have been subjected to diverse interpretations over the centuries (e.g. Giorgini 2013). Both American founding father John Adams and iron-fisted Soviet premier Joseph Stalin were influenced by the thought of Machiavelli yet in the pursuit of vastly different projects (Thompson 1995; Kuromiya 2013: 208–209).

Machiavelli's perspective on political ethics emphasizes the *ends* over the *means*. In this sense, it is utilitarian or consequentialist in nature, and so when asked the question of whether a political leader has committed a moral act, we look to the consequences of that act rather than the way they did it. Many philosophers of the Enlightenment embraced this perspective of morality, much as they did in thinking about political legitimacy (see section "The Legitimacy of Leaders"). Political leaders themselves often embrace consequentialism as justification for their actions – even if their actions stray from the polite, conventional or ethical. Yet consequentialism as a moral guide in politics has many significant issues that are hard to resolve (see Sinott-Armstrong 2019). For example:

- **Consequences for Whom?** For whom are we justifying the consequences of our actions? Who is the leader obligated to consider the consequences for?
- **The Relative Value of Consequences?** How do we rank and value all the various kinds of consequences? Is freedom or equality worth more and is it moral to sacrifice one to provide the other? Who determines these values?
- **Foreseen Consequences?** Are leaders morally responsible for things that they did not intend? Can leaders accurately predict all the consequences of their actions or policies – if they can't, then how can they adopt consequentialist ethics?

Machiavelli makes a powerfully simple statement about political morality – that ultimately, it is outcomes that matter, and a leader should be free of moral constraints so they can provide the best kind of stability, order and society for their subjects. But arguably it provides nothing more than a convenient moral fig leaf for every kind of leader from do-gooder to demagogue, and such a conception of morality can justify almost anything imaginable.

Means: Immanuel Kant

In counterpoint to Machiavelli, the moral philosophy of Immanuel Kant (1724–1804) shifts focus onto means. For Kant, *how* a leader does something counts, and counts more than the character of that leader or the consequences of their actions.

Kant establishes a series of maxims for moral conduct which he collectively calls the *categorical imperative*. The imperative has four formulations:

1. *Act only according to that maxim whereby you can at the same time will that it should become a universal law.*
2. *Act in such a way that you treat humanity, whether in your own person or in the person of any other, never merely as a means to an end, but always at the same time as an end.*
3. *Thus the third practical principle follows as the ultimate condition of their harmony with practical reason: the idea of the will of every rational being as a universally legislating will.*
4. *Act according to maxims of a universally legislating member of a merely possible kingdom of ends.* (Kant 1785/1993: 30–44)

The first formulation is perhaps the most powerful one and calls upon the individual to only act if that action could become a 'universal law'. A politician making a promise to their citizens they cannot keep, for example, cannot be universalized because if everyone in the world made promises that weren't kept then promises would become meaningless. A politician lying about their promise only works because *most* people keep their promises, and thus by Kant's formulation is immoral. The second maxim, that humanity is an end in itself, effectively prohibits the use or abuse of people by political leaders to achieve some specific end, and no action is moral if it does not respect the humanity of others (see Hill 1980). The third and the fourth maxims provide clarification to the first two, seeing the moral being as one who is rationally drawn to moral action rather than compelled to do so, and that a moral society is that which follows the universal laws a hypothetically just society of rational, moral beings would create.

Kant's ethics were criticized by contemporaries like Georg Hegel and Arthur Schopenhauer; however, his influence has been undeniable and two of the most influential moral philosophers of the twentieth century – Jürgen Habermas and John Rawls – were influenced by Kant's work and developed theories of their own that shift the focus of moral calculus to considering *means* (Alexander & Moore 2016). *Deontological ethics,* an umbrella term for means-orientated moral theory, provides a far clearer moral compass than the vagueness of consequentialism, and establishing rules for moral conduct is now the backbone of how we formally implement ethics into our politics. Constitutions and laws usually proceed on this basis, outlining the moral imperatives by which our leaders should act and the duties they have.

Yet like consequentialism, there are dilemmas inherent to deontological ethics (see Alexander & Moore 2016). What if, for example, moral duties and obligations conflict with each other? (Vallentyne 1987) Torture, for example, is expressly forbidden by many international and domestic laws, being deemed a morally unacceptable means for any political leader to use for any reason. And yet, in a situation where torture may coerce a terrorist to reveal information necessary to prevent death and destruction, at what point does adhering to deontological ethics become unsustainable? In contemporary debates around the use of torture in the fight against terrorism, the public, scholars and politicians alike (Carmichael 1982; Gutting & McMahan 2015) have held mixed views, but with sizable numbers seeing the potential end of saving lives as providing sufficient justification for its use.

Some have consequently developed the concept of *threshold deontology,* in which deontological moral norms should generally apply to all our behaviour, but when the consequences of doing so reach a certain threshold, at that point moral consequentialism takes over. Such a system probably makes intuitive sense for most of us – we would expect our leaders to act morally and legally in normal circumstances but would be willing to accept transgressions when the well-being and lives of many were at stake. But of course, there is no clear way to define where that threshold is, nor who should do the defining (see Zamir & Medina 2010: ch. 2).

Problem of dirty hands: Michael Walzer

Returning to the torture example, American ethicist Michael Walzer posits the example of a political leader who is recently elected in the aftermath of civil war. They have promised peace and an end to violence and torture. Yet soon after they are elected, a hold-out is captured who has planted bombs around the capital that will detonate within 24 hours. With no leads, little time, and virtually limitless places where the bombs might be hidden, the only practicable hope of preventing disaster is to torture the bomber to attempt to gain the information necessary to find the bombs. Should the leader authorize it? (Walzer 1973: 167–169).

Walzer argues this is an example of the 'problem of dirty hands'. We ask, and indeed expect, our political leaders to safeguard our interests, our communities, and our livelihoods. They have unique responsibilities and make decisions that affect the lives of millions. "It is easy to get one's hands dirty in politics and it is often right to do so" (Walzer 1973: 174) because we give political leaders unique sanction to get their hands dirty when the situation requires it, if only so that the wider population may be spared it. This creates a paradox where sometimes political leaders apparently must do wrong in order to do right. Unlike Machiavelli though, Walzer believes that political leaders must acknowledge and ought to feel guilt for doing wrong, even in the service of doing the public good, as doing that ultimate good does not alter the immorality of the act itself (Walzer 1973).

The dirty hands problem is the price of leadership. In fact, it's often naïve, selfish, or even irresponsible for a leader to try keep their hands clean when they are entrusted by the public to dirty them for the greater good (Oberdiek 1986). A leader elected to lead a country during a war for its survival would be reckless in the extreme if they shied away from morally tough decisions necessary to defend the nation, much as it would be reckless for a doctor to assume an emergency room position if they were unwilling to make life-and-death decisions (e.g., Case 3.1).

And yet, placing political leaders in a special moral category, exempt from the usual considerations we place upon ordinary citizens, creates the great hazard of enabling rulers to justify anything and everything in the pursuit of the 'public good'. Just what is the threshold for justifying the dirtying of one's hands? How certain does a politician need to be that a terrorist has life-saving information before torture can be justified? Many have observed a slippery slope in the justification of immoral action - what starts as a `state of exception' to deal with threats and dangers can easily become business-as-usual (Agamben 2005: 1–31).

Moreover, some ethicists reject the idea that we can meaningfully separate the dirty hands of leaders from our own hands (Thompson 1987: 11–39; Walzer 2006: 287–303). "Political actors, duly appointed within a legitimate state, have an authority deriving finally from the people. Currently that means from you and me.... When their hands get dirty, so do ours" (Hollis 1996: 146–147). Such a concept means that we can't elect our leaders to do our moral dirty work and expect to stay clean - that we as citizens must still wrestle with the morality of our leaders and take responsibility for them.

The problem also occurs in the reverse formulation – what obligations does a leader have to morality if his or her own citizenry who are demanding immoral action? As a representative of the people, how obligated are they to follow the demands of those they represent? Jeannette Rankin of Montana, the first woman elected to the United States Congress, was an avowed pacifist and the lone vote against the United States' declaration of war on Japan in 1941. Taking a moral stand against war in the face of overwhelming public sentiment, the decision ended her career and she was widely seen as betraying her constituents. Yet 1,553 people from Montana died in WWII, to say nothing of the 400,000 from the rest of the United States killed in that conflict. Was her act in trying to prevent their deaths truly a betrayal of her constituents?

Figure 3.1 Jeannette Rankin, US Congresswoman and pacifist

Problem of many hands: Dennis Thompson

The potential culpability of the public in the immoral acts of their leaders leads to the second major problem that distinguishes political ethics from other arenas, and that is the issue of 'many hands', prominently advanced by American political scientist Dennis Thompson.

Governments are vast institutions with many decision-makers, and no leader rules alone. Government policies that prove to have immoral (or even just undesirable) consequences may have been the *ultimate* responsibility of the leader, but in a democratic government those policies passed through many hands, from a cabinet that designs the policy, to a legislature that approves its funding, to the vast bureaucracy that implements it. Indeed, many of those hands may have been well-intended and unable to foresee the implications of their contribution (Thompson 1980, 1987: 40–65; Poel et al. 2015). And if those policies were subject to, or even at the behest of, prevailing public sentiment, then arguably the public has some culpability as well.

The notion of a *collective* moral responsibility in government though has often proved unsatisfying, and not just from a scholarly standpoint (e.g. Downie 1969; Sverdlik 1987) but also from a societal one. Those who have been wronged have little means for recourse against an amorphous collective in which individual responsibility cannot be assigned, and the "fact that no one can be meaningfully called to account after the event also means … that no one need feel responsible beforehand" (Bovens 1998: 49). Subsequently, blame games and scapegoating are common in politics if only because "everyone is jointly responsible" seems to deny a satisfying answer.

In 2010 the Australian government under Prime Minister Kevin Rudd introduced a scheme to commercially incentivize the installation of home insulation to encourage domestic energy efficiency. It created a boom in the insulation industry, but to meet demand insulation companies hastily hired new installation staff that were often poorly trained. Four such installers died in workplace accidents in quick succession, due to a lack of training, experience and safety provisions. Undoubtedly the Australian government had no intention of causing death through the program, but the conditions created by the policy and the lack of oversight in its implementation were critical contributing factors. Debate raged in the Australian media as to who was to blame for the program's failings. Though a year-long Royal Commission investigating the matter ultimately found no single factor or individual in the government responsible, the court of public opinion nonetheless focused much of its blame on the minister and prime minister as the most visible parties (McAuley 2014).

Often, politicians will be made to take responsibility for failings, moral or otherwise, that were created collectively by many hands. This is one of the hazards of political leadership, as rightly or wrongly, our political leaders are the chief focal point of government and are ultimately held to account for what it does, even if it did so inadvertently, and even at our behest.

Moral disengagement: Albert Bandura

Societies have laws and conventions which set out how we expect our leaders to rule. Yet it is ultimately up to elites and the public to invigilate and enforce these standards. While we would hope that political leaders would police themselves and act morally, as we all should, we know it is not always so.

Canadian psychologist Albert Bandura has extensively developed the concept of *moral disengagement* to explain how as individuals, and as societies, we routinely subvert standards of morality, finding ways to justify why such standards don't apply to our own conduct (Bandura 2015).

There are many mechanisms by which we morally disengage and find acceptable justification for immoral behaviour (Bandura 2002, 2015: 2–3).

- **Moral Justification:** We justify inhumane actions by arguing a moral purpose for those actions.
- **Euphemistic Labelling:** We use language to minimize or disguise the moral implications of our actions, or to change the terms of a moral debate. Bombing becomes 'surgical strikes' and terrorism becomes 'freedom fighting'.
- **Advantageous Comparison:** We can justify our actions and minimize their moral implications by comparing them with a far worse alternative.
- **Minimizing Consequences:** We tend to minimize or disregard the negative consequences of our actions.
- **Dehumanization:** We are tempted to think of our opponents as lacking human or civilized qualities, and thus unworthy of moral or humane treatment.

Such tools are readily used by political leaders to justify their actions to themselves and their followers, and they are frequently effective at doing so. Political elites have powerful platforms from which to provide moral justifications or conceal the moral consequences of their actions, which the public has limited capacity to question (McGraw et al. 1995; McGraw 1998).

Yet even when the public has fuller information, and immoral acts are revealed on the part of our leaders, the public itself is often partisan in its judgements. *Cognitive dissonance* is the phenomenon by which individuals experience discomfort when their beliefs clash with evidence from the real world. When it comes to deeply held beliefs, humans often resolve this dilemma not by abandoning their views but by selectively interpreting evidence or creating mental justifications that will allow their beliefs and reality to harmonize (Festinger 1957). Political views are amongst those often deeply held, and cognitive dissonance in politics is commonly observed (Mullainathan & Washington 2009; Druckman et al. 2013). The result of this can be, when faced with uncomfortable revelations about their party or political leaders, rather than morally sanction them faithful voters will tend to use the same techniques listed above to justify and defend their parties or leaders. It is also common, in deeply divided polities or periods, for people to dehumanize their political opponents, and thus make much easier the justification of any action, even immoral action, by their leaders to defeat them (Cassese 2019; also Mason 2018).

The consequences for moral politics can be dire, as instead of elites and society acting as a check on the behaviour of leaders, they may ultimately act as enablers in the name of the partisan cause. Processes designed to police political leaders and ensure moral conduct may in the process become dysfunctional. Jacob Zuma, President of South Africa (2009–2018), faced near-continuous personal scandals and charges of corruption and illegality during his several terms, yet was able to circumvent legal charges and moral sanction until his elite and public support waned in the final years of his rule (Hartley 2016). The impeachments trials of Romania's Traian Băsescu, Paraguay's Fernando Lugo and America's Andrew Johnson proved to be tests of political support rather than considered moral examination, with little confidence in the aftermath that justice was done. In such circumstances, the morality of leadership lies in the eye of the beholder.

However, despite the obvious complexities as to devising and enforcing moral standards for our political leadership, this has not given license to wanton immorality on the part of our leaders. A flawed but functional system of checks and balances has emerged in most systems, such that it would be rare to go a month in most nations without reading stories of politicians being shamed, penalized, prosecuted or removed over moral infractions. That said, whilst the moral standards of Confucius and Kant remain laudable goals, it is easy to place unrealistic moral expectations on leaders that we ourselves would struggle to meet. As Dick Gephardt, Democratic Minority Leader during the impeachment trial of US President Bill Clinton in 1998 stated:

> Our founding fathers created a system of government of men, not of angels...no one standing in this House today can pass a puritanical test of purity that some are demanding that our elected leaders take. If we demand that mere mortals live up to this standard, we will see our seats of government lay empty and we will see the best, most able people unfairly cast out of public service. (Mitchell 1998)

Case 3.1 The morality of destruction

Harry Truman

United States President, 1945–1953

Figure 3.2 Harry Truman in 1945

Few political leaders have been asked, as Harry Truman was in 1945, to make a decision that would determine the fate of so many lives. The American atomic bombs dropped on the Japanese cities of Hiroshima and Nagasaki killed over 100,000 people almost instantly, and many more through lingering illnesses. Most of those who died were civilian non-combatants. Establishing the morality of Truman's decision has been the subject to ceaseless debate ever since and demonstrates many of the concepts discussed in the previous section.

The primary justification for their use has always been that they were necessary to end the war with a militaristic Japan that had vowed to fight to the bitter end. Truman said "it was done to save 125,000 youngsters on the U.S. side and 125,000 on the Japanese side from getting killed and that is what it did. It probably also saved a half million youngsters on both sides from being maimed for life" (Lambers 2006: 11).

Truman, and many American leaders, saw the moral calculus as largely consequentialist, a matter of adding up the casualties of different choices and choosing the lowest. But can such reasoning really justify the means? And how certain should Truman have been of the consequences of his choices? Questions remain as to whether Japanese surrender was as distant as claimed, with mixed views on whether the atomic bombs (rather than the Soviet invasion of Manchuria) were the decisive factor behind the Japanese surrender. And yet, every day's delay in making the decision meant casualties continued to rise in the Pacific theatre.

Judging the morality of the means rather than the ends invites similar debate. The indiscriminate destruction of civilian life is considered a war crime and outside the boundaries of moral conduct even during times of war. Radhabinod Pal, the Indian jurist on the Tokyo War Crimes Tribunal, saw no moral difference between the Japanese and American leadership and equally guilty of crimes against humanity in their prosecution of the war.

Even American generals involved in the authorization of the bombings have admitted that had they lost the war, the bombings would have been prosecuted as a crime against humanity (Turan 2003). Yet are there any truly moral means to carry on a war? How do you distinguish between civilians and military combatants in a condition of total war, in which nearly every household and civilian institution was involved in the war effort? Strategic aerial bombing was used by all sides during the war, collectively accounting for over a million deaths. What makes the nuclear bombings so morally different other than scale? And is conventional warfare any more justifiable? The invasion of Okinawa just prior to the bombings was extraordinarily bloody, killing more than 200,000 Americans and Japanese, half of which were civilians who either threw themselves into the battle or committed suicide before capture.

Assigning moral responsibility is also a problem of many hands. Though Truman ultimately authorized their use, he became president only after the unexpected death of his predecessor who had authorized their construction. Truman had been kept in the dark as vice president and played no part in their development. Scientists Leo Szilard and Albert Einstein were amongst the strongest critics of the dropping of the bombs on Japan, yet it was their joint letter to President Roosevelt in 1939 that urged their development in the first place. Committees of scientists, bureaucrats, generals and politicians were involved in both recommending the use of the bombs and the sites where they should be dropped (Rhodes 2012: 617–651). And perhaps there is no greater temptation for moral disengagement than during times of war, for once developed, political leaders and the public alike soon found moral justifications to support the use of nuclear weapons against a dehumanized enemy (Rhodes 2012: 696–699; Stokes 2015). As nuclear scientist Edmund Teller remarked in 1945, "I have no hope of clearing my conscience...if we have a slim chance of survival, it lies in the possibility to get rid of wars...actual combat-use might help convince everybody that the next war would be fatal...the responsibility must in the end be shifted to the people as a whole" (Barlow 2019: 197).

Speaking after the war, Truman said "As President of the United States, I had the fateful responsibility of deciding whether or not to use this weapon for the first time. It was the hardest decision I ever had to make. But the President cannot duck hard problems—he cannot pass the buck" (Truman 1948). Although it is easy to debate from the comforting position of bystander, Truman alone was forced to make the final decision. To end the war through the bombings, or to continue it through conventional means, inevitably left the blood of hundreds of thousands on his hands. It is a mercy that most of us are spared from ever having to take on such responsibility.

From Confucius to Rawls, debating the legitimacy, morality, and role of leadership in our society is unceasing. Every generation struggles with new variations of these age-old debates as institutions are amended, laws are changed and new experiments are tried. Context greatly influences these debates. Faced with tyrannical dictators philosophers warn of the dangers of unrestrained leadership and popular or elite revolt curbs their power. In times of civil strife, instability and deadlock, strong leaders come back into vogue to save the state. Although institutions and thinking have evolved over the millennia, there are still no easy answers to the big issues posed above, and each generation and every society must find answers for themselves.

Chapter Summary

- Legitimacy is the perceived *right* to power and authority, as established and verified by wider society. Political leaders must engage continuously in justifying the legitimacy of what they do. There are three common justifications used to establish the legitimacy of authority:
  - Consequentialism: Political legitimacy stems from the good it creates, or the harm it prevents, in wider society.
  - Consent: Political legitimacy stems only from public consent, and/or what is done to uphold the public will.
  - Public Reason: Political legitimacy is rooted in common human values and reason and is justified through procedures that produce genuine deliberation and consent.
- The appropriate role of a leader in society has undergone continuous debate, ranging from seeing leaders as being necessary and central to happy societies, to leaders being a necessary evil that must be carefully constrained, to leaders playing no legitimate role in society. Philosophical debates over the role of leadership are often heavily influenced by prevailing political conditions and historical experience.
- Morality presents a unique challenge for political leadership, as it is the subject of intense public scrutiny yet also an area where general rules of morality may be difficult to apply. The three common bases for judging the morality of political leadership are:
  - Character: The morality of a leader's action is rooted in their personal moral character.
  - Ends: All actions can be morally justified on the basis of the ends they produce.
  - Means: Morality is based upon the nature of the actions taken themselves, regardless of ends.

- There are three problems however in adjudicating the morality of political leadership in our society:
    - Dirty Hands Problem: We routinely ask, and require, our leaders to wield coercive powers and take actions for the good of society that ordinary citizens cannot.
    - Many Hands Problem: Government is large, and decisions and actions are implemented by many different actors, making true responsibility for successes or failures hard to assign.
    - Moral Disengagement: Moral assessments tend to be self-serving, and heavily influenced by political beliefs and partisanship, which often compromises the moral policing of political leadership.

4 DEMOCRATS AND DICTATORS

Chapter Outline

- How can we compare the role political leaders play across different political systems? How can we measure the degree to which leaders dominate their respective systems?
- What are autocratic and democratic systems? Are there grey areas between the two? How do autocratic and democratic systems differ in empowering and constraining leaders?
- What are the challenges faced by autocratic rulers? How do autocrats maintain power and rule their polities?
- What are the challenges faced by democratic rulers? What are some of the drawbacks of democratic rule?

Whilst philosophers have debated the ideal nature of political leadership for eons, those debates have influenced (and been influenced by) its practical application in systems of government that have evolved in parallel. It is here that idealized principles run into the hard realities and human frailties that so often arise in the drama of politics.

Consider the French Constitution of 1848. Written in the aftermath of a string of increasingly disastrous dictatorships, philosophers and politicians came together to write a new constitution that would prevent an autocrat from emerging ever again. They sought to implement the philosophical ideas of Rousseau and Montesquieu, enshrine extensive political and social rights, and learn from best practice by adopting an American-style presidency with strict separation of powers. But for all their careful planning, it failed spectacularly in its primary goal. Within just four years its first elected president Louis-Napoleon Bonaparte, with significant public support, abolished the republic and crowned himself Emperor Napoleon III.

Thus, when looking at systems of government, we must consider both the theoretical design and the practical reality which has resulted to truly understand how exactly political leadership fits within.

Comparing systems

Political systems are commonly classified according to the power of leaders within them. Despite many variations, most systems can be distinguished by considering where power and authority are concentrated, and with reference to just two polar forms – autocracy, which is the 'rule of the one', and democracy, which is 'rule of the many'. In a democracy, power and authority tend to be dispersed, and legitimacy is verified through popular consent. In autocracies, power and authority tend to be concentrated, and the legitimacy and survival of the leader are maintained through elite consent.

Not all systems can be mapped easily onto this continuum. There are many 'grey zone' regimes, sometimes termed 'anocracies', which blend autocratic and democratic rule (Ezrow & Frantz 2011: 8–12). The long-standing Polity datasets classify political regimes by scoring them for both levels of autocracy and democracy, and although most systems are clearly one or the other, a sizable minority have features of both (Marshall & Elzinga-Marshall 2017).

Further differentiation between systems is usually made by examining the relationship between the executive, legislative and judicial functions of government. Autocratic systems tend to blur the lines between these functions, and potentially concentrate them into the hands of the same people, whilst more democratic systems tend to separate out these functions (O'Neil, Fields & Share 2015: 9–15).

Autocratic systems

In the Biblical story of the Judgment of Solomon, King Solomon of Israel adjudicates a dispute between two women who both claim to be a baby's mother. After listening to their arguments, Solomon claims to be unable to decide the true mother and states the solution is to divide the baby in half. One of the women agrees, while the other begs Solomon to give the baby to her rival so that it at least might live. Solomon, believing only the true mother would nobly sacrifice her own interests to save her child, rules that the baby is in fact hers (1 Kings 3: 16–28). The story is a moral parable, but the keen observer will note that the executive, legislative and judicial functions are all merged in King Solomon's system of rule – the law is what he says, he judges each case personally, and he is able to execute (quite literally) his rule on the spot. Only as societies evolved and became more complex did these functions diverge as separate institutions. As such, autocracies were the dominant form of government until the second half of the twentieth century (Tullock 1987: 1–5), and by most measures democratic systems have only become the most numerous globally since the 1990s (Marshall & Elzinga-Marshall 2017: 31). As the traditionally dominant style of political system, there are many historical variations of autocracy, from archdukes to zamindars. Schemes for categorization are numerous (e.g. Hadenius & Teorell 2007; Lidén 2014), but several types are commonly described in the literature (Ezrow & Frantz 2011: 2–24), which I'll summarize here (Table 4.1):

Table 4.1 Classifications of autocratic regimes

System	Brief description	Current examples
Absolute monarchy	A monarch is head of state and directs the affairs of government. Legitimacy established through birthright.	Brunei Eswatini Saudi Arabia Qatar
Theocracy	Functionally similar to a monarchy, but legitimacy established through reference to divine sanction.	Vatican City
Military	A regime enabled through military domination of coercive power. Legitimacy often weak and established idiosyncratically.	Myanmar (1962–2011) Sudan Thailand (2014–2019)
One-party	Only one political party is legal, and members of that party occupy all the positions of power. Party and state leadership are merged, legitimacy is established through fidelity to the party and its organizing ideology.	China Cuba Eritrea Laos Vietnam
Competitive	Legitimacy is established through elections, but electoral competition is limited. Leaders effectively rule as autocrats over societies that are not sufficiently free to sustain democratic checks on leaders (Schedler 2006; Levitsky & Way 2010).	Afghanistan Cambodia Cameroon Egypt Russia Venezuela
Personalist	All power structured around a single individual or family. Personalist regimes often incorporate personality cults and a hand-picked elite. Legitimacy established idiosyncratically.	North Korea Syria

Another well-developed distinction between autocracies regards the regime's goals. *Totalitarian* regimes are those which seek massive state intervention into the economy and people's lives, often with an ideologically driven agenda of societal transformation, such as fascism. *Authoritarian* regimes lack this agenda, focusing instead on keeping the regime and its allies in power, and intervening into the lives of citizens only as much as necessary to keep that power (Wintrobe 2000: 43–45). Fascism is functionally little different from any other form of autocracy, but its totalitarian ambitions and ideological agenda do make it historically distinctive. However, scholars have noted the distinction is rarely useful, as there have been few truly totalitarian regimes (Brooker 2013: 18–20).

Democratic systems

As Francis Fukuyama pronounced in *The End of History*, the end of the Cold War seemingly cemented liberal democracy and free-market capitalism as the only credible foundations for a society, and millennia of debate over political ideology were at an end (Fukuyama 1992/2006). This also entailed a decisive shift away from autocracies to democratic systems in which power is dispersed and legitimacy established through popular consent.

Yet despite this shift, we still live in a world fascinated by and devoted to our political leaders, even if no longer beholden to them to the same degree. And therein lies a paradox that bedevils the study of leadership in democracy, insofar as democracy and leadership seem to be concepts diametrically opposed to each other (Cronin & Genovese 2012: 125–128). Democracy entails the dispersal of political power to the many, whilst leadership concentrates it in the few. Democracy suggests that all voices in the community are inherently equal, whilst leadership projects and promotes the voices of the few over the many. Democracy embraces collective decision-making and debate; leadership embraces singular visions and individual action. "In a truly democratic society, the leader is the odd one out" (Hendriks & Karsten 2014: 41). Kenneth Ruscio notes that much of our political evolution towards democracy has been underpinned by a need to constrain and provide checks upon our leaders. And yet at the core of modern democracy we still find leaders, some more powerful than their autocratic forebears (Ruscio 2008).

Hence, democratic systems do not necessarily render political leaders less dominant than they are in autocratic systems even though the legitimation of their authority and the nature of their powers are different. Leadership structures in democracies vary almost as widely as they do in autocracies, and democratic systems are usually categorized with respect to the relationship between the executive and legislature (Table 4.2).

Different political arrangements create different opportunities and constraints for political leadership, and encourage different strategies and leadership styles in order to be successful. It is often helpful when thinking about political leaders within systems to consider what kind of behaviours and strategies are incentivized by different arrangements. In parliamentary systems, for example, the prime minister's position is not fixed or secure – they serve only at the behest of the legislature and their party. Prime ministers must maintain the confidence of both to stay in power, and thus must work at least somewhat collaboratively with their colleagues and legislature. Presidents within full presidential systems, on the other hand, are independently elected and cannot be easily removed by legislature. They are less dependent on the legislature to survive, and indeed, will more readily adopt a combative stance against it, especially if doing so is likely to be popular with the electorate.

Table 4.2 Classifications of democratic regimes

System	Description	Current examples
Presidential	Executive branch is completely independent of the legislative and judicial branches. The president is elected by the public and is directly accountable to the electorate. The president is both head of state and head of government. They have a high degree of control over the executive branch, appointing their own cabinets and running the executive government. They have far less control over the legislative/budgetary process though, relying on cooperation with independent legislature.	Brazil Chile Ghana Indonesia Mexico Nigeria Peru USA
Parliamentary (Westminster)	The executive is chosen from the ranks of the legislature to form a government. The executive is responsible to the parliament – it can govern only so long as it can command a majority in the legislature. A prime minister leads the government. There is a separate head of state, though with a largely ceremonial role. In the Westminster variation, the executive tends to dominate over the legislature, politics is dominated by just a few large parties, and usually just one party forms the government (Lijphart 1984: ch. 1).	Australia Canada India Jamaica Japan Singapore UK Vanuatu
Parliamentary (consensus)	As above. However, in the consensus variation, there many more parties in the legislature and it is rare for any party to hold a majority, so governments tend to be formed by coalitions of several parties, and the executive and legislature tend to share power more equally (Lijphart 1984: ch. 2)	Belgium Denmark Germany Iraq Netherlands Spain

(continued)

Table 4.2 (continued)

System	Description	Current examples
Semi-presidential (president-parliamentary)	A hybrid system where there is both an elected head of state and head of government. The president appoints the prime minister and cabinet and shares some executive powers with them. President-parliamentarianism is a variant of semi-presidentialism where the prime minister and cabinet, once appointed, are collectively responsible to ***both*** the legislature and the president (Shugart & Carey 1992; Elgie 2011: ch. 2).	Azerbaijan Congo Mauritania Namibia Palestine Peru Portugal Taiwan
Semi-presidential (premier-presidential)	As above. Premier-presidentialism is a variant of semi-presidentialism where the prime minister and cabinet, once appointed, are responsible ***only*** to the legislature (Shugart & Carey 1992; Elgie 2011: ch. 2). Across both types of semi-presidentialism, there is great variation in the relative power of the president, prime minister and legislature within the political system.	Algeria France Haiti Lithuania Mali Poland Sri Lanka Ukraine

Semi-presidential systems vary in this manner too. In premier-presidential there is more incentive for the president to negotiate with the legislature, as the legislature has the sole power to remove the appointed government and will readily do so if the president refuses to accommodate at least some of the interests of the legislature. In president-parliamentary, the government is responsible to both president and legislature. As such, the government may be caught in a tug-of-war between the interests of the president and legislature. It has been observed that in such systems, there is more ambiguity and rivalry over who holds authority over the government, leading to greater instability and political clashes, than in premier-presidential arrangements (Shugart & Carey 1992: 106–130; Elgie 2011: 30–36).

Leader dominance

Within democracies

Although it seems a given that autocratic systems have more dominant executives than democracies, and presidential systems more dominant executives than parliamentary, in practice these labels are not always a reliable guide. Even within systems of the same type, there can be significant variation. This is particularly so in semi-presidential systems, in which the relative strength of the legislature, president and prime minister may be ambiguous or mercurial (Elgie 2011: 26–28). To clarify the power of the executive across systems, metrics have emerged that provide some comparative insight. One that has reached particular prominence was developed by Arend Lijphart (1984, 2012), who employs 'cabinet duration' (i.e., the average length of time a cabinet stays in power) as a proximal measure, developing an index using this metric alone for parliamentary systems, and with certain adjustments and other controlling variables for non-parliamentary systems (Table 4.3).

Lijphardt's index suggests there is not a clear relationship between the formal arrangement of a political system and the degree of executive domination within it, and instead we must look to other factors.

Table 4.3 Patterns of executive dominance across democracies

Country	Executive dominance index	Average cabinet duration	Democratic classification
Israel	1.46	1.46	Parliamentary
Finland	1.55	1.55	Parliamentary
Mauritius	2.39	2.39	Parliamentary
Netherlands	2.91	2.91	Parliamentary
Costa Rica	3.00	5.15	Presidential
Portugal	3.26	3.26	Semi-presidential
United States	4.00	7.05	Presidential
Greece	4.45	4.45	Parliamentary
Sweden	5.61	5.61	Parliamentary
Trinidad	6.95	6.95	Parliamentary
France	8.00	3.22	Semi-presidential
South Korea	8.00	2.77	Presidential
Malta	8.85	8.85	Parliamentary
Jamaica	9.64	9.64	Parliamentary
Botswana	9.90	45.33	Presidential

Source: Lijphart (2012: 120–121).

A common alternative explanation of executive dominance is the arrangement of political parties. Systems featuring many small parties that must form a coalition in order to govern tend to have more unstable cabinets and shorter-lived or less powerful political executives when compared to democracies that have only two or three major parties (Laver & Schofield 1998; Dodd 2015). This difference is particularly striking when comparing Westminster-style and consensus-style parliamentary systems. With the latter often requiring coalitions of several parties to command a majority in legislature, executive dominance is generally low, and successful political leaders in such systems tend to be less bombastic and more diplomatic than their Westminster counterparts (see Case 4.1).

Significant ideological distance between parties and coalition partners also undermines government stability (Warwick 1992). Giovanni Sartori postulates that larger numbers of parties in a legislature leads to more extremism, fragmentation and generally make it more difficult for political leaders to negotiate majorities to pass policy and legislation, leading to weaker executive government (Sartori 2005: ch. 5–6).

Herbert Döring postulates that the degree of control over the legislative agenda is another key to understanding executive dominance. The power to decide which bills to present to the legislature, the power to change or amend bills, how budgetary bills are managed, and control over the legislative timetable are his most relevant factors. Döring finds huge variations in these powers across 18 democracies. In Ireland and the United Kingdom, the executive has great control over the legislative agenda and timetable, and largely controls what issues are discussed and voted on. In the Netherlands and Sweden, the executive shares this power with the legislature and is far less able to control the legislative agenda (Döring 1995: 223–247).

Another perspective is offered by George Tsebelis, whose work on the concept of 'veto players' has been highly influential in recent decades. Veto players are defined as institutions (executive agencies, courts, legislatures etc.) or actors within a political system (political parties and factions) that have the power to *stop* a policy or prevent political change (Tsebelis 2011: 2). And Tsebelis's core claim is that the more veto players there are in a political system, the less potential there is for change (Tsebelis 1995). And by extension, the more veto players in a system, the less powerful the executive or any single political leader will be. Other factors are incorporated into the model, particularly the ideological distance between veto players and the internal cohesion of veto players, which may moderate the impact of veto players on the system (Tsebelis 2011).

Using veto-player theory allows many different types of political systems to be compared more directly and offers a unified framework for understanding the inertial forces in a political system. Although defining exactly who or what a veto player is in a system at any given time can be complicated (Hallerberg 2010), there is evidence that when used to analyse issues like executive dominance in a system, more veto players correlates with lower cabinet duration, the measure of executive dominance first noted in this section (Saalfeld 2010).

All this variation in executive dominance has significant implications for the practice of political leadership. The styles of leadership likely to succeed

Case 4.1 Rule by consensus

Wim Kok

Prime Minister of the Netherlands, 1993–2002

Figure 4.1 Wim Kok in 1994

What does leadership look like in a political system in which executive dominance is low? The Netherlands is one such example. Historically highly fragmented both socially and politically (Andeweg & Irwin 2014: ch. 2), no single party has won a majority in the Dutch legislature since 1897. What has developed as a result in the Netherlands is a 'consensus democracy' or 'Polder model' (see Hendriks 2018), in which a leader must form a cabinet with many disparate voices to govern and must work collaboratively to get things done. Historically, this had led to pragmatic and 'down to earth' leaders who prefer collegiality over confrontation and using tactics to depoliticize issues and find reasonable compromises on policy (Swinkels et al. 2017: 165–167). In this way, the Dutch prime minister is more like a chairman than a director (Andeweg 2000).

The son of a carpenter, Wim Kok was a trade unionist who assumed the leadership of the Dutch labour party (PvdA) in 1986. His presence as leader was measured, to the point where at many points in his career his leadership was not obvious (see Klein 1998). His ascent to the top of Dutch politics was unusual, becoming Prime Minister in 1994 after elections in which his party lost a quarter of their seats. However, the government lost even more, leaving PdvA in a leading position. He formed the first of the 'purple' coalitions, bringing together three parties from left and right to form a government after months of negotiations. Kok was a master of keeping these disparate forces together, maintaining a stable governing alliance through two terms. His was a quiet government that focused on steady economic management and united around liberalization, one of the few goals all coalition partners shared. His style was consciously low-key, eschewing a significant public character or popular profile (te Velde 2002: 241–243)

The advantages of the consensus model in the Netherlands are that most decisions by the government have a high degree of legitimacy attached to them, since they have generally been thoroughly vetted by all interests. Moreover, there is a high degree of policy stability and continuity between governments, a stability that has been seen as beneficial for attracting business and talent to the country (Andeweg 2000: 703–704). The Wassenaar

Agreement of 1982, masterminded by Prime Minister Ruud Luubers and Wim Kok while he was a national trade union leader, brought government, employers and trade unions together to agree on labour market reforms, including wage restraint and flexible working hours. The reforms were widely credited with ending the wage-price spiral in the Netherlands that beleaguered many Western economies in the 1980s, yet did so by consensus, rather than the confrontation and sometimes bitter clashes with labour seen in the United States and United Kingdom (see Case 2.1), earning the appellation 'the Dutch miracle'.

The fragmentation of the political landscape, and high degree of heterogeneity in cabinets, means there are many political veto players in Dutch politics. Making policy is often a slow and measured process, and there is sometimes significant frustration at the glacial pace of change (Hendriks 2018). Though this was a criticism frequently levelled in the Kok era, there were major breakthroughs, and indeed, Kok negotiated the legalization of prostitution, euthanasia and same-sex marriage after years of careful work, and with less political and social discord that would emerge over these issues in other democracies.

But "the involvement of so many agents in policymaking may result in convoluted compromises that are sometimes deliberately vague in order to keep everyone on board" (Andeweg & Irwin 2014: 276). Kok's government earned the reputation of being overly cautious and managerial. Indeed, it was often openly described as 'boring', much the same as the politics of the era, in which the left-right coalition meant there was little formal opposition (te Velde 2002: 241–249). Critics contended that Kok and the PvdA shed much of its ideological footing to keep that governing coalition together, pursuing middle-of-the-road policies rather than long-held party goals. Moreover, highly contentious policy issues – most notably healthcare, rising concern about crime, and growing distemper over immigration and asylum policy – were avoided by the Kok cabinet in order to maintain amity given conflicting cabinet views (Albertazzi & McDonnell 2007: 153–158).

A major public backlash against this kind of consensus politics came at the 2002 elections, with the public and media raising those issues that the political class were avoiding, and the PdvA lost much of its support to Pim Fortuyn, a highly divisive and populist political leader who openly criticized Kok and the Polder model (see Pauwels 2014: 71-85). The consensus system of politics in the Netherlands, however, has largely endured, and Dutch prime ministers have continued to garner reputations as uncharismatic and managerial, while "peer-oriented, backstage leadership skills, relations, and reputation appear to remain more important than mass-oriented ones" (Swinkels et al. 2017: 178). Though populist confrontational politicians are continuing to make a mark on Dutch politics, it has not, it seems, altered the fundamental logic of governing in a state with weak executive dominance.

in weak executive systems are different from those with strong executive dominance (see Case 4.1).

For instance, the European Union has many veto players, from powerful individual member states to various decision-making bodies and courts (Tsebelis & Yataganas 2002). Major policy change and decisive action are thus rarer and more difficult to achieve, especially as ideological differences between different veto-players have grown. In consequence, collaborative and diplomatic leaders who can build consensus and navigate the complex institutional environment are perhaps favoured (Nugent 2017: 10–11). Herman Van Rompuy, the first permanent president of the European Union after the Treaty of Lisbon, was just this – a leader who necessarily specialized in negotiation, persuasion and transactional leadership in order to get things done in a crowded veto-player environment (Dinan 2017; Tömmel 2017). Unsurprisingly, this was Van Rompuy's strength, having served previously as Prime Minister of Belgium, a country with one of the weakest executives by all the measures mentioned above. By comparison, Van Rompuy's successor, former Prime Minister of Poland Donald Tusk, was predicted by many to be a poor fit for the role, having much less experience and skill as a consensus-builder and coming from a country with high executive dominance and a tradition of strong political leadership (Redei 2014).

Within autocracies

Despite outward appearances, autocracies too may have great variation in leader dominance. Regardless of form, all autocrats rely upon a system of elites underneath them to implement their rule and maintain power (see section "Elites"). The nature of this elite, and its relationship to the leader, are the principal determinants of how dominant the leader actually is.

In personalist regimes where the elite is hand-picked, the leader is highly dominant as there is little difference between the interests of the elites and the leader, and there are few, if any, veto players to block the will of the leader (Ezrow & Frantz 2011: 114–121).

In single-party systems, by contrast, there is usually a broad structural elite made up of party careerists, often with backgrounds, constituencies and interests different to the leader. Lacking other political parties to compete with, competition over power and ideology instead happens within the ruling party, usually leading to *factionalism* (see Taras 1989), and as such the leader will find themselves having to negotiate with opposing factions within the elite to maintain authority and govern. Indeed, factionalism within single-party states is often entrenched and severe, creating numerous veto players in the policymaking process and rendering leadership much weaker than is apparent. Slow, incremental changes in policy and budgeting – a hallmark of democratic politics where there are many veto players and interests to contend with – have been similarly observed in mature Communist states (Bunce & Echols 1978). Indeed, in such systems leaders may even have less power and authority than their counterparts in democratic nations. Vietnam, for example, has been cited as an example where severe factionalism and disagreement within the ruling Communist party have rendered both major policy change and decisive leadership very difficult, and gridlock a common state of affairs (Abuza 2002; Koh 2001).

Hence, although we might reasonably expect autocracies to feature more powerful and dominant leaders relative to their democratic counterparts, this is not necessarily the case. Determining leader dominance within political systems is deceptively tricky, and often requires a strong knowledge of both institutional settings and politics on-the-ground.

The challenges of autocratic rule

Maintaining power

Like all leaders, autocracies must legitimize their authority. Although autocrats may appear all-powerful, and they may even cultivate such an image of themselves, there are elites within an autocratic state just like any other, and the autocrat must maintain their confidence to rule (see section "Elites"). Maintaining the confidence of the armed forces is usually critical, as they play a much larger role in upholding a leader's rule in an autocracy than a democracy (Finer 1962). It may also be the party (in a one-party state), major economic interests, or regional/local powers who are most consequential.

Democratic leaders must also tend to elites. Party factions, major donors, corporations and trade unions are often powerful in democratic systems and most leaders will court them. But a major point of difference between autocratic and democratic rule in maintaining power regards what Bueno de Mesquita and Smith call the first 'rule for rulers' – *keep the winning coalition as small as possible* (Bueno de Mesquita & Smith 2012: 17). It is a good idea for rulers in all contexts to adhere to this rule, as the broader and larger the coalition, the more complicated and expensive it is to keep it together, and the more opportunity there is for it to fail.

An autocrat can potentially narrow their ruling coalition to a great degree, relying on perhaps just a few key institutions (like the police and military) to monopolize power. Not so in democratic systems, where there are far more veto players and independent institutions involved in policy-making, and in order to win elections and maintain popular support to rule, you must have a broad coalition of voters, constituencies, interest groups and elites to succeed (Bueno de Mesquita & Smith 2012: 17–20; see section "The Challenge of Democratic Rule"). Yet the logic of the rule still holds. In parliamentary systems, governing coalitions made up of many parties and ideologies are generally less stable and less decisive than those made up of just a few, or a single, party (Strøm & Müller 1999; Kaarbo 2012: 13–17).

Yet a narrow governing coalition comes with its own challenges. As autocrats generally have weak authority claims, other aspirants can usually push the leader out and make similar claims of legitimacy just as easily (Dukalskis & Gerschewski 2017). Furthermore, as autocracies generally weaken or remove other veto players in a political system (such as courts, legislatures, political parties, trade unions and other civil institutions) to concentrate power in the centre, aspirants for leadership may need only sway a relatively small section of the elite (usually key sections of the military, police or wealthy interests) to seize enough power to depose the leader. As autocracies generally lack fidelity to legal-rational authority or independent political institutions, power relationships can shift quickly.

Although popular revolutions are a possibility to overthrow a dictator, since 1945 over two thirds of leaders in autocratic regimes have been removed through *coups d'etat* (Svolik 2009: 477–478). Hence in autocratic regimes, it is intra-elite power struggles that pose the most serious threat to the leader (Tullock 1987: 9–10). Autocrats must focus on keeping elites happy, whether it is the military, the governing party or other institutions like industry and religious authorities, in order to remain in power (Ezrow & Frantz 2011: ch. 4). Because by their nature a coup requires swiftness, secrecy and strong organization to succeed, autocrats don't necessarily know where threats to their rule lie, and thus must invest significant time into continuously countering the ever-present but often hidden danger. The methods by which they do this might vary. In military and personalist dictatorships, there is often an emphasis on economic and material outcomes for the power elite (Bueno de Mesquita & Smith 2012: ch. 6). In one-party dictatorships, particularly communist systems, the ruler must also be seen to be upholding and progressing the ideological mission of the party, and indeed, ideological purity may even rival the importance of material benefit (Brooker 2013: 114–116).

This does not necessarily mean a wanton disregard for the public. A booming economy and a stable government are both a public good and of value to elites, and moreover create the financial basis upon which a regime might survive in the long term (Bueno de Mesquita & Smith 2012: ch. 4). Poverty and low levels of economic development are strongly correlated with coups and political instability, as both are spurs for popular and elite unrest (Londregan & Poole 1990). Popular overthrow of the autocrat is very possible when thresholds of dissatisfaction have been reached (Tullock 1987: 10), and hence the autocratic leader cannot completely ignore their legitimacy in the public eye. Usually, autocratic rule must be sustained publicly through promises of security and material benefit for the population, and a veneer of democratic legitimacy may be created through uncompetitive elections and referenda (Soest & Grauvogel 2017; Cassani 2017). Such authority though is brittle, easily contested by rivals and may collapse rapidly in the face of shocks or crisis.

Yet the unsettling reality is that public revolt is in practice a relatively remote threat to the rule of an autocrat, whilst a coup is near certain if the autocrat loses critical support amongst the power elite (Svolik 2009). Thus an autocrat who focuses on furthering the public good and improving national conditions isn't guaranteed survival – indeed, if they do so at the expense of the power elite, they will hasten their own demise (see Case 4.2). With a narrow coalition supporting their power, it makes more sense for the autocrat to concentrate policies and investment on just enough public goods like basic education, healthcare and infrastructure to stave off popular revolt and provide a basis for economic growth and revenue, which in turn can be reinvested in maintaining the loyalty of the power elite (Bueno de Mesquita & Smith 2012: ch. 5). Leaders in democratic systems must generally do the opposite and try to hold together the largest possible coalition of support to win elections, minimize opposition and pursue their agenda. A strong economy and increasing public goods will broaden your popular appeal and coalition strength. Tax cuts and public infrastructure are popular with all sides of politics and are a common strategy to endear the leadership to the widest possible audience.

Autocratic regimes are far less forgiving of leaders who fail to find the right balance between keeping the public and the elite happy. The survival rates of autocratic leaders are in fact poorer than democratic leaders in the early years of a new regime. Over time though, autocratic leaders who successfully find the right formula to allocate rewards, manage public and elite expectations, and narrow their ruling coalition have the potential to hold power far longer than democratic leaders (Svolik 2009; Bueno de Mesquita & Smith 2012: 72–74).

Fragile regimes and weak governance

Autocratic regimes are often fragile. Many rely heavily on the personal and charismatic authority of individual leaders, which often makes succession and transfer of authority from one ruler to another problematic. Monarchical systems try to alleviate the problem by preparing royal heirs with a childhood of education and training in preparation for a life of rule. But unexpected or unprepared succession, or untalented heirs, will cause problems. Similarly, single-party states attempt to create a more enduring system of legitimacy by enshrining a party and ideology as the highest political authority, rather than the singular leader. Yet factionalism and infighting within single-party systems are endemic, and successions are major power struggles that can be extremely destabilizing, even violent (see Rush 1974; Taras 1989). Many autocratic regimes, like Falangist Spain, Communist Yugoslavia and the Portuguese Estado Novo, have not lasted long beyond the life of their founding leaders.

Indeed, this situation is almost a feature of autocratic rule, as in order to survive, it is usually in the interests of autocrats to neutralize other talented leaders who might become rivals for power. One side effect, though, is depriving the state of talented leadership successors, as well as depriving the state of a competent leadership class and policymaking establishment (Bueno de Mesquita & Smith 2012: 58–60). Since a falling out in 2012, Turkish President Recep Tayyip Erdoğan has staged a series of purges against followers of former political ally Fethullah Gülen. These purges intensified after a failed military uprising in 2016, which was blamed on Gülenists. Erdoğan's increasingly autocratic regime has removed or arrested hundreds of thousands across the civil service, education, media, military and judiciary. Though it has solidified Erdoğan's rule over the country, the mass purges have significantly disrupted the economy and have weakened governance as thousands of top administrators and experts have been purged (Habibi 2016). Erdoğan's increasingly unrestrained rule has also proved disastrous for economic policymaking, as expert guidance has given way to erratic presidential fiats (Daragahi 2018).

This speaks to a broader problem of autocratic regimes – that of the 'weak state' (Ezrow & Frantz 2011: ch. 6). Put simply, the institutions and

Case 4.2 Keeping power

Thomas Sankara

President of Burkina Faso, 1983–1987

Figure 4.2 Thomas Sankara in 1987

Thomas Sankara was president of Burkina Faso for just four years in the 1980s, coming to power in a military coup staged by radical revolutionary officers of the national army. His rise and fall illustrate some of the perverse logic that undergirds autocratic leadership survival discussed in the previous section.

Sankara was young, energetic and fiercely determined to change the course of one of Africa's most underdeveloped nations. He oversaw the mass mobilization of the country through local revolutionary committees, which saw millions of Burkinabe build new schools, hospitals, roads, dams, wells and public amenities. He enacted ambitious agricultural reforms that fostered widespread land redistribution and the rapid expansion of irrigation and fertilization – within four years Burkina Faso had nearly doubled its wheat and cotton production and reached food self-sufficiency. A mass immunization campaign saw 2.5 million children vaccinated and the virtual disappearance of polio, meningitis and measles, which had claimed thousands of lives annually. Millions of trees were planted in attempts to arrest the desertification of the country and restore soil health. And he oversaw major programs of literacy, education and national pride – even changing the country's name from the French colonial "Upper Volta" to "Burkina Faso" – land of the upright people (Harsch 2014: 71–107).

Sankara's revolution and political base were mobilized through the creation of the Committees for the Defence of the Revolution (CDRs), populist organizations that aimed at mass mobilization against the established power of the elites of Burkina Faso. Sankara frequently used these organizations across the country to defeat the organized power of trade unions, tribal chieftains, the bureaucracy and business interests. The CDRs were powerful but they were a broad and unwieldy coalition of diverse interests and ideologies. Sankara soon struggled to maintain control over them, and many overstepped their initial goals and engaged in class violence (Kandeh 2004: 124–135). Sankara himself would eventually acknowledge the failures of the CDRs, but did not follow up to create an effective political party or umbrella organization that might have shifted his source of power to an organized civilian political structure and a narrower governing coalition.

Sankara moved fast and upset many. He pushed a revolution in women's rights in a society scandalized by such concepts. He staged anti-corruption and austerity campaigns within the government that angered bureaucrats, tribal chiefs and the military. He was a fierce anti-imperialist who wanted to spread revolution across Africa, worrying neighbouring countries and Western powers. He became a hero to many ordinary citizens, but within a few years he had alienated most of the country's elite (Martin 1987).

Within this popularity among citizens lay the seeds of his regime's downfall. Sankara had sought popular revolution, yet his regime was largely a dictatorship built around Sankara himself, often resorting freely to coercion to achieve the ends of the revolution. Without an established system of democratic institutions or rule of law, Sankara thus ignored political realities that would result from his marginalization of the nation's elite, whose network of power and authority his own ultimately relied upon (Kandeh 2004: ch. 6). Sankara himself acknowledged the danger in 1985, noting that through his dogged pursuit of corruption and equality, and his insistence upon the austerity of the leadership, he was challenging the petty bourgeoisie, who had been the socio-economic strata who had effectively made the revolution a possibility in the first place (Harsch 2014: 142–143).

Sankara's foreign policy was one of revolutionary agitation, which alarmed many neighbouring countries as well as France, whose post-colonial influence in West Africa continued to be strong. With foreign help, eventually various sections of the disempowered elites of Burkina Faso, and in particular a now disloyal faction of the military, violently overthrew Sunkara and stopped much of the revolution in its tracks. Sankara had achieved enormous popular prestige but ignored the fact his own power rested on autocratic elite structures rather than democratic institutions. Despite a great talent for leadership and revolutionary policy legacy, in pursuing reform that so quickly impacted every established interest in Burkina Faso, whilst failing to create a replacement structure of power and authority to oversee the revolution, Sankara ultimately set himself on a collision course with the vested interests to whom he was doomed to lose power.

mechanisms by which autocrats rule over their nations tend to be much shallower and less effective than their equivalents in democratic systems, particularly in personalist and military dictatorships. Policymaking and decision-making structures are often emaciated within an autocratic system, as the high degree of individual control means there is a significant limitation on how much can be done at any one time. Autocrats often surround themselves with hand-picked loyalists who will not question their judgment or authority, and hence are able to make erratic, hasty or poor decisions with few impediments (Geddes et al. 2018: 222–226). Moreover, decision-making is often compromised by poor information flows throughout the system. In a system built on elite loyalty rather than legal-rational authority or the public good, lower-tier officials primarily seek to curry favour (or avoid sanction) with the leadership, and hence there is often significant incentive to distort what is reported to those above (Jiang & Wallace 2017). The effects can be calamitous on the decision-making capacity of autocratic leadership, who in the absence of reliable information from below, may be unable to understand the situation on the ground. Such was the case with the Chinese Great Famine of 1959–1961, in which local officials competed for promotions by exaggerating food production, whilst in reality there were enormous deficits, leading to a catastrophic famine that took years for the central government to fully realize and respond to (Fan, Xiong & Zhou 2016).

Furthermore, because autocratic regimes are often built around patronage relationships and corruption in order to keep key power elites happy, cultures of corruption and patronage spread throughout the system. The lower tiers of officialdom are those that are needed to administer policy, distribute resources and maintain the day-to-day functioning of the regime and yet may have limited incentive to work for the public – and more to work for themselves – especially if lines of authority are unstable (Geddes et al. 2018: 226–229). As such, autocracies often struggle to administer their states effectively, and petty fiefdoms and local tyrannies tend to emerge as distance from the centre increases, and in practice the reach of autocratic government often weakens rapidly once outside the capital cities. The personal rule of an individual has the capacity only to reach so far within a nation, especially when their ruling coalition is narrow, and there is limited capacity for such regimes to actually govern in response to public problems or foster economic and institutional development (Jackson & Rosberg 1982: ch.2).

Yet such regimes can still be grimly effective. Mobutu Sese Seko, dictator of the Democratic Republic of the Congo from 1965 to 1997, effectively ruled through a patronage network of local strongmen enabled by monopolization of the country's natural resources. The state apparatus was barely functional, with many regions running largely as independent fiefdoms only nominally under Mobutu's authority, yet his kleptocratic regime proved to be one of the longest, helped greatly by Western support due to Mobutu's fiercely anti-communist stance at the height of the Cold War (Reno 1997).

Not all autocratic systems are necessarily weak states, and if they survive long enough single-party states can endure. The use of a party allows the autocrat to create broader institutions of governance over a nation, more effective systems for elite training and circulation, and hence greater capacity for effective policymaking and implementation. It also creates systems whereby new leaders are legitimated, and a foundation for authority that goes beyond the charisma of the leader to the ideology, traditions and laws of the guiding party. Yet there is a trade-off. In doing so, autocrats must cede at least some power to other actors within their own parties and must create many more leadership positions within that structure in order to manage it effectively. As discussed previously in section "Comparing Systems", this leads to systems with more veto players, which in turn become somewhat more democratic (or at least oligarchic) in nature – the ruler can no longer ride roughshod over his or her colleagues but must consult and rule collectively with other factions of the party, other regions of the country or other experts and institutions within the government.

The challenges of democratic rule

Broad coalition politics and gridlock

Just as a narrow coalition and shallow governing apparatus presents challenges to autocrats, so too do crowded institutional environments and broad coalition politics present challenges to democratic leaders. In democratic systems, there are many stakeholders and institutions involved in the political process, and consequently, many veto players. Decision making and policymaking in such arrangements are generally slow, deliberative, and have multiple opportunities to be blocked or derailed. Although this can be a strength of democratic systems, acting as a safeguard against tyranny and oppression, it is also a hindrance to governments and leaders being able to respond effectively and quickly to problems.

Political gridlock has become a hallmark of modern democracies, in which various parties, branches of government and stakeholders find themselves in entrenched opposition, giving leaders limited opportunities to progress an agenda. There are manifold opportunities in a democracy for dissatisfied parties to frustrate the agenda, from lobbying legislators to funding public campaigns of opposition. A result of this, when faced with large, heterogeneous coalitions and many veto players, is that leaders are more likely to need to pursue uncontentious policies that will meet with the least resistance (Martin 2004). Across twenty-first–century Western democracies, there are significant problems faced in managing welfare policies (such as healthcare, retirement, and social insurance), climate change and budgetary deficits (Allan & Scruggs 2004; Chen 2011). Yet proposing substantive reforms to these areas, whilst technically necessary, is politically volatile and likely to fracture political coalitions and spur significant opposition from interest groups who deem change disadvantageous to their own interests. Broad policy agendas and divided control amongst branches of government are also well-established precursors to gridlock (Binder 2004: ch. 3).

Even when pursuing a narrow focus with united control of government, success is not guaranteed. United States President Barack Obama, governing in a rare period where Democrats controlled the White House and both houses of Congress, chose to focus on passing landmark healthcare reform in 2009–2010, one of the most contentious policy issues in the country. Despite favourable conditions and lessons learned from past attempts, the resulting legislation took almost 18 months to secure, wiped out much of the president's political capital, and was still a complex patchwork of compromises and concessions to various stakeholders and interest groups, resulting in an improvement but far short of wholesale reform that would address deep problems within the system (Oberlander 2010; c.f. Cahn & Johnston 2018). Moreover, since its introduction, 'Obamacare' has been systematically undermined or distorted by other institutions and interest groups, from courts to state governments, leaving it only partially effective (Oberlander 2019).

Gridlock is a major frustration in democratic politics, to politicians and the public alike (Binder 2004: ch. 6), and it seemingly deprives politics of the promise of leadership. Leaders do not win elections preaching modest achievement – they sell grand visions, transformative change, defending values and progressing an agenda. Though anointed by the electorate to be agents of change, leaders in democracies will often find themselves quickly ensnared in political quagmires with limited powers to create said change. Indeed, the problem may have worsened over time as democratic polities have broadened suffrage, legal and bureaucratic oversight has strengthened, and political society has become more inclusive (Laing 2012). Undoubtedly such changes have strengthened civil society and made politics more inclusive. And yet it may be rendering strong political leadership, and hence decisive and effective responses to society's ills, more elusive. As veto players and stakeholders proliferate, and policy issues become more complex and interconnected, "more has to be changed to break from the past, and those adversely affected by the changes will be able to put up more formidable resistance" (Skowronek 1997: 56).

The dilemma for modern democratic leaders is potent. Australia has had no fewer than seven prime ministers since 2007 and has witnessed the perils of both sides of the problem. Julia Gillard (2010–2013), for example, bravely tackled climate change and took bold actions which had been promised, but not delivered, by her predecessors. It soon created a maelstrom of resistance from negatively impacted stakeholders and became a rallying point for the opposition, such that she was ultimately deposed by her own party in the face of a deeply divided public. One of her successors, Malcolm Turnbull (2015–2018), took the opposite tack and avoided controversial policies or big agendas to keep his fractious party together, yet soon lost public support as he appeared 'gutless' and lacking in leadership (Hartcher 2017).

Resolving or bypassing gridlock in democracy is not impossible, but it requires perhaps a different set of skills and talents to what is traditionally required to campaign and win elections in a democracy. Charisma and soaring rhetoric are amongst the characteristics often rewarded in electoral politics, yet neither is necessarily very valuable in working through a gridlocked political system – a lesson quickly learned by Barack Obama, who despite his undeniable skill in rhetoric and campaigning, was bogged down in gridlock for much of his term (Coates 2016). By contrast, Republican President

George H.W. Bush presided over one of the least gridlocked legislative periods in recent history (Binder 2004: 55), passing a higher than usual number of significant laws and major tax reforms, as well as successfully leading a broad international coalition to preserve the independence of Kuwait in the first Iraq War, despite both houses of Congress being held by the opposition. Bush was well regarded as a pragmatic politician and a bipartisan negotiator and took a particularly brave stance against his own party in brokering a bipartisan budget deal that raised taxes and controlled spending to reduce the national deficit (Sinclair 2014). Yet he lacked charisma and struggled to inspire the public. Despite his policy successes, he was soundly defeated for re-election by Bill Clinton in 1992.

Democratic legitimacy

What are leaders *for* in a democracy? What does a good *democratic* leader look like? And where is the line between a good democratic leader and just another autocrat (see Case 4.3)?

These dilemmas exist because pure democracies in which everyone takes part in decisions equally are exceedingly rare. Throughout history it has often been feared that too much public participation can descend into 'mob rule', and that a leadership class is needed to temper outcomes. Ancient Athens, the most celebrated case of a pure democracy, is often subjected to this criticism. "The actual history of Athens in the period of its democratic government is marked by numerous failures, mistakes, and misdeeds—most infamously, the execution of Socrates—that would seem to discredit the ubiquitous modern idea that democracy leads to good government" (Samons 2007: 6). Thucydides criticized Athenian democracy, observing citizen-led decision-making was often woefully ill-informed and dismissive of experts on critical issues, which led to poor decision-making (see Pope 1988). Indeed, Athenian democracy helped trigger its own demise, after a jingoistic popular assembly voted for a disastrously ill-advised military expedition to Sicily, the catastrophic defeat of which crippled the city-state and led it to ruin.

In the 1920s, Walter Lippmann infamously argued the same weakness was true of modern democracies. Citing the lack of general expertise on complicated policy issues, the ease of which news and information can be manipulated, a lack of interest and engagement from the average voter, and their emotional and cultural biases, Lippmann contends that the public interest is much better served by a technocratic elite than by the public making decisions for itself (Lippmann 1922, 1925: 198–199). A century later, it's hard to argue that any of these factors are any less relevant today – indeed, policy issues are arguably even more complicated, fake news and misinformation are rampant, while cultural and ideological divides still heavily bias how we see the world around us.

American philosopher John Dewey, responding to Lippmann, defends democratic rule and the notion of a public, but nonetheless sees leaders playing a critical role in counteracting some of the inherent imperfections of a democratic system (Dewey 1927). Austrian economist Joseph

Schumpeter famously expanded on the argument in the 1940s, arguing that the public's capability to both articulate their own interests and design policy or embrace ideas to achieve them is illusory. Schumpeter's model of an ideal democracy is thus a thin one – elites and leaders still rule and should do so fairly unfettered by public participation, but be periodically subjected to elections and public approval so that legitimacy is maintained, and egregious breaches of the public trust can be punished (Schumpeter 1942; also Popper 2014: 351).

Yet regardless of what truth there to such scepticism of public participation in government, it cannot be denied that in modern democracies expectations are high that elected leaders can and will represent the public foremost and translate public interest into policy. "Unless mass views have some place in the shaping of policy, all the talk about democracy is nonsense" (Key 1961: 7). Consequently, leadership authority in democratic systems is intrinsically tied to perceived public support – we constantly monitor opinion through polling, constituency engagement, elections (of every sort) and the media. A leader's approval rating is virtually a de facto statement of their democratic legitimacy (Lepore 2015). Political leaders riding high in the polls will have great political capital to negotiate with other actors and broaden their coalition, whilst leaders in the polling doldrums will soon find their political allies abandoning them and their authority to lead compromised.

So how to navigate this tension as democratic leader – between the need to genuinely represent the public interest and yet make the best decisions and most effective policies, regardless of public sentiment? Irish statesman Edmund Burke describes the ideal politician thusly:

> It ought to be the glory of a representative to live in the strictest union, the closest correspondence, and the most unreserved communication with his constituents. Their wishes ought to have great weight with him; their opinions high respect; their business unremitted attention... But his unbiased opinion, his mature judgment, his enlightened conscience, he ought not to sacrifice to you, to any man, or to any set of men living... Your representative owes you, not his industry only, but his judgment; and he betrays instead of serving you if he sacrifices it to your opinion. (Burke 1774/1899: 95)

Achieving this ideal is much harder in practice. Although surveys show that voters want leaders who are principled and willing to fight for what they believe in, even if unpopular (Pew Research Center 2018; also Tavits 2007), there is scant evidence that political bravery is greatly rewarded at the polls. The best-selling *Profiles in Courage* (1956), written by John F. Kennedy and Ted Sorensen, offers short biographies of eight US politicians who took principled yet unpopular stands, but nearly all did so at great cost to careers and public standing. Juan Manuel Santos, President of Colombia (2010–2018) spent much of his term brokering a peace deal with the FARC movement with whom the Colombian government had been engaged in devastating guerrilla warfare for over five decades. However, the final deal met with significant resistance from sections of the public, for whom the deep scars left by decades of war made forgiveness difficult. The peace treaty was put to a national referendum but was narrowly defeated. Santos negotiated minor adjustments to the treaty but did not resubmit it for public approval before signing. Peace with FARC was secured but at a high cost: Santos's personal approval plummeted, and his party's vote collapsed at subsequent elections (Cobb & Casey 2016; The Economist 2018).

Public backlash at Santos's decision to prioritize peace over public opinion is an example of "twofold politics [in democracies]: a politics as usual, concerning the merits and mechanics of specific political decisions; and a politics of legitimacy, which calls into question [the leader's] authority in making particular decisions". The democratic leader must chart a course between what is in the public interest and what meets with public approval, and then engage in a battle to justify their choices to those who question them. Constant scrutiny of that process is institutionalized through the presence of a free press, opposition parties and other branches of government (Kane & Patapan 2012: 45–47).

This dynamic has strategic repercussions as well. A leader who pursues unpopular stands will likely face erosion of their public support. Once that has happened, their political capital will diminish – other stakeholders, parties and political leaders have little reason to work with a leader whose perceived popular (and hence democratic) authority is low. And a leader who loses an election has no authority at all. An unpopular decision may soon be repealed by successors, even if the leader is able to implement it in the face of public dissent. Many political leaders may reason that political martyrdom will help no one in the end, and continuing to influence from the inside – even if that means compromising on beliefs or principle – will do more good (see Case 4.3). Such was the case arguably with Theresa May, who took office as the Prime Minister of the United Kingdom after the Brexit referendum in 2016. May had both believed in, and backed, the Remain campaign, yet in the wake of the Leave campaign's win, she chose to run for the leadership regardless and take charge of implementing the policy she opposed. May believed her best opportunity to make a positive contribution lay not in obstructing the inevitable and that which had been democratically decided, but rather in trying to limit the negative impact that Brexit might have through negotiating a less damaging exit strategy than her pro-Leave colleagues might otherwise (Seldon 2019: ch. 1).

Of course, not every decision a democratic leader takes is a choice between doing right and doing popular – happily, they frequently overlap. And when they don't, good democratic leaders argue, cajole, bargain and campaign so good policy also becomes good politics. American political strategist Dick Morris suggests that despite the sometimes high personal cost of idealistic leadership, the alternative is "timid, tepid, meek governance that leaves the initiative to others…a politician can do what he thinks is right; he just has to be sophisticated in how he goes about it" (Morris 1999: 82, 87).

Case 4.3 The limits of democratic leadership?

Lee Kuan Yew

Prime Minister of Singapore, 1959–1990

Figure 4.3 Lee Kuan Yew in 1968

Few leaders in world history can claim to have transformed their societies as dramatically as Lee Kuan Yew. A Cambridge-educated barrister, Lee returned to Singapore and became one of its leading political figures, founding the People's Action Party (PAP) in 1954. Lee was elected the first post-colonial Prime Minister of Singapore, and successfully campaigned to unify the island with Malaysia in 1963, a cause Lee had passionately worked towards throughout his early career to ensure the tiny city-state's survival.

Just two years later though, Singapore was expelled from Malaysia, due to demographic differences and growing concerns about Singapore upsetting Malaysia's political and economic balance. Devastated over the defeat of his great political cause, Lee was now leader of a country unexpectedly independent. A tiny island surrounded by potentially hostile nations with no natural resources or even its own supply of freshwater, Lee chose to fight on as leader, and his new cause became survival of the fledgling nation. He turned to embrace globalization, realizing the only resources that Singapore possessed were its harbour and people, and providing trade and services to the international economy was its best option.

Lee turned this cause into a collective and communitarian ethic for Singaporeans and sought this ethic to be the centre of the new state's politics. "You will need to work hard and save...the road will be very demanding... we need to be better than others, just to survive" (Hyman 2015). Lee undertook an ambitious socio-economic program and reorientated the PAP around state-directed economic development, over three decades transforming Singapore from an isolated island to a global economic powerhouse, increasing GDP per capita by more than 1400 per cent and improving every metric of quality of life.

Lee's PAP won every single election by a landslide after 1965, in many elections winning every seat in the legislature. Though undoubtedly a popular hero for his transformation of the country, Lee nevertheless saw political stability and continuity as essential to national survival and developed a political system in Singapore that was only partially democratic. For his part, Lee avoided describing Singapore's regime on the democratic/autocratic scale, instead terming the system 'meritocratic' or 'technocratic' insofar as the system is designed to secure both stability and public approval, whilst ensuring that talent rose to the top (Tan 2016: ch. 2). Yet without credible democratic opposition and fairly limited checks on authority, many have observed that 'meritocracy' increasingly came to be 'aristocracy' with declining elite circulation and a self-supporting ruling class associated with the PAP, particularly after the accession of Lee's son Lee Hsien Loong to national leadership in 2004 (Barr 2014: ch. 4–5).

The Singaporean regime does not meet the expectations of a truly democratic state, and the ruling party Lee built maintains structural dominance over the political system and the media, subtly but effectively maintaining political domination (George 2007). And yet Singapore has maintained regular and free elections since independence, and by most accounts Lee Kuan Yew and his successors have maintained overwhelming public confidence. Indeed, this state of affairs has been often described as a social compact, in which most Singaporeans have effectively consented to the soft paternalism of the governing regime in exchange for the societal progress, economic prosperity and social harmony it provides (Tan 2010). On most metrics of an open, free and inclusive society, Singapore scores well – it is consistently rated as one of the safest and least corrupt countries in the world, and its parliament and cabinet have made credible efforts to strike racial and religious balance in line with the nation's demographic makeup. Moreover, Lee's regime transformed Singapore from a colonial backwater to one of the world's most prosperous and developed states.

Was Lee Kuan Yew a good democratic leader? Do the great achievements ***for*** the public justify a government that is not entirely ***by*** the public? If leaders improve the lives of their citizens, and are able to do so in a manner that secures broad public consensus, is that not consistent with the ambitions of democratic philosophy, even if it does not take the most democratic of forms? "Lee Kuan Yew leaves students and practitioners of government with a challenge. If Churchill was right in his judgment that democracy is the worst form of government except for all the others, what about Singapore?" (Allison 2015).

In reviewing how political systems operate in application, we see a gulf between theory and practice. Neither autocracies nor democracies are completely at peace with their leaders. What leadership looks like in practice can vary greatly between autocracies and democracies, as does the degree of leader dominance within the system. Of course, democratic and autocratic leaders are far from incomparable, and indeed, in many political systems the line between a democratic leader and an autocratic one is vague. The tools, theories and tasks of leadership described elsewhere in this book are generally applicable when considering either democratic or autocratic leaders.

But institutional arrangements matter, because they incentivize political leaders to behave differently, depending on who determines their power and political survival. Subsequently, understanding political leaders and their behaviour starts by understanding the institutional context.

Chapter Summary

- Political systems are generally categorized as autocratic (the rule of one) and democratic (the rule of many); however, the specific powers of leaders within each category can vary significantly.
- The powers of the executive branch, the nature of the party system, and the number of veto players within a system tend to be better predictors of leader dominance than the formal structure of a system.
- Strong democratic systems with weak executive branches tend to incentivize consensus-building and 'chairman' leadership styles, while unstable autocratic systems may require decisive and forceful leadership in order to endure.
- Autocratic regimes pose two distinct challenges to political leaders:
    - Firstly, maintaining power is a constant struggle, as autocratic leaders usually have weak claims to authority, relying instead on a narrow coalition of elites to maintain their rule. Autocrats must keep their ruling coalition constantly happy in order to survive.
    - Secondly, autocratic regimes are generally fragile and suffer from weak governance, as their narrow ruling coalitions often limit policymaking capacity and the ability to implement a leader's rule. Alliances are often transactional, encouraging corruption rather than public service.
    - Autocratic leaders are thus highly incentivized to invest significant resources into protecting their position and narrowing their governing coalition, while often having a limited governing apparatus to effect policy and change.
- Democratic regimes have two distinct challenges of their own:
    - Firstly, broad coalitions of voters, elites and institutions are required to win elections and make decisions in democratic systems with many

veto-players. Such coalitions are fragile and easily broken, making strong and decisive leadership difficult to bring about, and political gridlock common.

- Secondly, democratic leaders must constantly work to maintain public approval and democratic legitimacy. This often leads to tensions between that which is effective, right or necessary, and that which is popular.
- Democratic leaders are thus incentivized to create broad governing coalitions and pursue positions and policies that will best meet with their coalition's approval and distribute benefits widely.

5 BIOLOGY, CULTURE AND GENDER

Chapter Outline

- Are our responses to leaders instinctual? How much of leadership rests on biological and evolutionary imperatives?
- Are people born political leaders? Do genetics and ancestry play a role in our fitness to lead?
- What has driven humans to evolve systems of leadership? What can anthropology show us about its origins and its present form?
- How much does cultural background shape political leadership? Which traits are universal, and which are culturally specific?
- What role does gender play in leadership? Are there meaningful differences between how men and women lead, and how their leadership is perceived by others?

In his 1973 masterwork *The Interpretation of Cultures*, anthropologist Clifford Geertz declared that "there is no such thing as human nature independent of culture" (Geertz 1973: 49). Just two years later naturalist Edward O. Wilson published *Sociobiology: A New Synthesis,* which made a contrary case, proposing an evolutionary basis for a staggering array of social and cultural traits, from the way we communicate to the ethics we practice. The age-old 'nature versus nurture' debate has waged continuously since. It spread into political studies in the 1960s and *biopolitics* – the exploration of the interaction between biology and politics – was born (e.g. Somit 1968; Thorson 1970). At the same time interest in cultural studies of political life underwent similar growth (e.g. Seaton & Claessen 1979). Second-wave feminism, emerging in parallel, also turned its lens to the political world. Works like Kate Millet's *Sexual Politics* (1970) inspired a comprehensive re-evaluation of the highly gendered and patriarchal structures that dominate politics.

Biological, cultural and feminist perspectives provide vital insight as to how human nature, whether naturally or socially evolved, influences our political behaviour. The implications for political leadership are enormous, and a full picture of how it unfolds in our world requires a keen appreciation of its biological and social determinants.

Biology and evolution

Leadership in non-humans

Leadership is not unique to humans. Many species are capable of highly complex organizational behaviours that serve as an eerie, if distant, mirror of modern human society. Observing leadership behaviours in animals, particularly primates, may help establish a biological and evolutionary basis for leadership behaviours we observe in human society today.

For instance, Norwegian zoologist Thorleif Schjelderup-Ebbe was intrigued by the behaviour of chickens and was particularly puzzled as to why there was seemingly so little aggression between them. Through many decades of observation, he uncovered an elaborate system of social hierarchy within chicken clutches. He coined the term 'pecking order' to describe it, inspired by the sharp pecks that dominant chickens would use to remind subordinate chickens of their status. The most dominant chicken (which Schjelderup-Ebbe termed the 'despot') received great benefits as a result of their status, most notably preferential access to food and mates (Schjelderup-Ebbe 1922).

The 'pecking order' is an example of a *dominance hierarchy,* which is common across the animal kingdom (Wilson 2000: ch. 13). Dominant individuals receive preferential access to mates and food. Yet studies have found *all* individuals in a dominance hierarchy tend to have better rates of survivability, even if the dominant members receive more benefits than subordinates (Ward & Webster 2016: 121–122). The pecking order in chickens, for example, greatly reduces the need for fighting over food, mates or territory – an energy-consuming activity with uncertain outcomes – and allows even the weakest chickens a chance at survival in a group of stronger individuals. Pecking orders increase the efficiency with which chickens consume food too. Even though dominant chickens get more, the group as a whole eats more also, whilst groups without a pecking order eat warily and spend more time fighting each other (Wilson 2000: 279–280).

Does such dominance imply leadership – individuals influencing others in the pursuit of common goals? For many species the answer is yes. Birds and bees, for instance, have evolved elaborate systems of communication which allow individuals to signal danger or opportunity to others and in doing so help ensure their collective survival (Wilson 2000: 213–214).

In primates, leadership becomes more distinct and nuanced. Studies have established, for example, that baboons do not determine dominance solely through a ranking of physical prowess. Often older males well past their prime will continue to hold leadership positions, likely on the basis of their superior knowledge and experience in leading the group rather than their physical capacity (DeVore 1965; Rowell 1969). Different 'leadership styles' can be observed across groups of primates based on the characteristics of the dominant male and can lead to different strategies towards other primate groups, relationships within the group and movement patterns (van der Dennen 2011). Cooperation between primate groups, and alliance formation, has long been observed (van der Dennen 2011). Far from being aggressive free-for-alls with constant battles for dominance, many primate groups are extremely stable, and the political order is seldom challenged. Infighting within primate groups is motivated primarily by enforcing expected social behaviour and preserving the status hierarchy, even by those ranked lowly within it, rather than by attempts to reorder the hierarchy or equalize resource distribution (Bernstein 1970).

Fred Willhoite concludes much of what we call leadership today has likely evolved from behaviours our distant ancestors adopted: "There seem to be good reasons to believe that man's biological nature incorporates strong propensities to establish and sustain dominance-deference hierarchies…the stratification of political authority, power, and influence may be by nature intrinsic to human social existence" (Willhoite 1976: 1110).

Evolved leadership behaviours

Observations of animal groups may help explain why humans adopt subservient and follower roles, often willingly and without resistance. Although there are often circumstances when it is rational and beneficial to do so, humans have likely evolved to be on some level predisposed to seek out leaders and respond to them in certain ways (Bastardoz & Van Vugt 2019). The *service-for-prestige* theory, for example, sees leadership as initially emerging as a solution to coordination and communication problems in large groups. Over time it may have evolved into a system of exchange where followers can reward leaders for providing them with goods that would otherwise be too costly or chaotic to obtain individually by giving the leader status and/or preferential access to group resources (Price & Van Vugt 2014).

Evolutionary Leadership Theory (ELT) seeks to explicate the evolutionary basis of leadership in humans. ELT theorists note that several key cognitive processes are critical for individuals to engage in leader-follower behaviour, such as:

- The ability to perceive the need for coordination, not just in immediate crises but also to face long-term or distant threats.
- The propensity for groups to agree on courses of action and conform to group standards willingly.
- The ability to recognize leadership potential in others.
- Specialized forms of communication, including perspective taking and conflict management.

Humans possess these and many other leadership-necessary abilities quite naturally and practice them almost unconsciously, as various studies have found (see Van Vugt, Hogan & Kaiser 2008). Indeed, a well-developed line of inquiry in evolutionary biology has focused on the idea of 'role taking' or 'social sensitivity', in which humans anticipate the expectations of others and respond accordingly. Though often seen as a purely social feature of how humans are raised, recent research has revealed that there is significant neural architecture to support role-taking (Judge & Hogan 2015), which in turn may reinforce leader-follower roles.

Some of these evolved traits may have dramatic implications. Leader-follower dynamics during periods of crisis are a notable example. Numerous studies have demonstrated that people are more likely to submit to authority when faced with dangerous situations (Hamblin 1958; Baumeister et al. 1988), and that group support for leaders who reinforce group cohesion is also preferred when facing a perceived threat (Van Vugt & De Cremer 1999). We can see this disposition in the 'rally around the flag' effect, in which during times of war or crisis, the popularity of political leaders and nationalist sentiments tend to improve dramatically.

Leader-follower relationships may become considerably more intense and even irrational in times of crisis. Facing the widespread destruction of their culture and population, many native tribes in the American West during the late nineteenth century turned to the Paiute mystic Wovoka, who espoused a prophecy that the whites would disappear if Native Americans followed his teachings and performed ritual dances. The 'Ghost Dance' movement became a 'crisis cult' built around Wovoka for decades, though no material improvements resulted (see Overholt 1974). Crises and danger activate neurological responses in humans through an involuntary 'threat system'. These responses impair our cognitive abilities, impel us to quick decision-making, and lower our emotional self-control. Though helpful in basic survival situations, when faced with more complex problems these responses increase the risk of irrational or extreme reactions by leaders and followers (Narayana & Prasad 2015: 121–124). Some of our worst politics, that which embraces prejudice and discrimination against minorities and outsiders, may have its roots too in evolved behaviours long in our past (see Case 5.1).

These propensities do not mean that we have evolved to take set positions automatically. There is significant evidence to suggest that our propensity towards dominance is matched by a balancing propensity towards egalitarianism. We have also evolved some democratic instincts, desiring a choice in our leaders and the ability to remove them when they no longer serve to advance the group (Boehm 2001; Van Vugt et al. 2004). Moreover, there seems to be a strong biological foundation for an innate disposition towards fairness when judging and consenting to the actions of those who lead us, although the rules of what constitutes 'fair' may be more individually and culturally determined (Price & Van Vugt 2014: 183–185).

Evolutionary biology can also help explain how leaders behave or misbehave. Hubris, risk-taking and overconfidence in decision-making, for example, are ever-problematic aspects of political leadership. Yet some models have demonstrated that overconfidence is not a flaw of individual temperament but an evolved feature of human decision-making that served to benefit our evolutionary fitness (Johnson & Fowler 2011). Neuroscience research has illuminated significant limitations faced by humans in decision-making, and when faced with short time-horizons, complex problems, and information overload (as many political leaders inevitably are), neural shortcuts necessarily result (Losco 2017: 275–278; see Chapter 8). Self-confidence is

Case 5.1 Our worst instincts

Slobodan Milošević

President of Serbia, 1991–2000

Figure 5.1 Slobodan Milošević in 1994

One of the most powerful and commonly observed political principles that finds its roots in the natural world is that of xenophobia. Little will motivate a group to close ranks and unite behind its hierarchy more than the appearance of outsiders who threaten the status of those within in. For long periods of evolutionary time, all species, humans included, lived in relatively small and closely-related groups whose survival and evolutionary success were best served by cooperating with other members of the group, clan or tribe whilst defending against outsiders. The animal kingdom abounds with such behaviours, with newcomers to groups, from chickens to monkeys, relentlessly harassed by the group members until the outsider is defeated, dissuaded or forced to assume the very lowest rung of the established hierarchy (Wilson 2000: 286–287).

Sociobiologists have seen parallels between these behaviours and the widespread predilection of human societies towards expressions of racism, nationalism, discrimination, and xenophobia (Reynolds, Falger & Vine 1987). Whilst not necessarily an inevitable feature of political society, the recurrent appearance of xenophobic politics has raised the prospect that fear or distaste towards outsiders may lie deep within human instincts. Neurological experiments have revealed automatic and unconscious activation of the fear centres of the brain when presented with cues like unfamiliar faces, races, cultures or names (Blank 2011: 219–220), with some studies even suggesting these reactions evolved as an immune response that once helped protect groups from unfamiliar diseases (Aarøe et al. 2017).

Few countries invested as heavily in deprogramming such deep-seated parochial sentiments than did Communist Yugoslavia (1945–1992), which was composed of numerous ethnic, cultural, linguistic and religious sub-nations. Its ***Brotherhood and Unity*** program implemented strict quotas to ensure fair representation of all groups across government and the public sector, and an education system that attempted to indoctrinate a unified Yugoslav identity and equality between religions and ethnicities for half a century. Expressing nationalist or ethnic sentiments was a political crime and attempts to revive them were stridently punished (see Bertsch 1977).

As the Communist system began to collapse, a generation of new politicians emerged who were quickly and cynically able to exploit nationalist sentiments that were dormant but far from vanquished. Slobodan Milošević, a bureaucrat and Serbian Communist functionary, soon recognized the opportunity and sought to fan ethnic tensions to advance his own career. Many of those who knew him saw his politics as entirely self-serving, seeking to use nationalism to take political control while personally having limited commitment to Serbian nationalist ideals (Sell 2002: 170; Zimmermann 1999: 25–27).

Yet his approach proved effective, with many Serbs quick to embrace nationalist sentiments and blame rival ethnic groups for long simmering economic, political and social problems. Milošević encouraged Serbs to see themselves as the victims of bias and inequitable treatment within Yugoslavia and that Serbia itself faced a threat to its traditional and territorial integrity from the other nationalities (LeBor 2012: ch. 7). Milošević harnessed fear and resentment as the political and economic crisis within Yugoslavia grew. Rhetoric demonizing other nationalities soon became commonplace across the Yugoslav republics, redrawing the political battle lines, further empowering leaders like Milošević who seized upon nationalist policies, and laid the groundwork for what would eventually become political violence and civil war (Thompson 1999; LeBor 2012: ch. 10). The forces unleashed would see Milošević greatly empowered within Yugoslavia in its final years, yet it also hastened the breakdown of the county into warring republics and unleashed ethnic violence that would leave over 100,000 dead.

The rapidity with which half a century of relative internal peace and solidarity broke down into violently xenophobic factionalism, and the role political leadership played in activating these sentiments and fomenting fear, raises troubling questions as to the innate receptivity communities have to xenophobic politics, particularly in times of great change and crisis.

essential for leaders to make decisions and lead convincingly in environments of great uncertainty.

Indeed, some of our greatest disappointments in political leadership – egotism, self-serving behaviours, and tyrannical tendencies – may not be purely moral failings. There is reason to believe that these too have a footing in evolution, perhaps because for eons autocratic leadership served to create disciplined groups that could best survive (Smith 2007; Judge et al. 2009).

Many of these phenomena may be evidence of what ELT scholars call the 'mismatch hypothesis'. That is to say, a lot of the seemingly irrational, flawed, and problematic aspects of leadership today could be the result of our cultural and political evolution far outstripping our biological evolution. 'Mismatches' are common in all areas of contemporary human behaviour – our taste for fat, salt and sugar are evolutionary dispositions for survival that are only now backfiring as their availability becomes widespread. So too crisis-orientation, overconfidence, deception and dominance were all once far more beneficial to the practice of effective leadership in prehistoric societies than they are today (White 2017: 239–240), and popular attraction to leaders with those traits may similarly harken back to earlier instincts (e.g. McAdams 2017). As a result, many of the worst and seemingly self-destructive propensities of leaders that rear their heads from time to time may be holdovers of evolved instincts that are poorly adapted to our current political environment.

Genetics in leadership

Aristotle, in one of his most contentious and fiercely debated statements (see Levin 1997), states in Book One, Part V of *Politics* that:

> For that some should rule and others be ruled is a thing not only necessary, but expedient; from the hour of their birth, some are marked out for subjection, others for rule ... the lower sort are by nature slaves, and it is better for them as for all inferiors that they should be under the rule of a master.

In a contemporary context, Aristotle's words seem discriminatory, paternalistic and undemocratic in the extreme, though for most of human history, 'born to rule' was the norm, and the mantle of political leadership was the exclusive province of just a handful of family dynasties. Even today, political dynasties are exceedingly common, not just within traditionally autocratic political systems like the Middle East (McMillan 2013), but also in thriving democracies like India (Chandra 2016). In the Irish county of Kerry, for generations nearly all local politicians have been drawn from just a handful of families (O'Shea 2012).

Whilst it is well documented that those in power have a variety of tools and resources at their disposal to help promote the political aspirations of their heirs, can there be any truth to Aristotle's contention that some are simply born to lead by virtue of their nature? Do some inherit traits that make them better disposed to political leadership?

Dominance in various species has a strong genetic component, in large part because the traits that determine who is dominant in a pack (like physical strength) are genetically determined (Moritz & Hillesheim 1985; Dixson et al. 1993). The same is at least partially true in human society. Studies have repeatedly established, for example, that comliness is a statistically significant factor in elections, with more physically attractive candidates generally garnering more votes (Banducci et al. 2008; Rosar, Klein & Beckers 2012). Taller and more physically imposing candidates tend to be more popular and electorally successful than candidates of average stature, and interestingly, those of greater physical stature are also more likely to perceive themselves as good candidates for leadership than those of average stature (Murray & Schmitz 2011; Sorokowski 2010). Even the pitch of a leader's voice can be important – lower pitched voices tend to be preferred by voters amongst candidates in elections, and in studies of voter reactions deeper voices were more strongly associated with positive leadership qualities like strength and integrity (Klofstad 2015). British Prime Minister Margaret Thatcher took the lesson to heart and had voice coaching in her early career, developing a tone and style of delivery in the 1970s that was much deeper than her natural voice.

Evolutionary leadership research has suggested the existence of 'cognitive ancestral leader prototypes' (or CALPs), which prime us to continue to associate traits like physique with leadership. Evolutionary survival in historical situations was improved by deferring to various types of leader. Those with strong physiques and youthful confidence helped us survive in times of conflict, while those of wisdom and temperance might have helped us find and conserve food in times of hardship. Over successive generations, these CALPs became instinctive in our minds, and in the modern world our thinking may still default to these archetypes (Van Vugt & Ahuja 2011: ch. 6; Price & Van Vugt 2014: 181–182). The uncompromising and domineering Winston Churchill achieved heroic popularity as British Prime Minister during World War II. Yet in the first post-war election in 1945, the world was stunned when Churchill lost in a landslide to the mild-mannered and contemplative Clement Attlee of the Labour Party. Journalists speaking to voters found that though Churchill was widely beloved and respected for winning the war, the public could not see him as a peacetime leader or of the right temperament to rebuild the country (Ingersoll 1940). Biological instinct may have played as much a role as rational analysis by the voters.

Ralph Stogdill, one of the early pioneers of leadership studies, examined the results of 124 studies investigating the traits commonly associated with, or found in, leaders across a wide variety of contexts, from urban gangs to large corporations. Out of innumerable leadership characteristics identified across these studies, 15 traits consistently appeared as desirable in leaders in just about every context (Table 5.1).

Contemporary research has discovered strong genetic links to many of these traits. Responsibility, initiative, persistence, self-confidence, sociability and cooperativeness have been found to have at least some genetic origins (e.g. Power & Pluess 2015; Lo et al. 2017). Other studies have uncovered the possibility that even partisan attachment amongst followers might be partially explained through genetics, giving rise to the prospect that some

Table 5.1 Stogdill's 15 'universal' leadership traits

Intelligence	Scholarship	Responsibility
Activity	Socio-economic status	Initiative
Persistence	Experience	Self-confidence
Situational awareness	Cooperativeness	Popularity
Adaptability	Sociability	Communication skill

Source: Stogdill (1948: 63).

political parties and leaders may expect stronger support from certain genotypes and not others (Alford et al. 2005; Hannagan 2011).

One study has even found there may be a genetic disposition for a person's likelihood to assume a leadership position in a group – a variation on the CHRNB3 gene – though such studies are in their infancy (De Neve et al. 2013). If true though, it might lead us to re-evaluate political dynasties. Though frequently nominated as examples of how privilege and nepotism distort a meritocratic society, they might also be examples of how leadership traits can be inherited over generations. The Udall Family, the descendants of Western pioneer David King Udall, have produced three generations of prominent American politicians across four states, including three US Senators, despite notable variations in socio-economic status, education and political beliefs across branches of the family. Modern genetics may yet prove some truth in Aristotle's contention.

Anthropology and culture

Biology and evolution offer a starting point for understanding leader-follower behaviours, and how we may be instinctively programmed to be receptive towards, or suspicious of, different styles of leader. But there is a large gulf between these biological rudiments and the complex political cultures we observe today. Political anthropology bridges the gap between our instinctive inheritance and contemporary society by examining human social systems and processes, and their evolution over time.

Furthermore, while there are many things about political leadership that are recognizable across countries and societies, it's nonetheless true that there are significantly different expectations of leadership across cultures. Whilst anthropology can find much about political leadership that is common to the human experience, it has also revealed the very real ways in which leadership is shaped by culture. As anthropologist Margaret Mead notes:

> The aggressive, efficient, ambitious Manus leader in Oceania would have been rejected by the Dakota Indians, who valued mutual welfare, conforming to the group, generosity, and hospitality. (Bass 1990: 785)

Culture thus cannot be ignored in our understanding of leaders, and like biology is foundational to how we perceive, practice and respond to leadership.

Examining systems

One of the first major contributions to political anthropology came from *African Political Systems* (1940), which examined the political structures of eight African cultural groups. The authors found just one major distinction between the cultures studied – whether they had created a system of centralized government and a leadership class that had accepted authority over the entire community, or whether they lacked clear government or leadership (Fortes & Evan-Pritchard 1940: 5). There seemed to be no obvious demographic reason for this divide – the size and density of the population, economic activity and territorial relationships did not predict the nature of political organization. Yet in practice the two groups of societies operated very differently – those with centralized leadership had systems of law, justice and policy that could be enforced by leaders, could coordinate major society-wide projects like settlement, construction or warfare, and were relatively peaceful internally. Those without such structures tended to lack enforceable laws or widespread cooperation – various clans and segments banded together over disputes to determine the outcome, and coordination between segments of the society was often poor, while conflict was high.

To be sure, even those without clear political leaders had leaders of various sorts – family elders and religious figures were accorded great deference. Yet as the editors of the book conclude "herein lies a problem of world importance: what is the relation of political structure to the whole social structure?" (Fortes & Evan-Pritchard 1940: 23). Though later criticized as overly simplistic, culturally biased and theoretically incomplete, *African Political Systems* sparked great interest in using anthropology to explain the evolution of systems of leadership (Lewellen 2003: 6–11).

Marshall Sahlins, an anthropologist who studied the cultures of the Pacific Islands, famously compared two common types of political leadership found there – the 'big-men' and the chiefs (Sahlins 1963). Big-men ruled predominantly in Melanesian cultures and tended to do so through *personal* power and authority. They were the strongest, most capable or most charismatic, and attracted a loyal following, but their leadership authority was limited usually to only a small clan. Moreover their authority was fragile, fleeting and often reciprocal, and when the big-man could no longer deliver material benefits to his followers his authority quickly waned. Many Polynesian cultures by contrast had made the jump to 'chiefs' – systems of leadership authority that were predominantly *positional*. Leadership was now formalized and could be inherited; it accrued to the position not the individual. Leaders no longer needed to invest constantly in maintaining their following through personal interactions or kinship ties or fighting off contenders (Allen 1984: 35–36); and could focus more on coordinating more complex projects, like construction and agriculture. Centralized leadership over larger areas could pursue higher-order economic activities that provided benefits to the entire group, such as storing food surpluses and releasing them in times of need, or reducing inequality through food and resource redistribution. Much larger societies with more economic and social specialization could be supported as a result (Lewellen 2003: 55; Sahlins 1963). Economics has thus been cited as a key reason human societies 'jump' from more immediate, kinship-focused leadership (the prevailing form in the animal kingdom) to the much more structured and positional authority seen in contemporary political systems (e.g. Polanyi 2001).

Political economy continues to be relevant to thinking about the fitness of political leadership structures today. For instance, it has been observed in some circumstances that more authoritarian regimes are *better* at fostering economic development than more democratic ones. The logic goes that a strong state that is insulated from the narrow and sectional interests pursued by individuals and interest groups in a democracy has much greater opportunity to pool collective resources and pursue large-scale projects that will benefit everyone in the long run (Przeworski & Limongi 1993: 55–56). Indeed, state-led economic development often involves unpopular sacrifices and sometimes aggressive policies that are hard for leaders to sustain in a democratic system (Silva 2014). There are some notable examples where this logic seems to have proven true – particularly the Asian tigers of Taiwan, South Korea and Singapore – though overall the evidence is mixed (Przeworski & Limongi 1993). 'Authoritarian capitalist' regimes like China, able to pursue long-term economic policies and projects little fettered by democratic pressures, have experienced rapid economic growth in recent decades, and have proven increasingly alluring to those disillusioned with democratic regimes. Especially so as economic growth slows, inequality rises, and the welfare state weakens amongst the mature democracies (Horesh 2015).

Yet there are other drivers behind the historical development of leadership structures, such as technology, environment, demographics and culture (Kurtz 2001: 133–137). Some early societies came together under unified leadership to coordinate against external threats, others to reduce internal conflict and instability, and others still to solve organizational challenges caused by growing populations (Lewellen 2003: 47–56; Fried 1967). Elman Service espouses a popular four-tiered classification of human societies based on the nature of its political leadership – bands, tribes, chiefdoms and states – with increasingly institutionalized forms of government and leadership driven primarily by population growth and density. As people shift from nomadic to urban lifestyles and the specialization of labour increases in the economy, so too does politics and the role of political leadership become more structured and formalized (Service 1975).

Examining processes

The *processual approach* in anthropology sees conflict, tension, power-seeking and dynamic change as constant features of human society, even within broader systems that may be relatively stable (Lewellen 2003: 86). Ambitious individuals driven to obtain status and power are recurring constants as well, even when leadership positions may confer few benefits and involve significant costs or sacrifices to obtain (Kurtz 2001: 157).

F.G. Bailey provides an exemplar of this kind of anthropological analysis, finding that political leadership is a process or 'game' that plays out with striking similarity and with a common set of strategies across cultures and contexts. Leadership games involve:

- **Prizes**, culturally defined, that incentivize people to play, like a leadership position, a policy outcome and the perks of rule.
- **Personnel**, including a political community (electorate), political elites who vie for the prizes (politicians), and political teams who cooperate to compete (parties).
- **Leadership**, including individuals who lead their teams in competition and the rules concerning who can lead and their powers.
- **Competition**, which occurs within a set of agreed rules so that it remains bounded and reasonable (like an election versus a civil war).
- **Control**, which includes judges, checks and balances that enforce the rules of the 'game' (Bailey 2001: 19–33).

Leadership 'games' are constantly being played and are not resolved definitively – when one ends with one team defeated, the teams reform, new leaders in competition emerge, and a new game begins. Teams form around leaders on either a *transactional* basis or a *moral* basis. Moral teams are driven by ideology and principles, like nationalism or religion, whilst transactional teams are built around the personal gains followers believe they can get from following the leader. Moral leaders tend to have more devoted and secure followings but face significant constraints in terms of how they are expected to play the game. Transactional teams are entirely pragmatic and will do anything to win the game, but the teams are brittle, and followers readily abandon the leader when a better prospect comes along. These tensions play out not only between teams but also within them – political leaders must constantly walk a line between playing by *normative rules* or by ruthlessly *pragmatic strategies* (see Bailey 2001: ch. 3,9). We can think of such games playing out in modern party politics. Followers in strongly value-driven political parties – like those within the Green, Libertarian or Communist movements – tend to demand ideological purity from their leaders and expect them to play the game righteously, or they will defect. Larger political parties tend to be more transactional in nature, and their leaders are more likely to be able to compromise on principle, bend the rules or change course in the pragmatic pursuit of winning without losing significant support (though there are limits).

Anthropologists have found symbolism too is a critical aspect of explaining how political leadership becomes entrenched. Elites in all societies cultivate not just wealth but the symbols of their power – their mode of speech and education, manner of dress and appearance, recreational activities, ceremonies and so on that set them apart from the rest. Power and symbolism are inseparable, and leadership deploys both interdependently (Cohen 2016;

also Kertzer 1988). Royal families consciously cultivate the symbols and rituals of their role in society that draw enormous interest and veneration, but also separation, from followers. In every political speech made by a politician in an open democracy, symbolic ideas (whatever they actually mean) form the most powerful and ritualistic core – words like freedom, equality, order, nation, justice, family and so on.

Leaders may also serve symbolic roles that resonate with the deepest recesses of our psyche. Joseph Campbell's *The Hero with a Thousand Faces* (1949) found that mythological and religious narratives across vastly disparate cultures centre upon hero stories with many similarities in form and structure. Campbell linked the seeming ubiquity of hero stories to an *archetype* – a concept advanced by psychiatrist Carl Jung – which posits that humans have certain innate images and roles imprinted in the mind from birth like mother, father, child, devil, god and so on (see Jung 1981). The archetypes are given a particular expression through our individual experiences and social context, leading to may cultural variations of the same basic concepts. Jung and Campbell both argue that the 'hero' is one of the most powerful archetypes that seems to spring from a deeper psychic belief in, and need for, heroes.

> The hero, therefore, is the man or woman who has been able to battle past his personal and local historical limitations to the generally valid, normally human forms. Such a one's visions, ideas, and inspiration come pristine from the primary springs of human life and thought. Hence they are eloquent, not of the present, disintegrating society and psyche, but of the unquenched source through which society is reborn. (Campbell 1949: 19–20)

Political leaders are often accorded mythic status by their followers and praised or hated far beyond the scope of the functional roles that they serve. Much like the heroes of myth, they become vessels for the hopes and dreams of followers, and what we think of 'charisma' may be a reflection of how much a leader succeeds in tapping into this instinctive psychic attraction towards hope and salvation (Smith 2000; see Case 5.2).

Examining culture

Finally, we come to culture, the customs, traditions and institutions particular to a society that make them distinct from others. Many have attempted to discover what constitutes a 'political culture' within a society, and how they compare with others. Almond and Verba's *Civic Culture* (1963), for example, found three different typologies of political culture:

- **Parochial**, in which people have low interest in politics and whose interactions with their political systems are limited and pragmatic.
- **Subject,** in which a community has a high interest in the political system and policy outcomes but does not see their input into either as necessary.

"The law is something he obeys, not something he helps shape" (Almond & Verba 1963: 118).

- **Participant**, in which citizens are interested in the political system and what it does, as well as how it is run and their own active role within it.

Such variation has enormous implications for political leadership – while subject cultures seem more positively disposed to strong rulers who 'get things done', participant cultures have much higher democratic expectations and prefer working *with* their leaders to create outcomes. Though their findings have been critiqued from a variety of angles (see Simeone 2010), research into how cultural differences translate into leadership and politics continues to be popular, especially in business studies, which in an era of globalization has become particularly interested in questions of leadership across cultures. The implications for political leadership, whether managing a party, government, or campaign, are readily inferred though.

Geert Hofstede established six value scales that he felt best explained different leadership expectations across cultures: (1) power distance index, (2) uncertainty avoidance, (3) individualism versus collectivism, (4) masculinity versus femininity, (5) long-term versus short-term orientation and (6) indulgence versus self-restraint (Hofstede 2011). His ideas were tested in the GLOBE study of culture, which surveyed tens of thousands of members of organizations across 63 countries and tested responsiveness to leadership traits to see which were culturally contingent and which were universal.

22 'universally positive' and 8 'universally negative' traits were identified. Regardless of culture, respondents valued leadership traits like 'honesty', 'problem-solving', 'confident' and 'motivational'; while traits like 'egocentric' and 'ruthless' were universally disliked. Yet a further 35 traits were found to elicit very different responses depending on cultural background. For example, 'cunning', 'risk taking', and 'sensitive' varied enormously in survey responses as to whether they were perceived as desirable or undesirable in leadership (House et al. 2004). This GLOBE data was then used to isolate nine culturally-specific dimensions to leadership:

(1) **Performance orientation** – how concerned are they with rewarding and improving performance?

(2) **Assertiveness orientation** – how assertive and confrontational are they?

(3) **Future orientation** – how much do they think about and plan for the future?

(4) **Humane orientation** – how important is being fair, friendly, caring, and kind to others?

(5) **Collectivism I: Institutional collectivism** – how much do they value collaboration over individual achievement?

(6) **Collectivism II: In-group collectivism** – how loyal and proud are they towards the group?

(7) **Gender egalitarianism** – how equal are gender roles?

Case 5.2 The caudillo legend

Simón Bolívar

South American Independence Leader and President of Gran Colombia, 1819–1830

Figure 5.2 Simón Bolívar

Simón Bolívar was a military leader and politician who played a key role in leading six South American nations to independence, and ultimately would serve as president of four. Born into privilege in Spanish Venezuela, he was inspired in his youth by the principles of the Enlightenment and the American War of Independence. Bolívar made his early career in the colonial military but would become a revolutionary and lead his armies against Spain, fighting a long and bitter series of independence wars throughout the first three decades of the nineteenth century. His dogged persistence, widespread popularity, enormous charisma and daring intelligence eventually prevailed and saw the creation of Gran Colombia, a state encompassing today's Colombia, Venezuela, Panama, Ecuador and parts of Brazil, Peru and Guyana.

Bolívar came to position himself as a populist authoritarian, declaring himself "President for Life" and rejecting partisan politics in favour of a system built on stability and the constancy of internal checks and balances. He was principled, enforcing unpopular ideas like the banning of slavery, but was increasingly iron-fisted. His vision for a united South America was only a reality for 11 years, before the Gran Colombian state collapsed under internal pressures and ambitious politicians, and Bolívar died soon after aged 47, in poor health and relative poverty.

Bolívar remains a hero in South America, with monuments and images of him found across the continent. However, what he represented and his style of rule have themselves become both a cultural symbol and a functional type – a military strong-man form of leadership known now as the ***caudillo.*** The ***caudillo*** has proven to be a recurring appearance in South American politics, and the continent's turbulent political history has been frequently marked by the emergence of ***caudillos*** like Bolívar – of military origin, fusing authoritarianism with populist appeal. Nineteenth century South America is sometimes known as 'the Age of the Caudillo' (Scheina 2003).

The *caudillo* phenomenon has been extensively studied, and cultural and anthropological theories can help shed light on it. Some have pointed to the circumstances and political economy of nineteenth century South America. The departure of the Spanish left behind a power vacuum and underdeveloped states in which the military and the church remained the only widespread organizations. Colonial economies were fragile, largely agricultural and highly stratified, with a landowning elite controlling most of the means of production. Instability and class conflict seem to have reliably led to the emergence of popular *caudillos* who emerge to save their countries from chaos but also to protect the lopsided economic order (Lynch 1992). Others might contend that *caudillos* represented a controversial but necessary step in the political evolution of South America – lacking the infrastructure, economic security, education levels and political institutions of the United States, democratic government over such vast and underdeveloped states frequently proved destabilizing, and *caudillos* represented one of the few institutions strong enough (the military) to provide a framework for political evolution and economic development.

Some have argued that the *caudillo* is more unique to the Hispanosphere. For example, Spanish Catholicism may play a role in reinforcing the *caudillo* idea, from its hierarchical conception of social order to its personalist style of rule, with religion and leadership style going hand in hand (Dealy 1992). Others have contended that Spanish history, marked by its five century Reconquista of the Iberian Peninsula and the conquistador's violent conquest of the New World, created a unique martial framework of rule that became entrenched in the Spanish-speaking world. Even today the GLOBE studies provide some substantiation of this – Latin American countries are amongst the most accepting of strong authority and high power distance between themselves and their leaders. Latin American countries also rank 'charisma' as one of the most essential qualities of leaders and are much more receptive to paternalism and personalist styles of rule (Chhokar, Brodbeck & House 2007: 655).

Bolívar and the *caudillo* itself have also become powerful symbols and parts of the popular mythology of South America. In Venezuela particularly, political leaders across the spectrum – from right-wing dictator Marcos Jimenez to socialist demagogue Hugo Chávez – have attempted to seize the Bolivarian mantle and mould themselves in his image. Indeed, Bolívar's own skeleton has been exhumed multiple times and venerated by Venezuelan leaders as a direct symbol of their connection. Most potent of all perhaps is the myth of Bolívar and the *caudillo.* A leader who gives up everything – money, status, and ultimately their health – to lead the people and save the nation. It is a powerful and perhaps preconscious dream that seems to keep recurring – a 'hero with a thousand faces' as Joseph Campbell might opine (Campbell 1949).

(8) **Power distance** – how much social distance between leaders and the led is desired?

(9) **Uncertainty avoidance** – how comfortable are they with risk and uncertainty?

The use of this system of dimensions to score expectations of leadership across 63 countries has allowed the study authors to reveal where true differences in leadership styles lie across cultures. Turkey, for example, was one of the highest scoring countries on in-group collectivism. This can be observed culturally in Turkey's high emphasis on family and local community, and strong patterns of obligation to both in every-day practice (Kabasakal & Bodur 2007: 846–847). This is seemingly reflected in Turkish political leadership, where politics (particularly at lower levels) is extremely local in nature, and one of the most important qualities for office tends to be the depth of a candidate's ties to the local community. Aspiring leaders build political careers through in-group associations and community work (Joppien 2017: ch. 3). Factionalism, though present everywhere, is particularly strong and pervasive in Turkish politics, and *who* and *what* you are associated with within a party are critical parts of your identity as a political leader. Factional associations are a significant part of progressing as politician in Turkey (Massicard & Watts 2013).

Assertiveness, another dimension studied, provides many clues to political leadership behaviour across countries. For example, in the Nordic countries like Sweden and Denmark, assertiveness is not particularly valued by people or practiced by leaders, meaning that politicians tend to avoid being aggressive, confrontational, emotional or angry in the practice of politics, and tend towards consensus-driven political leadership styles (Holmberg & Åkerblom 2004: 47; Goldsmith & Larsen 2004). This is in stark contrast to the United States, in which assertiveness is more valued and more practiced, to a degree that often surprises or offends in less assertive cultures. American politicians and leaders are expected to speak their mind and be confrontational when the situation demands, and assertive political leadership styles tend to dominate American politics (Hoppe & Bhagat 2004: 503). This also finds expression in Latin American politics, most notably in the *caudillo* tradition (see Case 5.2).

Naturally, there are caveats to using culture to understand patterns of political leadership. As nations become increasingly multicultural, diverse sub-cultures proliferate that may have different expectations of leadership than the mainstream. Furthermore, some cultural theories have not held up well over time, and culture does change. For example, East Asian culture has long been remarked upon for its predilection towards hierarchy and order, in part due to the abiding influence of Confucianism (Jelonek 2005; Zhang 2016). It was a popular myth for a time that true democracy was neither valued nor feasible in East Asian cultures (Dae Jung 1994). In recent decades though, numerous East Asian nations (e.g., South Korea, Taiwan and Japan) have progressively democratized and public expectations have shifted away from traditional deference to political leadership. Some have observed there a fusion of values and cultures as a result of globalization, which is diluting its substantive political differences with the West, even whilst traditional forms, symbols and practices might persist (Compton 2000).

Thus, culture and anthropology, like biology and evolution, provide lenses critical to understanding what we observe in political leadership, but by themselves cannot paint the full picture.

Gender and feminism

Figure 5.3 Statue of Hatshepsut

In 1478 BCE, Hatshepsut (Figure 5.3) ascended to the throne of Egypt and became pharaoh, reigning for 20 years until her death. She is considered one of the most successful pharaohs, embarking on an ambitious program of construction and economic development, with great temple complexes and new trade routes to distant lands standing as some of her most notable accomplishments. As one Egyptologist would remark, she is "the first great woman in history of who we are informed" (Breasted 1908: 217).

Female political leaders are as ancient as male political leaders, and in every era and civilization powerful women, ruling overtly or covertly, have existed. Yet leadership has also been heavily gendered for as long as it has been practiced. Hatshepsut, in order to distinguish herself from merely a consort, adopted all the masculine traits of rule after becoming pharaoh, and in her official statues and portraits is often portrayed donning a male kilt and head cloth, and sometimes the false beard as well. In official statements she routinely sought to reinforce her authority by speaking of the *male* gods and ancestors who had willed her to rule. Then, as now, the political system struggled to reconcile Hatshepsut's femininity with her status as a ruler. Some years after her death, much of her public memory, including statues and cartouches bearing her name, were destroyed – an extreme act completed under the supervision of her son that ensured that it took Egyptologists over a century of study to rediscover her existence in the pharaonic timeline.

History is full of examples of female leaders who have held political power and wielded it successfully, and yet women are vastly underrepresented in politics internationally. In 2019, women made up just 24.5 per cent of all national legislatures, and only three countries had national legislatures with chambers that had reached 50 per cent female representation (International Parliamentary Union 2019a, 2019b). Female representation is worse still when considering the senior positions of political leadership, even in countries with strong records of gender equality in other regards. For example, the Netherlands has frequently topped the United Nations Gender

Equality Index, yet at the 2017 Dutch general elections, only 1 of the 13 parties that won seats in the legislature was led by a woman.

The problem of female underrepresentation in political leadership, as well as the unique challenges female political leaders have faced in office, have been the subject of extensive study and debate in recent decades. Feminist and gender theory have provided important, if sometimes controversial, insights into the gendered nature of political leadership and laid bare practical quandaries that women face when seeking to lead. It also goes to the heart of the nature vs nurture debate – are the gendered differences in leadership perceptions a result of societal and cultural conditioning, or are there essential differences between the sexes that manifest in how leadership is practiced and received?

Feminist theory and leadership

As Lisa Pace Vetter argues, there is no 'feminist' theory of political leadership, and instead there are two ways in which women in political leadership have been studied. The first is through the lens of feminist theories as it has sought to explain related concepts, like power, authority and ethics. The second is through a largely empirical or observational perspective of female leadership in action, often with comparative or 'gender informed' approaches (Vetter 2010: 3).

Feminist theories of power and authority have questioned the foundations of both concepts. Carole Pateman in *The Sexual Contract* (1988) takes aim at political philosophers like John Locke, arguing that ideas like the social contract that underpin obligations to leadership and government are structures which have perpetuated gendered and ultimately oppressive sexual politics. Radical feminism rejects the concept of political leadership as anything more than a manifestation of oppressive patriarchal relations:

> Power is ... a primal relationship under patriarchy. The identity, the very personality, of the man depends on power and on power in a certain, specific sense: that of power over others, beginning with a woman and her children. (Rich 1995: 64)

The distinction between 'power-over' and 'power-with' was illuminated a century earlier by management studies pioneer Mary Parker Follett. Follett argues that *power-over* is the traditional, hierarchical and ultimately masculine form of rule, whilst *power-with* is collaborative, egalitarian and democratic. Follett and feminist theorists have argued for a wholesale reappraisal of power, seeing traditional forms of 'power-over' as irredeemably gendered, coercive and non-inclusive (see Pearce 2010: 525). Although radical feminism in its early stages often rejected power structures and concepts of leadership entirely, even feminist movements soon found that attempts to eliminate power-structures and leadership merely masked de facto forms of both, and instead feminists began working towards reconceptualization of leadership in ways that could escape masculine *power-over* forms (Carroll 1984: 140–141).

Feminists in the 1960s and 1970s turned their attention to the seemingly patriarchal structures of human society. One of the most influential voices was Kate Millet, who in *Sexual Politics* argues that all government and political power is upheld either through violent force or through socialized consent, the former being a traditional tool of masculine oppression, the latter being a gendered process by which women have been socialized to accept a lower status in society. She argues that the foundation of the socialization process is the family – led by a paternal authority – which becomes a microcosm of a broader society in which women are conditioned to accept a subsidiary role. State, society and family are all interlocking patriarchal institutions that constitute a cradle-to-grave process of gender stratification and masculine leadership reflected in every facet of social life (Millett 1970: 23–58).

This interconnected dynamic means that establishing legal gender equality alone is unlikely to produce true gender equality. Susan Moller Okin, for example, argues that even whilst the public arena, including politics, may have progressively removed barriers to female equality, it is private life – the family – that remains highly discriminatory and compels women into inequitable roles, and that inequity will inevitably prevent women from equality in public life (Okin 1991; also Lipman-Blumen 1984). Cultural institutions – like religion, nearly all of which are built around male gods or male-dominated pantheons – are also argued to entrench acceptance of male dominance at a deep level (Daly 1985). Others have pointed to the pervasiveness of gender inequality in other economic and social structures – power, wealth and social connections are often found together and are self-reinforcing, such that gender inequalities in one regard may hobble gender equality in all of them (e.g. Carbert 2009).

Thus far, these are all arguments for the nurturing of gender bias in leadership. However, there are those who have argued that gendered differences in leadership have their roots in our biological nature. Steven Goldberg has been one of the foremost proponents of the 'inevitability of patriarchy'. He argues that nearly all known societies and cultures have been patriarchies, and that human physiology, and particularly the male sex hormone testosterone, are central drivers of both dominance behaviours and leadership instincts. This would mean that regardless of our attempts to socially engineer otherwise, patriarchies will inevitably resurface (Goldberg 1973, 1999). Goldberg's controversial thesis is, like all iterations of the 'nature vs nurture' argument, difficult to definitively substantiate or disprove. Anthropologists have pointed out that male dominance is not, in fact, inevitable, and societies do vary significantly in the degree to which men predominate both public and private life, perhaps as a result more of environmental and contextual factors than of innate biology (Sanday 1981; Lerner 1986). Yet by the same token, documented examples of genuinely female-dominated societies – matriarchies – are very rare in human history, and some have argued the concept itself is more a socially desirable myth than a documented reality (Eller 2001).

Another observed difference that may have biological roots is the 'ambition gap'. It has been well documented in numerous democratic systems that gender inequalities in political leadership begin with a lack of candidates – women are less likely to run for public office and less likely to run for leadership positions in politics than men, even though female candidates are seemingly as successful in competitive elections as male candidates (Lawless & Fox 2010; Lawless 2010; Drummond et al. 2016). So, are women biologically less disposed to be ambitious or are they socialized to be so? The evidence is mixed and often contradictory. Studies have long shown that women tend to appraise their ability and fitness to be leaders poorly, even when their education, experience and skills are equal to or greater than their male colleagues, and even when they achieve career advancement (Clance & Imes 1976; Salmond & Fleshman 2010), though research is inconclusive on the role gender plays in this phenomenon (Bravata et al. 2020). Confidence and competitiveness have been shown to have at least some foundations in physiology, particularly testosterone (Kay & Shipman 2014: ch. 3; Eisenegger et al. 2017; Dalton & Ghosal 2018). Yet there is equally well-established evidence that gendered social expectations and sex roles significantly distort the expression of female ambition (Fels 2005 pt. 2; Fox & Lawless 2005; Lawless & Fox 2010).

Women as political leaders

Putting to one side the complex questions of whether leadership and political structures are inherently gendered, important questions have also been raised as to whether female leadership is in practice different to that of men. Do women lead differently to men? Are our perceptions and expectations of leadership gendered? Must women and men follow different rules or approach leadership differently in order to succeed?

In 1405, Cristine de Pizan, a writer and philosopher in the court of King Charles VI of France, published *The Book of the City of Ladies* and *The Treasure of the City of Ladies*. In them, she highlights important contributions made by powerful women throughout history, as well as offering advice to women (and in other works, men) who might find themselves in positions of power and wished to rule effectively. Throughout her works, the tactics and insights she offers on leadership are similar to those which Machiavelli would offer over a century later (de Pizan 1405/2018). As early as the fifteenth century it seems, the rules for gaining and holding power were not obviously perceived as any different for women than for men.

More recent studies, on the surface, seem to confirm this. In 2015 the Pew Research Center conducted a large survey on gender and leadership perceptions, and found that respondents saw women and men as equally capable of leadership, and of the seven key traits respondents felt were most important for leaders to possess, a majority felt that women and men were just as likely to have such traits, except for 'organization' and 'compassion', which respondents felt women were *more* likely to possess. Indeed, respondents rated women higher performing than men on several key tasks of political leadership, such as forging compromises, being honest and ethical, and standing up for their convictions (Pew Research Center 2015b).

Yet scratching below the surface reveals that in practice, female leadership, particularly political leadership, is often evaluated on different standards. The Catalyst study of female leadership uncovered a phenomenon the authors termed a 'double bind'. Leaders are expected to take on traits like decisiveness, goal-orientation and strength, or may need to be competitive and ambitious, to succeed in their roles. When women display these traits, however, they are far more likely to invoke negative reactions and be judged by others to be too 'tough'. Yet when women display traits more in keeping with gendered expectations, such as compassion or relationship-orientation, they are perceived as 'too soft' and thus not leadership material by others (Catalyst 2007: 9–15). The same report also found that women are often held to much higher standards than men to prove they are competent to lead, and women who do get ultimately judged as competent are much more likely to be personally disliked than male counterparts (Catalyst 2007). Psychologists have termed the problem 'role congruity theory' and have found that gendered expectations of female behaviour make it significantly harder for women to both lead and be liked (Eagly & Karau 2002; Johnson et al. 2008).

This hidden and deep bias seemingly extends to both men *and* women when rating leaders. Some studies have found that both female and male employees say they are less satisfied under female managers and express preferences for male bosses (Liden 1985; Artz & Taengnoi 2016). Even if the less patriarchal 'power with' methods are tried in organizations, in practice they are hard to operationalize and follower expectations tend to gravitate towards 'power over' methods (Salovaara & Bathurst 2016). In specifically political arenas, the evidence is mixed and contradictory (see Campbell & Heath 2017). There is at least some evidence that when female and male candidates go head to head in competitive democratic elections, all things being equal, female swing voters will *not be more* likely to vote for candidates of their own gender, but conversely male swing voters are *more* likely to vote for the male candidate (Fulton 2014). However in some contexts, women running on platforms around female-specific issues have garnered stronger support from female voters (Hernson, Lay & Stokes 2003).

Even successful female political leaders, such as German Chancellor Angela Merkel and Philippine President Gloria Arroyo, have tended to be 'respected' more than 'liked'. Press coverage of female political candidates tends to be biased and distorted along gender lines (Kahn 1994; Fowler & Lawless 2009). Though female candidates are triumphing with increasing frequency in contemporary politics, and the electoral disadvantages female candidates face appear to be declining, there are still significant gender disparities in the expectations placed upon female politicians.

When they do succeed in obtaining political office, do women practice leadership any differently to their male counterparts? Answering this question has proved to be challenging also. In the first instance, so much of leadership scholarship – from biographies to theoretical analyses – is based on a history of male dominance and masculine expectations of leadership, which makes it challenging to establish an ungendered baseline of what 'good' leadership looks like (Stead & Elliott 2009: 15–39; Sjoberg 2014).

Studies of female political leaders have not found gender stereotypes to be reliable predictors of how they will behave in office or interact with others. For example, it is commonly perceived that female leaders will be more likely to be consensus-builders, peacemakers, and 'doves' rather than 'hawks' on war and security (Pew Research Center 2015b). There is evidence that, across a variety of contexts, women emphasize consensual styles of leadership and a preference for 'power-with' rather than 'power-over' tactics (Rosener 1995; Daum 2010: 81–83), and that women lead more democratically and men more autocratically (Eagly & Johnson 1990). Several female political leaders have achieved electoral breakthroughs in the aftermath of conflict or political crisis, being seen perhaps as more likely to heal divisions and restore stability, such as Maria de Lourdes Pintasilgo of Portugal, Claudette Werleigh of Haiti and Violetta Chamorro of Nicaragua (see Case 5.3).

Yet in practice these supposed patterns seem difficult to establish, and prominent counterexamples abound. Comparing the political leadership of Madeline Albright and Condoleezza Rice as the US Secretaries of State, one study found that they differed significantly, with Albright conforming to a more 'feminine' style of leadership but Rice not at all, and both oversaw major armed conflicts regardless (Dolan 2010: 92–93). An analysis of US State Department officials too found females no less likely to suggest aggressive policy options than peaceful ones when compared with their male counterparts (McGlen & Sarkees 1993), and similar findings have been made of female political leaders generally (Holsti & Rosenau 1981). Indeed, modern female leaders have so frequently defied these stereotypes it's almost discredited: look no further than the 'Iron Ladies' such as Dominica's Eugenia Charles, Israel's Golda Meir, Britain's Margaret Thatcher and India's Indira Gandhi.

On domestic matters too, the evidence is mixed. Whilst some studies have demonstrated that female politicians are more likely to pursue policy agendas around welfare, education and social policy, the actual differences in policy outcomes are often modest (Eswaran 2014: 354-360); and many female political leaders have quite prominently spurned such agendas (see Case 5.3).

Complicating any systematic study is the fact that, until recently, there have been only a small number of female leaders who have ascended to the top roles of national politics as independent politicians and free of extenuating factors. South Asia is prominent for producing some of the world's first female heads of government – Sirimavo Bandaranaike of Sri Lanka, Indira Gandhi of India, Khaleda Zia and Sheik Hasina of Bangladesh and Benazir Bhutto of Pakistan. All, however, came to office as the daughters or widows of prominent male politicians, often in extreme circumstances (such as political assassination).

Other prominent female 'firsts' in political leadership were the product of politically calculated manoeuvres when a party or government's fortunes were in dire straits (Sykes 2014: 694–695). Gerraldine Ferraro was selected by the Democratic Party in 1984 to be the first female vice-presidential candidate in the United States, but it was a calculated move by the Democrats to try turn around the almost impossible odds of beating the incredibly popular Republican incumbent Ronald Reagan (Ferraro & Francke 2004: 73–75). Kim Campbell, Canada's first female prime minister, ascended to the role in 1993 as leader of the governing Progressive Conservative Party, yet did so in the wake of the resignation of Brian Mulroney, who had become one of the most unpopular politicians in Canadian history. The party election to succeed Mulroney had few candidates, and many saw the leadership as a poisoned chalice just months before a federal election the party was expected to lose. "Taking over the party leadership from Brian was a lot like taking over the controls of a 747 just before it plunges into the Rockies" (Ferguson 1999: 284). Though Campbell was initially popular, the novelty seemingly wore off quickly. Voters reacted negatively to her when switching into campaigning mode, and gender-bias in press coverage quickly saw the party's unpopularity return. Campbell's frankness and honesty, a popular trait for male leaders, was interpreted in her case as condescension and callousness. At the 1993 election, Progressive Conservatives lost nearly two thirds of its support and 152 of its 154 seats, including Campbell's own. Some female leaders have even been selected by autocratic regimes to deflect criticism or garner positive attention internationally, such as Elisabeth Domitien of the Central African Republic and arguably Ana Brnabic of Serbia.

However, in recent decades, female leaders have progressively shed gendered leadership expectations. Angela Merkel, Chancellor of Germany (2005–), is arguably the most successful democratic leader of the twenty-first century, steering both Germany and the European Union through enormous challenges, from the European debt crisis to the migrant crisis. Merkel has notably done this without resorting to traditionally masculine tropes of leadership. She is considered a consummate negotiator, collaborator, networker and 'power with' leader. Yet she has not embraced traditional feminism or femininity either, and despite significant media attention to her ambivalence towards both, it does not seem to have undermined her electoral support nor greatly impacted perceptions of her leadership (Ferree 2006). She has gained a reputation as a restrained, unassuming leader who does not necessarily need to lead from the front, and yet has been notably steadfast in key moments where others have not, holding firm on difficult positions, earning her enormous respect, if sometimes temporary unpopularity, on the domestic and international stage (Lagarde 2019). Though gender still plays a role in how Merkel is perceived, it has not been the defining feature of her leadership for colleagues or voters alike as it may have been for previous generations of female leaders.

All this suggests that although gender is an important lens through which to analyse political leadership, it is also an exceedingly complex one with many intervening factors. Moreover, as political leadership remains nearly everywhere the domain of men, there is still much we do not know, both in theory and practice, about the relationship between gender and political leadership. But there is great change at hand. The first two decades of the twenty-first century have seen more women serve in top political roles than the entirety of the century previous, and in 2020, more serving concurrently than ever before. Early research has suggested, for example, that female political leaders have outperformed male counterparts on the handling of the Coronavirus pandemic, potentially the result of a combination of decisiveness, empathy and emotional intelligence not commonly found in male leadership (Taub 2020). As female political leaders become commonplace, so too will our understanding of if, how or why it differs.

Case 5.3 Defying expectations?

Violeta Chamorro

President of Nicaragua, 1990–1997

Figure 5.4 Violetta Chamorro in 1990

As the first elected female head of state in the Americas, Violeta Chamorro's term as President of Nicaragua both confirmed and defied gendered expectations of political leadership.

Her rise to power, like many female firsts, was unique. Running in the 1990 election in the midst of a bloody civil war, a country weary of conflict elected Chamorro primarily on the promise to restore peace and rebuild society, a promise seemingly made more credible by Chamorro's gender and the Latin American ideal of ***marianismo*** – a belief women have divine properties and are morally and spiritually superior to men (see Stevens 1973). Women are often perceived in Latin American society to be nurturers and peacemakers, contextually important traits in 1990. Yet women were also assumed in Nicaragua to be apolitical and to have domain over the private, rather than the public realm, thus Chamorro's candidacy also defied many of the ***marianismo*** ideals. Chamorro's election was heavily influenced by her deceased husband, a prominent opposition leader who had been assassinated. His image continued to be used as a symbol of political opposition in Nicaragua during the 1980s, and Violeta's political identity was inextricably linked with her husband's, especially as popular beliefs in Nicaragua stipulate that the dead live on in spirit through others (Saint-Germain 2013).

In office, again Chamorro both seemingly confirmed and defied gendered stereotypes and assumptions about political leadership. As often found in organizational settings led by women, her administration was more consensus-orientated, less hierarchical, and emphasized 'power-with'. She appointed prominent political opponents to important posts, granted widespread political amnesty, ran a largely non-partisan administration and a adopted a consensual style of leadership that sought to unify the disparate viewpoints and political forces in the country at that time (Close 1999: ch. 3). She held together a fractious coalition and proved strongest at negotiation and consensus-building, successfully navigating the nation through a constitutional crisis and overseeing the first democratic transition of power in half a century. The most potent symbol of 'power over' – the Nicaraguan military – was partly dismantled, with military conscription abolished, millions of weapons destroyed, and over half of the armed forces demobilized. Forging a complex but durable peace proved to be Chamorro's great legacy and strength as leader. Gendered imagery fed into this leadership, as she was often termed 'Dona Violeta' (Mother Violeta), and was portrayed as the loving mother who reunites an angry and torn-apart family (Kampwirth 1996). Even visual symbolism – such as Chamorro's trademark of dressing in white during rallies and public campaigning – aligned strongly with gendered expectations of feminine purity and goodness in Latin America.

And yet other gendered expectations were routinely defied. Despite a widespread belief in female political leadership's proclivity towards social and welfare priorities, Chamorro pushed for the privatization of state assets, pursued monetarist polices and neo-liberal economic reforms, and made large cuts in all forms of social spending, including support for the poor, elderly and disabled. These policies impacted poor and vulnerable women the very hardest (Metoyer 2000: 2–5). Women's rights were not advanced by Chamorro, who did not see herself as a feminist – she upheld rigid bans on abortion, restrictions on contraception and divorce, and did not appoint women to government positions or encourage their participation in political life (Skard 2014: 261–264). Indeed, Chamorro routinely adopted anti-feminist rhetoric, describing herself as a 'loyal wife and mother' and praising the traditional role of women in the family (Kampwirth 1996). Chamorro was not a social progressive, and under her reign some of the strictest anti-homosexuality laws in the Americas were passed. Chamorro also proved capable of tough and confrontational politics and fought hard to maintain a strong executive presidency structured around herself and only reluctantly agreed to share power with the legislature after an extended political standoff. Chamorro retired after a single term in 1997, leaving a contradictory legacy around gender and leadership, both reinforcing and rejecting traditional gender roles in Nicaragua.

Though there continues to be significant debate over how much biology, culture, and gender influence political leadership, that they all do to at least some degree is beyond question. They are not deterministic – there have always been extraordinary leaders who have defied biological, cultural and gender expectations. Moreover, society and culture do change and evolve, and with them the social expectations of leadership. Yet there is still much that is innate and instinctive about leadership that perhaps goes back to the very beginning of humanity and is perhaps not so easily overcome. Seeing our worst selves in politics and leadership (e.g., Case 5.1) can be a potent reminder of the basic instincts that we've inherited from millions of years of evolution to survive, yet others (e.g., Case 5.2) illustrate how a society fosters and mythologizes the leaders it wants to see. The tension between nature and nurture continues to play out in our politics.

Chapter Summary

- Because of the advantages for group survival, leadership has strong evolutionary roots and can be observed in the organization of many other species. Evolutionary leadership theory argues many cognitive processes necessary for leadership behaviour are likely the products of evolution.
- Moreover, many traits deemed desirable in leaders are strongly influenced by genetics, and there may even be a gene that affects a person's proclivity towards seeking a leadership role.
- At the same time, anthropological studies have established that many human societies have reliably evolved systems of political leadership in response to environmental, economic and social pressures.
- Many aspects of leadership serve common functions and follow familiar rules across cultures. However, large-scale cultural studies have established that cultures do vary in the expectations they have of leadership in certain respects.
- Feminist perspectives on leadership have argued that traditional views of the concept are paternalistic and associate leadership too much with power relations.
- There may be some biological differences in the way leadership manifests between genders. However, there is much more evidence that social expectations of leadership are gendered.

6 BIOGRAPHY, PSYCHOLOGY AND PERSONALITY

Chapter Outline

- What is biography? How has it been used to shape our understanding of political leadership over time? How reliable is it as a method to profile a leader?
- How have psychological approaches been used to understand political leaders? How do beliefs and motivations drive the behaviour of leaders?
- What role does personality play in determining how leaders react to the circumstances presented to them?
- What traits of personality do we find most commonly in leaders? Are some traits more necessary than others for effective leadership?
- What are some of the theories and frameworks commonly used to analyse the psychology of leadership, and do they have predictive power for explaining how political leaders will behave?

Politics and leadership are not just institutional structures that operate like clockwork. They are dynamic phenomena that feature individuals whose personalities and backgrounds matter. Whilst biology, gender or culture might give us some broad patterns that hold over time, individual leaders and followers can and will deviate from those patterns based on their own unique character. Similarly, although philosophers might debate whether it is better to empower or constrain leaders, in practice how each individual leader uses their powers is highly variable, depending on the individual's own motivations and personality.

Indeed, this is where studying and understanding leadership can become terribly complex. Each leader has their own life-story and multifaceted personality, and how a leader reacts to, say, a challenge to their authority might be the product of hundreds of factors, from their childhood relationship with their father to the amount of sleep they had the previous night.

Unravelling these many threads and exploring the leader as a unique, complex individual is the task of biographers and psychologists.

Biography

The lives of leaders

Since time immemorial, people have loved reading about leaders, from their heroic exploits to their lurid personal lives. This is the domain of biography. Biography is a method rather than a specific discipline, yet before there were formal disciplines like psychology, biography was effectively the only window into political leaders as individuals. They remain today the principal means of studying and understanding political leadership for the public, and indeed, should be so for any scholar of leadership as well. To quote Harold Lasswell, "political science without biography is a form of taxidermy" (Lasswell 1962: 1).

Two of the very first biographers were the classical historians Plutarch and Suetonius. Their works *Parallel Lives* (c.80 CE) and *Lives of the Twelve Caesars* (c.121 CE) sought to tell the stories of great leaders of their age and identify factors that explained why they succeeded or failed. In an era before accurate records, Plutarch and Suetonius relied heavily on scattered accounts, popular legend, historical fragments and gossip to write their biographies, many of which are interwoven with superstitious elements and moralistic judgement. But they take every opportunity to highlight the traits of their subjects they felt were ideal for leadership. For example, Plutarch describes Alexander the Great's supposed reaction to the discovery that his generals had taken to extravagance and laziness after the defeat of Persia:

> he was surprised that men who had fought so often and in such great battles, did not remember that the victors always sleep more sweetly than the vanquished, and that they did not perceive, when they imitated the luxury of the Persians, that indulgence is for slaves, but labour for princes...'do you not know, that our career of conquest will come to an end on the day when we learn to live like those whom we have vanquished?' He himself, by way of setting an example, now exposed himself to greater fatigues and hardships than ever. (Plutarch 1906: 342–343)

Modesty, humility, and self-sacrifice are traits widely associated with good leadership even today. Yet with all biography there is a tendency for accounts to become distorted, and often leaders have a mythology built around them beyond their life that exaggerates their strengths and obscures their failings. Ancient biographers were unceasingly praising of Alexander, seeing all of the very best qualities in his character. Suetonius' description of the unpopular Roman Emperors Nero and Caligula, however, ascribes to them every possible vice and character flaw, many of which were often little more than unverified rumours. For the ancients, the division was simple: good leaders were good people, and bad leaders were bad people.

It is therefore challenging to know how to deal with people who do not fall snugly inside these boundaries. Take the Roman Emperor Claudius. He was described by historians of his age as a poor leader with many problematic traits – a bad temper and bloodthirst, a stutterer, was overly trusting and manipulated, and suffered from what modern historians now believe was a form of cerebral palsy. However, the modern record attests to numerous achievements – the formal conquest of Britain, development of the judiciary and bureaucracy, improved administration of the growing empire, tax reform, and innumerable public works including canals, aqueducts, roads and ports. Claudius had many obvious flaws in his character, and yet was one of the most productive emperors of his age.

So, what do the life and character of a leader teach us about leadership? How do we know what aspects of their character were consequential to their successes and failures? Plutarch, for example, describes many of his successful leaders as having simple diets, sleeping in the open air, and practicing moderation in pleasure and drink. Self-control is nearly universally respected as both a positive human and a leadership quality (Wilson 1995: 79–98), so it's hardly surprising that Plutarch would choose to highlight this trait in leaders he perceived to be good. Yet we know of plenty of examples of successful leaders who eschewed such self-control – Winston Churchill, Itō Hirobumi and John Curtin were high-functioning alcoholics, for example (Ludwig 2002: 226–223). So even if self-control seemed important to Plutarch in explaining why his leaders were successful, did he actually uncover something universal about leadership?

More method-driven biographies that sought to analyse leadership style and personality nuances did not appear until the eighteenth century. These biographies adopted ideas from the rapidly advancing fields of sociology, psychology and medicine to guide their work. Lytton Strachey's *Eminent Victorians* (1918) was a landmark example that explored some of the hidden qualities that drove four prominent Britons. For instance, General Charles Gordon, one of the most celebrated military leaders of the Victorian Era who served as inspiration to a generation of young men, was judged by Strachey to have risen to the top due to his insatiable ambitions, restlessness, fanatical religiosity and possibly a mild psychosis. Strachey also alluded to hidden aspects of his character, including homosexuality and alcoholism, and drew attention to the hypocrisy of a man devoutly dedicated to Christian charity, grace and compassion who spent his life as a mercenary general and oversaw the slaughter of thousands in colonial wars (Strachey 1918: ch. 4).

Psychology took on a greater role in biography, particularly as the emerging discoveries in that field gave biographers more tools to uncover aspects of personality in leaders of the past. Karl Abraham, one of Sigmund Freud's students, diagnosed Amenhotep IV, one of Egypt's most dramatic pharaohs, with an Oedipal Complex in which repressed resentment of his father and unconscious attachment to his mother were purported to be the driving forces behind many of his acts as leader, particularly the significant reforms to the art, religion and ethics of his reign (Abraham 1915). Psychology's predictive capacities were also exciting. Henry Murray, working for the American Office of Strategic Services during World War II, conducted a psychological analysis of Adolf Hitler's personality and leadership in 1943. Concluding he was a 'counteractive narcissist', Murray accurately predicted that as the war turned against Hitler he would become increasingly irrational and ineffective, and if faced with certain defeat would likely commit suicide. Psychobiography waned in popularity with the decline of the credibility of psychoanalytic techniques in the 1960s; however, biographies in general remain one of the most popular literary genres.

The problems of biography

Biographies are both methodologically and theoretically troublesome. Firstly, because it is impossible to know the mind of others, the biographer's interpretation of their subject will always be subjective on some level. Biographers will research intensively and use a wide variety of tools and theories to shape their inquiries, but all approaches have limitations (see Bornat 2008). Even those who can negotiate access and directly observe leaders in action can never be sure they are seeing the 'real' leader or just their public persona (Gains 2014). There is also the problem of attachment. As Leon Edel once commented, writing a biography is like 'falling in love' – can the biographer who will often spend years studying their subject stay objective? (Jokinen 2013).

Autobiography – writing by the leader themselves – does not ameliorate the problem. Human memory is notoriously unreliable (Shaw 2016), and autobiographical accounts have often been shown to be incomplete, unreliable or distorted when compared to the public record, even when there is no intention to deceive on the part of the author (Berghegger 2009). Furthermore, it is extraordinarily difficult for humans to objectively appraise their own performance. Accounts of ourselves tend to emphasize our best intentions and we are liable to attribute our successes to our own actions and talents, while dismissing our failures as the fault of external factors rather than our own shortcomings (see Chapter 8). Political autobiographies are particularly problematic, as they are often marketing tools to further the career of the author or provide retrospective justifications for controversial or unpopular decisions. Some see the genre as so deeply flawed and unreliable that it should be largely ignored (O'Brien 1998).

Secondly, the degree to which biography can contribute to the study of leadership more generally has been questioned. Leadership studies, in politics and elsewhere, strive for rules, laws and guidelines that help explain the theory and practice of leadership as a whole, whilst biographies provide explanations that are unique to that individual (Walter 2014). Biography is a diverse genre that relies on its author to decide what factors, among the countless that form a person's life, are most relevant to their story. Biographers pursue different angles when studying their subjects and employ different styles (France & St Clair 2004). Because of the idiosyncratic nature of the genre, it can be hard to do comparative studies of leadership from biographies.

Because of these problems, in the 1980s there was a movement away from biography towards institutional analysis of leadership, and 'new institutionalism', which tends to deemphasize the individual character of leaders and instead focus on how structures, rules and contexts shape the behaviour of political actors (Walter 2014: 318; Jackson 2010). This has fostered a major debate in the study of political leadership, with a significant school of thought believing that structures are better predictors of what an actor will do than their personality (see Chapter 7). As Aaron Wildavsky surmises "when you know more about what a third baseman is likely to do by knowing his personality than by understanding the rules and customs of baseball, one of you is crazy" (Wildavsky 2006: 279).

Yet politics is not baseball, because the 'rules' of politics are not fixed but are often changed by players as they go along. Donald Trump, during his 2016 presidential campaign and his subsequent administration, routinely defied conventions and broke many of the so-called 'rules' of American politics. Trump's success has created a wave of leaders emulating his style, and biographical insight into Trump's persona proved far more enlightening than expectations based on political institutions and structures, which Trump defied throughout his term (Lemire 2018).

Just as importantly, biographies serve as symbols to others on how to lead. One of the reasons biographies of leaders are so popular is because others read them as inspiration and instruction for their own leadership. Napoleon Bonaparte idolized Julius Caesar and modelled many aspects of his leadership on him (Wyke 2008: 287). Nikolay Chernyshevsky, the mid-nineteenth century leader of the revolutionary democratic movement in Russia, wrote during imprisonment *What Is to Be Done?*, a semi-autobiographical novel idealizing total self-sacrifice and dedication in the cause of revolution. The book was profoundly influential on the next generation of radical leaders, mostly notably Vladimir Lenin, whose own leadership was modelled on Chernyshevsky's example, with far-reaching consequences for the revolution Lenin would lead (Figes 2017: 130–131).

Leadership cannot be studied in the absence of its practice and attempts to do so promote an attractive but unhelpful illusion that politics and leadership are predictable, orderly processes. Leadership is a product of both broader context and individual personalities and style, and despite its many flaws, biography is still the principal genre through which that combination can be explored.

Psychology and personality

In 1908, Graham Wallas wrote in *Human Nature in Politics* that "we are apt to assume that every human action is the result of an intellectual process … [but] whoever sets himself to base his political thinking on re-examination of the working of human nature must begin by trying to overcome his own tendency to exaggerate the intellectuality of mankind" (Wallas 1908: 21). Notwithstanding some of their inherent problems, biographies of the twentieth century increasingly began to embrace this understanding. The great leaders of the past were not morally pure and brilliant thinkers whose careers evidence the triumph of man's better selves. When authors began to scratch the surface of the personal lives and motivations of political leaders, they found they were just like ordinary people – they could be emotional,

Case 6.1 The child as leader

Mustafa Kemal Atatürk

President of Turkey, 1923–1938

Figure 6.1 Mustafa Kemal Atatürk

Mustafa Kemal Atatürk is a pivotal figure in Turkish history. A talented military officer who played a key role in the Ottoman war effort in World War I, he rose to national prominence in the war's aftermath. With the Allied nations planning to carve up the dying Ottoman Empire, Atatürk took the lead in a nationalist revolutionary movement that successfully expelled the Allied forces and dissolved the Ottoman Empire, forming the modern, secular and democratic Republic of Turkey in its place. Of enormous energy and ambition, Atatürk transformed Turkish society. He set up thousands of schools and made education compulsory, created a modern system of justice, promoted the arts and sciences, extended civil rights to women and reformed the Turkish language. He invested enormously in infrastructure, banking, mechanization and technology to modernize Turkey's largely pre-industrial economy. His name today, Atatürk, means 'father of the Turks', an appellation awarded by the Turkish Parliament in 1934, and he continues to enjoy heroic status amongst the Turkish people.

How do we understand what drives a man to take so prominent a role on the stage of history? Although many standard biographies of Atatürk have been written, Volkan and Itzkowitz (1984) attempt to answer that question more directly through psychobiography, using psychoanalysis to unpack his deeper motivations.

Four of Atatürk's five siblings died in childhood, and as the only surviving son he was greatly indulged and protected by his mother. She instilled in Atatürk a pervading sense of his own specialness and that he was saved from death for a divine purpose (Volkan & Itzkowitz 1984: 34). Atatürk's relationship with his mother was publicly and privately devotional, and he felt compelled to act as father and protector towards her, particularly in the wake of his father's early death which left the family in material want. Volkan and Itzkowitz argue that Atatürk would later project these feelings into his mission for the nation – to save and protect the Turkish people from predatory outside forces, backwardness, superstition and weak rulers, and his drive to be the father he never had is in no small part responsible for the role he would eventually assume as 'father of the nation'. Atatürk would bear no biological children of his own but would go on to adopt 13 over his lifetime. He was drawn to a military career, even over the objections of his mother, again to honour his idealized father who had served in the militia and had planned for his son to serve in the military and gain a secular education (Volkan & Itzkowitz 1984: 35).

Perhaps more crucially, the psychobiographers identify Atatürk as having developed a narcissistic personality through his mother's childhood obsession with him, and that personality led him to enormous feats of energy to place himself at the centre of events. As Atatürk wrote in his diary as a young man: "Why, after my years of education, after studying civilization and the socialization process, after spending my life and my time to gain pleasure from freedom, should I descend to the level of common people? I will make them rise to my level. Let me not resemble them: they should resemble me" (Volkan & Itzkowitz 1984: 104). Atatürk would spend most of his adult life doing just that. "When Atatürk's grandiose dreams were thwarted by the constraints of reality in his world, he transformed the world to sustain his self-image, in the process gaining the hero-worship of his nation" (Post 1987: 674).

Yet as one historian argues, the circumstances of his formative years were hardly unique. Infant mortality was high in Turkey during his childhood, as were mothers doting on sons, who were highly prized as providers and heirs. Paternalism was a predominant cultural trait of Turkish society in this time, and military careers commanded great respect and were attractive to ambitious men. Many of his reforms were not merely feats of transforming Turkey into his own image – most had long been proposed or discussed prior to Atatürk's administration and any post-Ottoman government might have reasonably been expected to pursue them.

Arguably then, Atatürk's circumstances were far from unusual in the times in which grew up, leaving us to question whether his psychobiographers uncovered clues from his early life that genuinely explain the leader he was to become, or whether this is just selective interpretation and broader sociopolitical and historical factors make these aspects of Atatürk's character unremarkable.

irrational, cruel, egotistical and foolish just as often as they were brave, self-sacrificing, intelligent and perceptive.

Psychology is the study of the human mind and behaviour, both of which are at the very centre of how politics is practiced. Political psychology has become a large and diverse sub-discipline with theoretical implications for every aspect of politics (see Jost & Sidanius 2004: 1–13). It offers theories and tools that allow us to probe political leaders from just about every conceivable angle, three of which I will explore in the rest of this chapter:

- **Motives and Beliefs**: Why do leaders seek to lead? Why do followers allow them to lead? What explains the political ideas and beliefs leaders hold?
- **Leadership Traits**: What aspects of character and traits of personality make leaders effective? What traits attract followers?
- **Leadership Behaviour**: How do personality and psychology help us explain and predict how leaders lead and perform in office?

Because psychology has powerful ramifications for just about every aspect of leadership, reference to psychological theories and perspectives won't be confined to this section alone, but here we can cover some of the major frameworks and theories that have helped develop a much more sophisticated picture of leadership, and some of the fascinating, and at times dysfunctional, psychology at its core.

Leadership motivation

Why do leaders lead? A career in politics, at least in most contemporary democracies, is not particularly lucrative compared to a job in a large corporation or successful legal practice. The hours of a politician are usually very long, especially at the top, and there is no such thing as a holiday in politics – the phone is always ringing, and the dramas of a political career are never far away. At the lower rungs, a political career can be extremely unsatisfying – endless fundraisers, party functions, policy briefings, constituent meetings, election campaigns and legislative sessions with very little power to influence the party, government or policy. Numerous studies have found politicians incur significant psychological strain, family problems and health problems as a result of their work (Weinberg 2011: 123–141). Moreover, there is no job security. In democracies there is the ever-looming threat of elections or internal party machinations that will cut your career short, and in autocracies the leader must nearly always watch their back for rivals who will depose them at the first opportunity. All the while, you are constantly criticized by the media, the public and your political opponents for your every misstep. So why would any rational individual pick such a career?

Power

Harold Lasswell, a pioneer of political psychology and psychoanalysis, sums up the power-seeker (*homo politicus*) as a person who "pursues power as a means of compensation against deprivation. Power is expected to overcome low estimates of the self, by changing either the traits of the self or the environment in which it functions" (Lasswell 1948: 53). The concept goes back to Alfred Adler, who coined the concept of the *inferiority complex* and determined that feelings of inadequacy, and the need to compensate for them in other areas of life, were central motivators of human behaviour.

Alexander George, an early psychobiographer, tested the concept on American President Woodrow Wilson. Despite initial reservations, he found there was much to suggest that Wilson's political career had been (at least in part) motivated by feelings of inferiority due to a strict and hypercritical father, and he was defined by a strident and sometimes compulsive need for power. From adolescence he sought leadership roles, from organizing his teenage friends into a club with a constitution to a succession of powerful roles in academic, state and federal politics. George noted that this need for power was not a constant fixture in his career, yet it frequently absorbed him and motivated much of his leadership style. He jealously guarded his power and was often stubborn and combative with those who opposed him. It was a drive that helped Wilson fight tough battles to win the presidency in 1912 and win the day on key domestic reforms such as the introduction of income tax and the Federal Reserve system. Yet it also appears to be behind some his troubles as president, including his rancorous relations with Congress, his unwillingness to delegate key policy portfolios, the defeat of the League of Nations and refusal to give up office after being incapacitated by poor health (George 1968; George & George 1964).

However, the compensatory motivation to lead has not proven universal by any means. Many other psychological motivations behind leadership are possible, and some political leaders only find themselves as such after much reluctance. Stanley Renshon notes that, as least as often as leaders seek power as compensation, leaders seek power as *validation* of "high estimates of self... the attainment and exercise of political power is viewed as a natural and legitimate consequence of their talents" (Renshon 2014: 136).

Needs and desires

James Davies offers an alternative perspective on the primary motivators of political behaviour by considering the *hierarchy of needs* that was famously developed by James Maslow (1954). Maslow's hierarchy is a series of needs that humans will seek to satisfy in order of necessity. At the base of the hierarchy are physiological necessities for survival, like food, water and shelter. Then comes the needs for safety and security. Then belongingness, love and friendship. Then self-esteem and the feeling of accomplishment. And finally, at the top, self-actualization, in which one can strive to achieve one's creative needs and full potential.

Davies believes such an approach can be used to explain political behaviour, including political leadership (Davies 1986). Consider that a politician must at all costs survive in order to be a politician – they must be re-elected or otherwise keep their position because once they are out of office their influence and ability to satisfy any other interests of a political career are gone. And it is readily apparent in most political systems that politicians will do what it takes to survive – they will even compromise beliefs, policies, and relationships to stay in the game. Security and safety are relative measures, but politicians, even if not faced with immediate re-election, will go to great lengths to feel politically safe. Politicians are highly responsive to opinion polling, for example, often avoiding actions they believe will jeopardize their chances of political survival.

Going up a step of the pyramid to social needs – allies, parties and ideological associations are surprisingly strong in politics and politicians are capable of displaying great loyalty to their colleagues and their team. After these needs are met achievements and prestige-seeking become more relevant – politicians will seek to get things done and have their name next to policies, plans and outcomes. Self-actualization – perhaps the very thing that drove someone to politics in the first place – is likely a fleeting opportunity during a political career. Only after you have met the need for survival, security, alliance and achievement can a political leader arguably afford the luxury of thinking about their ideas, philosophies, beliefs and visions for a better world, and how to actualize a political career in that context.

But of course, political leaders do sacrifice their political survival frequently for the higher goals. Zhao Ziyang, General Secretary of the Chinese Communist Party, gave up his career and his freedom in 1989 when, defying nearly all of his colleagues, he famously walked among the student protestors in Tiananmen Square and made a speech sympathetic to their cause. Principled stands in politics are common enough to render a Maslow hierarchy an imperfect predictor of leader behaviour.

David Winter has also written extensively on the psychology of political ambition, and in his work identifies three core ambitions that drive leaders:

- **Achievement:** excellence, accomplishment and innovation.
- **Affiliation:** friendship, collegiality and to be loved.
- **Power:** prestige, impact and consequence.

Winter developed a method for discerning which of these motives most drove individual politicians, analysing public statements, speeches and writings for recurring images, concepts and linguistic patterns (Winter 1991). Winter sees all three motivations as present to some degree in political behaviour and mixed motivations are common, yet the relative strength of these motivations within a character is instructive for understanding their behaviour (see Case 6.3).

For example, those with high achievement orientations tend to be outcome-driven in politics and approach political problems with rationality and moderation. They are inclined to be cooperative and less partisan, seek advice from policy experts, strive for informed decision-making, and take risks or play politics only when necessary to advance goals. Yet they tend to be frustrated as politicians due to the slow and chaotic nature of politics. Affiliation motivations are common in those who seek public life, and those most motivated by them tend to be popular team-players who gain energy from public adulation, seek stable government, are peacemakers and avoid confrontation, yet are often vulnerable to being manipulated or having their trust abused by colleagues and advisors. High power affiliation leads to the classic 'strong man' archetype of leadership. Such leaders are often charismatic and confrontational, warrior politicians who confront and agitate; they are risk takers, even revolutionaries, and yet their aggressiveness often leads to hawkish foreign policy and obsessive behaviours (Winter 2005).

But for Winter, it is the mix of these motivations that proves most interesting in creating varied political personalities. Winter's analyses of US presidents rated John F. Kennedy as the highest scoring on affiliation motivation, a strong fit seemingly for one of the most publicly beloved presidents and one who loved the social aspects of politics. Yet he also scored highly on power, and indeed was an ambitious and at times highly combative politician who rarely shrank from a political fight and stood toe-to-toe with the Soviet Union during the Cuban Missile Crisis – an interesting blend of both the peacemaker and the warrior (Winter 1987).

Followers

As discussed previously (Chapter 2), leaders are enabled and given power and authority ultimately by followers, who on some level choose to follow them. Social psychologists in recent years have sought to refocus the study of leadership onto the social relationships between leaders and followers that underpin it. Social identity theory in particular has been used to this end, recasting leadership as a process whereby groups create norms and identities, and the group members who best exemplify those norms and identities appear to have influence because others within the group aspire to be what they exemplify. "The appearance of influence becomes a reality through depersonalized social attraction processes that make followers agree and comply with the leader's ideas and suggestions" (Hogg 2001: 184).

Haslam, Reicher and Platow (2011) elaborate on this process, specifying the social needs of groups that leaders satisfy in order to become leaders:

- Be seen as "**one of us**", and representing the ideals and identities of their group, especially in contrast with 'others'.
- Be seen to be "**doing it for us**" and understood as leading for the common good of the group rather than for personal gain or interest.
- Be seen to be "**crafting a sense of us**" by understanding and implementing the values of the group whilst actively articulating and shaping those values in the face of change.
- Be seen to be "**making us matter**", in which the group's values and ideals find expression and advancement in the real world.

In this way, the authors argue that the effectiveness of leadership is inseparable from social identity relationships, and leadership in the broader sense is much more a question of "we" rather than "I" as a result (2011: xxi). Although how a leader's own motivations may have great bearing on how they go about leading, the social identity theory perspective is an important reminder that at a basic level, followers must be motivated to follow as well in order for leadership to exist at all.

Leadership personality

Political leaders have complex personalities that incorporate many features, from the way they interact with others to the way they think about problems. A staggering array of models for the political personality, and methods for discerning it, have been developed in this field. The study of the leader personality arguably had its heyday in the 1940–1960s (McGuire 2004), yet it continues to capture both public and scholarly imagination. The study of political personality is complicated by issues of access, evidence, interpretation and theory; however, increasingly sophisticated methods have evolved to study personality 'at a distance' and provide rigorous substantiation behind complex theories and dramatic findings (see Greenstein 2004).

Psychoanalysis

The psychoanalytical approach was one of the first major contributors to the study of political personality and led to the popularization of the psychobiography. The validity of psychoanalysis has been fiercely debated, and many of its methods have been criticized even within the field of psychology (see Cocks 1986). However, its influence on the study of leadership persists, and many of its works have become popular classics in the understanding of leadership.

Psychoanalysis sees "human beings acting out of a complex combination of rational and irrational impulses formed by memory and environment" (Cocks 1986: 144). Psychoanalysis sees human behaviour as powerfully driven by the *unconscious* mind, and personality as primarily determined by developments in childhood (Renshon 2014: 134–135). The psychoanalysis of leaders thus focuses heavily on their early lives, and often finds that conflicts within families, first sexual experiences, early education, childhood role models and identity crises in youth are essential to understanding the deeply embedded and often unconscious aspects of personality that are expressed in adulthood.

Psychoanalytical approaches generally take the form of individual case studies that seek to uncover hidden aspects or conflicts within leader personalities and the formative experiences that help explain their later behaviours (see Cases 6.1 and 6.3). The psychoanalyst Wilhelm Reich believed early psychosexual development in childhood was critical in this respect. One of his personality types developed from these ideas was the "phallic-narcissist". Freud first describes the so-called 'phallic' stage of psychosexual development, whereby between the ages of three and six, children become aware of and often fascinated by their own genitalia and pre-sexual exploration of the bodies of others. Boys face the infamous Oedipus complex at this stage, in which they unconsciously desire their mothers and see themselves competing for her attention with their father, though they cannot defeat their stronger, grown fathers and instinctively fear defeat at his hands. This inner psychic conflict, if not resolved and passed from the unconscious in a healthy manner, is a precursor of Reich's phallic-narcissist – a man who compensates for this childhood defeat and insecurity through obsessive compensation, hyper-masculinity and aggressive competitiveness, as well as the search for power and domination (Reich 1933/1972). Reich saw many political leaders, like Napoleon and Mussolini, as these psychologically stunted archetypes, pursuing power as compensation with little regard for consequences or social norms (Reich 1972: 198).

There are, however, some more general frameworks and typologies for explaining political leadership that rest on psychoanalytical ideas. James David Barber's *The Presidential Character* (1972) stands out in this respect. Barber believed that studying political leadership could be done most effectively by observing the development of three stages:

- **Character** in childhood, where basic outlooks, experiences and estimations of self-worth emerge.
- **World View** in adolescence, where an individual develops their sense of justice, morality, human nature and society.
- **Style** in early adulthood, where patterns of behaviour in the performance of their roles and jobs become embedded.

These elements are progressively layered upon each other to form a political personality, with elements dynamically interacting with each other, though Barber felt that the initial stage – character – was the most important. Indeed, Barber felt that the most critical and defining aspect of personality was the development of an individual's political character with respect to two criteria.

The first is *energy* or drive towards politics – how motivated is the political leader towards achievement? How energetically do they seek power and advancement? Are they passive or active in this regard? The second is *outlook* or emotional engagement with politics. Do they enjoy the exercise of power and the careers they sought? Are they emotionally fulfilled when they achieve and advance? How do they emotionally respond to the ups and downs of political life? Arraying these two criteria together, Barber developed a fourfold personality type he felt best separated out political leaders (Table 6.1).

Table 6.1 Barber's personality matrix from *The Presidential Character* (1992)

	Positive emotional outlook	Negative emotional outlook
High activity level	**Active-positive** Self-confident, flexible, creates opportunities for action, reflective, optimistic, power used as a means to achieve beneficial results.	**Active-negative** Power as a means to self-realization, manic, preoccupied by success and failure, self-critical, rigid, poor self-esteem and pessimistic.
Low activity level	**Passive-positive** Receptive, compliant, seeks affection, directed towards helping others, easily manipulated, ingratiating personality to overcome low self-esteem, reactive	**Passive-negative** Responses to a sense of duty, avoids power, reactive, avoids conflict, emphasizes procedure and principle, dislikes uncertainty

Case 6.2 Finding Nixon

Richard Nixon

President of the United States, 1969–1974

Figure 6.2 Richard Nixon in 1973

Richard Nixon "was one of the most fascinating figures to occupy the Oval Office and his personal traits were the author of his doom. Like most humans Nixon was a complex person, only more so" (Drew 2015). Richard Nixon served as president during some of America's most turbulent times. An experienced politician of great intellect and drive, his administration would see many breakthroughs, including détente with the Soviet Union and the opening of relations with China, as well as the establishment of the Environmental Protection Agency and the first large-scale integration of schools in the South. Yet nearly all of this would be overshadowed by Nixon's abuse of power in the pursuit of advantage over his political opponents. Those abuses, and their coverup, would snowball into the Watergate scandal that played out in courts and the media for two years and eventually forced Nixon's resignation in disgrace, and the indictment of many of his administration's aides and officials. As one of the most infamous politicians of the twentieth century, scholars have long struggled to understand the character and psychology of Nixon and to understand his contradictory and ultimately self-destructive actions.

Born into a poor family in California, Nixon was driven to succeed and worked furiously to gain the access to opportunities many others took for granted. He was unpopular with much of the political and media elite during his career, and he keenly felt, and even promoted, his outsider status his whole life. He was an unnatural politician in many ways – he was socially awkward and anxious, nervous in large groups and had few close friends (Farrell 2017: 203–205; Thomas 2015: 30–31). Yet while he was weak in human relationships, he was a cunning strategist and proved his detractors wrong many times, carving out successful electoral victories. Indeed, Nixon conceded in his later life the drivers that led to his political rise and likely fall: "what starts the process really are laughs and slights and snubs when you are a kid...but if you are reasonably intelligent and if your anger is deep enough and strong enough, you learn that you can change those attitudes by excellence, personal gut performance".

Nixon lived this mantra. When hounded in 1952 by media allegations of financial impropriety with his campaign funds, Nixon took the unprecedented step of going on television and candidly releasing his personal finances, revealing himself to be of very modest means. Though media reactions were mixed, Nixon received thousands of supportive telegrams and the sympathy of many voters and was elected Vice President that year. Yet he lost his first run at the presidency in 1960 to John F. Kennedy, who in many ways represented the privileged elite he had struggled against his whole life, in a very close election in which he felt media bias and dirty campaigning by his old enemies had cost him the election (Farrell 2017: 294–300).

This contradictory character went to the very heart of his leadership. As Nixon's speechwriter Ray Price wrote of his boss, "the light side and the dark side are both there, and over the years these have been at constant war with one another" (Thomas 2015: 527). Nixon was a tender and loving husband and father yet could be unceasingly spiteful towards his enemies. He advanced religious and racial equality through many of his policies, and yet was often viciously anti-Semitic and racist in private. He was an active and enthusiastic politician driven to seek power, yet seemingly drew no satisfaction from it and never shrugged off his fears and insecurities despite reaching the highest office (Barber 1992: 150–167).

That fear and self-doubt plagued his political career and ultimately brought down his presidency (Thomas 2015: xiii). Psychologists and biographers have debated the morality and specifics of Nixon's behaviour during Watergate, yet near universally agree that the scandal's origins lay in Nixon's paranoia and obsession with staying on top. Nixon maintained an 'enemies' list and created a climate of suspicion and intrigue, which at least indirectly led to his subordinates breaking into the Democratic Party headquarters in 1972 to steal intelligence, and then a two-year saga in which Nixon abused his power repeatedly to obstruct the investigation before resigning from office once his impeachment became a certainty. Nixon himself seemed to acknowledge his tragic fate – in his farewell address he stated "Always remember. Others may hate you, but those who hate you don't win unless you hate them, and then you destroy yourself" (Nixon 1974).

Nixon's rise from obscurity and dramatic self-destruction continues to fascinate. Dozens of biographies have been published, and whilst the key aspects of his psyche and personality seem clear, finding a satisfying summation of his life has remained elusive. Yet so much of Nixon's own words and deeds are matters of public record that in studying him we come closest perhaps to seeing the real human behind the mystique of the leader, and what we find is ourselves – complex, flawed and contradictory.

Barber's typologies were designed to provide a key to understanding the United States presidents he'd studied. The active-positive presidents were the most well-adjusted and were in some ways the typical politicians – they both sought power and enjoyed its exercise. Happy in their roles and motivated to achieve in them, many of the most successful presidents are in this category, such as Thomas Jefferson, Franklin Roosevelt, and John F. Kennedy.

Other typologies, however, provide interesting points of difference. Passive-positive presidents, for example, liked power and politics but were reactive and accepted power perhaps as compensation for low self-esteem rather than having a healthy drive towards it. Barber cites several presidents who fit this type and played the role of the cheerful amateur in politics, serving as president happily but with little real energy or ambition within the role. They were often popular with the public but were easily manipulated by others and deceived by their subordinates. Ronald Reagan, Warren Harding and James Madison stand out in this typology.

Passive-negative presidents are perhaps the most confusing, as they neither like political power nor seek it, yet for reasons of history and circumstance, and perhaps out of a sense of duty, reluctantly become political leaders. George Washington is the most prominent example, as a general who disliked politics but took on the first presidency to ensure the stability of the system, yet like his hero Cincinnatus gave up power voluntarily after two terms to return to his farm.

For Barber, active-negative presidents are the most problematic – they seek power compulsively but derive no joy from it. They tend to be manic, emotionally conflicted, pessimistic or paranoid as a result of the mismatch between drive and happiness, and this inner turmoil can be highly unpredictable and possibly destructive in positions of political power. Erratic behaviour and aggressive outbursts are common. Barber cites John Adams and Woodrow Wilson as classic examples in this category, but became famous when he published his book in 1972 for predicting that Richard Nixon also exemplified this type and, inevitably, this would lead to conflicted behaviour in the role and perhaps even a tragic showdown (see Case 6.2) – all of which would become publicly apparent as the Watergate scandal began to unfold the year after *The Presidential Character* was published (Barber 1992: 123–168).

Trait approach

Another early and influential means to exploring the personality of leaders can be termed the 'trait approach'. Beginning in the 1940s, some leadership scholars drifted away from biography as the primary method of investigating the personality of political leaders and turned instead to quantitative methods to distil what character traits were most crucial to successful leadership. Surveys of experts, surveys of leaders, content analysis, comparative biography and meta-analysis of leadership studies have been used to collect large amounts of data on the attributes of leaders and to analyse which attributes,

Table 6.2 Core leadership personality traits from five studies

Study	Leadership traits
Stogdill (1948)	Intelligence, alertness, insight, responsibility, initiative, persistence, self-confidence, sociability
Mann (1959)	Intelligence, masculinity, adjustment, extraversion, conservatism
Bass (1990)	Adjustment, adaptability, aggressiveness, alertness, dominance, emotional balance, independence, creativity, integrity, self-confidence
Kirkpatrick and Locke (1991)	Drive, motivation, integrity, confidence, cognitive ability, task knowledge
Zaccaro, Kemp and Bader (2004)	Cognitive ability, extraversion, conscientiousness, emotional stability, openness, agreeableness, motivation, social intelligence, self-monitoring, emotional intelligence, problem solving

particularly personality traits, most strongly correlate with effectiveness (or ineffectiveness) in leadership (see Bass 1981: 43–96; Judge et al. 2002).

As summarized in Table 6.2, there is often significant variation in the findings of these studies. Although some traits are nearly always cited, such as self-confidence and intelligence, others have come in and out of favour. For example, emotional intelligence and empathy have long been studied as to their association with successful leadership. Results of studies have been mixed and inconclusive, and highly dependent on what method of analysis was used and what kinds of leaders were studied (Bass 1981: ch. 7).

In recent years, trait and personality studies of this kind have moved towards a more unified framework of studying personality known as the *Five Factor Model (FFM)* (Table 6.3), which several leadership scholars have found works well as a distillation of previous trait approaches and as a method for analysing leadership personality (Judge & Bono 2000).

The FFM, in its application to leadership (Judge et al. 2002; Bono & Judge 2004), has found that the majority of leaders most positively correlate with extraversion and most negatively correlate with neuroticism – i.e., most leaders are outgoing and self-confident, two personality traits that have in just about every trait study been associated with leadership.

Yet many subtleties in these studies emerge upon closer inspection. For example, there are differences between personality traits that predict the *emergence* of a leader and the *effectiveness* of a leader. Extraversion is strongly associated with leader emergence but less so effectiveness. An amiable and outgoing politician is perhaps ideal for winning elections, but such traits are less useful in running a government. The inverse is true of agreeableness, which does not predict leader emergence but is associated with effectiveness.

Table 6.3 The Five Factor Model and its personality implications

Factor	High scorers		Low scorers	
Openness to experience	Creative	Unfocused	Cautious	Pragmatic
	Curious	Risk-seeking	Risk-averse	Calculating
	Adventurous		Traditionalist	
Extraversion	Sociable	Attention-seeking	Reserved	Aloof
	Energetic	Domineering	Reflective	Self-centred
	Expressive		Independent	
Contentiousness	Organized	Stubborn	Flexible	Sloppy
	Disciplined	Obsessive	Easy-going	Careless
	Efficient		Spontaneous	Disorganized
Agreeableness	Friendly	Naïve	Assertive	Suspicious
	Compassionate	Submissive	Competitive	Mistrustful
	Cooperative		Independent	
Neuroticism	Sensitive	Anxious	Stable	Inscrutable
	Reactive	Emotional	Self-Assured	Boring
	Engaging		Confident	

Source: Matthews et al. (2009: 23–26).

Voters are often attracted to a warrior with a single-minded platform at the polls, but that lack of agreeableness tends to be problematic when having to share power and negotiate with other political players in government. Moreover, context matters – in business, for example, the openness trait and creativity are much more strongly associated with good leadership than in politics (Judge et al. 2002: 772–773).

These findings may not be as profound as they first appear. Extraversion is positively associated, and neuroticism negatively associated, with career advancement and personal success across the board, not just in leadership (Seibert & Kraimer 2001; Sutin et al. 2009). Moreover, it has been conceded that there is significant variation in desirable leadership traits across contexts, meaning that just about any potential mix of personality traits may find itself desirable in leadership at a given moment. US President Abraham Lincoln was famously both introverted and prone to bouts of depression, anxiety and neuroticism, and yet was the leader America needed during its darkest hour and proved successful at keeping the nation together and inspiring a generation amidst the horrors of the Civil War. Indian Prime Minister Manmohan Singh and British Prime Minister Clement Attlee were famously introverted and unlikely politicians yet were widely respected and successful in their roles.

Indeed, some have contested the neuroticism finding altogether. Nassir Ghaemi in *A First-Rate Madness* (2011) specifically links depression and mania, two otherwise negative personality disorders, with leaders who do exceedingly well in times of crisis because a certain amount of mental abnormality gives rise to unique qualities that help with crisis leadership – realism, empathy, creativity and resilience are strongly correlated with these two disorders. In this sense, even neurotic personalities can possess uniquely useful features ideal for leadership in certain circumstances (Ghaemi 2011).

Not all traits are necessarily inborn aspects of personality either. Recent studies of personality have increasingly made a distinction between distal traits (disposition, personality, character), which are innate to a person, and proximal traits (skills, expertise, communication), which can be learned over time. Research has found that traits from both categories are predictive of effective leadership outcomes, indicating that at least some important leadership traits (like skills and expertise) can be learned or sharpened (Hoffman et al. 2011). Recently trait theories have combined both the FFM the proximal/distal trait approach, as well as controlling for situational needs and environmental factors, to provide a much more nuanced model of how a leader's personality interacts with its context (e.g. Zaccaro et al. 2004).

So, although quantitatively we can verify that certain traits and dispositions are more *likely* to appear in effective leaders, there are many caveats and exceptions. Traits have limitations insofar as they tend to be a static snapshot of a leader. Although proximal traits suggest that leaders might progressively improve in some regards, history tells us that political leaders, if anything, lose their instincts and their popularity over time – something hard to explain given their personalities have presumably little changed. Personalities are not simply aggregates of various traits, but rather the product of dynamic interactions between them, and expressed variably depending on context and interactions with other people.

Style approach

The style approach focuses more on *how* a leader leads – how they relate with followers, communicate, make decisions, negotiate, respond to opponents and so on. Aspects of leadership behaviour may be an outgrowth of personality, and in this sense 'traits' may inform 'style' to some extent, but the style approach is more interested in how those traits interact with context and influence the way a leader thinks, communicates or acts in practice.

There are dozens of typologies of leadership style that have been generated, some that make simple distinctions between how leaders behave and some that plunge deeply into their personality and mindset. One of the most influential, and yet simplest, was first described by James Macgregor Burns (1976), who identified just two key styles of leaders – *transactional* leaders and *transformational* leaders.

Transactional leadership motivates followers by appealing to their self-interest. Transactional leadership is reactive and about wheeling-and-dealing, rewarding or punishing, supervising, organizing, focusing on goals and outcomes, setting rules and standards. On the other hand, transformational leadership is about inspiring followers through higher ideals and moral values. Transformational leadership is proactive and stresses ideas, intellectual stimulation, creating positive change and individualized needs and considerations (Gill 2011: 83–84). A classic distinction in style can be seen by comparing US Presidents Barack Obama and Donald Trump. Obama is often seen as a classic example of someone who adopted a publicly transformational style of leadership – his emphasis on lofty ideals, a central theme of 'hope' during his 2008 presidential campaign, his emphasis on unity and togetherness, his seeking international agreements like the Paris Accords, and the way many of his followers interacted with him are trademark aspects of Burns's original definition (Greenberg 2017). By comparison, his successor Donald Trump, although not without appealing to higher ideals like "Make America Great Again", adopted a more squarely transactional style, appealing much more to the self-interest of voters and supporters (jobs, security, immigration restriction), casting himself as a deal-maker and businessman, and seeking the maximization of national gain at the expense of high-minded ideals (Gillespie 2018).

What drives a leader to adopt a transformational or transactional style? Studies have generally shown a weak relationship between personality characteristics and leadership style; however, transformational leaders tend to be stronger on the extraversion factor than transactional leaders (Bono & Judge 2004). Motivations can be relevant, as those driven to seek power or advancement are more likely to pursue those goals by transacting with those who can deliver them, whilst affiliating leaders will want to genuinely inspire and connect with followers rather than simply 'buy' them. How a leader sees the world matters too. Is it a 'jungle out there' with competition and rivalry the norm? Or is the world a fundamentally good and harmonious place? Donald Trump, coming from a business background and in training much of his life to succeed in a world where fierce competition and cut-throat deal-making are the norm, and in which most other players are in the game to make money, would seem naturally inclined to lead transactionally. By contrast Barack Obama was a scholar, community organizer and civil rights attorney who spent much of his early career working towards equality and social change. We might only expect a person of this background and outlook to assume a transformative posture in a leadership role.

Although transformational leadership sounds instinctively more appealing than transactional, in truth both styles have their strengths and weaknesses and a heavy preference for transformational styles in business literature isn't necessarily supported by evidence from practice (Foley 2013: 53–57). US President John F. Kennedy was an archetypical transformational leader who inspired a generation to re-engage with the big ideals of American democracy like the civil rights movement and the Peace Corps. Yet it was his successor Lyndon B. Johnson who actually achieved much of what Kennedy had sought. Johnson was a master of transactional leadership, who cajoled, struck bargains, made trade-offs, and threatened punishments to finally get the landmark civil rights and Great Society legislation passed (see Burns 2009: ch. 4).

A more comprehensive model of leadership style is provided by political psychologist Margaret Hermann. She posits three criteria as most relevant for understanding how leaders operate in practice:

1. How they respond to constraints or opposition.
2. How open they are to new information.
3. Whether they are focused more on problems or relationships.

The model uses seven measures of personality, beliefs, motivations and emotion to answer to these questions: need for power, belief in their ability to control events, self-confidence, conceptual complexity, task focus, ingroup bias and distrust of others (Hermann 2002). The way in which these measures are used to determine the answer to these questions is more nuanced than previous models I've described. For example, openness to new information is determined through the measurement of self-confidence and conceptual complexity. If the first is higher, then the leader tends to dogmatically adhere to their pre-existing beliefs and ideas. If the second is higher, the leader knows how much they do not know and will search for information.

Depending on where leaders fall across these three spectra, Hermann nominates eight core leadership styles which help explain and perhaps predict how different leaders operate when faced with similar situations (Table 6.4).

Table 6.4 Hermann's leadership styles

	Problem focus	Relationship focus
Challenges constraints + Closed to information	**Expansionistic** Focus is on expanding one's power and influence	**Evangelistic** Focus is on persuading others to accept one's message and join one's cause
Challenges constraints + Open to information	**Incremental** Focus is on maintaining one's flexibility and options while avoiding obstacles	**Charismatic** Focus is on achieving one's agenda by engaging others and persuading them to act
Respects constraints + Closed to information	**Directive** Focus is on personally guiding policy and political ideas, while working within the norms of the role	**Consultative** Focus is on monitoring others who will support one's agenda and maintaining social status
Respects constraints + Open to information	**Reactive** Focus is on assessing what is possible given circumstances, nature of the problem and what followers will allow	**Accommodative** Focus is on reconciling differences, building consensus, empowering others and sharing accountability in the process

Adapted from Hermann (2002).

For example, Hafez al-Assad, President of Syria from 1971 to 2000, was analysed at a distance by Hermann in 1986 using this framework. Similar to other strongmen in the region, Hermann determined that Hafez challenged constraints and was problem focused. Yet in contrast with neighbouring dictators his cognitive complexity and self-confidence were both high, indicating openness to new information, and thus he was an 'incremental' or 'independent' style of leader. She predicts such a leader to be assertive and goal-orientated yet also pragmatic, adaptive and rational in the face of challenges and changing context (Hermann 1988). Her prediction proved to be prescient. For example, although outward rhetoric made Hafez seem like he was an implacable opponent of Israel, over his long period of rule he switched positions on the issue depending on circumstances – he was a leader in the Yom Kippur War against Israel in 1971 yet by 1991 was a party to the Madrid Conference. He had pragmatically manoeuvred to a more advantageous side, extracting the optimal concessions for Syria in the process (Wigington 1992: 11–12). As predicted by this type, Hafez was single-minded in his consolidation of personal power and his attempts to strengthen

Syria's domestic and international position, but again proved to be pragmatic and flexible in his thinking about how to reach those goals, demonstrated amply by Hafez's shifting alliances during his three decades of rule, with both Russia and the United States courted as regional circumstances shifted.

Hafez's son Bashar inherited much of his father's leadership style when he became Syrian President after the former's death in 2000, except commentators have noted that Bashar lacks the self-confidence, wariness or flexibility of his father. He prefers action, tradition, and tends to adopt a dogmatic posture or react emotionally when challenged. Thus he is potentially more liable to manipulation by advisors and prone to knee-jerk reactions, despite a generally high level of cognitive complexity (Spitaletta 2014; Council on Foreign Relations 2016). Subsequently, Bashar's personality may be more 'reactive' due to these factors, and perhaps increasingly so as his agenda has shifted from reform measures in his early reign to a focus on maintaining the regime's control in the wake of the Arab Spring. Yet at the same time Bashar's higher cognitive complexity, low personal need for power and low in-group bias (Spitaletta 2014: 74–75) may help explain why Bashar al-Assad has been able to manoeuvre pragmatically to maintain enough alliances and support to hold onto power in Syria despite nine years of bloody civil war in a decade where most of his hardline contemporaries in the region were deposed.

Hermann's model relies on 'personality-at-a-distance' measures similar to those described previously, such as content analysis of written and spoken material, and like many of these models there can be legitimate questions as to their accuracy. However, a review of Hermann's use of her own model of leadership style found her predictions matched fairly closely with observations by journalists, biographers and experts who had direct insight into the leaders she profiled (Hermann 2002: 39–41; see also Case 6.3).

Biographers and psychologists have long been interested in analysing political leaders to see what makes them tick, and it will continue to be a popular area of leadership inquiry. Although there are limits to what we can see and know for sure about our leaders, it is a natural starting point in studying any leader to consider their personality, traits and leadership style.

However, the popularity of biographies and psychological portraits means there is always a danger of overemphasizing the role of individual character and personality in leadership outcomes – as demonstrated throughout this book, individual psychology is just one of many potential factors that come together in the expression of leadership. And as explored in the next chapter, the impact of the individual character and style of a leader in some circumstances may be of little importance against the tides of history.

Case 6.3 Unpacking a leader

Saddam Hussein

President of Iraq, 1979–2003

Figure 6.3 Saddam Hussein

How would various approaches to political psychology work when brought together in a single case? Saddam Hussein, a central player throughout three decades of Middle Eastern politics, provides a rich case study for psychologists and political scholars.

From a psychoanalytic or biographical perspective, his childhood and early development are of critical interest. Saddam was an unwanted child – his father died before he was born, and his mother attempted to abort him, only to be prevented by a family of Jewish benefactors. She refused to see Saddam after he was born, and it wasn't until three years later she returned to raise him with her new husband, who was abusive towards Saddam. As Jerrold Post speculates, Saddam's painful early childhood hardened his heart, diminished his capacity for empathy, and set him on a course to avenge his 'wounded self' in adulthood (Post 2003: 336). He would run away from home at ten years of age after being denied the ability to get an education, and instead went to live with an uncle, who had fought against the British in the Iraqi Uprising of 1941 and encouraged Saddam to believe that he was destined for greatness, as well as inspiring in him a deeply xenophobic worldview (Post 2003: 337).

Post believes that Saddam developed 'malignant narcissism' – an obsession with his own greatness fuelled by a need to compensate for a scarred and tragic childhood. Saddam was not irrational in his pursuit of power – he responded aggressively but strategically to exploit opportunities. Yet his narcissism prevented him from acknowledging mistakes. His narrow worldview, paranoia, and belief in his own greatness also dissuaded him from accessing unbiased perspectives on his plans and actions – and many major miscalculations, such as the Iran-Iraq War and the Gulf War, followed. Moreover, his lack of empathy and tendency to react with extreme aggression when confronted led to terrible atrocities under his rule. And yet, his unceasing belief in himself also bred patience and shrewd calculation, and a canny ability to politically survive for over two decades (Post 2003: 340–348).

David Winter found much agreement in Saddam's spoken, written and available biographical material, and found he scored very highly in power motivation. Risky gambles in foreign policy, overestimation of his own plans, and dogged holding on to office all correlate with this view. Yet a moderate affiliation score also appears in content analysis, and although counterintuitive for a dictator, is perhaps consistent with Saddam's other great passion for Arab reunification – i.e., affiliation with those he trusted and felt common cause with (Winter 2003: 371–373). Walter Weintraub found that Saddam rated highly on explanatory language yet low on linguistic qualifiers, indicating that he had high self-confidence and would eagerly rationalize his own ideas and decisions rather than admit defeat or face unpleasant truths (Weintraub 2003: 367–368).

Margaret Hermann's model indicates an expansionist – Saddam had low openness to new information, a high problem focus and challenged restraints. Hermann finds Saddam similar to leaders like the hero of his youth Gamal Abdul Nasser in that he constantly strives for power, both personally and for the nation he believes he embodies, and will connive and compete in order to obtain goals. Hermann's model also matches a man who is opportunistic and uses friends and foes alike to advance his own goals. Yet her scoring also indicates a possible change over time – his conceptual complexity apparently decreased as he aged – leading him to become even more dogmatic, self-convinced and stubborn towards the end of his reign, perhaps best evidenced by his dramatic miscalculations during the Gulf War of the 1990s (Hermann 2003: 375–386).

The aforementioned profiles were all published prior to Saddam's downfall during the 2003 Iraq War. Though the US-led invasion coalition was justified on faulty premises, undoubtedly Saddam's political personality had made him an easy target. In the aftermath of the Gulf War, Saddam declared victory over the United States publicly on the basis that his government had not been toppled by the war, and began restyling himself as a hero of Islam and resistance leader to American imperialism (Esposito 1997: 56–58). Perhaps Saddam's greatest miscalculation then was that he could continue to play a pariah on the international stage forever. Even during his final trial in 2006, Saddam refused to accept the authority of courts over him and adamantly maintained he was still the true President of Iraq.

Chapter Summary

- Biography is the traditional means by which leaders have been studied and is an extremely popular and influential genre for reading and learning about leadership.
- Psychobiography merges biography with psychoanalysis and was a popular approach in the early twentieth century, often focusing on the formative years of leaders to find clues about their later motivations and actions.
- However, both biography and autobiography suffer from several methodological problems, making their reliability, particularly prior to the twentieth century, questionable.
- Psychology has played a major role in expanding the field of leadership analysis, and has yielded particular insights into:
    - Motivations, particularly the need for power, but also other psychological needs like achievement, affiliation and self-actualization, which can help explain why leaders seek their offices in the first place.
    - Trait approaches, which help paint a picture of the personalities of leaders, and how various traits of those personalities impact their behaviour and effectiveness as leaders.
    - Style approaches, which examine how personality and individual psychology influence how leaders behave and how they will interact with followers and their environment. They also try to anticipate how certain personalities and styles will react when faced with various opportunities or challenges.
- Numerous models have been developed that offer typologies of leadership personality and style. They often employ methods like content analysis to gain insight into leaders who must necessarily be studied 'at a distance'.

7 CONTEXT, INSTITUTIONS AND CHANGE

Chapter Outline

- Do leaders really matter in history? Do leaders shape their times or do the times shape their leaders?
- Do all leaders get the same opportunities for success? How much are context and history responsible for enabling or constraining political leaders and the options they have for action?
- What are institutions and how do leaders operate within a broader institutional context?
- What are the key institutional and contextual mechanisms that shape a leader's actions? How do leaders adapt their styles to match their historical, contextual or institutional environment?

In the previous chapter, our focus was upon leaders as individuals. This is perhaps the natural focus, as we tend to judge leaders on their successes and failures, strengths and weaknesses, as individuals. It may also be an outgrowth of how we tend to learn about leadership. After all, biographies of individual political leaders sell much better than textbooks trying to explore the concept more broadly. This intense focus on the individual, though, obscures a more nuanced reality in which leaders are couched within much broader institutional structures and historical context. These structures and contexts enable or constrain the options for action a leader has, how effective their actions are, and how we perceive them as well. While leaders may outwardly appear to be in complete control, many aspects of political leadership are routine, constrained and even predictable through the lens of the structures they operate within.

So in this chapter, we take a different tack and question how important leaders really are in the broad scheme of things. To what extent are the successes and failures of a leader the product of their own individual actions, and to what extent are their actions the product of structures and circumstances they find themselves operating within?

Context and circumstance

Do leaders make history?

Thomas Carlyle declared in *Hero and Hero Worship* that "the history of the world is but the biography of great men" (Carlyle 1849: 26). Putting his gendered assumptions of leadership to one side, Carlyle sparked with this statement a debate that has long raged amongst historians and those interested in leadership – to what degree is history influenced by the actions of individuals? Carlyle's contemporary Herbert Spencer rejected the notion entirely, stating:

> you must admit that the genesis of a great man depends on the long series of complex influences which has produced the race in which he appears, and the social state into which that race has slowly grown. ... before he can remake his society, his society must make him. (Spencer 1880: 34)

Spencer is contending that all great people are the product of the environment in which they have grown, and that historical change is ultimately driven by large social and structural processes over which individual leaders have but marginal influence. Leo Tolstoy agreed, wryly observing in the epilogue of *War and Peace* that kings and generals are deluded into thinking their actions are determining the fate of the world, when in fact they are merely "slaves to history".

Consider the example of German Emperor Friedrich III. Coming to the throne in 1888, Friedrich was a committed reformer and liberal who wished to radically change the course of the German Empire from its militaristic Prussian roots to a modern constitutional monarchy, with a parliamentary government and an open economy in the style of Great Britain. Friedrich III was a fierce critic of Germany's punitive actions towards minorities and was noted for his advocacy of the rights of Jews while Crown Prince, to the horror of the imperial court. He abhorred war, opposed the 'blood and iron' policies of Chancellor Otto von Bismarck, and sought to turn Germany instead into a centre of learning, culture and democratic rights. Yet tragically, after waiting 56 years for his chance to rule and change Germany's course, he developed a tumour in his larynx shortly before his accession and succumbed to cancer just 99 days into his reign. As a result, his son Wilhelm II, who had taken after his grandfather's militarism and rejected his father's liberal attitudes, became Emperor and would continue Germany's path towards expansionism and war.

Had he lived, would Friedrich III have changed the course of history? This is a question that scholars have debated for over a century (see Kollander 1995). Some have contended that World War I, and even World War II, could have been avoided entirely had Friedrich III had a chance to liberalize Germany. Others have contended that one man, even if emperor, could not have unwound the deeply entrenched social and cultural values of the times, and its militaristic politics were unlikely to have been dismantled.

The importance of context

At a broader level, these questions are really about *what* political leaders are influencing, changing or doing when they are leading. Most scholars agree that individual leaders *are* important and have an impact on history, and comparative analysis of the role leaders have played and how they have responded in similar circumstances over different polities can demonstrate convincingly that 'who leads matters' (Hermann et al. 2001; Byman & Pollack 2001). But by what mechanisms do leaders create change? And *how much* change are they able to create given their circumstances and contextual limitations?

Part of the problem of answering this question has been unearthed by the *romance of leadership* concept. Scholars studying this phenomenon have found that leaders and leadership issues are the most likely things to be identified as responsible for organizational successes or failures, even when there is little evidence to back up such contentions. Moreover, perceptions of leadership within an organization strongly influence how people feel about its performance – if leaders are liked, organizational outcomes will be deemed to be better, and if leaders are disliked, so too do perceptions of organizational outcomes decline (Bligh & Kohles 2010; Meindl et al. 1985). This romance of leadership entangles political leadership as well. Not only are the public very heavily focused on political leaders, and tend to deem them far more responsible for the state of the nation, the economy and their own lives than they really are; but so too do scholars and the media, who tend to be biased towards individualistic and personality-based explanations of outcomes rather than exploring the contextual constraints placed upon leadership (Felfe & Petersen 2007; also Elgie 2018: 41; Haslam et al. 2011: 200–204).

Wren and Swatez provide a simple conceptual model for thinking about different levels of context that may constrain the leader. There is the *immediate context,* and this is the most obvious for political leaders – every day they wake up to various crises and problems they must deal with, events that have happened, or goals and agendas their government, party or movement are supposed to meet. *Contemporary context* is a little more removed, but important – what the economy is doing, what other political actors and institutions are doing, the rules of office (such as constitutions and laws), and other structures sit around the leader and immediately influence their choices and options. *Historical context* is the farthest removed, but still important – the political leader must contend with the weight of social, historical and ideological forces that are present in their society and shape what they can do (Wren & Swatez 1995; see Case 7.2).

These nested layers provide a starting point to think about how context might influence the ability of a political leader to actually lead. Consider the example of James Buchanan, who became President of the United States on the eve of the American Civil War in 1857. His immediate context was problematic – he was elected as a compromise candidate at the head of a party deeply conflicted on slavery. His goal was to preserve the Union, but his party and cabinet were divided on how to do it, and so Buchanan could not afford to move too far in either direction without risking losing many of his supporters. Yet the immediate context did not allow him to avoid the issue either – the Dred Scott case, fugitive slave laws, John

Brown's raid, and the Kansas-Nebraska crises during Buchanan's term forced the President to weigh in on the issue of slavery time and again. The next level of context – contemporary – was also crucial. The Supreme Court early in Buchanan's term had found limits to what the Federal Government could do to regulate slavery in US territories. The balance of power in US politics meant Buchanan had limited options for addressing the ruling or passing of new laws. Buchanan also had to share power with Congress, despite it being hopelessly deadlocked on slavery along regional lines. Moreover, the US political system in this time was structured such that even relatively small numbers of elected opponents could frustrate attempts to negotiate a settlement to the slavery issue. Economically, the South was poorer and dependent on slave labour whilst the North had become wealthy and industrialized, a state of affairs central to the political problem of slavery but not one that could be quickly solved by Buchanan. Historical context, the top band, was also vital. After all, the Civil War did not develop overnight, and the issues that led to it had been burning for almost a century. Ideas and public attitudes towards slavery and race had changed over the decades, whilst the South and North had culturally, economically, and socially diverged, making compromise and cohabitation increasingly difficult. Buchanan was one of the most experienced politicians of his generation, yet in this light we might appreciate how his choices, opportunities and actions were from the very beginning heavily constrained by institutional and historical context.

Ralph Stogdill, in his review of trait-based research into leadership (Chapter 6), concluded, as many others subsequently have, that the importance of context is so overwhelming that it cannot be ignored. "An adequate analysis of leadership involves not only a study of leaders, but also of situations" (Stogdill 1948: 65). This has led to the development of what some have termed the 'interactionist paradigm' of leadership scholarship, which accepts that the study of how leadership works must include both individual and contextual factors, and how they interact (Elgie 2018: 39).

Situational leadership models

Situational leadership models have become increasingly popular expressions of this interactionist paradigm. These models share the assumption that traits and personality by themselves do not predict an effective leader – effective leadership is about matching the right traits and style to specific situations, depending on what those situations demand.

Situational Leadership II (SLII) for example (Blanchard 1985; Blanchard et al. 1993) is a popular model used in business and organizational contexts that considers the nature of the leadership task when prescribing the skills required to lead. The model starts by considering the 'development level' of followers – do followers have (a) the skills and (b) the confidence or motivation to achieve their desired goals? It then matches leadership styles to those development levels. For example, highly motivated but poorly skilled followers require more hands-on management and a 'directive' style of leadership, whilst highly motivated and competent followers are better off with 'supportive' leaders who are happy to delegate rather than micromanage (Blanchard 1985; Northouse 2016: ch. 5).

Despite being created in a business context, this model has much relevance to politics. Think about the difference between a political movement trying to influence politics and a governing political party. Managing the former is often very challenging – followers are frequently very motivated initially but poorly organized and politically unskilled. Leaders need to be able to thoroughly coordinate and resource the movement if it is going to have any impact. Building a new movement requires giving it direction and structure so that enthusiasm can be converted into targeted political impact, but also inspiration and 'supportive' leadership to attract people to join. On the other hand, a government in power is usually composed of highly competent politicians and bureaucrats, and those leaders who try to micromanage and be overly 'directive', instead of delegating and supervising, will face resistance/resentment from their colleagues and be overwhelmed and bogged down in the minutiae of governing.

Another way of looking at the situational demands of leadership is to consider the nature of the specific tasks or problems being tackled. Fred Fiedler (1967) and Roland Heifetz (1994) both see key differences between 'structured' tasks (clear problems that have known solutions) and 'unstructured' tasks (unclear problems that have disputed or unknown solutions), with significant implications for how a leader can (or should) lead. Consider the difference again in politics. A well-structured problem could be a natural disaster – everyone recognizes immediately that there is a problem to be solved, and the key challenge is coordinating response efforts. Subsequently the best leader in such a circumstance is a director who will coordinate and manage from the front, offer comfort and solace to the public, allocate the right resources and experts, and pursue technical solutions. On the other hand, a problem like climate change is more unstructured. While there is widespread expert consensus that there is a problem, there are also very vocal interest groups and sections of the population who do not agree. And even amongst those who do agree there is a problem, there are disputes over the precise nature of the problem, who is responsible for the problem, what the best solution to the problem is, and how to implement it. The leader in this situation therefore needs instead to build consensus, negotiate with stakeholders, provide a vision and bring people together – an entirely different style of leadership and requiring quite different skills.

Some problems may be semi-structured, in that there is widespread agreement over the problem but less agreement over solutions. Consider the Global Financial Crisis of 2007–2008 – every politician knew there was a crisis and what had caused it, but what did that crisis mean? Was it a systemic problem that required wholesale reform of the financial system, or just a particularly bad bubble in the market requiring relief to those affected but no major reform? The diverging nature of these problems clearly highlights the need for different leadership styles depending on the task faced.

This need for adaptivity applies broadly across the different tasks of political leadership. For instance, getting legislation passed or a treaty signed is an act of negotiation, communication, patience and strategy, whilst running the executive branch and implementing laws are often more managerial, evaluative and consultative – very different leadership skills are likely to be required to excel in both. Fred Fiedler (1967) stipulates the importance of the power and authority of the leader. Leaders with lower reserves of both generally cannot maintain 'directive' styles of leadership to the same degree as those with high amounts of both. This dimension is highly relevant when considering political leadership, and it is commonly observed comparatively. Charismatic and individualistic leaders who rule with passion and single-mindedness can thrive in systems where authority and power are concentrated around the ruler. This style is unlikely to work though in a system where power is diffuse, and where negotiation, persuasion and inclusiveness are more important to maintain the consensus of stakeholders and other powerholders (see Case 4.1).

Robert House (1996) developed a synthesis of some of the above approaches, considering the nature of both followers and tasks. House sees the leader's job as guiding followers to choose the best paths to reach their goals, but the leader must adapt their leadership style to suit the needs and ideals of followers, compensate for the weaknesses of followers, and consider the task or goal that followers want to achieve (House 1996). For example, House's framework (Table 7.1) considers the preference of followers for both structure and affiliation. Do followers want to feel like they belong to a community and build social relationships, or are they happier following orders and living in a hierarchy? Do followers need to have their world structured and orderly? Do they want to have a say in how they are led? The answer to those questions will determine the kinds of leaders that are most likely to win the confidence of that group, satisfy their needs and address the task before them.

Leaders are not static in their leadership style, though, and can adapt to circumstances, and House's framework also allows us to think about the different styles that are applicable given changing tasks and groups of followers (House 1996). For example, campaign staff must engage in repetitive, unchallenging, and often mundane tasks – making thousands of calls, distributing election material, meeting voters and so on. Yet many get involved in political campaigns because they believe in their candidate and want to be more involved in civic life. Hence a good politician likely needs to be *supportive* as a leader with their staff and campaigners. This is entirely different to what they will require if they are elected and find themselves with a position in the party leadership, where *achievement oriented* leadership is more likely to be demanded, or if leading executive government where *participative leadership* is often expected in a group of peers and experts (Table 7.1).

Understanding the nature of followers and their specific needs is very much a function of what political leaders do, and why some succeed and some fail. Authoritarian leadership has been much studied from this perspective. In *The Origins of Totalitarianism,* Arendt suggests that social isolation and loneliness are follower characteristics that engender attraction to authoritarian leaders (Arendt 1973: 474–478). Feelings of uncertainty and helplessness, and a desire to feel special and secure, are other powerful drivers (Lipman-Blumen 2005: ch. 2). These characteristics are not created in

Table 7.1 Robert House's path-goal leadership style matrix

Follower characteristics	Task characteristics	Best-suited leadership style
Dogmatic, low-skilled, desiring structure and order, external locus of control	Ambiguous and complex tasks with unclear rules	**Directive leadership**, providing guidance and structure, and making clear the path to goals
Looks for support and empathy, highly capable, internal locus of control	Simple or structured tasks, repetitive and mundane, unchallenging	**Supportive leadership**, where the leader nurtures, attends to well-being and treats subordinates as equals
Want to be involved and inspired, internal locus of control, high ability and skill	Ambiguous and complex tasks with unclear rules	**Participative leadership**, where leaders consult, seek input, and act as chairperson rather than ruler
Want to succeed, external locus of control, high ability and expectations	May be simple or complex, structured or unstructured, mundane or novel	**Achievement leadership**, which creates high standards of excellence, seeks continuous improvement, provides framework to 'win'

Based on House (1996).

followers by leaders but are exploited by them to enable their own ends, and often with great effect during times of war and crisis, yet even in times of stability there will be disaffected groups vulnerable to such appeals. The Islamic State of Iraq and Syria (ISIS) during the 2010s attracted not only hundreds of thousands of followers from across the Middle East in the wake of the Iraq War and civil war in Syria, but also nearly 20,000 from otherwise stable states, with scholars citing isolation and ideology as the key motivators for the latter group, rather than the economic or political conditions in their countries (Klor & Benmelech 2018).

Examples, though, need not be so extreme. Different political parties in democracies are often characterized (particularly in multiparty systems) by different types of followers. Green and progressive left parties generally attract followers who privilege participative leadership that maintains the autonomy and grass roots involvement of party members – many Green parties subsequently have internally elected leaders with constrained authority and sometimes limited political experience, and collective leadership of such parties is common. This can create challenges as Green parties grow in popularity and their leaders must pivot from activism and community

Case 7.1 No man for all seasons

Lech Wałęsa

President of Poland, 1990–1995

Figure 7.1 Lech Wałęsa in 1991

In 1980, Lech Wałęsa and a group of trade unionists at the Lenin Shipyard of Gdansk founded Solidarność ('Solidarity'). It was the first trade union in Communist Poland not controlled by the communist party. Wałęsa would spend much of the next decade in a constant struggle against the ruling regime. He was imprisoned and harassed but maintained a strict policy of non-violent civil resistance. In the process, Wałęsa became a national hero, triggering a series of strikes and widespread societal resistance to the regime that led to the peaceful restoration of democracy and collapse of the one-party state in 1989.

Wałęsa's appeal as leader of the Polish anti-communist revolution was readily apparent – he was an ordinary working-man, the very type that was supposed to be served by a workers' state. He was plain-spoken, direct and clear in his opposition to the regime and able to articulate the problems and anger of millions of fellow Poles. He was brave and daring in resisting an oppressive government and willing to risk his own safety and freedom to do so, which emboldened others to join the cause. His openly Catholic faith appealed in a deeply religious nation where religion had been suppressed by the communist authorities. And Wałęsa's talent for leadership was obvious as he steered the movement – he was a masterful organizer of its underground resistance yet maintained the group's cohesion and prevented the outbreak of violence. He proved a canny negotiator and strategic campaigner, outfoxing his political opponents, and winning a string of public relations coups that made him a national and international hero (Dobbs et al. 2013: 86–125).

As the leader of the movement that successfully brought down the communist regime and brokered the return to democracy, it was only natural that Wałęsa would be the first post-Communist president of Poland, and he was elected as such with 75 per cent of the vote in 1990. Yet as president, Wałęsa was far less successful than he had been as leader of the resistance movement. His ordinary and plain-spoken manner could easily become vulgar and distasteful as president. His direct and confrontational style much lauded as a resistance leader came off as crass and rude in office, and he struggled to transition to the diplomacy and tact required to hold together a fragile new regime (Millard 2000). His lack of education and working-class background endeared him as a resistance leader yet was a major liability as president – Wałęsa struggled to master the complex policy landscape faced by a nation transitioning to a liberal democracy. He was manipulated by his advisers and proved an erratic decision maker on complex issues (Zubek 2007). On some fronts he struggled to differentiate between a social movement and a government – he was nepotistic and personalistic as president, often ignoring institutional norms and appointing unscrupulous or inappropriate friends and former allies into key positions. He stayed a fighter, intriguer and political strategist, but in government it led to frequent internal crises, interpersonal conflicts and instability amongst his team (Zubek 2007). Poland faced a painful transformation from a planned economy to a market economy as it opened to the West. Wałęsa was a stabilizing force in these difficult years, yet in most respects lacked the experience or expertise to ensure a smooth transition.

Wałęsa's popularity, astronomical in 1989, had collapsed by the end of his term as president – he lost re-election in 1995 and his party disappeared from Polish politics soon after. Wałęsa's influence had disappeared entirely by 2000, when in the presidential election of that year he polled just 1 per cent of the vote. Pivotal to the collapse of communism in Poland and its downfall throughout much of the Eastern Bloc, Wałęsa's leadership style and talents proved much better suited to leading a revolution than to leading a government (see also Lussier 2010).

organization to negotiation, policy development and even leadership within government (see Burchell 2002: ch. 5; van Haute 2016).

Political leadership and its effectiveness are thus inexorably linked with the context in which they operate and the followers they have. The mercurial nature of politics creates a wide array of potential contexts and followers (and hence required leadership styles and skills), and it is not uncommon to see successful 'teams' in political leadership, often pairings, where leaders with differing styles compensate for the weaknesses of the other. An example is provided by Francois Mitterrand and Pierre Mauroy, who served as President and Prime Minister of France respectively in the 1980s. Mitterrand was a charismatic, larger-than-life figure in French politics who sold a grand plan of socialist reform to the nation and reoriented French foreign policy, whilst Mauroy was a hardened trade-unionist and who hammered out domestic policy and legislation to make the vision happen, and this proved to be one of the most effective partnerships in modern French politics, even amidst a shifting economic paradigm (Morray 1997: ch. 7). Executive structures in many political systems are designed or intended to allow for multiple leadership roles, specialized leadership in policy portfolios, and shared power and authority across areas of decision-making. Semi-presidentialism in France prescribes a divided executive, which can lend itself to fruitful partnerships and contrasting capabilities and talents within the executive government.

Yet it can also create tension and rivalries. Building a leadership team that is diverse and multitalented enough to deal with any circumstance yet maintains its solidarity and support for the top leader, is a great challenge. Mitterrand frequently clashed with his prime ministerial partners, including with Mauroy, and despite policy successes their partnership fell apart after four years (Cole 1994: ch. 6). Often, it is just as tempting for political leaders to resist sharing power and attempt to be all things to all situations, impossible as that may be.

Political opportunity

We might take as a given then, that leadership effectiveness is at least partially determined by circumstance, and that good leadership outcomes occur when the right mix of leadership style, followers and circumstances comes together. But is the influence of context constant? Does every political leader, given the right skills, get the same opportunity to create change and lead effectively?

Some theorists have contended that there are hard limits on what is within the realms of possibility within a given period or context. For example, Joseph Overton describes the concept of the 'window of discourse', which states that although there is a theoretically long list of policy options that can be implemented for any problem (in Overton's examples, they range from totally statist to totally free-market), there is actually only a relatively narrow band of policy options that are politically acceptable, which are undergirded by the values that a society holds (Mackinac Center for Public Policy 2019). Even the most talented political leaders cannot shift social values singlehandedly. The United States' experiment with Prohibition is a prime example. The success of the Anti-Saloon League and Women's

Temperance Union in getting alcohol banned nationwide in 1920 was testament to one of the most sophisticated and effective political campaigns in American history, led by master strategist Wayne Wheeler. Yet the policy in implementation was a resounding failure and turned millions into lawbreakers, and even a Constitutional amendment could not change the underlying social values around freedom of choice that ordinary citizens held.

Sociologists studying political and social movements have used another phrase – *opportunity structure* – to describe the external circumstances that limit or empower collective actors. Studies of major political movements have found that even the best led movements require certain contextual factors to arise before the opportunity for success emerges. Commonly cited examples include shifting social and political alignments, division within the elites, or the development of new political alliances (McAdam, McCarthy & Zald 1996: 23–40; also Meyer 2004). Lech Wałęsa (Case 7.1) was not the first anti-communist activist to rise to prominence in Poland – there had been major uprisings in Poland in 1956 and 1970, and Wałęsa himself led the Solidarity movement for nearly a decade before a critical mass was reached. Wałęsa's success was predicated on deteriorating economic conditions and changing global politics, as well as emerging divisions within the ruling Communist elites across the Eastern Bloc, which critically weakened Communist regimes and pushed millions of Poles towards rebellion, creating an opportunity for Wałęsa's revolutionary leadership.

Adding to the complexity, however, is how political opportunity is *perceived*. Even with privileged access to information and expertise, it is far from easy as a political leader to accurately gauge what is happening around them and identify the best opportunities and strategies for action. Quite often vital warnings are missed, and contextual clues are misinterpreted. The Revolutions of 1848 in Europe were massive protest movements in the context of their day, but movement leaders misjudged the depth of their popular support and unity, and the strength of the absolutist regimes they were opposing. By contrast, the Arab Spring uprisings of 2010–2012 were underestimated by their opponents but rapidly and unexpectedly toppled several seemingly impregnable militarist regimes across the Middle East. Learning how to recognize political opportunity and timing action accordingly is thus an essential but infrequently discussed skill of political leadership (Tarrow 2011: 163–165).

John Kingdon in *Agendas, Alternatives and Public Policies* develops a model that highlights the role of opportunity, arguing that multiple streams of events (policies, problems and politics) are running concurrently in the contextual background and are often outside of the control of leadership. When these streams come into alignment, an 'opportunity window' opens, and only then does the political leader or 'policy entrepreneur' have a chance to make a major change (Kingdon 1995). However, such alignment is rare, and a leader willing to push the change when the opportunity arises is not always present when it occurs. Baumgartner and Jones provide some substantiation for this staccato model of change with their theory of *punctuated equilibrium,* demonstrating that public policy tends to be highly stable, with only occasional bursts of major change and reform. Despite every political leader promising change and reform in major policy areas, it seems only every so often do the right circumstances align such that they might be successful at doing so (Baumgartner & Jones 1993).

Evidence suggests that political leaders are aware of this dynamic and will try and exploit political opportunities to maximum effect when they arise. For example, in a study of successful tax increases (always politically unpopular but sometimes utterly necessary), one study found that they were usually timed by politicians to coincide with certain opportunities, such as a long period of time before the next election, the existence of a fiscal crisis or the adoption of a tax by another neighbouring jurisdiction (Berry & Berry 1992). Crises in particular can present opportunities for major shifts in policy and politics that aren't usually possible, and political leaders often seek to frame or even manipulate crises in such a way that can make this happen (see Boin et. al. 2008; 2009). A deft ability to interpret and exploit events to political advantage is often found in the stories of successful political leaders. King Chulalongkorn of Siam, a reformer who wished to rapidly Westernize his nation during the nineteenth century, faced entrenched opposition amongst the traditionalist elites and his own court. A seemingly innocuous fire that broke out in the royal palace in 1874, however, was used as an opportunity by the king to create a showdown with the nobility, and a pretext for outside intervention in his favour that saw many of his royal opponents weakened. Other threats and crises, including a war with France and rampant European colonialism in the region, were also used by Chulalongkorn to justify radical reforms of the military, political system and society, including the abolition of slavery (see also Case 7.2).

Political time

One theory that articulates how political leadership interacts with the historical and contextual constraints around it comes from Stephen Skowronek, who in *The Politics Presidents Make* (1997) sets out three temporal patterns that have affected how the US presidency has operated and its opportunities for creating change. The first is the *persistent pattern,* which is constant. The president is a paradoxical force in the US political system, because each president must simultaneously seek to uphold the political order, but also change and partially destroy it to solve problems and move the nation forward – to lead is to create, maintain and dismantle order all at the same time. The second is the *emergent pattern* which is linear – the office of the presidency has changed as a political institution amongst others, its powers have risen and fallen, and the way it operates in the twenty-first century is dramatically different from its eighteenth century origins.

The third pattern, the *recurrent pattern,* is the most complex but further reaching in its implications for understanding presidential action. Skowronek stipulates that the opportunity and warrant for presidents to remake the political order are different depending on the nature of the times in which they are leading. Skowronek contends that politics and policy operate in 'paradigms' – fairly stable sets of commitments, values, ideas and debates that dominate politics for a given period. For example, the period following the Great Depression in the United States (and in fact most Western nations) until the late 1970s was dominated by a Keynesian paradigm – a collection of economic and social ideas rooted in the work of economist John Maynard Keynes. Keynesian approaches to economics, budgets and public policy were the cornerstone of the New Deal in the United States and remained as an accepted foundation of much of what was done in the United States for decades afterwards, with both Republicans and Democrats generally working within the parameters of the paradigm.

Skowronek calls these paradigms 'regimes' and believes that their strength is crucial to understanding a leader's opportunity to create change. Popular, well-functioning regimes that provide effective solutions to public problems are not going to be easily defied by a leader. Weak, dysfunctional regimes on the other hand give greater than usual opportunity for a leader to challenge the political orthodoxy. And when a regime is in crisis, leaders are given huge warrants of power to change course and remake politics, and thus they have the greatest opportunity to create change. Democratic President Franklin Delano Roosevelt, for example, coming to power at the height of the Great Depression in 1933, was elected in a landslide by a public who were desperate for a solution to the crisis. Roosevelt's New Deal, which transitioned the United States towards a Keynesian policy orientation, was one of the most radical and far-reaching changes in American political history – changes achieved by Roosevelt in just his first term are far beyond what most presidents could expect to achieve in two.

How a president is positioned vis-à-vis the current regime is also crucial. Those who are allied with, and dependent on, the dominant regime as their basis of power will not be able to repudiate that regime, even if it is weak. Herbert Hoover, Franklin Roosevelt's Republican predecessor, was in office when the Great Depression hit, and was head of a party committed to the existing regime of neo-classical economic policy and small government. Hoover, despite understanding the magnitude of the problems Americans faced and even having laid some of the groundwork for Roosevelt's later policies, was not truly able to grasp the scale of change necessary. Nor was he able to convince the public he was committed to systemic change, or to convince his party (and thus his own base of political power and authority) to go along with these changes (Laing & McCaffrie 2017). Instead, it takes someone *opposed* to a weak regime to recreate it. The opportunity must be there though – brilliant reformers who are elected while regimes are strong are not going to get much accomplished and will constantly fight against the allies of the regime, having only weak mandates for change.

The combination of regime strength and presidential allegiance creates a 2 × 2 matrix of historical possibilities for presidential action (Table 7.2).

For Skowronek then, the opportunity for presidents to be great leaders is highly contingent on the historical moment. Most of America's 'greatest' and most respected leaders came as 'reconstructors' – regime opponents elected at a time when an old regime was collapsing. Andrew Jackson at the end of the Era of Good Feelings, Abraham Lincoln at the outbreak of the Civil War, Franklin Roosevelt during the Great Depression, Ronald Reagan during the decline of the Keynesian era and 'stagflation'. And importantly, they accomplished major change in these roles as president despite a wide variation in their political talents – perhaps even an averagely talented leader may seem 'great' when coming

Case 7.2 The tides of history

Cixi

Empress Dowager of China, 1861–1908

Figure 7.2 Dowager Cixi in 1900

Few figures in Chinese history have a legacy as fiercely debated as Cixi, who ruled the Qing Empire in its final decades. Though of humble status when selected as a concubine to the Xianfeng Emperor, Cixi gave birth to the dynasty's heir and became a shrewd political operator at court. When the emperor died during her son's childhood, Cixi manoeuvred to take power as regent in 1861. She relinquished the regency briefly in 1873 upon her son (Emperor Tongzhi) reaching an age of majority, but by 1875 she resumed power when the young emperor suddenly died, until his 4-year old cousin (Emperor Guangxu) could rule. Once again, in 1889 Cixi 'retired' in favour of her now grown nephew but continued to be a major power behind the throne. In 1898, the Guangxu emperor embarked upon the 100 Days of Reform, a radical program of change in the wake of China's humiliating defeat in the Sino-Japanese War, but the nobility and the court revolted and had the emperor placed under house arrest. Cixi was installed as ruler once more until her death in 1908.

The Qing Empire at its peak was one of the greatest empires in world history, however by the nineteenth century it was in terminal decline. When Cixi first assumed the regency in the 1860s, it was in the aftermath of the Taiping Rebellion, a massive civil war that had crippled the empire. Cixi and the court undertook the Self-Strengthening movement, designed to arrest the Qing Empire's decline through internal improvement and receptiveness to Western technology and military tactics, yet it failed to reform the moribund nobility or bureaucracy, and came amidst the crumbling of centralized power as local warlords with private armies increasingly represented the ultimate authority outside the capital (Rodzinski 2017: 182–194). Cixi's reign was marked by repeated skirmishes amongst the ruling elite between reformers and traditionalists, with prominent reformers ultimately losing out to conservative forces.

Cixi at many times in her reign acted as the agent of stability and tradition. She had repeatedly, and forcefully at points, intervened in political events (in alliance with the generally conservative Manchu nobility) to stem major reform movements such as the one initiated by her nephew. Yet Cixi was not blind to the problems of the nation, and late in her reign attempted to make reforms that went even further than those her deposed nephew had begun. The millennium-old imperial examinations system was finally abolished in 1905, ministers and students were sent abroad to study Western technology, and military training was professionalized. Constitutional and political reform began in earnest too after 1905.

However, like the Self-Strengthening movement, the impact was slow, limited and patchy as the elites of the regime and provincial warlords openly flouted the authority of the palace. The fragility of the regime's authority was revealed whichever way it tried to move – attempts to reform the army and develop the railroads incurred major resistance from conservative and nationalist forces, whilst constitutional and political change was not fast enough to satisfy reformers (Spence 1990: 249–256). Indeed, the context of her rule was profoundly disjunctive – the prevailing regime run by a traditional Confucian bureaucracy and Manchu nobility had outlived its ability to cope with new threats and could not adapt in the face of industrialization and colonialism. Yet as her own authority rested solely on that decaying structure, it was virtually impossible to repudiate that regime. In any case, her times were greatly driven by force of events now seen as far outside her control, such as foreign intervention by technologically superior opponents during the Boxer Rebellion, which spiralled out of control in the country late in her reign (Silbey 2012: 29–30; 52).

Cixi's historical place has genuinely perplexed scholars, who have ranged from seeing her as an obstinate traditionalist who thwarted reform and stopped at nothing to maintain her own power, to more recent histories, which have taken a more sympathetic tone (e.g. Chang 2013). Undoubtedly, her position was incredibly difficult – her legitimacy to rule was never very solid and she relied heavily on the conservative Manchu elites to maintain her power. She had recognized, and attempted, to implement reform, yet had seen all too well what had happened to those who gone too far too quickly. Some have argued that the continuation of the Qing regime at all beyond the calamity of the Taiping Rebellion in the 1860s was remarkable, and perhaps owes something to the great political skill of Cixi and her ability to find a path between the forces of tradition and the forces of reform (Rodzinski 2017: 182). However, if we can attribute such regime survival to Cixi's leadership, then it seems it was only delaying the inevitable, as the Qing regime collapsed entirely with the Xinhai Revolution within a few years of her death.

Table 7.2 Leader authority in political time

	Affiliated with regime	Opposed to regime
Strong regime	**Politics of affiliation** Average authority presidents who maintain regime commitments and espouse the political orthodoxy	**Politics of pre-emption** Opposed to a strong regime, they have variable authority but clash with context in trying to make change
Weak regime	**Politics of disjunction** Weak presidents with little authority, associated with a failing regime, no capacity to repudiate regime	**Politics of reconstruction** Opposed to a failing regime, they are given high authority to comprehensively reshape the political orthodoxy

Based on Skowronek (1997).

to power in times of reconstruction. By the same token, many talented presidents have existed in either 'preemption' or 'disjunction' and thus with limited contextual authority to enact the changes they've sought.

Skowronek's theory has been widely discussed and critiqued. However, it remains one of the more comprehensive ways to conceptualize how we might reconcile the role of leaders as individuals against the backdrop of context. In this case, regimes rise and fall with the sweep of history – they are the major shifts in society, ideology and the economy that no single leader can really control; and because of these shifts, some otherwise brilliant leaders are rendered helpless whilst modestly talented leaders find themselves with incredible warrants to remake politics. That said, most presidents are the affiliating type, operating in periods of relatively stable regimes, and as such they have much more scope to be differentiated on the basis of individual leadership qualities and presidential performance. Arguably, the recent presidencies of George W. Bush and Barack Obama are cases of affiliation, in that neither attempted major regime change but rather pursued change within the bounds of the orthodox neo-liberal framework that has continued since the 1980s. Yet they were obviously very different leaders in terms of their leadership styles, what they achieved in office, and how they're publicly remembered. Thus, perhaps in periods where the tides of history are calm, individual leadership traits are much more consequential.

Institutional analysis

Situations and historical context are not the only factors that work to constrain and shape the behaviour of political leaders. Political leaders also operate within an institutional environment. The boundaries of what is possible are governed both by formal institutions (constitutions, laws, systems of government, cabinets, legislatures) and informal institutions (conventions, mores and orthodoxies). In this sense, political leaders play 'roles' within an institutional setting, and those roles are subject to both formal rules and laws, and informal conventions and expectations. "Political actors organize themselves and act in accordance with rules and practices which are socially constructed, publicly known, anticipated, and accepted" (March & Olsen 2008: 7). Understanding political leadership thus requires us to understand the institutional settings in which it operates, and institutional analysis provides a variety of tools designed to elucidate the role institutions play in shaping how leaders behave.

Institutionalism

Traditional institutional analysis considers how the structures of political systems affect how leaders behave within them. As discussed previously (see Chapter 4), political systems vary enormously with regards to how they empower and constrain their leaders, and understanding those variations is critical to understanding how leaders behave within them. For instance, one of the great psychological motivations for any political leader is survival (see Chapter 6) – once you have achieved your position, you must fight to keep it, or the game is over. But *how* you survive and *who* determines if you survive depends on the rules and institutional settings around you.

One framework for understanding the role of institutional settings on the survival behaviour of politicians is provided by Bueno de Mesquita et al. in *The Logic of Political Survival* (2004). They nominate three groups that make up the 'selectorate' for a leader – the *nominal* selectorate (consisting of everyone who has a say in the choosing of a leader), the *real* selectorate (consisting of the influential few who have the greatest actual power in choosing the leader), and the *winning coalition* (the combinations of support will translate into taking and keeping power). A large selectorate but a small winning coalition is a characteristic of dictatorships, where a narrow *real* selectorate of military generals, businesspeople or bureaucrats exists. Leaders are incentivized towards rewarding their coalition through private goods – using the wealth of the state to keep their coalition happy to maintain power (see Chapter 4). A large selectorate and large winning coalition tend to be found in democracies, and thus leaders must reward voters with public goods through policy and budgets since it is no longer possible to individually reward enough people to stay in power (Bueno de Mesquita & Smith 2012).

Yet even within democracies, there are multiple 'selectorates' with differing rules and norms that greatly impact the choices political leaders have if they want to survive and implement their goals. Westminster systems, like Canada and Jamaica, have a prime minister (PM) who serves at the pleasure of their party. To survive, the PM must keep their party happy or risk being deposed, and thus in such systems the rules and structures by which leaders and their parties interact are of great importance (see Blais & Cross 2012). In presidential systems such as in the United States and Brazil, the president is directly elected, cannot be easily removed by any other institution and parties do not serve as a check on the behaviour in the same way as Westminster systems. In such systems, presidents "have little to fear from their own colleagues" (Samuels & Shugart 2010: 15), which gives license to very different behaviours (see Samuels & Shugart 2010: ch. 1–2). Institutional settings do evolve, though, and in doing so change how political leadership manifests. For instance, Canada's shift in recent decades from conventions of party delegates selecting leaders to direct election by the party membership has accordingly seen a shift in the types of candidates produced and the style of leadership practiced (Courtney 1995: 289–293). However, the impact institutional changes will have on leader behaviour is not necessarily easily to predict. For example, there has been a contemporary trend in democracies to widen the selectorates that choose party leaders, usually in the hopes of increasing public participation and the responsiveness of leaders to party supporters. Yet ironically, such institutional changes have generally increased the degree to which leader dominate their parties rather than the reverse (Schumacher & Giger 2017).

Various other institutional settings have been found to be relevant to explaining differences in political leadership across polities, such as the strength of judicial review of executive decisions, relative powers of the legislature versus the executive, party discipline and the leader's degree of control over the executive branch and bureaucracy (Helms 2005, 2014: 200–202). In consequence, it is observed that in Westminster systems, the leader tends to need to be more collegial, collective and diplomatic – after all, they must keep their colleagues satisfied to stay in power (Rhodes, Wanna & Weller 2009: ch. 4). Whilst in presidential systems "the institutional imperatives of the presidency lie on the side of independent political action" (Skowronek 1997: 49). This is much the same for legislative leaders, leaders of political movements and leaders of political parties – each institution has specific features and rules that will determine how leaders can or cannot act (see Helms 2012: ch. 1–4; 2014).

However, emphasis on institutional rules and structures must be balanced with the acknowledgement that individual leaders can and do have the capacity to bend these to their own designs from time to time. *Actor-centred institutionalism* (Scharpf 1997), for example, places more emphasis on the power actors have to structure their environment around them. After all, political leaders are dynamic and creative, and continually find new ways to use institutional settings to their advantage, or to reshape them to suit their own ends. Deng Xiaoping, serving as paramount leader of China throughout the 1980s, achieved far-reaching economic and social reforms, yet did so without holding any of the top institutional leadership positions. He often bypassed the traditional top-down control of Chinese policymaking by quietly allowing local policy experimentation and then supporting wider adoption if experiments successful. Even after retiring, he embarked on an influential but unorthodox 1992 southern tour of China, building support for continued economic and political reform, yet doing so outside the normal institutional channels.

Path dependence

Moving beyond the rules and structures of politics, historical institutionalism (Hall & Taylor 1996) can help us understand how time and history empower or constrain leaders. Political leaders do not come to office with a blank slate. They inherit a vast legacy of decisions and policies from their predecessors, which over time citizens, businesses, governments and other organizations have become accustomed. Much as they might like to, political leaders cannot simply undo what was done in the past, and their own options for action may be greatly constrained as a result (Rose & Davies 1994). This concept is known as *path dependency*. Choices political leaders make in the past are often increasingly difficult to deviate from as time goes on (Pierson 2004: ch. 1). For example, in 2009 US President Barack Obama passed the Affordable Care Act (ACA), a comprehensive overhaul of the American healthcare system that proved highly controversial and was vehemently opposed by Republicans at every successive election. When Republicans finally had a majority in both chambers of the legislature and a Republican president in 2017, attempts to overturn the reforms failed. Within less than a decade, the new system had become entrenched: public opinion had warmed towards the reforms, health insurers and providers had adjusted to the system, as had state governments, and the public – happily or grudgingly – were using the new system. Repealing the changes was by 2017 considered a radical step as the ACA had gone from highly controversial to business-as-usual.

Path dependency is not destiny, however. Firstly, given the sheer scale of modern government, leaders cannot possibly review the great majority of laws, policies or processes they inherit when they take office. Much will carry on the same with a new leader as it had with the previous, leaving leaders instead to focus efforts on the most problematic areas where there are opportunities for change. And secondly, leaders have multiple strategies for pursuing policy change even within a dense institutional environment, including (Streeck & Thelen 2005: ch. 1; Mahoney & Thelen 2010):

- *displacement*, when existing rules are removed and new ones are introduced.
- *layering*, when existing institutions or rules are not replaced but new ones are added over the top of them..
- *conversion*, where pre-existing institutions or rules are interpreted and implemented in new ways.
- *drift*, when changes in external conditions leads to policies, rules or institutions having a different effect than was originally intended.

In a complex area such as the US healthcare system, this can be readily seen, as most presidents have been unable to generate the political consensus for wholesale reform. Instead, a complex patchwork of laws and rules have been layered on top of old ones, while pre-existing laws and rules have been differently enforced and in some cases have drifted some way from their original intent – strategy for change that might have been predicted by Mahoney and Thelen due to the strength of veto players in this policy subsystem (2010: 18–22; see also Case 7.3).

Case 7.3 Leading under constraint

János Kádár

General Secretary and Prime Minister of Hungary, 1956–1988

Figure 7.3 János Kádár in 1962

János Kádár was a political survivor. Born to a poor single mother in the last years of the Austro-Hungarian empire, Kádár became a typewriter mechanic and then Communist organizer during Hungary's Great Depression, and then a member of the underground resistance during World War II. Arrested and purged at several points during his early career, Kádár managed to survive and ultimately thrive within the post-war Hungarian Communist Party.

Kádár was installed as leader of Hungary by the Soviet Union in the wake of the 1956 Hungarian Uprising, during which Prime Minister Imre Nagy had attempted sweeping reforms and withdrawal from the Soviet-dominated Warsaw Pact. Nagy's regime was brutally removed by a Soviet-led invasion.

Kádár faced an extremely constrained leadership position for most of his reign. The Soviet Union would not countenance significant deviation from the policies set in Moscow and had now demonstrated its willingness to use devastating force against those out of line.

Yet, throughout most of his rule, Kádár attempted to exploit his limited institutional opportunities to deliver material improvements in Hungary. Although he faithfully carried out the draconic punishments demanded by the Soviets against the participants of the '56 uprising – actions that would weigh on his conscience until the end of his life (Powers 1989) – Kádár bided his time, faithfully following orders on the surface whilst building up political credit to introduce piecemeal reforms. Over time, restrictions and oppression were softened, and various freedoms afforded that were exceedingly rare in other Communist nations. Kádár slowly built up trust with Soviet authorities until he was able to announce a general amnesty for the great majority of political prisoners in 1963 (Gough 2006: 141–143). In 1968, Kádár argued stridently against the Warsaw Pact intervention in reformist Czechoslovakia, and yet when unable to change the course of events, committed Hungary to join in the intervention rather than risk his own regime being the next target of suspicion (Gough 2006: 166–169).

Other notable deviations occurred in economic policy. On the surface, Kádár was careful never to stray far from orthodox Communism, emphasizing constantly the need for political and economic continuity across the Eastern Bloc (Gough 2006: 152–153). Yet beneath the surface, Kádár adopted several strategies to reform economic policy. ***Drift*** was common – Kádár would allow the reality 'on the ground' to deviate from official policy as farmers and businesses found ways to improve local conditions through bypassing inefficient economic controls (e.g. Gough 2006: 132).

Conversion was another tactic adopted by Kádár. Although a committed Communist himself and surrounded by a Hungarian Central Committee that was frequently very conservative and anti-reform, Kádár nonetheless found ways to reinterpret the orthodoxy to support moderate change. The New Economic Mechanism (NEM) of 1968 was the most significant development, which allowed a degree of private enterprise and decentralized planning to return to the Hungarian economy (Swain 1992: 99–113). Gradually other changes were introduced as well – greater interaction with the West, the encouragement of Western tourism, a much stronger focus on the production of consumer goods and agricultural products within the Hungarian economy (rather than the Warsaw Pact preference for heavy industry), and an improved human rights record. Collectively, these reforms became known as 'Goulash Communism' – a somewhat more liberal and consumer-orientated variant that allowed for a standard of living and level of personal freedom that was relatively higher than the rest of the Eastern Bloc (Benczes 2016).

Kádár would tread a fine line and avoided the fate of his predecessor, achieving in some measure the reforms that Nagy attempted in 1956 over a much longer timeframe. Yet Kádár's relative liberalism and reforms were not enough to overcome the major challenges all Eastern Bloc economies faced in the 1980s, nor did the regime depart too far from its fundamentally authoritarian nature. There were significant achievements by the Kádár regime, but not enough to placate the demand for democracy and major economic reform that brought down Hungary and her communist neighbours in 1989 (see Swain 1992).

Kádár's legacy is challenging to assess, and like many Eastern Bloc leaders he was responsible for numerous acts of oppression and state-sanctioned violence. However, as West German Chancellor Willy Brandt once commented, "he did the best possible, given his knowledge of the realities as they were then" (Gough 2006: 250). Kádár on at least some level managed to navigate an extremely constrained institutional environment and shield Hungary from the very worst seen elsewhere in the Eastern Bloc. And indeed, this is seemingly his legacy in popular memory post-1989, as large majorities of polled Hungarians continue to hold Kádár in high regard (Gough 2006: 254–255). Kádár choose the following inscription for his tombstone: "I was where I had to be, I did what I had to do."

Jawaharlal Nehru, Prime Minister of India from 1947 to 1964, provides a simple reconciliation of the opposing forces of context and leadership. "Life is like a game of cards. The hand you are dealt is determinism; the way you play it is free will" (Moodian 2008: 30). Historical circumstance and institutional context provide leaders a hand of cards with which to lead. Some hands will virtually determine the outcome – even the most skilled poker players cannot win every hand, and even the most unskilled can win if dealt a royal flush. Yet most hands are middling, and a good player knows how to bluff, stand and fold to turn even a poor hand into a victory. Though a simplistic analogy, sometimes the complexity and intensity of contextual, situational and institutional theories make leadership outcomes appear more pre-determined than they really are. Leaders do have choices and frequently manage to buck the constraints of context and pull off the unexpected.

Thomas Aquinas, in *Summa Theologica* (1485/1920), describes prudence as the ability to make the right judgments on how to act in specific situations. Of the aspects of prudence, Aquinas describes important skills such as *sollertia* (an ability to quickly assess your context), *providentia* (foresight and the ability to connect goals with action), *circumspection* (ability to take all relevant circumstances into account), and *memoria* (accurate memory of past experiences and an ability to learn from them). Many of these skills are integral to 'contextual intelligence' (Nye 2008: ch. 4) and working effectively within a leadership environment that is inevitably constrained. As one scholar notes, effective leadership is not beholden to structures, but rather about 'structuring the world so you can win' (Riker 1986: ix).

Chapter Summary

- The immediate, contemporary and historical contexts all act upon a political leader and work to enable or constrain their leadership. There is ongoing debate over the degree to which leaders and individuals shape history.
- Situational Leadership theories, like SLII and Path-Goal Theory, demonstrate how different leadership styles, traits and approaches are required by different circumstances, and there is no leadership style that will suit all occasions or please all types of followers.
- Leaders do not get a free hand to remake the world around them. Political opportunity is key, and leaders must be able to recognize and exploit them to be effective. Opportunity windows are a confluence of contextual factors, most of which are not within the control of leaders, but they may help to create them.
    - The theory of political time proposes that large-scale historical, economic and social processes are strong determinants of the amount of authority individual political leaders will have in any given period, and these are far outside the control of leaders.

- Institutional analysis also places emphasis on the rules and systems leaders operate within as critical to understanding their behaviour. Political leaders are incentivized to pursue certain actions based on the institutional environment. However, leaders do have some capacity to attempt to bend or manipulate these institutions to their own design.
- Path dependence shows that 'history matters' and leaders do not begin with a blank slate. A leader's policies and actions are pursued in the context of a long history of prior actions by other leaders which limit their choices. However, leaders do have viable strategies for handling a dense institutional environment.

8 DECISIONS, POLICY AND ADVICE

Chapter Outline

- What is the governing role and why does it form the core of what political leaders do? How do political leaders vary in their approach to that role?
- How rational is the decision-making process, and how do limits to rationality impact political decision-making?
- What is the core executive and how do leaders govern through it?
- How does collective decision-making differ? What are some of the challenges unique to it within government?
- How do leaders influence the policymaking process and the decisions it makes? How much control do they really have in the end?

US president Harry S. Truman kept a plaque on his White House desk that bore the phrase 'the buck stops here'. Truman is describing the core task of political leaders: they are responsible for making decisions, setting goals, implementing policies, allocating resources and coordinating government (Elcock 2001: 105). Making decisions and policies that advance the needs and aspirations of the group is at the heart of what we expect our political leaders to do, and we hold them accountable for their decisions and if those needs and aspirations aren't met.

Such responsibility is a heavy burden. Declarations of war, international trade deals or even the legalization of a pharmaceutical product are the kinds of decisions that may affect the lives of millions of people. And yet to make these decisions, political leaders must overcome numerous limitations, both cognitive and structural, to the decision-making process and find effective courses to pursue amongst limitless choices. They must coordinate the operations of large, sprawling governments and bureaucracies to carry-out those choices. And they must be able to do so facing significant constraints on time, resources and authority.

The governing role

At the most basic level, political leadership exists so that there is a decision-making structure to resolve disputes, allocate scarce resources and coordinate the operations of a community. Anthropological studies (see Chapter 5) have long established that having such structures greatly enhance the stability and prosperity of a community. Modern governments are sprawling evolutions of these original decision-making machines, now charged with decision-making on a mass-scale, resolving disputes, allocating resources and coordinating the operations of communities with millions or even billions of members.

For the contemporary political leader, it is humanly impossible to oversee any but the tiniest fraction of government operations. The President of Gabon, sitting in Libreville, is unlikely to be aware (absent a major scandal) of how farm subsidies are being allocated in Ngounié Province, how mine safety disputes are being resolved in the Haut-Ogooué, or how airport schedules are being determined in Tchibanga.

Instead, political leaders set the goals for whey want to achieve, and formulate guidelines, create programs and allocate resources to achieve those goals. It is then the job of bureaucracies and elites further down the chain to implement the decisions within their areas of specialty or localities. The broader term used to encapsulate what political leaders and their governments do, or intend to do, in this way is 'policy'. This is an important development in political leadership – as communities and their governments become larger, leaders become more distant from the on-the-ground reality.

Our President of Gabon may have been elected with a goal of improve the quality of healthcare across the country. Yet consider some of the most basic challenges they face in trying to make decisions and policies that will achieve this goal:

- **What should we be aiming for?** Where do you start? What problems need to be solved to improve Gabonese healthcare? In a large country like Gabon, there might be some obvious national issues, but every community will have its own unique struggles with health.
- **What are the options?** The president of Gabon is a politician, not an expert on health policy. Without a depth of knowledge and experience in this area, how do leaders come up with policies that are going to effectively solve those problems and improve conditions?
- **Can you account for everyone?** There are thousands of healthcare workers, clinics and hospitals treating uncountable conditions for millions of patients. How can policy be crafted that will account for all innumerable variations and local conditions across a large country?

Case 8.1 Deciding by not deciding

Golda Meir

Prime Minister of Israel, 1969–1974

Figure 8.1 Golda Meir in 1973

Although much of the emphasis is on studying decisions that are made, sometimes it is the decisions that are ***not made*** that are just as important. Because political leaders have the final responsibility to determine policy, both as it is written and as it is practiced, 'deciding not to decide' can sometimes be just as powerful as an overt decision.

This concept has been applied to the actions of Israeli leaders with regards to the occupied territories. Obtained after the 1967 Six Day War, Israel quickly faced a major decision over how the new territories were to be administered, particularly the legitimacy of new villages that were being established by Israeli settlers in newly occupied areas. A variety of views emerged within the Israeli government, the ruling Israeli Labor Party, and across broader society. Conflicting views over the proper handling of the territories were the subject of political debate for some years.

Coming to power in 1969, Golda Meir soon gained a reputation amongst her people as the strong-willed 'Iron Lady', a fearless and unapologetic defender of Israel. Domestically and internationally she was greatly, if not sometimes begrudgingly, respected for her decisiveness and clarity of purpose. Yet she faced a political maelstrom over the issue of the occupied territories, which came to a critical point during her administration. Meir's position was a difficult one. On the one hand, Meir was not a supporter of annexing the occupied territories to Israel and saw them as a bargaining chip – something to hold onto and exchange back to the Arab world in exchange for peace (Burkett 2008: 300; Klagsbrun 2019: 512). Yet on the other hand, events were increasingly taking the situation beyond government control. Israeli settlers began to pour into the occupied Palestinian territories and were building settlements regardless of government policy. Meir used the military to restrain some settlers, but even minor cases of doing so proved politically explosive, as many Israelis, and members of her own party, saw annexation of the occupied territories and expansion of Israel's holdings and population as the best means to safeguard the nation against a coterie of hostile neighbours (Ranta 2015).

Ultimately, Meir avoided confronting the issue directly, and no long-term decisions about the status of the territories, or the new Israeli settlements within, were concluded. Wishing to maintain her party's unity and believing time was on Israel's side with regard to establishing the long-term status of the territories, Meir's 'non-decisions' pragmatically delayed resolving this thorny issue (Burkett 2008: 293–300, 351–353).

Yet by strategically avoiding making big decisions on the issue, these 'non-decisions' themselves eventually created the government's policy, which ultimately constituted a neutrality allowing Israeli settlements to continue without official sanction. Moreover, the lack of authoritative decision-making by the prime minister on the issue gave an opening for other political leaders to promote their own perspectives and plans for the region. Though not Meir's stated intention, the lack of a decision effectively became a de facto decision that was increasingly difficult to reverse as time wore on, as unsanctioned Israeli settlements swelled in the West Bank and created a situation much harder for future governments to resolve peacefully (Ranta 2015; see also Gorenberg 2007).

- **How do you make it happen?** The President cannot directly enforce their policies in every jurisdiction – they will rely on a large sprawling bureaucracy to do so. The policy has to be flexible enough so that it can be adjusted by local officials to suit local conditions, and yet be strong enough so that real change occurs.
- **How do you know it worked?** Where does feedback come from? The President cannot personally visit every hospital, doctor's office or patient to see if their decisions worked out – so how do they evaluate their policies?

This thought experiment highlights the challenge of modern political leadership – while it exists to make decisions and administer policies on critically important issues that affect everyone, it does so in an environment often quite removed from on-the-ground realities, and the relationship between a decision or policy made by a political leader, and what is experienced by a citizen, can be a very indirect one. Running a government then is not like commanding a battalion, and hence we cannot think of political decision-making in quite the same way either. As Harry S. Truman, who opened our chapter, once famously said of his successor in the office, General Dwight D. Eisenhower: "He'll sit here, and he'll say, 'Do this! Do that! And nothing will happen. Poor Ike – it won't be a bit like the Army. He'll find it very frustrating" (Nelson 2015: 472).

Yet because they represent the apex of political authority, the decisions leaders make, or even the decisions they do not make (see Case 8.1), have profound ramifications on the issues of the day. Consequently, understanding how leaders think and make judgments as individuals as well as the broader structures through which they collect evidence, consider advice, and develop policy; is central to understanding how political leadership operates.

Making decisions

Decision-making is a process, done individually or collectively, in which a course of action is chosen from available alternatives. There are many theoretical models used to explain the process, but most have similar elements within them and broadly agree on five basic stages:

1. Identifying problems or establishing goals
2. Generating options or alternatives
3. Searching for information to make a judgment
4. Making the best choice based on the evidence
5. Implementing that choice and evaluating the effects.

Policymaking, which describes the broader process of how governments decide what to do, may involve many individual decisions made by different political leaders. But these processes are often described in much the same way and involve similar stages to that of individual decision-making. The *stages heuristic* used to explore the policymaking process revolves around a similar five-step cycle of:

1. **Agenda-setting**: identifying problems and setting goals.
2. **Policy formulation**: collecting information and evidence, establishing. what the available policy options are.
3. **Decision-making**: choosing the policy to follow.
4. **Implementation**: enacting that policy into reality.
5. **Evaluation**: seeing how well the policy worked.

These five basic stages can be found in most models and they have become the conventional way to describe the policy process (Jann & Weigrich 2017), though some models try to break down these stages into smaller sub-processes (see Howlett & Ramesh 2003).

In trying to simplify something complex, the stages heuristic may give a misleading sense of orderliness. It's readily observable that decision-making and policymaking are not unidirectional processes, and sometimes stages are repeated, pursued in a different order, or skipped altogether. Sometimes developing and evaluating the options provide undesirable choices, and decision-makers will go back to information-gathering to see if they can find more options. Problem diagnosis, or even recognition, may change as situations evolve or new evidence appears. Some problems and policy conflicts are continuous, and so the cycle never really ends (Sabatier 2007: 6–7). Thinking about decisions and policy as progressing through stages is just a starting point for understanding something that is much more chaotic.

Rationality and its limits

So how do political leaders proceed through this process? The most established model of how decision-makers proceed is expressed in the *rational choice model.* The starting point for this model is *homo economicus* – economic man – who seeks to extract the maximum utility from his or her environment, subject to the rules of their institutional surroundings. An individual's strategy hinges on his or her valuation of costs and benefits associated with anticipated outcomes, and accordingly they can establish preferred courses of action. In earlier applications the concept of rational utility was relatively narrow (generally focusing on economic rewards or costs) but has expanded over time to include other types of motivations (Persky 1995: 223–226).

If we take this assumption, then, that decision-making is foremost a rational balancing act of anticipated costs and benefits, the decision-maker thus needs the following information:

1. What are my possible courses of action?
2. What are the events that might follow from these actions?
3. What is the likelihood of each event?
4. What is the value of each event to me?

With this knowledge in hand, any decision-maker theoretically has what they need to make the best choice, though not everyone will necessarily make the same choice since the estimation of value or utility from certain outcomes will vary between individuals (Connolly et al. 2003: 4–7).

But is this how it happens in reality? There have been many criticisms of the rational choice assumption. Deborah Stone in *Policy Paradox* (2012) argues that rational choice models will never properly account for political life because so much of it is fundamentally incoherent, chaotic, paradoxical and vague. For example, political leaders have many goals that conflict with each other – on the one hand, they want to win election or stay in power and advance their careers, yet on the other they usually have strong ideological beliefs they want to see codified into policy. When these goals come into conflict, political leaders face quandaries that aren't easily resolved through purely rational estimation of utility.

Herbert Simon, in *Administrative Behaviour* (1997), thus notes that although rationality is a starting point for decision-making, in practice our rationality is compromised because of contextual limitations. Simon outlined a theory of *bounded rationality*, offering three main reasons why policy and decision-making falls short of rational expectations:

1. Rationality requires a complete knowledge and anticipation of the consequences that will follow from each choice. In fact, knowledge of consequences is always fragmentary.
2. Since these consequences lie in the future, imagination must supply the lack of experienced feeling in attaching value to them. But values can be only imperfectly anticipated.
3. Rationality requires a choice among all possible options. In actuality, only a very few of all the possible alternatives ever come to mind (Simon 1947/1997: ch. 5).

From Simon's work came a plethora of other studies of decision-making in political and policy contexts, and a great deal of other limitations on rational decision-making have been studied, which have opened new doors to understanding how political decision-making works in practice. We can see some of the prominent limitations in how decision-makers obtain information, process information, calculate risk and handle emotion.

Obtaining information

In order to make an informed rational choice, a political leader should have all the relevant information available before they make a judgment, at least in theory (Cartwright & Hardie 2012).

Yet in practice, there are hard limits on the ability to obtain information. Simon offers a clear example: consider the distribution of resources for a city fire department. To make the most accurate distribution of firefighting resources, the fire marshal would need to know probabilities of fire and the logistics of fighting fire in every single district, even every single structure, within a city. Even if it were theoretically possible to gather this information, the process would cost a fortune and likely take many years, and the database would need near-constant updating as buildings changed. Yet the danger of fire is ever-present and fire departments cannot wait for the perfect data to arrive before distributing critical firefighting resources, so they must use approximations and whatever data they can get in a short period of time to make allocation decisions, imperfect as they will be (Simon 1997: 94–97).

Democratic politics is particularly prone to this problem, as the constant cycle of polling and relatively short electoral timeframes places enormous pressure on political leaders to get results and deliver on promises to voters quickly, or risk losing the faith of voters. Time pressure and stress lower the quality of decision-making overall, with information searches usually becoming more limited and cursory (see Svenson & Maule 1993).

Further complications present when there is genuine ambiguity, or where information is functionally unknowable or unobtainable. Leaders making foreign policy decisions involving North Korea, for example, have very limited reliable knowledge of that state's intentions, capabilities or attitudes, meaning that any policy is often based on educated guesswork.

Processing information

After information is obtained, there are significant limitations on the decision-maker processing it. James March offers four examples:

1. **Attention**: there are limitless potential issues that need attention from a political leader, but only a limited number that can be dealt with at any one time. And the problems that end up getting attention are not always the ones that most need it.

2. **Memory**: leaders do not possess perfect memories of what has occurred before and hence learning is always partial and incomplete. New governments take the place of old and often end up making the same mistakes as their predecessors.

3. **Comprehension**: leaders are fed huge amounts of information and data, but humans are not supercomputers, and we can only process a limited amount at any given time. Moreover, much of the information we are given is of uncertain relevance to solving a problem, so leaders do not always know what information to privilege in making a decision, and what to discard as background noise.

4. **Communication**: experts have trouble communicating and translating between their fields of specialty. Even if a political leader or policymaker has relevant scientific data to help make a decision, will they understand it sufficiently given limited personal expertise? (March 1994: 10–11)

Ahmed Ben Bella, who was the first President of Algeria after it gained full independence from France in 1963, chaired a government that was immediately presented with an inexhaustible supply of complex issues, all of which demanded immediate attention – recovery from the war, land and agricultural reform, water supply, unemployment, industrial development, establishing new relationships with other nations and so on. Each of these issues on its own would require years of study and experience to master. Yet Bella and his cabinet were novices in government. Most of the bureaucracy were Europeans who departed after independence, taking their collective administrative memory with them, leaving few to advise and assist the new government. Indeed, there remained not even enough trained typists to prepare reports or operators to run the telephone exchange (Ottaway & Ottaway 1970: 9–26). In such circumstances, there are clearly severe limits on the ability to collect and process information, and despite good intentions and great ambitions to rationally reform the country, post-independence government in Algeria's early years was understandably characterized by improvised and sometimes naïve policy-making (Stone 1997: 43–57).

Human limitations on information processing have given rise to the study of *heuristics* and *biases* – mental shortcuts that people make when considering information in order to make a decision quickly and in the absence of complete information, a mental mechanism likely necessary for our survival in an evolutionary context but potentially problematic in our modern world (Kahneman, Slovic & Tversky 1982). Some prominent examples include:

- **Availability and familiarity heuristics:** Decisions are heavily influenced by the examples or information that first come to mind. Research has found that when faced with complex, new or confusing situations, decision-makers tend to be strongly guided by examples or historical analogies that appear similar and provide some experiential guidance, even though there is often no clear correlation between circumstances (May 1975; Vis 2019).
- **Confirmation bias:** There is a pervasive tendency for people to interpret new information, or search for new information, in such a way that will support their preconceived ideas or notions. This is particularly true in politics, where strongly held political ideologies and partisan identification tend to the colour our ability to impartially assess new information (Lodge & Taber 2005). Humans are generally averse to admitting error or changing their minds. In the face of evidence that might undermine our decisions or positions, we often try and interpret the evidence in such a way that supports our original decision or position. Or we simply reject or ignore the evidence outright (Nickerson 1998). "People see what they want to see—information that provides a convenient rationalization for their underlying political interests and that minimizes their emotional discomfort" (Levy 2018: 180).
- **Self-serving bias***:* When analysing our own decisions, we tend to see positive outcomes as the result of our own clever efforts or brilliance, whilst negative outcomes we tend to blame on other people, situational factors or just bad luck (Dobbins & Russell 1986). While helpful for maintaining personal self-esteem, this bias can have disastrous impacts in politics, preventing leaders from recognizing their mistakes.

These and many other biases are at work in our minds all the time and seeing through them is not always easy. They can be readily appreciated as influencing decision-making behaviour even in the most consequential decisions (see Case 8.2).

Risk and probability

To make an informed decision, political leaders must weigh up the consequences of various courses of action, and the risks associated with each. Because the future is unknowable, at best the impact of a policy or political decision can only be predicted. A rational choice model of decision-making would assume that political decision-makers are good at this.

However, cognitive research has shown that people generally make decisions based on a distorted perception of risk and probability. Amos Tversky and Dan Kahneman developed *prospect theory* based on their research, which demonstrates that people are generally risk averse when they are in a good position but are more willing to take gambles when they're not (Kahneman & Tversky 1979). In other words, the more you have to lose, the more risk-averse you are, and vice-versa.

However, people are generally *loss averse* as well, meaning that fear of losses is more powerful in motivating a decision than the possibility of gains (Quattrone & Tversky 1988). This can be seen in the 'negativity bias' in politics – voters tend to be more sensitive to potential losses from a policy than they are to potential gains (Weaver 1986). Hence avoiding bad outcomes, or at least the blame for them, can be very useful in explaining political decision-making. "Because costs and benefits are perceived asymmetrically, policymakers fear that new policies will not win them as much support as dismantling the old ones will lose" (Weaver 1986: 394).

Such theories can be used to explain why, for example, politicians avoid reforming popular policies or making hard choices in times of relative stability (e.g. Vis & van Kersbergen 2007), yet may be attracted to bolder and riskier action when facing a crisis or electoral oblivion (e.g. Weyland 1996; also Case 8.2).

Emotion and hubris

Political judgements are influenced by emotion at every level, and most political issues elicit emotive responses (Marcus et al. 2000; Taber & Lodge 2006). Yet emotions are not easily studied because they often influence decision-making subconsciously, making their role hard to isolate and their impact hard to control for (Marcus 2000: 231).

Emotion is not necessarily antithetical to effective decision-making. For example, caring about the impact a decision has on others can motivate ethical judgments (Houghton 2015: 151–154), and sociopathic political leaders who eschew emotion in favour of ruthless maximization of gain have been some of the most terrifying dictators in history. Nevertheless, its impact can be profound and ultimately unpredictable, as emotional responses are rooted in personal history and thus unique to the individual.

Depression is not an uncommon trait amongst political leaders, yet it is clearly linked with poorer decision-making and cognitive function (Murphy et al. 2001). Fear and anxiety, such as might be stimulated by a crisis, alter cognitive processing as well, heightening learning and awareness but also changing the way we judge risk and available options (Houghton 2015: 153–154). Fear when faced with new or unclear risks is a tool of survival in

Case 8.2 How bad decisions become history

Anthony Eden

Prime Minister of the United Kingdom, 1955–1957

Guy Mollet

Prime Minister of France, 1956–1957

Figure 8.2 Anthony Eden

Figure 8.3 Guy Mollet

Emotions and hubris, heuristics and biases, and limits on information collection and processing, can all be seen in the disastrous decisions made by British and French leadership during the Suez Crisis (Brady 1997). In 1956 President Gamal Abdel Nasser of Egypt announced a bold but popular decision to seize control of the Suez Canal, one of the world's most important waterways and of vital strategic interest to Britain and France, who jointly operated the canal and relied upon it to maintain their global empires. In response, British Prime Minister Anthony Eden and French Prime Minister Guy Mollet hatched a secret plan to invade Egypt and retake the canal, and potentially topple the Nasser regime at the same time. In October 1956, in a secret agreement with Israel, Britain and France invaded Egypt, but within just 9 days, despite complete military success, Britain and France were forced by intense international and domestic condemnation to abandon the plan and withdraw.

Britain and France were humiliated, and both leaders lost their careers. The fallout of the crisis was profound, and the invasion ultimately precipitated the final collapse of the French and British Empires, as well as doing irreparable harm to their international reputations. So how did these two leaders decide upon such a disastrous course of action? Common cognitive biases and decision-making limitations provide some important insight.

Availability and familiarity heuristics: Nasser was an entirely new breed of politician on the world stage and neither Eden nor Mollet understood him or the movement he represented. Coming just a decade after World War II, both applied analogical thinking, and saw Nasser as another Hitler, and the Suez seizure as similar to Hitler's annexation of Austria and Czechoslovakia, which had not been challenged in the 1930s by Britain or France but had proven a disastrous miscalculation of Hitler's expansionist ambitions.

Confirmation bias: Critically important to the Anglo-French plan was the support of the United States. Eden and Mollet assumed that the 'special relationship' between the United States and United Kingdom, as well as American interests in the Middle East, would deter them from opposing an invasion. Yet Nasser's actions and the status of the Suez were not interpreted the same way by other countries. Indeed, the United States made it clear at several points in the lead-up to the invasion that it did not support military action over the canal. Yet Eden and Mollet ignored the warnings and selectively interpreted US communications as supporting their original assumptions, a mistake with enormous consequences (McDermott 2001: ch. 6).

Collecting and **processing information** presented further limitations. Both Eden and Mollet had a limited time frame for action, knowing that the longer they waited the stronger Nasser's position became. Both leaders focused heavily on the military aspects of the operation and its aftermath, as evidenced by the very successful execution of the military phase that overwhelmed Egyptian forces within nine days. Yet the leaders had failed to plan for the diplomatic and economic ramifications of the invasion. Britain particularly faced financial ruin in the aftermath. The canal was shut down and several oil exporting nations boycotted the United Kingdom. The United States threatened to sell its holdings of British bonds and devalue the Pound Sterling, a step which within weeks would have made it difficult for Britain to even import enough food to feed its people, giving it virtually no choice but to abandon the invasion.

The months it took to make an invasion plan also meant that information that was true at seizure in July was not true by October. Domestic political support to retake the canal was initially strong. Yet the British and French public had come to accept the loss of the Suez by October, particularly as it became clear that little had changed as a result. When the invasion came in October, there were now significant public protests, especially as it came in the wake of the Soviet Union's invasion of Hungary that year, and parallels between the two were quickly drawn, inciting international furore.

Emotion and **hubris** also come into play. Mollet had been a former captive of the Nazis and a resistance fighter. He saw Nasser's writings as similar to ***Mein Kampf,*** and subsequently was highly emotional in his response to Nasser's actions rather than even-keeled. Across the Channel, Eden was addicted to amphetamines in this period, which drove him to manic episodes and sleep deprivation, as well as creating augmented feelings of hubris and invulnerability (Owen 2008: ch. 3).

Finally, altered **risk perception** arguably played a role. When the Suez Canal was seized, Britain and France were facing the twilight of their status as world powers in the new Cold War world. Neither leader had come to terms the end of imperialism, and hence in the face of a potentially fatal blow to their empires in the Suez, were willing to take a great gamble in order to maintain the status quo and recover their losses, whilst the potentially disastrous consequences of failure may well have deterred the invasion plan in more ordinary times of risk calculation (McDermott 2001: 147–156).

a dangerous world, but in modern contexts may have profound policy ramifications, perhaps witnessed in political responses to new but poorly understood issues, like recreational drug use in the 1950s and 1960s, and the HIV/AIDS epidemic in the 1980s.

Another disposition that greatly affects decision-making is hubris. Charisma, intelligence, confidence and courage are personality traits strongly correlated with effective leadership (see Chapter 7), yet they also give rise to feelings of arrogance and overconfidence on the part of leaders. Indeed, because those traits are often found in successful politicians, hubris is a commonly observed side effect, and hubristic behaviour may intensify over time when political leaders are successful or unchallenged for long periods (Owen & Davidson 2009). And it can be followers themselves, who in the process of supporting their leaders, engender hubristic feelings within them:

> Many of us look to leaders who project an aura of certainty—real or imagined—that we lack within ourselves. And if they are not actually knowledgeable and in control, we convince ourselves that they truly are, to satisfy our own desperate need. In the process, we sometimes push leaders into believing in their own omniscience. (Lipman-Blumen 2005: 53)

Hubris can be a useful disposition, insofar as it enables the confidence to lead even in the face of opposition, and yet may severely undercut rational decision-making, insofar as hubristic leaders are prone to ignoring advice and criticism, sometimes allowing them to push forward on courses of action that may have disastrous consequences (Sadler-Smith et al. 2017; see Case 8.2).

Decision-making structures

The reality of modern government is that it is too large and complex for any one leader to control, particularly when faced with the cognitive restraints on decision-making by individuals. Much larger decision and policymaking structures are thus required to operate the machinery of government.

There are two distinctive and clear benefits to making decisions collectively. The first is that of *information integration*. Put simply, the information processing capacity of a group is significantly greater than a lone individual, and accordingly most collective decision-making in executive contexts is differentiated on this basis. Cabinets are composed of ministers or secretaries who have portfolios so that they may specialize in certain areas of policy and contribute specialized perspectives to discussions. Ministers in turn have departments and advisors beneath them that further specialize and coordinate the collection and processing of information, as well as the implementation of policy. Committee systems are ubiquitous in legislatures and party organizations, which allow certain groups to articulate goals, collect information and develop alternatives on specific areas of government interest and report back to the larger body. Groups also have a greater collective memory and more individual experiences to draw upon (Forsyth 2009: 319–320).

The deliberative debate stimulated by group decision-making can help clarify goals and options, guard against individual cognitive limitations or biases, and through critical evaluation make more accurate judgments about possible choices (Forsyth 2009: 321).

The second benefit of group decision-making is *consensus building*. Individuals are far more willing to accept a decision, and abide by it, if they have taken part in the decision-making process (Nijstad 2009: 123). In political contexts, collective decision-making is often an expectation or even a requirement of governance, insofar as collective decision-making can incorporate diverse voices and represent a commitment to democratic, rather than authoritarian, rule. For these reasons, as well as practical considerations, broad decision-making structures are usually required by the laws or conventions of a political system – cabinets, executive councils and legislatures are examples of bodies that formally split decision-making responsibility and reduce leader dominance within the decision-making process (see Chapter 4).

However, just as frequently leaders themselves create informal structures around themselves – advisors, colleagues or peers become an 'inner circle' – to assist with the decision-making process but also solidify their control over government. How leaders assemble, manage and involve themselves in these decision and policymaking processes around them is an integral part of leadership style and the contemporary leadership challenge.

The core executive

In recent decades, when studying political leadership (at least in executive government), the term 'core executive' has often been used to capture the heart of political decision-making in modern government. Dunleavy and Rhodes define it as:

> all those organizations and structures which primarily serve to pull together and integrate central government policies, or act as final arbiters within the executive of conflicts between different elements of the government machine. (Dunleavy & Rhodes 1990: 4)

The core executive is made up of formal elements (like cabinets and senior bureaucrats) as well as informal ones (like political advisors). But it is best thought of not as a fixed cluster of institutions, but rather a web of relationships at the heart of government (Buckley 2006: 186; Lecy, Mergel & Schmitz 2014). As such, what constitutes the core executive is fluid, and patterns of influence are ever-changing.

Subsequently the power of political leaders is not monolithic within the centre. The core executive often includes independent centres of influence over which leaders may have limited authority. Senior bureaucrats, for example, are usually key players in policy and decision-making; however, their positions are often legally protected from everyday politics, and they have expertise, loyalty and powers that political leaders may not have ready access to or they rely upon. In Westminster systems, prime ministers must make many decisions and policies through cabinet and their parliamentary party, with other parliamentarians who are political leaders in their own right and collectively have the power to remove the prime minister.

As such, political leaders must use authority and power, both positional and personal (see Chapter 2) to influence the operations of the core executive. To be sure, leaders at the apex have significant resources at their disposal – they have the democratic authority of their election and the other prerogatives of their office as institutional tools (Heffernan 2003, 2005). And they can also seek to restructure the core executive around themselves, placing key allies in influential positions within the government while marginalizing those who are likely to hinder their goals (e.g. Stehr 1997).

Leading the core executive

How a political leader manages their core executive is a strategic choice. Some will attempt to dominate and micromanage as much as they can, while others might adopt a laissez faire approach, content to delegate most decisions and policy matters to subordinates. Two broad approaches have been commonly described: the *circular*, in which the leader is like the hub of a wheel; and the *hierarchical*, in which the leader sits atop a pyramid of relationships. Circles are dynamic and creative, and they allow the leader to receive far more information and be much more involved in executive management. Yet circles can also foster competition between staff, lead to unclear lines of authority and tend toward the chaotic. Hierarchies are more orderly, clear and predictable, and allow the leader greater space and independence, yet can leave a leader aloof from the operations of the core executive and tend to make staff at the top of the pyramid extremely powerful due to their control over access to the leader (Nelson 2015: 476–477).

Taking an approach inspired by leader personality and motivation (see Chapter 6), Thomas Preston in *The President and His Inner Circle* (2001) offers an 'at a distance' model for understanding the executive management style of leaders. Three dimensions are relevant:

1. **Need for Power:** How much does the leader seek to control and dominate the decision-making process?
   - High: the leader dominates decision-making, centralizes procedures, prefers hierarchies and suppresses open debate.
   - Low: the leader facilitates rather than controls decision-making, decentralizes procedures, prefers loose arrangements, delegates tasks to subordinates.
2. **Cognitive Complexity**: How good are leaders at processing information, exploring options and understanding nuances?
   - High: the leader undertakes broad information searches, listens to multiple viewpoints, has a nuanced view of context, is less decisive and more deliberative.

- Low: the leader conducts limited information searches, makes greater use of biases or mental shortcuts, has a black-and-white view of context, is more decisive and less consultative.

3. **Prior Experience/Knowledge**: How much do leaders know about the area they are making a decision on?
   - High: the leader is highly interested, listens to independent viewpoints, has high confidence in their ability to understand.
   - Low: the leader is less interested or less able to grasp the details, is dependent on advisors, has low to moderate confidence in the decision-making capacities.

Preston argues that the combination of these three dimensions determines a leadership style in the management of government. For example, Bill Clinton (US President 1993–2001) is thought to have been one of the most intelligent American presidents, with staff and colleagues attesting to his high cognitive complexity, allowing him to process vast amounts of information and make himself a virtual expert on just about any area. His strong grasp on policy usually made for high-quality decisions. Yet it also led to indecisiveness, as Clinton would tend to search for more information and continue debate, rather than close off issues and move on (Woodward 1994: 328). He selected a diverse cabinet and advisory team with different viewpoints, yet sometimes this process would become chaotic as debate and argument became the norm between conflicting groups. Many of his senior staff and his own vice president saw his cognitive complexity and intelligence as a problem for quick and decisive action (Preston 2001: 227–231).

By contrast, Lyndon Johnson (US President 1963–1969) had a high need for power, but low cognitive complexity and low prior knowledge on foreign policy – a combination that led him to dominate the decision-making on the conduct of the Vietnam War through tightly managed hierarchies. However, his low cognitive complexity led him to vastly oversimplify the conflict, see things in black-and-white terms and arrive at decisions too quickly, and without the experience or knowledge to question the advice he received or the way his subordinates implemented decisions (Preston 2001: ch. 5).

Managing the policy process

Assuming, however, that a political leader seeks to be involved and active in the decision-making processes of their government, we can see at each step of the theoretical policy cycle (see "Making Decisions"), the levers political leaders have to exert influence and the trade-offs they make to do so.

Agenda-setting

In democratic systems, the policy agenda is determined through public debate, media discourse and elections. Political parties and their leaders develop platforms that they take to the public, and if theirs proves compelling, they are elected into government and expected to pursue those platforms during their term of office. Of course, there are no guarantees that such goals are achievable or realistic when in office. Indeed, political parties outside of government generally do not have access to bureaucrats and experts within government that might help them formulate realistic policy goals and ideas (Elcock 2001: 113).

Once in government, political leaders must drive the policy-making process towards achieving their stated agenda (Brady & Catterall 1997: 510, 518–519). This requires energy and commitment on the part of leadership to overcome the inertial forces of government. A prime minister leading a cabinet, for example, has as colleagues other political leaders who have their own agendas they will want to advance. Legislatures can also seize the agenda and push their own issues rather than the government's. Leaders also face a constant stream of issues and problems that divert attention and frustrate agendas. Allegedly, when asked by a reporter what was most likely to blow a government off course, British Prime Minister Harold Macmillan replied "events, dear boy, events". A natural disaster, a crime wave, an outbreak of disease, a viral YouTube video highlighting the problems of poverty in the inner city – all these and more conspire to seize control of the agenda.

Political leadership must somehow maintain steady progress towards its goals even while contending with a constant stream of events and other political forces that wish to see their own goals prioritized. This requires leaders, usually through persuasion and rhetoric, to maintain their issues at the forefront of the public and their government's attention ('t Hart & Tummers 2019: 108–109). The challenge of course is that policymaking can take a long time, and political attention can move on quickly, especially if a government has a large agenda it wants to achieve. As Lord Armstrong observed of Margaret Thatcher: "there was so much to do and not enough time to do it, and if she was going to get it all done while she was still in office she really had to keep up a tremendous pace and, if necessary take short cuts to do so" (Lawson & Armstrong 1994: 447).

As government by its nature tends to become fragmentary and 'siloed' (Peters 2018), driving policy agendas also requires political leaders to play an essential coordinating role (Calvert 1992). Usually they do so through a well-ordered core executive which oversees the vast machinery of government and ensures it works towards the same ends.

Policy formulation

Once the agenda is set, achieving it is the next major challenge. Unless the leader is an expert in the field, how do they know what policy options exist to solve a problem, and how do they establish the merits and risks of each option?

John Kingdon in *Agendas, Alternatives, and Public Policies* found that when it comes to policymaking, political leaders set the agenda, but often it is bureaucrats that have far more power in determining what policy options are considered to achieve that agenda (1995). Leaders rely heavily on the advice they receive from their departments and subordinates in areas with which they have limited expertise. Leaders are of course briefed to try and gain an understanding of the issues they want to tackle, but even the most cognitively sophisticated leader has only a limited ability to gain expertise on all the relevant policy areas they might be involved in.

Leaders thus have long sought to surround themselves with trusted voices who can effectively advise them. In contemporary politics, we tend to think of 'inner circles' or other informal arrangements that describe relationships within the core executive through which a political leader receives information and advice. These are often the most informal parts of a government's decision-making processes, insofar as formal bodies may exist to determine an agenda or make a decision (like a cabinet), but there's no similarly formal process to determine who a leader listens to.

In modern governments, there are large bureaucracies whose job it is to provide professional and formal advice to political leadership, with the professionalization of policy advice and implementation greatly influenced by the thought of German sociologist Max Weber (e.g., Nass 1986). Bureaucrats often face a challenging position in this regard – they must on the one hand be responsive to the agenda of the government-of-the-day, yet on the other maintain their independence and serve the public interest, rather than political interest (Mulgan 2008). What results is not always an advice structure that political leaders entirely trust – indeed, as famously satirized in the television series *Yes, Minister,* the bureaucracy often has its own agenda and limited loyalty to that of political leadership.

In response, political leaders often attempt to appoint people they believe are loyal to them into positions of influence or as part of their own 'inner circle' to provide advice they believe they can trust, or alternative perspectives. Often generically termed 'advisers', they have been of increasing interest to scholars in recent decades (see Ng 2018) but are not without their shortcomings either. Whilst the politicization of advice and use of appointment to create allies across policy bureaus strengthens the leader's control over the policy process, it does not necessarily increase the quality of their decision-making. Firstly, because political appointees come and go as governments change, they tend to lack technical expertise in policy (compared with public servants) and are oriented more towards the provision of political and media advice (Christiansen, Niklasson & Öhberg 2016). Though desirable for a political leader wishing to stay in office, policy processes that focus on what is politically expedient, rather than what is likely to be effective at solving problems, are not necessarily in the long-term interests of leaders or their constituencies.

Secondly, the appointment of a loyal inner circle and network across government can cause problems for group dynamics. As stated previously, the core executive is at its heart a web of relationships – if those relationships are contingent on loyalty to the leadership, then this can compromise the nature of advice given. There is "a thin line between advisers offering emotional support and becoming sycophants to a dominant leader. If consensus and mutual support becomes the norm, an absence of critical thinking and self-reflection may take hold" ('t Hart & Tummers 2019: 66). Thus, a loyal and hand-picked inner circle may give rise to a phenomenon identified as *groupthink,* in which instincts to maintain group harmony and protect the leader lead groups towards defective decision-making. Articulated by Irving Janis (1972), groupthink most often manifests as:

- Feelings of invulnerability amongst group members.
- Rationalizing or ignoring feedback that challenges group assumptions or thinking.
- Discounting or demeaning outsiders who disagree with the group.
- Self-censorship amongst members who may doubt the group's consensus but fear being the odd one out.
- Placing pressure on dissenting members of the group to be 'loyal'.
- Restriction of information or alternative viewpoints that might challenge the group consensus. (Janis 1972; 't Hart 1994)

Groupthink can hinder effective policymaking and has been cited as a major factor behind misguided decisions, such as the disastrous Bay of Pigs invasion. It likely played a role too in the questionable decisions taken by Anthony Eden and his cabinet during the Suez Crisis (Verbeek 1994; Case 8.2). Moreover, if the leader surrounds themselves with hand-picked loyalists or ideological allies, who think and feel as they do, will they receive the kind of alternative viewpoints and dissenting advice that is needed to make balanced decisions? The Chinese idiomatically refer to this problem as 'three men make a tiger' – if the leader hears the same thing from enough people they trust, regardless of how irrational, then they are likely to believe it.

An alternative approach is to assemble a 'team of rivals', who are likely to challenge each other and the leader, and thus provide a robust forum in which a variety of advice, information and policy options are vetted (e.g., Kearns Goodwin 2006). However, this too has its own dangers. *Polythink* can result from a high degree of disunity in a decision-making group, in turn creating deadlock and an inability to find consensus on key issues. Such groups tend to take compromised and watered-down positions to secure a majority position amongst a diverse group, or else simply provide confusing and conflicting advice to their leaders (Mintz & Wayne 2016). Thus leaders face a critical challenge – to create circles around themselves that can provide trustworthy advice and can help them reach their and the public's goals, while avoiding group dynamics that will undermine the quality of policy development and decision-making processes.

Decision-making

Once information and advice have been gathered, and policy options identified, then decisions must be made about what options to pursue. Most major policy decisions in contemporary government are required, at least formally, to be made collectively. Many of the facets of group dynamics discussed in the previous section apply similarly to the decision-making process.

Collective decision-making bodies sit atop executive government in most nations. Although they are often composed of peers or even rivals to the political leader, there are many ways in which the leader can influence the operation of a decision-making body. For example:

- What issues will be considered by the group and in what order.
- Who gets to speak, and in what order, and for how long.
- What information group members receive before meeting.
- How information is shared, and the number of options considered.
- How choices are arrived at – by consensus, majority vote, or does the leader maintain the final say?

The degree to which a leader seeks to control the decision-making processes of government goes to the core of their leadership style. Australian Prime Minister Billy Hughes (1915–1923) was infamous for his domineering style and manipulation of his cabinet, by encouraging rivalries amongst his ministers, strictly controlling the flow of information, keeping a tight personal control of the agenda and sometimes even ignoring or reinterpreting its decisions altogether (Weller 2007: ch. 3). Subsequent prime ministers have had varied approaches, adopting tactics both overt and covert to influence their government's decision-making (see Weller 2007).

The degree to which decision-making is made consultative and collective, though, is also a practical consideration by leadership. As argued by Vroom & Yetton, genuinely collective decision-making is necessary and optimal in scenarios where acceptance and buy-in from subordinates are important, and/or the problem is complex, unstructured, or requires a variety of views and options to be vetted in order to produce a high-quality result. Yet in the absence of these requirements, collective decision-making may create needless conflict and be time-consuming and unpredictable, and autocratic decision-making may be preferable by contrast (Vroom & Yetton 1973: ch. 3).

Indeed, as collective decision-making increases in scale, it becomes much harder for all voices to be heard and for a common position to be found amongst the group. Hence large groups often struggle to come to decisions and tend avoid difficult issues by debating trivialities and focusing on areas that engender less conflict (Forsyth 2009: 326–329). Cyril Parkinson in *Parkinson's Law* (1958) observes that executive power is ideally expressed in a collective decision-making body of a dozen or less, and then when decision-making bodies become too large, new smaller sub-bodies are created that ultimately become the new primary forum. For example, in the Communist Party of China the Central Committee is the ultimate executive authority for all major decisions, yet as this body over time has grown to hundreds of members, power has successively devolved to ever smaller groups, first to the Politburo and then to its Standing Committee (currently five to nine members). Political leaders will often pursue greater manageability and influence over policy by forging close relationships between key colleagues and devising smaller and hence more manageable decision-making bodies.

Implementation

Making a decision is not the same as that decision being realized in reality. Nothing will happen unless the enormous machinery of government and its bureaucracies, agencies and other associated arms work to implement decisions on the ground. And while the public and media tend to place emphasis on the pronouncements and decisions leaders make, the long tail of implementation can be much harder to track.

Managing implementation is an enormous task. The sheer scale of government is such that it is impossible for any leader to be fully across the agendas, operations and procedures of its innumerable departments. Leaders do have significant scope to use their appointment powers and own staff to create networks of authority and information flows that allow decisions at the top to be transmitted across the government and provide oversight to its workings. Yet control is arguably only ever partial, and the further from the centre you go, the weaker the influence of the leader becomes (Nelson 2015: 471–475).

Many policy decisions – especially in areas such as health, welfare, trade, economics or agriculture – may take months, years or decades to fully realize. And often political decisions are implemented incompletely, or perhaps not at all. As Pressman and Wildavsky explore in their landmark study *Implementation* (1984), many excellent ideas and decisions made by political leadership using the best advice and brightest minds available can still lead to poor or unintended outcomes on the ground in distant corners of the country (see Case 8.3).

Others have noted that some problems simply aren't conducive to straightforward policy options that can be easily implemented. Rittel and Webber (1973) described these as 'wicked problems' – unique or multi-faceted problems that have no clear or widely accepted definition, aren't easily solved, and have little opportunity for trial and error. They tend to be politically charged and difficult to find public and/or elite consensus on as well (McConnell 2018). Leaders try to tackle them, but soon find that little is 'solved', political agreement is fleeting, and at best there is merely improvement – think of complex social problems like poverty, racism or obesity. The concept of 'super wicked' problems has been presented in the context of climate change, a crisis made even more difficult for leaders to solve due to time pressures, insufficient authority to enforce a solution, and the fact that those who caused the problem must also create the solution (Levin et al. 2012).

Furthermore, the policy options available to political leaders are not limited by their imagination, but rather by what they can reasonably or legally implement. Good economic management, for example, is a key priority for any political leader wanting to be re-elected. But economies are massive, complex entities that in practice are extremely difficult to steer. Many economic levers, like interest rates or exchange rates, are outside of a leader's control and are set by central banks and currency markets. Prices and wages are difficult to control and attempts to do so by political leaders have generally failed to produce the desired results (Schuettinger & Butler 2009). Tax rates and trade tariffs may be adjusted by governments, but it is often hard to predict what impact such changes will have on an economy, and they are

Case 8.3 The challenge of implementation

Julius Nyerere

President of Tanzania, 1964–1985

Figure 8.4 Julius Nyerere in 1965

Like many anti-colonial activists who found themselves in power in post-independence Africa, President of Tanzania Julius Nyerere faced the daunting task of transforming his country from a subjugated colonial territory to a prosperous modern state. Educated in Scotland in history and economics, Nyerere returned to become the leading figure in the Tanzanian independence movement, committed to a peaceful and inclusive transition to independence. High-minded and idealistic, Nyerere was distinguished by his personal integrity and commitment to Tanzania, hoping to lead Africa to become "a continent of hope for the human race".

After taking power Nyerere was confronted with an underdeveloped nation, dependent on agricultural cash crops with very limited infrastructure or public education. In 1967, Nyerere made the Arusha Declaration, which revealed to the world a radical blueprint for development he termed ***ujamaa*** ('family-hood' in Swahili). Ujamaa was Nyerere's plan for an African form of socialism – it proposed the nationalization of key sectors of the economy, the collectivization of the rural population into communitarian villages, compulsory education, a spirit of self-reliance and community sharing, and shifting the Tanzanian economy away from foreign dependence and cash crops for export.

Ujamaa was the product of decades of study by Nyerere (see Pratt 1976). It was a revolutionary concept that generated great excitement throughout the Tanzanian population and across the continent (Bjerk 2017: 82–83). Nyerere would spend the rest of his rule passionately working towards its ideals, setting a personal example by living humbly and self-reliantly himself. Yet whilst Nyerere had successfully sold his vision and persuaded a nation to follow him, making that vision a reality was to prove the disappointment of his life.

To implement such an ambitious transformation of the economy took a capacity that Tanzania simply did not have. The ujamaa model moved Tanzania towards a centrally-planned economy as sectors were nationalized, yet its post-independence civil service had limited economic expertise and were ill-prepared for the scale and complexity of ujamaa (Bjerk 2017: 85). At the village and local level, development plans from the state were woefully inadequate and sometimes amounted to little more than unrealistic production targets. Civil servants from the cities had limited understanding of the reality of life in the rural provinces, and often struggled to find common purpose with the farmers and villagers they were trying to direct (Raikes 1975: 42).

Also lacking was the implementation infrastructure to mobilize the population towards self-reliance and new ideals. Tanzanian education levels were low, so mobilizing the population to understand Nyerere's complex policy ideas and implement new techniques or technologies was extremely challenging and very slow. Nyerere's ruling party elite (TANU) was only loosely held together under very general principles, and had limited reach in rural areas, with local political leaders themselves often having a limited understanding of, or commitment to, the ujamaa concept (Raikes 1975: 39). Thus, policies were applied haphazardly and inconsistently, and many villages simply added the word 'ujamaa' to their name without implementing any change.

Moreover, the creation of a planned economy gave the bureaucratic elite vastly more power over the economic livelihoods of citizens. In a poor nation where civil service wages were declining, what resulted was rampant corruption that had spiralled out of control by the 1970s (Sedigh & Muganda 1999: 152–160). Bureaucrats were often elitist and uninterested in the opinions of uneducated rural Tanzanians, setting targets or pursuing projects that had little relevance or chance of success due to a lack of local knowledge (Ergas 1980: 388–398). Though Nyerere continued to energetically promote his policies and oversaw some model projects personally, it proved to be a drop in the ocean. Nyerere himself critically misjudged the attitudes of the population – although the concept was popular in abstract, there was only limited autonomous movement of people into new communal villages. Few were as committed to the ideas of a society of family-hood and communal production as Nyerere was, and he could not personally oversee every village or program (Ergas 1980).

Ujamaa was not a complete failure – literacy and life expectancy improved significantly within a couple of decades. Yet by the 1980s Tanzania was facing widespread economic crisis and the government began abandoning Nyerere's vision, and Nyerere himself stepped down in 1985.

Few leaders worked so ardently towards a singular vision for their nation, but a leader cannot create change solely from the top. The challenge of implementation is perhaps the hardest and most remote from the leader's direct control. They must rely heavily on networks of elites, bureaucrats and citizens themselves to turn their visions into reality, and even the most principled visions may fail to be realized in the way the leader hoped. Yet as Nyerere himself commented in retirement; this is sometimes the destiny of the leader who dares. "They keep saying you've failed. But what is wrong with urging people to pull together? Did Christianity fail because the world is not all Christian?" (Mwakikagile 2006: 94–95).

not always fiscally sustainable. Some key economic variables – like consumer confidence, savings rates and entrepreneurial behaviour – are only indirectly influenced and not always in predictable ways (e.g. De Boef & Kellstedt 2004). Thus, despite the centrality of economic performance to a political leader's electoral success and popularity, they have much less control over the economy than we might expect (Irwin 2017).

Even when the right approach is found, effective implementation of a policy takes time and effort. Political attention quickly changes, and often when decisions are made and policy is set, political leaders have a tendency to move onto the next issue or idea. "Once in office, a president is much more concerned with choosing what to do than he is with how these decisions are implemented…or the conduct of program activities on a continuing basis" (Rose 1976: 23).

Successful policy implementation however requires ongoing leadership at numerous levels to maintain momentum, consistency and feedback (Sabatier & Mazmanian 1979). Political leadership must plan for this by creating trusted networks and relationships across government that can provide that ongoing leadership and the means to implement and adjust policy over the long-term.

The process in action

As stated previously, to break down the process of policy and decision-making into discrete steps can bely a much more chaotic reality. Three well-known heuristic models – *satisficing, incrementalism* and the *garbage-can model* – are alternative perspectives that may give a closer sense of how leaders, governments and information interact to make decisions and create policy in practice, and are worth considering here.

Satisficing. Herbert Simon proposed that instead of conducting a rational review of all available options, "the search is incomplete, often inadequate, based on uncertain information and partial ignorance, and usually terminated with the discovery of satisfactory, not optimal, courses of action" (Simon 1985: 295). Finding the optimal solution to a given problem may be exceedingly difficult and time consuming, or even functionally impossible. Hence once a viable option is found that meets the minimum requirements of acceptability to the decision-making group, a consensus tends to form and new evidence or concerns that question the suitability of that option tend to be downplayed (see Stevens 2019).

This phenomenon is readily appreciated in political negotiations, whereby in order to reach an agreement many parties have to compromise, and when there are many parties with widely varying positions, the first arrangement minimally acceptable to all parties is often the one taken, even if far from optimal (Thompson 2007: 89–94). For example, faced with the imminent threat of a civil war in India in 1947, the British raced through negotiations over the partition of their colony into India and Pakistan, seizing upon the first viable partition agreement that could be accepted by both sides. Major unresolved problems were ignored, and the hastily drawn border between the two countries led to horrific sectarian violence and one of the worst refugee crises in world history. Time, pressure, and the extreme difficulty of the negotiations between deeply divided parties led the British to take the first viable, rather than the best, option for partition (see Wolpert 2009).

Incrementalism. Charles Lindblom contends that the most likely courses for policy are ones of incremental change. When only limited options can be vetted, it is much easier to successfully model likely change and plan for implementation when just a few variables from the status quo are modified, whilst radical overhauls are far harder to plan, predict and implement. Politically, it is far easier to build consensus for small course adjustments than it is for total reform. Gradual and continuous change allows for learning and refinement, and small changes are much easier than large ones to reverse if they prove to be a mistake (Lindblom 1959).

This approach runs counter perhaps to the instincts of political leadership, which often desires big and exciting change to inspire followers, but in practice, Lindblom would argue, this is rarely successful. Achieving change is instead a long, hard grind and political leaders need to adjust their expectations and apply sustained effort, rather than short bursts of intense enthusiasm. And of course, incremental change can lead to major reform over time. Although demilitarized in its post-war constitution, Japanese defence capacity and spending have been incrementally but continuously expanded since the 1970s to a point where the Japanese Self-Defence Forces are once more one of the largest in the world, while constitutional provisions on its use have been progressively revised. By making incremental changes over a long period of time, Japanese prime ministers have collectively restored much of the nation's military capability, yet the incremental nature of change has avoided the significant domestic or international fallout a dramatic reform of military policy might have attracted (see Kapoor 2011).

Garbage Can Model. Cohen, March and Olsen take another approach entirely, describing policy development as:

> A collection of choices looking for problems, issues and feelings looking for decision situations in which they might be aired, solutions looking for issues to which they might be the answer, and decision makers looking for work. (Cohen, March & Olsen 1972: 2)

In other words, policymaking is more like leaders rummaging through a garbage can and finding what fits together. The decision-making process is far more chaotic in this model, with ideas, participants, situations and problems drifting in and out of focus. Government in this context is described as only an 'organized anarchy', with three general properties that undermine the rationality and/or predictability of the process:

1. **Problematic Preferences:** Leaders and their governments are a loose collection of values and ideas, rather than a hard-and-fast agenda. Different ideological forces within a party rise and fall, and thus so do policy preferences. Issues arise that leaders must deal with, and yet they may start doing so without a clear or consistent sense of the goals being pursued, or goals may change as more is revealed.

2. **Unclear Cause-and-Effect:** Leaders sit atop vast bureaucracies so complex that even those working within it have only a vague sense of how it all works. Policies are developed far removed from working realities, in environments where evidence for their effect is often theoretical at best. Trial and error becomes commonplace as leaders fumble through the process and try to figure out what actually works.
3. **Fluid Participation:** The policy-making process itself is unstable, and lines of power and authority are changeable. Advisors who have enormous sway over the leadership's thinking one week may be fired in disgrace the next. Leaders themselves may be powerful and dominant in cabinet early in their term and enfeebled and ignored by the end of it (Sabatier & Weible 2014: 26–27).

In such a system, political leaders do not necessarily even start with a problem – instead, they start with ideas, solutions, opinions and agendas and then scramble around looking for 'problems' to solve them with. For example, Shaukat Aziz, Prime Minister of Pakistan (2004–2007), was a long-time financier and banker whose total commitment to the neoliberal economic agenda saw his government dramatically increase the scale of privatization in Pakistan. Although nominally applied to solve the problem of low economic growth and reform state-owned corporations deemed to be underperforming, many profitable and otherwise properly functioning state corporations were privatized as well, only to produce worse public outcomes in the aftermath. Despite increasing evidence that privatization was not producing anticipated results, and significant public controversy and backlash, Aziz and his government continued to look for problems that privatization could 'solve' in the garbage can (Munir & Naqvi 2017).

Hence whilst idealized in theory as a logical, stepwise process, in reality decision and policymaking are complex and arguably chaotic phenomenon, marred by flawed and imperfect logic and a wide variety of human limitations – limitations that have enormous ramifications for policy and government. Whether conducted individually or collectively, these processes are subject to a variety of forces which mean that no two leaders would ever likely make the exact same decision in the same way on the same issue. And finally, making a decision is not the same as making it happen – the limitations of the decision-making process and the complexities of implementation ensure that even the wisest political leader can never really be sure of what exactly will result from his or her choices.

Chapter Summary

- Political leadership assumes a governing role to make critical decisions in a polity; however, that role is very much complicated by a lack of immediacy between political leaders and the on-the-ground reality.
- Decision-making, and the broader policymaking processes that encompass it in government, are of central importance to the governing role.

Though we strive for it to be an orderly and rational process, in practice its rationality is greatly limited by constraints, including cognitive and situational limits to our ability to obtain and process information; various cognitive biases that distort our perception of risks, probabilities and courses of action; and emotions and hubris, all of which make our rationality bounded rather than complete.

- Political leaders must oversee broader decision and policymaking structures. They shape and lead a core executive around them, however leaders vary greatly in style in this regard – some will seek to dominate policymaking personally while others may prefer a hands-off approach that delegates responsibility to subordinates.
- Leaders rely on their core executive to carry out their decisions and implement their policies. They draw in talent and expertise to help the leader develop effective policy. However, collective decision-making within these contexts can fall prey to various problems, such as groupthink, and leaders must create robust decision-making structures around them to avoid those problems.
- Observing the process in action, many scholars have offered models of the policy development process that highlight its complex, sub-rational and sub-optimal nature in which leaders may have far less control than is apparent. Satisficing, incrementalism, and the garbage can model are prominent examples of such.

9 PERSUASION, RHETORIC AND NEGOTIATION

Chapter Outline

- What is rhetoric? How do leaders use it to influence others, and why is it so central to political leadership?
- What is rhetoric used to do? Why do leaders rely on it so heavily?
- How is rhetoric structured to persuade? What tactics can leaders use to craft effective rhetoric?
- What is negotiation? What does it consist of in a political context?
- How are negotiations structured? What are hard and soft tactics? What considerations should leaders make when picking a tactical approach to negotiation?

Political leaders do not rule by fiat alone. In practice they must also persuade, bargain, cajole or even strongarm to achieve their goals. Politics gives leaders a platform to engage powerfully in the political discourse, define the agenda, build coalitions and negotiate outcomes.

Many of history's most effective political leaders have accomplished their ends even in the absence of the formal authority to make decisions, instead using rhetoric, persuasion and negotiation to influence those who do. Nelson Mandela, imprisoned for 27 years, nonetheless with allies and followers built a national and international coalition against the apartheid system in South Africa, and as leader of the African National Congress, peacefully negotiated the dismantlement of a regime that many had once felt would only end in civil war. Understanding the informal powers of political rule is essential to understanding political leadership.

Rhetoric

From soaring words of inspiration to logical argument, speech that is designed to persuade is known as *rhetoric*. In political leadership, particularly in modern democracies, rhetoric is the primary (and sometimes only) means by which a leader persuades others to follow. Though coercion, inducement or manipulation (see Chapter 2) are all potential means of securing compliance, history has shown time and again that it is the art of persuasion that has most enduringly built a following. As Napoleon Bonaparte once remarked of his loyal army: "a man does not have himself killed for a few half-pence a day or for a petty distinction. You must speak to the soul to electrify the man."

Rhetoric is about speaking to the soul. It is the bridge that connects leaders to followers most directly and intimately, and as such is a core skill of political leadership. Yet persuasion is not only the speeches and promises made on a campaign trail. It is also the speech a minister makes to the cabinet to build support for their policy proposals, the speech a president makes to the legislature to try and secure passage of a bill, or even the discussions a member of parliament has with a constituent at their local supermarket. Rhetoric is ubiquitous in politics, and it takes many forms, for many audiences and for many purposes.

"Persuasion is integral to politics because politics involves making judgments in contexts of uncertainty about what to do. To persuade in such contexts involves transforming, primarily by means of argument, a variety of possible options into a unified judgment, perhaps even a decision" (Martin 2014: 1). If the right way of thinking or course of action on any given issue were self-evident and uncontested, there would be little need for rhetoric to persuade people. Yet as we know this is seldom the case, as most issues in politics involve uncertainty, competing ideologies, trade-offs, risks and inertia that require discussion and persuasion to clarify options and build support for a way forward.

The word *rhetoric* in political contexts has suspect connotations for some. *Political rhetoric,* the kind we see political leaders using, is sometimes maligned as deliberately deceptive, false, self-serving or empty (see Martin 2014: 4–7). There is much of this to go around in modern politics, and many politicians are surprisingly bad at crafting rhetoric. Professional media training and speech-writing are now ubiquitous in contemporary politics, but that has created a style of political rhetoric that is often perceived by the public to be too polished, and lacking in authenticity or excitement (Kjeldsen et al. 2019: 184–185). Rhetoric that truly inspires and convinces is no mean feat, and it requires careful consideration of audience, purpose and context.

Persuasive methods

Rhetoric was much valued in the ancient world, where it was taught and studied at dedicated academies. Corax of Syracuse (C.5th BCE) and Isocrates (436–338 BCE) were highly influential in establishing its formalized study, but it was Aristotle's *Rhetoric* that more than any other work laid the foundations for the understanding of rhetoric.

Aristotle identified three means by which a leader's speech can be persuasive to those who listen: *logos* (logic), *pathos* (emotion) and *ethos* (character). Other contemporary practitioners added a fourth – *kairos* (right moment). More than two millennia later, these four dimensions still provide an excellent starting point for exploring political rhetoric.

Logos

Logos is persuasion using facts and reason. When a speaker uses logos, they use argument, structure and evidence to appeal to their audience's intellect and lead guide them towards logical conclusions (see Charteris-Black 2018: 12–14). Logos is a natural starting point for rhetorical appeals – when a politician mounts a defence of a policy or decision, they will usually start by presenting facts or logic that support their conclusions.

Central to logos is the selection and use of *evidence*, whether that be statistical (i.e., hard numbers, figures, facts) or narrative (i.e., stories, observations, examples). The effectiveness of using evidence to persuade people to take a certain opinion, believe a speaker or shift their opinion is well established (Reynolds & Reynolds 2002: 166–168; Stiff & Mongeau 2016: 427–428). The kinds of evidence used though can make a difference in how it persuades – statistical evidence is more likely to change the way the audience thinks about the issue at hand, whereas narrative evidence is more likely to produce an emotional reaction, which can be more powerful (e.g. Kopfman et al. 1998). While statistical evidence has been found to be generally more persuasive than other forms of evidence, the most effective rhetorical appeals overall employ *both* statistical and narrative evidence to make their case (Allen et al. 2000).

Yet there are many caveats as to whether evidence will persuade the listener. The effectiveness of logos assumes that the audience can follow the evidence and logic to arrive at the conclusion the speaker does. The complexity of modern policy issues is such that layman audiences may struggle to do this and might have gaps in their understanding (Bennett & Jennings 2011: 17–44). Areas like the environment and public health have been particularly notable in this regard, and thus part of the challenge of logos is not just constructing a persuasive, reasoned argument but doing so in a way so that a potentially less-informed audience can follow it as well. Political leaders in cabinet or amongst civil servants might discuss argue for a policy with a litany of facts, figures and projections, but for the general public will likely construct their reasoning through simpler metaphors and comparisons. For facts and evidence to work, they must also be recognized and seen as such by the audience, and their source must be trusted to be legitimate and valid (Reynolds & Reynolds 2002). In political debates, however, finding facts that everyone can agree upon is not always easy.

Thus, developing a compellingly reasoned, detailed and yet accessible line of argument in politics is rarely simple, particularly because political issues often involve conflicts over values and goals. A political leader may argue convincingly and demonstrate evidentially that needle exchange programs are proven to reduce rates of serious infections like HIV amongst drug users. Although the logic of the argument is compelling, the premises assumed in this argument are contestable. Some may believe that supporting needle exchange tacitly condones illicit drug usage and is therefore immoral. Others may question whether money spent on such a program is not better used to benefit addicts in other ways, like drug counselling and rehabilitation, or whether public money should be spent on helping drug users at all. Rarely, then, do political leaders have the freedom to construct an appeal based on *logos* free from values, emotions and beliefs.

Moreover, the nature of politics is such that a logical argument is not always the one that the public wants to hear. Upon accepting the Democratic nomination for President of the United States in 1984, Walter Mondale during his acceptance speech discussed the burgeoning federal deficit and concluded his remarks on the subject with "let's tell the truth. It must be done; it must be done. Mr. Reagan will raise taxes, and so will I. He will not tell you. I just did." Mondale's argument was sound – the US budget deficit was virtually unsolvable without some tax increases, and his Republican opponents would ultimately raise taxes during their successive terms. Yet Mondale lost in a landslide, with post-mortems analyses often pointing to his preference for logos (and his admission of an unpopular truth) as a key reason why he failed to inspire (e.g. Raspberry 1985).

In the right context though, logos can be incredibly powerful. Barbara Jordan (Figure 9.1), a Texas Democrat with little national profile, made a television address in July of 1974 during the impeachment hearings against President Richard Nixon in the wake of the Watergate scandal. Her speech, immaculately crafted to present the case against Nixon in thoroughly logical, straightforward and accessible terms, while eschewing partisan or personal arguments, is considered a masterpiece of modern political rhetoric and is widely thought to be a watershed moment in turning public opinion against the president (Rogers 1998: ch. 13).

Figure 9.1 Barbara Jordan in 1976

Pathos

Pathos is the use of emotion, feeling and drama to persuade. It has long been known as a powerful yet unpredictable dimension of rhetoric. The Greek philosopher Gorgias likened the effect of pathos to falling under the spell of a drug (Bizzell & Herzberg 1990: 40–42). Very few political or policy issues can be discussed without arousing at least some emotional responses, and how a speaker uses those emotions is a core element of rhetoric.

Pathos can involve either positive or negative emotions, though it is the latter that are most studied. Fear is one of the most powerful emotions, and frequently used by political leaders to heighten political engagement and motivation (see Robin 2004; Gustainis 1990). Appeals to fear are very effective if an audience can be convinced that they are threatened personally by something (Cap 2016: ch. 1). Closely related to fear is anger, which Aristotle argued has a place in rational discourse but requires careful handling by the speaker to confine its explosive effects (Zagacki & Boleyn-Fitzgerald 2006). Anger in rhetoric is particularly effective at raising support for retributive policies in areas like criminal justice or terrorism (Nabi 2002: 293). Fear and anger are often cynically exploited by political leaders though to quickly boost support or override other deficiencies of argument (e.g. De Castella et al. 2009). However, their volatile and unpredictable nature may unleash forces that political leaders cannot control.

Negative emotion is not necessarily destructive, nor is it always deployed in self-serving ways. Guilt, for example, can be one of the most compelling emotional appeals, and psycho-social research readily demonstrates its potential power in influencing behaviour (O'Keefe 2000). And as James Q. Wilson argues, certain beliefs, like *fairness, self-control* and *duty* are very deeply ingrained, if not instinctive, to the human character, and when those values are undermined or underserved we tend to be affronted and respond emotionally with contempt or outrage (Wilson 1995). Political appeals that make use of these facets of human character can be powerful forces for positive change. William Wilberforce, who successfully led the campaign to abolish the slave trade in Great Britain, frequently used descriptions of the horrors of the slave trade to elicit feelings of shame from his colleagues and the public:

> Never, never will we desist till we have wiped away this scandal from the Christian name, released ourselves from the load of guilt, under which we at present labour, and extinguished every trace of this bloody traffic, of which our posterity, looking back to the history of these enlightened times, will scarce believe that it has been suffered to exist so long a disgrace and dishonour to this country.

Political leaders of pressure groups and political movements, for civil rights and social reform, have often relied on highlighting injustice and invoking a sense of guilt or shame, or of duty and fairness, in their rhetoric to justify political change that may not directly benefit their audience.

And while perhaps less intensively studied, positive emotion has an equally powerful potential in rhetoric (Letts 2009). For example, humour and nostalgia are two means of inducing positive emotion that, when used well, are often difficult to counteract. Joy and happiness are disarming and harder to question than fear and anger, whilst positively disposing audiences to the speaker and their cause, if not their specific arguments (Benacka 2017: 3–5). But positive rhetoric is hard to master – it can easily feel trite or insincere to audiences. Humour particularly is a risky rhetorical device, as many political leaders are poor at it, and poorly executed humour readily falls-flat or backfires. Yet those who are skilled at it are some of history's most effective orators. Tommy Douglas, long-time leader of the New Democratic Party and one of the most successful politicians in Canadian history, was highly regarded for his use of humour, nostalgia and positive emotion in rhetoric:

> Thirty-five years is a long time to have been in public service. I now sort of feel like an antiquarian ... I can remember when grandma wore a night cap – now she drinks one. I can remember when I was a small boy, I would get a nickel for taking out the ashes – and now my grandson gets a quarter for turning up the thermostat. Sure things have changed. Hair has gone down and skirts have gone up. But don't let this fool you. Behind the beards and the miniskirts, the long hair, this generation of young people, take it from me, is one of the finest generations of young people that have ever grown up in this country. (Douglas 1970)

In the same vein, pride is a mainstay of political rhetoric, even though it is often hard to perfect is use or predict its effectiveness (Nabi 2002: 296–297). Undoubtedly though, many of history's greatest political speeches, from Churchill's exhortation to fight the Germans "on the beaches" to Nehru's "tryst with destiny", have emotions of pride and honour at their core. The inspiration of pride is often deeply resonating with audiences – anger, fear and guilt fade but pride often lingers. Against the backdrop of the extremely successful 1967 World Expo in Montreal, visiting French President Charles De Gaulle famously made a short speech in which he cried out "Vive le Québec libre!" The speech triggered an immense outpouring of French-Canadian pride that proved a major episode in the emergence of Québécois nationalism, which continues to be felt today.

Ethos

Ethos is how the speaker inspires trust in their audience. Even before a politician speaks, the listener will be prejudiced to what they say based on who is saying it. "Persuasion involves choice…it is directed to a man only in so far as he is free" (Burke 1969: 50), and thus whether we allow ourselves to be persuaded by a political leader's rhetoric will be strongly influenced by our perception of the authority behind that rhetoric. We are persuaded more by people we know or trust, and far less by those we do not. The words of a politician convicted of corruption carry little authority, regardless of how correct they are.

The use of ethos by modern political leaders is particularly critical because, unlike doctors or lawyers or engineers, there are no professional certifications that qualify a person to lead a government. In a democratic system where everyone has an opinion, how does a political leader establish their entitlement to speak and be listened to by the masses?

Leaders do this firstly by leaning on their prior experience, institutional positions and track record. And even a leader whose background and history are unknown to an audience has the capacity to define this through their rhetoric (Amossy 2001). Candidates running for office will stress their qualifications and their career accomplishments. Politicians running for re-election will list the achievements of their previous term. Establishing ethos is fine-tuned to the specific audience – leaders speaking to a religious community will undoubtedly stress their religious adherence or long-standing respect for their faith to build rapport.

Ethos is a frequent area of political contestation amongst politicians and using rhetoric to attack the character of other speakers is common in political campaigning (Wang et al. 2018). Yet, contestation over character highlights the real differences between leaders and keeps rhetoric in check. For example, during the 1984 United States Vice-Presidential debate, the Republican candidate Dan Quayle was asked by moderators to discuss whether, as a relatively young man with a short political career, he had the experience and character to ascend to the presidency should the situation require. Quayle responded by emphasizing his experience and noting that former president John F. Kennedy had as much experience as Quayle when he became president. His Democratic opponent, Lloyd Bentsen, responded with one of the most memorable lines of the campaign: "Senator, I served with Jack Kennedy. I knew Jack Kennedy. Jack Kennedy was a friend of mine. Senator, you're no Jack Kennedy."

It is not just politicians who contest ethos. In a contemporary globalized society of mass media and the 'monitory democracy' (Keane 2009: pt. 3) where everyone watches everyone else, it is ethos that will be the first to be scrutinized by the public. Fact-checkers and media commentators rapidly assess claims and hold leaders to account as to whether they have vested interested on the issue, whether their claims have been consistent with previous statements, and whether they have a sufficient moral, political or social track-record to speak on the subject authoritatively.

Leaders do not have an entirely free hand by which to define ethos – it is communally produced (Reynolds 1993). One of the ways this is most acutely felt is in the gendered nature of language in many cultures, and how the credibility of the rhetoric of male and female leaders is often differently perceived. Prejudicial gender attitudes may mean that regardless of their qualifications or background, female leaders in some communities will not be taken as seriously as men when speaking in political arenas. Many of our societal cues on gender come from differing expectations regarding diction, tone and rhetorical style, and usually it is 'masculine' forms of rhetoric that are associated with leadership rather than 'feminine' forms (Holman 2016; Jones 2016), such that female political candidates are often perceived as lacking traditionally admired leadership qualities such as 'strength' and 'confidence' (Huddy & Terkildsen 1993; see Chapter 6). Yet when female political candidates do employ more 'masculine' rhetorical styles in the pursuit of political office, it often jars with gendered public expectations and is not always considered credible. As Kim Campbell, Prime Minister of Canada, observed of her own treatment in politics:

> If I didn't speak the way I do, I wouldn't have been seen as a leader. But my way of speaking may have grated on people who were not used to hearing it from a woman. It was the right way for a leader to speak, but it wasn't the right way for a woman to speak. It goes against type. (Eagly & Carli 2007: 102)

Kairos

Kairos was not one of Aristotle's triad of persuasive means, but it is a related concept that translates as 'the right moment'. The concept encapsulates the idea of timing, and choosing the right words, or the right idea, in the moment to have maximum impact (Sipiora & Baumlin 2012: 2–7).

This can be a tricky concept to clearly define and practice – what do we mean by the 'right moment' in which to say something, and how do we know it when we see it? (see Muckelbauer 2008: 114–122). Instinctively though, we all know that feeling when an act of rhetoric seems to embody the spirit of a moment. When Martin Luther King Jr made his now famous "I Have a Dream" speech on the steps of the Lincoln Memorial in Washington, D.C. on August 28, 1963, it was just one of several speeches made that day, but was remembered because in the words of journalists and observers, his was the rhetoric that most captured the mood and aspirations of the crowd, and best captured the times in which he spoke (McGrory 1963).

Kairos underscores the importance of political leaders understanding their audiences. Rhetoric can only be persuasive if it is tuned to what audiences are susceptible to hear. A leader may persuasively make the case for a foreign military intervention to their cabinet and generals through carefully constructed logos, and make the same case to the public by use of inspirational pathos to unite the nation behind the cause. Kairos is critical though, because a nation that has just emerged from war will be weary of further conflict, and perhaps not even the most brilliant rhetoric can overturn a widespread sentiment for peace.

Canons of rhetoric

Aristotle's analysis of rhetoric and its persuasiveness was expanded upon by the Roman lawyer Quintilian into 'five canons':

- **Inventio (Discovery)** The substantive content of a speech, the discovery and construction of an argument.
- **Dispositio (Arrangement)** The structure of speech and how the arguments are arranged.

- **Elocutio (Style)** The linguistic style and techniques used.
- **Pronuntiato (Delivery)** How a speech is delivered and performed before an audience.
- **Memoria (Memory)** The ability to memorize and recall a speech.

The previous sections on ethos, logos, pathos and kairos implicitly cover *inventio* and the process of argument discovery. Let's briefly consider the other four canons and how political leaders consciously shape their rhetorical persuasiveness in this way.

Dispositio

Rhetoric often involves a narrative of facts and evidence to support a case, but how such evidence is selected and ordered in a speech can lead an audience to different conclusions. Unstructured or rambling speeches may be confusing and the point can be missed. Speakers are also faced with the challenge of how to maintain the attention of an audience. One way to do this is to begin with anecdotes or humour to 'warm up' the crowd yet build in seriousness to a crescendo to retain interest and provide catharsis. Structuring the speech carefully and engagingly can also help lead the audience to the conclusions the speaker wants them to draw. Take these excerpts from the Beira speech of Samora Machel, leader of the FRELIMO independence movement that overthrew Portuguese Mozambique in 1975:

> But colonialism has already fallen. Isn't that so? (Yes). Why did it fall, if colonialism is a superior race? If it is represented by the White race? Why did it fall, then? It proves that the people are stronger than any other force. Do you hear? (We hear). We defeated Portuguese colonialism here. Right? So, Portuguese colonialism was defeated by an 'inferior' race! Yes or no? (Yes).... The struggle in Mozambique didn't only free the land, it also freed mentalities, it freed complexes. Our struggle fought against superiority complexes and inferiority complexes and we have already won...Mozambique is a very rich country. We just need to use our strength correctly, our strength, our intelligence, our energy. And to use it correctly, it's necessary that we live organised, orientated and guided by FRELIMO. Do you hear? (We hear). (Darch & Hedges 2011)

Consider here how Machel builds his case in a stepwise fashion, soliciting active agreement from the audience through questions they would naturally agree with, to arrive at a logical conclusion that the audience would take great pride in. Namely, that Mozambicans of African descent are the equals of their former colonial masters. Once the audience is excited and in fierce agreement with the speaker, Machel ends on a conclusion that is less obvious and far more partisan (i.e. FRELIMO must necessarily guide the country post-independence), yet structurally is made to feel as if it is part of the broader point already agreed to (Darch & Hedges 2013: 56–59).

A modern trend in dispositio is the 'sound bite' – a short snippet of a speech that is memorable and encapsulates the main position. In the age of constant media coverage and short attention spans, modern rhetoric is often arranged in a more condensed fashion that allows for single-line summaries to be easily taken away and replayed (see Rinke 2016).

Elecutio

Language is not a neutral vessel for the transmission of political rhetoric – how words are used and in what way signal a great deal to the listener. For example, lexicon and accent: in Brazil there are dozens of dialects and accents of Brazilian Portuguese spoken. Traditionally many Brazilian political leaders have spoken, or have sought to speak, the *carioca* or *paulistano* dialect, which sounds the most 'correct' or refined to many Brazilians and is spoken by the educated elite in Rio de Janeiro and São Paulo (Tarallo 2009). Using one of these dialects immediately identifies the speaker to the audience as part of that elite. It may cut both ways, though – Lula Da Silva (Brazilian President, 2003–2011) possessed a notably unpolished and working-class accent, something that helped augment his credibility as leader of the Worker's Party and was a feature of his candidacy that endeared him to many working-class Brazilians (see Case 9.1).

Other cues in speech, like using certain phrases, examples or quotations are signifiers to an audience (Martin 2014: 63–64). The term 'green' for example has become explicitly associated with the environmental movement and few conservative politicians would use it, regardless of intent.

Pronuntiatio

Many studies have found that non-verbal cues have far greater impact on how rhetoric is received by the audience than the actual words used (see Natten 2020: ch. 6). Pronuntiatio is the use of paralinguistic tools, like body language, tone, pacing and setting to reinforce argument and augment the power of rhetoric. Italian fascist leader Benito Mussolini, for example, was master of using body language to convey strength and solemnity to his speeches – jutting out his chin, crossing his arms, staring intensely and cocking his head (Martin 2014: 84).

Take fashion as another example. When Augusto Pinochet, military dictator of Chile, spoke publicly he chose to always do so in his general's uniform. He had his peaked military cap tailored to be higher than the standard issue, and consciously adopted the insignia of 'captain general', a historical military rank used by Chile's independence leader (Coad 2006). Bolivian president Evo Morales cultivated a completely different image that stressed his common and indigenous roots by opting for casual or indigenous-inspired couture (Forero 2006). The power of paralinguistic cues is enormous and creates an impression in the audience's mind before the leader has even begun to speak.

Memoria

It may seem a banal topic to discuss how a politician memorizes a speech. But it can influence the perception of ethos. One of the modern devices used to avoid the problems of memory in speech-making is the teleprompter, a 'necessary evil' for contemporary politicians. However, audiences instinctively dislike politicians who seem too scripted, robotic or stilted in their delivery, often a symptom of teleprompter reliance (Oakley 2017: ch. 10). Political rhetoric that is delivered extemporaneously is likely to have some errors, lapses in memory or filled pauses (like um or ah), yet to audiences it often feels more natural and genuine. And many types of rhetoric still require memory and rehearsal. In political debating, the candidate's ability to remember and recall facts, figures or arguments on a wide range of topics is often the crucial difference between appearing to be credible and knowledgeable, or appearing to be flustered and uninformed.

Using rhetoric

Thus far we have discussed some of the approaches and techniques that leaders use to craft rhetoric. But to what ends do leaders employ rhetoric? There are endless potential applications, but four in particular – defining communities, setting the agenda, framing and explaining and campaigning – are central to political leadership and are worth exploring in depth.

Defining communities

One way in which a community might be defined is by what its members know, value or believe (Herrick 2017). Leaders offer visions, articulate goals, formulate plans, annunciate values, and in doing so appeal to others who share those visions or goals and believe in those plans. This process not only creates a followership for the leader, but often serves to explicitly define a community of interest built around that followership. Great political rhetoric may even help inspire and define an identity for an entire nation – when the first Prime Minister of the Congo Patrice Lumumba spoke about independence in 1960, he stated:

> no Congolese will ever forget that independence was won in struggle, a persevering and inspired struggle carried on from day to day, a struggle, in which we were undaunted by privation or suffering and stinted neither strength nor blood...I ask you all to sink your tribal quarrels: they weaken us and may cause us to be despised abroad.. We shall show the world what the black man can do when working in liberty, and we shall make the Congo the pride of Africa.

Lumumba, using rhetoric here and throughout his political career, attempted to build a unified Congolese community behind justice, freedom and social and economic emancipation, while diminishing the traditional tribal and ethnic divisions that existed within the newly independent nation. Through his words, Lumumba attempted to define what it is to be Congolese, and what that meant in the postcolonial world (see also Case 9.1).

Australian political scientist Graham Little argued that a leader's rhetorical style attracts and reinforces constituencies based on the psychosocial relationship between themselves and 'others'. Little's "strong" leaders, for example, set up a very distinct and adversarial tension between the *self vs other*: the other is to be challenged or feared, and the leader works to protect the group's interests against them. The "group" leader on the other hand sees the *self in others,* and thus attracts those who seek mutuality through open and accepting communities. The "inspiring" leader looks to the *self and other,* stressing creative partnerships, dynamism and power-sharing (Little 1985).

For example, Australian Prime Minister Robert Menzies built his early career around redefining a political community. In 1942 he famously spoke of the 'forgotten people' – the politically less-organized but growing middle-class of Australia – shopkeepers, small business owners, professionals, artisans etc. – and spoke to them as their champion, annunciating a view for Australia of ambitious individualism within a fair playing field. He did so by almost consciously avoiding the aggressive 'self vs other' politics that had dominated the Great Depression and World War II, and instead appealed to the creative, democratic and entrepreneurial spirit – a self-and-other project – that would inspire a generation as they focused on post-war rebuilding. Menzies helped redefine conservative politics and in doing so created a new middle-class political bloc that would become the backbone of his party's support for decades (Brett 2014).

Setting the agenda

Agenda-setting is one of the most powerful yet least obvious ways in which political leaders can use rhetoric to leverage their power. The "public agenda" consists of issues and problems dominating the public discourse at a given time. That agenda does not necessarily reflect the issues that are actually important or need solving, but rather a version of reality that is presented to them by the media and other sources (McCombs & Shaw 1972; Walgrave & Van Aelst 2016). The news media is particularly powerful in shaping opinion, and what it puts in its headlines tends to dominate public attention, regardless of any objective measure of an issue's importance.

And as those with the most vaunted political platforms, it is usually political leaders who have the greatest ability to dominate the media, and subsequently the public agenda. What top political leaders say or do will make the front pages almost automatically. Modern leaders have access to platforms to speak directly to the public *en masse* as well, from radio to Twitter, giving them enormous power to shape political discourse (Peake & Eshbaugh-Soha 2008). Donald Trump, running for the US Presidency in 2016, became most famous for his discussion of the need for a border wall between the United States and Mexico, and repeated this idea frequently. Even if only a minority were convinced of its actual need, discussion over the merits of a border wall and immigration issues generally dominated the period after his election, despite being far less prominent in political discourse in previous years.

In office, political leaders will use their soapbox to shape the public agenda and guide it towards issues and areas they consider priorities. This is especially true for large, complicated political landscapes with many independent institutions. Political leaders can help narrow the focus across the whole of government – legislatures, government departments and local governments can be encouraged to shift their attention towards goals and issues pushed by political leaders at the top.

This power can be abused. Propaganda is the term applied to unobjective and often extreme state-driven campaigns to manipulate the public agenda, which political leaders in states with limited media freedom have been able to use with extraordinary effect in the information age. Mao Zedong, for example, mounted the Four Pests campaign in China from 1958 to 1962, identifying flies, sparrows, rats and mosquitos as public enemies and a critical issue for mass public action. Many citizens responded to the state's ubiquitous propaganda and made eradication a priority, virtually wiping out the Chinese sparrow population and creating an ecological imbalance that caused locusts to breed unchallenged and wreak havoc for years.

Framing and explaining

Powerful as their platforms are, political leaders do not control the agenda, but merely influence it. And often they will find themselves reacting to an agenda driven by other forces. When a disaster like a nuclear accident occurs, for example, the media and the public inevitably discuss and focus on nuclear safety, regardless of the leader's interest.

Leaders do however use rhetoric to frame issues that emerge and influence how their followers think about them. A nuclear accident can be minimized and explained away by a pro-nuclear leader by advancing a narrative of a 'freak accident' or a 'one off' occurrence. Or it can be used by an anti-nuclear leader as evidence that nuclear power is systemically flawed and inherently dangerous to public health, and perhaps framed as justification for shutting the entire industry down. This is part of the 'sense-making' and 'meaning-making' of crisis, where leaders have great scope through rhetoric to influence how the public interprets events and issues that have arisen (Boin et al. 2005).

How successful they are relies on how persuasive their rhetoric is, though the credibility of the leader is particularly crucial if they are to successfully spin the public interpretation of issues to their advantage (Boin et al. 2005: 78–79). Robert Mugabe, ruler of Zimbabwe from 1980 to 2017, helped maintain his power over a period of dramatic economic and social decline by continuously scapegoating the nation's problems on Westerners and the legacies of imperialism (Meredith 2002: 17), and illusory social 'threats' such as homosexuality (Meredith 2002: 127), effectively distracting the public from the true problems the nation faced. This was made possible largely due to Mugabe's legendary stature in the country as a revolutionary hero, something he frequently reminded the public of through speech and symbolism.

Campaigning and building support

Political leaders do not just define their communities and then leave them – they must work constantly to maintain their support. Sometimes they might use various resources of power to benefit their followers materially or politically, yet most followers are beyond such immediate reach. Hence, maintaining support often means use of rhetoric and persuasion so that followers continue to believe in their leader.

But as new issues arise and conditions change, so too a political leaders' support will wax and wane. A leader's following is not fixed but fluid, and in large democracies often dramatically so. A new issue, completely unforeseen by politicians and the public alike, might emerge suddenly and without warning, and may divide a leader's following along new lines. The leader then must establish their position on the issue, and find ways to reunite their followers by reframing the issue or pushing it off the agenda, or by accepting the loss of some followers but perhaps attracting others, effectively redefining their community.

Every leader faced this challenge amidst the Coronavirus outbreak of 2019-2020. The standards by which leaders were judged shifted very quickly to their performance in managing the public health crisis, and whatever policies or issues leaders had been pursuing prior to the crisis were soon dwarfed in importance by comparison. Virtually every political leader globally had to redefine their policies and political mission in light of the crisis, and continuously refine those positions as the crisis wore on and public attitudes around lockdowns and acceptable risks changed. Leaders engaged in a continuous campaign to build support and encourage compliance for unpopular public health measures, maintain economic confidence in the face of significant downturn but also provide solace to an anxious and grieving public (e.g. Friedman 2020).

Rhetoric is the cornerstone of political leadership, and an essential tool in everything political leaders do, from setting agendas to passing policies. There is no set method or winning formula for the construction of rhetoric – only tools and approaches that a leader must choose from to match the audience and context. But when done well under the right conditions, rhetoric can redefine an issue, a community or even an entire era.

Negotiation

A leader can never completely monopolize power and must work with others who hold it to accomplish their goals (see Chapter 4). Rhetoric is a potent tool for building consensus behind a vision, but there will always be some with conflicting values and interests who cannot be readily swayed. Or even if a vision is agreed upon, there will inevitably be conflicting views amongst stakeholders on how to achieve that vision. A leader must thus turn to negotiation, the art of resolving disagreement, to find pathways forward. Barack Obama, when elected to the United States Presidency in 2008, did so having campaigned heavily on the need for comprehensive healthcare reform. Although successful in persuading many of this need, formulating and

Case 9.1 The word is mightier

Gamal Abdel Nasser

President of Egypt, 1956–1970

Figure 9.2 Gamal Abdel Nasser

Few leaders have galvanized a people, or articulated an agenda, so enduringly as Gamal Adbel Nasser, whose revolution in Egypt became a turning point in the history of the Arab world. The son of a postal worker from Alexandria, Nasser was a career military officer who came of age when the Arab world was almost completely dominated by European powers. Nasser became a leader amongst a circle of young officers who played the lead role in the revolution that deposed the pro-British King Farouk I in 1952. But more importantly, Nasser emerged as the chief ideologue of the movement, crafting a new purpose for Egyptians, and for the Arab world.

In ***The Philosophy of the Revolution,*** Nasser lays out a framework for the restoration of Egyptian sovereignty and power, through both a political and social revolution. Profoundly influenced by his service in the 1948 Arab-Israeli war, Nasser decried a history of European exploitation going back to the Crusades, and the perpetual failure of Arabs to unify in the face of outside interference. Nasser emphasizes the historical, religious and linguistic ties that unite Arabs, as well as a unified Arab world's potential for global strategic influence and economic prosperity, particularly through its oil reserves. In the coming years, Nasser would refine and proselytize this message, and by the time he assumed the Egyptian presidency in 1956, Arab nationalism had become his rallying cry (Jankowski 2002: 30–32) and soon dominated the Arab world's political agenda, sparking anti-colonial revolts and populist uprisings across the region.

Nasser was a savvy orator who had a commanding presence and charisma that drew millions of devoted followers. He was adept at speaking in different registers depending on his audience. Even within speeches, Nasser would often switch dialects, speaking Modern Standard Arabic when talking of broader Arab unity, then Cairene, a colloquial dialect, when speaking on local issues (Mazraani 2013: 48–52), allowing him to appeal to both domestic and foreign audiences simultaneously. He would frequently depart from his prepared speeches and speak extemporaneously, even casually. He made heavy use of personal pronouns – "I", "we" or "you" – and told candid personal anecdotes that helped establish rapport and familiarity with the audience. He would frequently ask rhetorical questions to the audience, as if in discussion with them directly rather than speaking down to them (Mazraani 2013: 88–91). He would modulate the tempo of his speeches precisely, slowing down when making solemn pronouncements or espousing important philosophical beliefs, and speeding up to a more lively pace when evoking nostalgia or telling stories (Mazraani 2013: 90).

He was skilled at using emotion. He could invoke anger or sorrow to rally passions and then easily switch to humour and storytelling to defuse tensions. He successfully walked a fine line in his rhetoric on religion – Nasser did not see Islam as the basis for Arab nationalism and sought to separate church and state. Yet when talking to religious audiences, Nasser was able to cloak his vision in religiosity and could quote the Quran at will (Jankowski 2002: 35). Even Nasser's appearance played a part. A tall and imposing man who exuded confidence, he nonetheless had bright eyes, a boyish look, and frequently smiled and joked, which disarmed his critics and endeared him to the masses (Lacouture & Lacouture 1958: 453).

Nasser fused his style with a powerful platform – radio – and created the ***Voice of the Arabs,*** a transnational broadcast service from Cairo that saw Nasser's rhetoric carried across the region to enormous effect (Boyd 1975). Nasser would enhance his broadcasts by pairing them with performances by Uum Kulthum, one of the most popular Arabic singers of all time. She was an active supporter of Nasser and composed numerous nationalist songs.

Nasser transformed Egypt, particularly through his economic policies, radically transferring much of the nation's land and wealth from the elite to the working classes, while undertaking massive infrastructure projects that rapidly industrialized the nation. Yet his most notable adventures in foreign policy were failures – his attempt to create a United Arab Republic collapsed within just a few years, and his support of a nationalist uprising in Yemen became Egypt's 'Vietnam War'. His attempt to forge a united Arab front against Israel in support of Palestine led to a disastrous invasion by Israel in 1967 in which Egypt lost the Sinai Peninsula.

Yet even Egypt's defeat in 1967 did not destroy his mystique, with Nasser's resignation in that year overturned after enormous crowds of Egyptians flooded the cities in support of their leader (Aburish 2004: 268–269). Indeed, Nasser had redefined the Arab community, articulated its agenda, and built support for his philosophy so effectively that Nasserism remains deeply influential in contemporary Arabic politics. During a speech in 1954, an assassin opened fire on Nasser. Chaos erupted in the room, though Nasser famously kept his composure and did not abandon the stage, instead continuing to speak and stating, "I am alive, and even if I die, all of you are Gamal Abdul Nasser!"

implementing such reforms took years of negotiation. Negotiations began initially with the United States Congress, within which there was a wide range of views on the direction reform should take. Building a consensus even within his own cabinet and party took considerable time and effort. And this was just the beginning – the administration then had to bargain with a wide variety of institutional players whose compliance and cooperation would be essential to any workable policy. Health insurers, hospitals, pharmaceutical companies, doctors' associations, unions, state and local governments, and so on, all of whom potentially had much to lose and little to gain by reform. Although rhetorical persuasion built a case, and a mandate, for reform with the public, negotiation and bargaining were fundamental to implementing actual policy change (Washington Post 2010; Brill 2015).

Fundamentals of negotiation

Negotiation is effectively a form of *joint decision-making* (Zartman 1988: 32). Negotiation is always necessary on some level when one party requires another party's consent or contribution to achieve something. The point of negotiation is to reach a common position, but that position may be a *consensus,* or it may be a *compromise.* A consensus indicates that all parties have resolved their disagreements and found a common position they can agree upon, whereas a compromise involves parties agreeing on a way to proceed through concessions or trade-offs, even as disagreement over values, ideas or goals remain unresolved (Rostboll & Scavenius 2017: ch. 1). Because politics is often a contest of competing values, ideas and goals, compromise is more common than consensus.

Negotiation is only possible when parties have a *zone of possible agreement* (ZOPA). The existence of a ZOPA means there is overlap between the range of possible outcomes that all parties to the negotiation will accept. Furthermore, parties to a negotiation will likely only accept an agreement that is better than what has been termed the BATNA – the 'best alternative to a negotiated agreement'. In other words, if a party at the negotiating table is going to get a worse outcome by accepting an agreement than it would by pursuing some other course of action (or doing nothing), their incentive to accept that agreement is low (Lax & Sebenius 2006: 164).

Successful negotiation is difficult in politics. There are many characteristics to negotiation in general, and *political* negotiations specifically, that impede successful compromise, as well as a wide range of tactics and strategies that leaders can employ to try to succeed in spite of these.

Distributive vs integrative

Two general types of negotiation have long been identified (see Walton & McKersie 1991). The first is a distributive negotiation, also known as a *zero-sum game.* It implies that there is a finite amount of benefit that can be distributed by the outcome. Any gain by one party in a negotiation will come at the expense of the other parties. The second is integrative negotiation, or a *non-zero-sum* game. The amount of benefit to be distributed is variable and expandable, and it is possible through negotiation to find outcomes that are beneficial to all parties. This is achieved through trade-offs which become possible when the parties to negotiation value potential outcomes differently and/or bring different resources, skills or interests to the table that when combined will provide far greater benefit to the parties than they would in isolation (Hudson 2010: 726–727).

By their nature, distributive negotiations tend to be adversarial and acrimonious. In a zero-sum game, the dominant strategy for any party is to adopt the position that maximizes their own gain and while conceding as little as possible. Because there is a fixed amount of benefit to go around, there is no incentive to give up any more than you absolutely must. By contrast, integrative negotiations have much more scope to be creative and dynamic in the search for outcomes that can mutually benefit all parties (win-win), and negotiation tactics are far more varied as a result (Fisher, Ury & Patton 1991: 15–81). Political leaders wishing to genuinely negotiate outcomes (rather than simply stare down their opponents) therefore need to look for ways to 'expand the pie' on issues so that all parties might be induced to an agreement in which mutual benefit is realized.

This is easier said than done, particularly in political contexts. Instinctively, we tend to see any negotiation as a zero-sum game. Some have cited this as a cognitive bias borne out of human evolution in environments where resources were scarce and survival depended on maximization of gain (Meegan 2010). Competitive environments have been shown to amplify that bias, and politics is an arena characterized by extreme competition between actors and heavily influenced by electoral politics, which in most nations is institutionally structured as a zero-sum game (i.e., there can be only one party who 'wins' an election and leads the government) (Mansbridge & Martin 2016: 126–127).

Moreover, some of the most contentious political issues, particularly social issues, are difficult to reframe beyond zero-sum. For example, abortion, same-sex marriage and euthanasia are binary choices – they're either legal or they're not. Policy steps towards either choice will likely be seen as a victory for one side and a loss for the other, and compromise between the two is unlikely to satisfy either side. During the height of same-sex marriage debates in the 2000s, many governments passed laws sanctioning civil unions that were functionally similar to marriage in an attempt to compromise between factions for and against same-sex marriage. However, in nearly all jurisdictions where this was attempted, civil unions were not seen as sufficient for equality by LGBT activists, nor were they accepted as happy compromises by marriage traditionalists (e.g., PACS in France), and these middle-ground options proved only temporary measures that were never popular with either side.

Negotiation strategies and tactics

Political leaders who want to secure power, accomplish a goal or make a change often face other actors who are oppositional and whose incentive to cooperate may be low. In democratic politics it is the elected government that will largely be held accountable for its successes and failures, and the public will judge whether its rhetoric and promises matched the reality. Minority parties and other political actors thus may have little incentive to work with them – if the government fails to achieve its goals then it is the governments opponents who stand to make gains from disaffected voters at the next election. In such circumstances, leaders must be willing to offer significant concessions or place pressure upon their political opponents to bring them to the negotiating table.

Integrative negotiation is one viable pathway for accomplishing major policy or legislative solutions if the political leader must work with others to accomplish it (Brazeal 2009; Hudson 2010). To accomplish an integrative solution, leaders must 'expand the pie' so that all parties find value in the agreement. The Peace of Westphalia of 1648, one of the most important diplomatic treaties in history that ended three decades of religious war in Europe, had over 100 parties to the negotiations. The negotiations increasingly 'expanded the pie' by involving territorial, economic and legal concessions that had virtually nothing to do with the original religious disputes. In the US Congress, the term 'Christmas tree bill' evolved in the twentieth century to describe this phenomenon, where in order to secure passage of legislation, leaders would attach numerous and often unrelated amendments and riders (like ornaments on a Christmas tree) to secure the support of key legislators (Safire 2008: 120). The critical challenge for political leaders in negotiation thus is finding options for an integrative solution, which often involves creative thinking and a good understanding of the interests, motivations and BATNAs of other parties (Fisher, Ury & Patton 1991).

In addition, leaders have both 'hard' and 'soft' tactics at their disposal to sway negotiations. Hard bargaining attempts to increase the pressure on other parties to come to agreement and/or make their BATNA unpalatable, whilst soft bargaining tries to sidestep confrontation and build trust and amity between negotiating parties.

Hard bargaining involves leaders taking a firm position and adopting an aggressive posture, with the intention of making other parties to a negotiation lower their expectations of what they might receive in an agreement. They may also use threats and bluffing to increase the pressure on negotiating parties and make their BATNA seem worse than whatever deal the leader is offering (Churchman 1995: 18). Hard bargainers often use negative emotions like anger or guilt to increase pressure, though research indicates that negative emotion is often unproductive in achieving viable agreements (see Allred et al. 1997). Hard bargaining can involve use of public rhetoric to increase political pressure on opponents, to attempt to shift political blame for a lack of an agreement and its consequences to other parties, or to otherwise increase the perceived political cost of a lack of agreement (see Case 9.2). More complex tactics include:

- **Bogeys**, where the negotiator tries to deceive other parties as to their real interests and their valuation of potential outcomes to the negotiation.

- **Chicken**, where extreme bluffs or threats are made to scare other parties.
- **Grandstanding**, where the negotiator publicly attempts to take the high ground in negotiation so that other parties appear unreasonable if they don't agree (see Lewicki & Minton 2003).

The so-called *going public* strategy is a well-studied example of hard bargaining that is used by leaders to pressure other political actors or institutions to sign onto the leader's agenda. Instead of negotiating directly with political opposition, the leader publicly campaigns on their position to try and worsen the BATNA for other negotiating parties and create public pressure in favour of the leader's position (Kernell 2007). Few institutions are immune to public pressure, but it is particularly effective against other elected actors like legislators (see Eshbaugh-Soha 2016). The going public strategy is largely made possible by the modern media age, insofar as political leaders have an extraordinary platform to broadcast to the public and usually one that is far more powerful than any other institution in the system. US President Ronald Reagan is often seen as a master of the strategy, using public campaigns to build popular support for policies both foreign and domestic to overcome Congressional resistance and strengthen his bargaining hand (Bodnick 1990; Eshbaugh-Soha 2016). However, a leader cannot use the tactic constantly – there are many limitations to its effective use (Canes-Wrone 2001), and the tactic is risky. The stakes rise when a leader goes public, and if the leader is ultimately unsuccessful in swaying their opposition as intended they will suffer a much more public defeat than they would have otherwise.

Hard bargaining tactics are only successful if other parties back down and there is a reputation to back the tactics up – if threats are made and not carried out, credibility is quickly dashed. Moreover, hard bargaining fosters resentment and erodes working relationships, meaning there will likely be less trust and fewer pathways for negotiation in the future with those parties. An agreement that has been coerced through hard tactics may also require constant vigilance to uphold. Parties compelled into an agreement they resent will try and avoid complying with it as much as possible (Johnson 1993: 76–80).

Soft bargaining is largely the opposite approach – the goal is to improve relationships and offer incentives to induce parties to the negotiating table. Soft bargaining is more akin to salesmanship, where a political leader uses a charm offensive to win over opponents and find grounds for compromise (Johnson 1993: 71–75). *Small-target tactics*, for example, involve purposefully finding agreement on easy or minor points first to build trust and agreeability before tackling the more contentious issues, or even delegating difficult issues to technical committees or third parties for arbitration. *Yielding* involves a party purposefully making a concession to other parties, which even if relatively minor in nature can demonstrate good faith and a willingness to sacrifice self-interest, which may encourage other parties to then do the same.

Expressing positive emotion and socializing with other parties have also been demonstrated to increase the likelihood of reaching mutual agreement and forging lasting compromises (Carnevale & Isen 1986; Barry et al. 2004). Yet soft bargaining is not necessarily without complex or deceptive tactics. *Mirroring*, for example, is the process of mimicking the behaviour of others and repeating what they say, which is an insincere but well-established method of endearing others to the negotiator (Lewicki & Litterer 1985: 289).

If successful, a soft bargaining strategy is much more likely to result in lasting agreements while avoiding irresolvable impasses (see Case 9.2). However, soft bargaining also requires the negotiator to make sacrifices, sometimes very significant, to achieve credibility and agreement with other parties – sacrifices that may play poorly with followers who wish to see their leaders be strong advocates for their side (Johnson 1993: 74–76).

That said, soft bargaining is ineffective and often at a major disadvantage against parties who engage in hard bargaining tactics. Moreover, soft bargainers face the prospect of 'bad faith' negotiation, whereby parties to a supposed negotiation have no actual intention of accepting an agreement as they believe their best interests lie in their BATNA. This is common in politics, with political leaders publicly espousing a rhetoric of reasonability but unwilling to make meaningful concessions in negotiations. Political opponents to a government are oft incentivized to take bad faith positions, as they will likely perceive any agreement as only to the benefit of a government's re-election chances, and a lack of agreement likely to benefit their own. Thus, the risk for a leader adopting a soft bargaining position is that they make concessions and offer carrots for nothing, undermining their own position whilst getting no closer to joint agreement.

Negotiation considerations

Agreements are hard-won and easily lost. Negotiation involves the somewhat counterintuitive act of sharing, or even relinquishing, power for the sake of a better outcome. A principal difficulty of the negotiating process thus often lies in overcoming our instincts and biases.

The 'self-serving' bias, for example, is a common mental trap that parties to a negotiation fall into. Any given party to a negotiation tends to think that their own position is stronger, their negotiation tactics better, their cause more righteous, and their willpower greater than that of their opponents (Mansbridge & Martin 2016: 127–131). Experimental evidence has indicated that impasses in negotiation are frequently caused by unrealistic expectations by negotiating parties, and only when forced to see the weaknesses of their own position does willingness to compromise increase (Babcock & Loewenstein 1997). Again, this is somewhat counterintuitive for political leaders, as to be successful, it is critical to have and express high self-confidence. And yet, to be an effective negotiator, leaders must also question that self-confidence.

Furthermore, Howard Raiffa (2002), an expert on negotiation analysis, cites some 'organizing questions' that present important considerations as to how leaders might approach negotiation and the likelihood of good outcomes:

1. **Are there more than two parties?** The more parties there are to a negotiated agreement, the more complex it is to find a zone of possible agreement between everyone, and the more challenging to find solutions in which all parties 'win'. Globally there are far more bilateral (i.e., two nation) free trade agreements than there are multilateral (i.e., three or more nations), in no small part due to the dramatic rise in the complexity of negotiations as more parties become involved.
2. **Are parties monolithic?** Often in politics, the parties at the negotiating table (like a political party) are not all of one mind and one interest, but a collection of potentially varying interests. In such situations, negotiators can appeal to certain interests within the opposition to break-up the coalition ('salami tactics'). In protracted negotiations or stalemates, the chances increase that the political coalitions on either side will falter under stress (Churchman 1995: 46).
3. **Is the game repetitive?** Negotiating with a party you expect to only deal with once is not the same as negotiating with one you will face repeatedly. In the case of the latter, using dirty tactics to coerce a bargain will not be forgotten and will likely decrease your perceived credibility and trustworthiness in future negotiations.
4. **Are there time constraints?** Negotiating under time constraint is suboptimal, as it puts the time-constrained party under pressure to accede to the first acceptable deal, rather than the best deal. This is surprisingly common in politics, as contentious negotiations are often delayed until a crisis is reached and agreement becomes crucial. Indeed, leaders will sometimes use this purposefully through the strategy of *brinkmanship* – trying to force an issue to a crisis point in order to make the BATNA as bad as possible and scare the other party into accepting a deal (Schelling 1980: 199–201).
5. **Are negotiations public or private?** The nature of negotiations will vary enormously depending on who is able to observe them. In public leaders face far more pressure from their followers, and there is more incentive to grandstand for political gain. In private there is more leeway for pragmatic compromise and genuine interaction between negotiating parties (Mansbridge & Martin 2016).

Effective negotiation by a leader thus requires careful consideration of the circumstances surrounding the negotiations, and the appropriate tactics to match them (see Case 9.2).

Case 9.2 Negotiating the impossible

Vallabhbhai Patel

Deputy Prime Minister of India, 1947–1950

V.P. Menon

Secretary of the Ministry of States, 1946–1951

Figure 9.3 Vallabhbhai Patel in 1939

At the time of India's independence from the United Kingdom in 1947, its new leaders faced an enormous challenge. Although over half of British India had been directly administered by the British, vast swathes and millions of people still lived under the rule of 554 'princely states', governed by hereditary monarchs who had sworn allegiance to the British Crown (Reddy & Mishra 2004: 184–185). Upon the dissolution of British India, these states were nominally free to declare independence. In order to create a unified Indian state post-independence, Vallabhbhai Patel and V.P. Menon, politician and bureaucrat respectively, were given the enormous task of negotiating the accession of ambivalent or hostile princely states to the new nation.

Patel and Menon employed every variety of negotiating stances and tactics. Patel himself was fond of soft rhetoric, describing himself to the princes he met "not as a representative of the old paramountcy or of any foreign power, but as a member of a family trying to solve a family problem" (Menon 1955: 110). Menon and Patel were unfailingly polite and affable with the princes, despite the often-hostile opposition from larger states to joining India.

Patel and Menon's standard approach appealed to the princes' national pride and took advantage of the euphoria of securing independence to get them on side. They carefully explained the logic of the BATNA for smaller states, for whom trying to operate as an independent entity and bearing the enormous associated costs would be untenable. They took a gradualist approach with integration, initially requiring only that the princes recognize Indian sovereignty and cede control of defence, foreign affairs and communications to the new nation. They provided for the self-interest of the princes by negotiating generous settlements for those who signed the Instrument of Accession, including a right to retain their noble titles and a privy purse, as well as a variety of other material benefits and special privileges (Copland 2002: 265–269). Princely states, traditionally ignored and underdeveloped in British India, were promised major expansions of public services and infrastructure to benefit the prince's domain (Menon 1955: 208). Princely states of common interest and language were allowed to join together as self-governing provinces within India, such as Rajasthan and PEPSU. Efforts were continuously made to 'expand the pie' and make accession a win-win. Many agreed to Indian accession without conflict.

Patel and Menon were not averse to hard bargaining when soft tactics failed, and they found numerous ways to worsen the BATNA for hesitant states. As Indian independence loomed, so too did the expectations of the population to live in a democratic state and become the beneficiaries of expanded government services. Patel and Menon, both subtly and overtly, helped raise these expectations and rally public opinion to place pressure on the princes to accede when private negotiations failed. Some princely states were already facing popular unrest and others could see its likelihood, which made a negotiated settlement the best chance to ensure political survival. While gracious and magnanimous by nature, Patel was very capable of unnerving his opponents and demonstrating an iron will, and he was sure never to make idle threats (Krishna 2007: 104–119).

Salami tactics were critical. Patel and Menon initially faced strong resistance from the Nawab of Bhopal and Maharaja of Indore, who attempted to create a confederation of princes that would be collectively strong enough to operate independently of the new Indian state. They had numerous allies and the support of Pakistan, but Patel and Menon approached each ally individually, and through a combination of personal diplomacy and careful leverage, pried them away one by one, eventually leaving Bhopal and Indore isolated and with little choice to but to accede (Krishna 2007: 104–119).

It was not universally successful and a zone of possible agreement could not always be found. Hyderabad, the most populous princely state and second largest by area, rebuffed all negotiations. Ruled by a devout Muslim who was one of the richest men in the world, Hyderabad already had the resources and infrastructure to operate as an independent entity, thus from the beginning its BATNA was far more promising than what India could offer in an accession negotiation. Ultimately popular unrest and political intrigue provided a pretext for India to invade and forcibly annex the wayward state. Such cases were the exception though, and by 1949, all but a handful of the princely states had voluntarily joined the new nation. The rapid and largely peaceful way in which Patel and Menon secured the integration of so many diverse and sometimes hostile interests into the new Indian state remains an incredible feat of twentieth-century politics (Copland 1991: 38–39).

Chapter Summary

- Rhetoric is speech that is designed to persuade. It is the cornerstone of how leaders exercise influence over others and is central to the practice of political leadership. It is used to define communities, set the agenda, frame events or change and to campaign and build support.
- Rhetoric may involve a variety of persuasive methods and approaches, the most important of which are:
  - Logos: The use of logic and argument to make a case.
  - Pathos: The use of emotion and feeling to influence others.
  - Ethos: The credibility and reliability of a speaker.
  - Kairos: How well rhetoric fits the times and circumstances.
- Furthermore, effective rhetoric by leaders involves considering aspects of how a speech is delivered, including in what tone and register, how a speech is memorized and how it is organized.
- When a leader cannot persuade through words alone, they must use negotiation to bring others around to their way of thinking.
- All negotiation requires finding a zone of possible agreement (ZOPA) in which parties can find areas in which their interests overlap, and agreement terms that offer better outcomes for the parties than what would result if no agreement was reached (the BATNA).
- The overall approach to negotiation rests on whether it is perceived as a zero-sum game or not – those that are will be more confrontational, but those that are not offer numerous opportunities to 'expand the pie' and create mutual benefit for all parties.
- The general approach to negotiation may be hard (in which leaders attempt to force parties to negotiate by worsening their BATNA) or soft (in which leaders attempt to build rapport and trust with parties). There are numerous considerations of the negotiating context, however, that determine which tactical approach is likely to succeed.

10 CONTEMPORARY TRENDS AND CHALLENGES

Chapter Outline

- What are some of the contemporary challenges that leaders in the twenty-first century face?
- How are presidentialization, populism and polarization reshaping the nature of modern political leadership?
- How does leadership fit into a modern egalitarian democracy? What do contemporary citizens want from their leaders?
- Why is the symbolic role of leadership so powerful?
- What can we conclude from our overview of political leadership?

Thus far, I have largely offered ideas, theories and paradigms that are broadly applicable to political leadership in any era. Political leaders have had to make decisions, conduct negotiations and craft rhetoric since civilization began, and psychology, culture, gender, institutions and history are lenses with just as much relevance to understanding political leadership in the past as they are to understanding political leadership today.

This is not to say that political leadership is the *same* in every era. The Prime Minister of Spain facing the Coronavirus crisis of 2020 is not the first leader to find themselves responsible for steering that nation through an epidemic – diseases have ravaged Spain periodically since the beginning of recorded history. Yet in each manifestation the constellation of policy options, political institutions, public expectations, technologies, societal norms, and of course disease pathology, is different. Pedro Sanchez, the Prime Minister of Spain in 2020, may take solace that King Philip IV faced a similar crisis with the Great Plague of Seville in 1647, but their governing contexts are so different, what the former can draw from the latter's experience is likely limited.

Indeed, as Nicholas Nassim Taleb argues, the 'black swans' that truly test leadership in a given age will almost by definition be those that were not predicted (and perhaps not even predictable) and catch us unprepared – studying the 'knowns' of the past will not always prepare us for the 'unknowns' of the future (Taleb 2007). A successful political leader in uncharted territory is a flexible one who can repurpose and retool the lessons of the past in creative ways to solve emerging challenges, but also one who is able to ignore those lessons when necessary and chart new courses amidst uncertainty. This final chapter examines some of those emerging trends and challenges that political leaders must contend with in the twenty-first century.

Presidentialization

Presidentialization is the term given to the observation that political leaders at the apex of the political system are claiming an ever-greater share of political power and authority in contemporary politics. In a landmark study of the phenomenon, Poguntke and Webb examined 14 democratic nations and found in nearly all there had been a moderate to strong increase in the dominance of the topmost leaders relative to other political actors and institutions over recent decades (Poguntke & Webb 2005: 337–339). This increasing domination has taken three forms:

1. **Executive Domination:** Greater dominance of executive decision-making processes by the leader, including greater control over the cabinet and bureaucracy, and a declining role of the leader's party in executive decision-making.
2. **Party Domination:** Increasing domination of the leader within their own party, especially over policy direction, candidate recruitment and internal procedures.
3. **Media Domination:** Intensification of media focus on the top leaders, and voter preferences increasingly determined by assessment of leaders, rather than policies or issues.

Scholars have observed these changes occurring even in democracies with traditionally weak political executives, such as the Netherlands (Fiers & Krouwel 2005; Garzia 2014), though *how much* and *how fast* do vary significantly across polities (see Passarelli 2015). Indeed, we might term the phenomenon more appropriately as 'personalization', as even within presidential systems, the degree of leader dominance over governments, parties and campaigns has increased (e.g. Wattenberg 2013; Siavelis & Field 2015).

These trends have been driven not by changes in how political systems are formally structured. Rather, presidentialization seems to be driven by changes in areas such as voting behaviour, partisan identification, media coverage of politics, and the policy-making process within government (Poguntke & Webb 2005). Changes in communication technology and the media are especially important drivers. In the 19th century, rulers were distant characters rarely seen by the public except through portraits in public buildings. Now we constantly see and hear our leaders through magazines, newspapers, television, radio and the internet. Social media has further reduced the perceived distance between leader and public, with platforms like Twitter allowing presidents and potentates to speak directly to millions of followers (Esser & Strömbäck 2014: 8–11). Political leaders in the process become "recognizable performers, but also intimate strangers" (Stanyer 2007: 72).

Another major shift in media coverage stems from the decline in both the availability, and interest, in local news in many countries – local or regional news outlets are steadily disappearing in the twenty-first century, giving way to just a handful of large news outlets, which tend to focus on national, rather than local, politics (Hopkins 2018). In conjunction with an increasing focus on political leaders in contemporary media coverage (Kepplinger 2002), the effect has been that coverage of national political leaders dwarfs coverage of all others.

The presidentialization phenomenon has been of particular interest in parliamentary democracies. In nearly all such systems, the head of government is not elected by the public, but instead the public votes for their parliamentary representatives, who in turn elect a government. Yet voters in parliamentary systems are increasingly voting for their representatives on the basis of their party's leader, rather than the candidate's qualities or positions, further cementing the centrality of the leader to a party's fortunes (McAllister 2007).

This increasing centrality of the top leadership has many potential consequences. One of the most notable is that political leaders across the political landscape, from legislators to local councillors, are increasingly swept up in national political issues, with voters tending to conflate local and national politics to a degree not seen previously. Donald Trump, for example, so completely dominated the politics of his time that even special elections for congressional vacancies, or elections for state legislatures, were often deemed 'referenda' on the president and covered in that light (e.g., Gabriel 2019). Another notable consequence has been the decline of the strength of traditional political parties, and political movements emerging on the basis of individual leaders, rather than ideologies or platforms. Consider France's Emmanuel Macron whose *En Marche* party, a movement largely built around himself, swept to power in 2017, displacing many of France's traditional parties in the process.

This has had significant flow-on effects with regards to the balance of power between different branches of government. Top leaders have not merely enjoyed more power *within* the executive and their parties, but they have shepherded the executive to greater power within the broader political system too. In many cases, this has come at the cost of the legislature, which has seen its relative influence decline significantly over recent decades in many polities (e.g., Kopecký 2004; Carmines & Fowler 2017). In some systems it is the judiciary too that has seen its ability to act as a check on power diminished by executive interference in its affairs (e.g., Davies 2018). These expansions of executive power have oft been endorsed, rather than resisted, by the public, particularly as leaders harness populist politics to justify such changes.

Presidentialization has arguably shifted the emphasis in political leadership too towards the performative and communicative aspects of the role. Certainly, no modern democratic leader can ignore the centrality of crafting a public image and maintaining strong relationships with mass and social media (Campus 2010: 220–223). With each leap in communication technology, it has often been the political leader who can best master new platforms that has seen their star rise fastest. US President Franklin Roosevelt's 'fireside chats' of the 1930s used the new medium of radio to connect with the public more intimately than any predecessor could. In the twenty-first century, it is social media that presents this same opportunity – India's Narendra Modi is one of the most followed political leaders in the world on Facebook, Instagram and Twitter, and his successful use of social media to shape his image and spread his message is widely thought to have been a 'game changer' in India's 2014 election, which saw Modi's party sweep to power (Pal, Chandra, & Vydiswaran 2016).

For leaders outside of the apex, presidentialization has significant consequences as well. If all politics is national, then local political leaders, from mayors to legislators, cannot ignore this trend, and increasingly must craft their message (and even their policies) with a view to the pulse of national politics. And their stock will rise and fall with it – when a national leader and their party are unpopular, it is reflected in sub-national and local races. The United Kingdom municipal elections of 2019, for example, were dominated by the issue of Brexit and the perceived performance (or underperformance) of the national party leaders on this issue (Castle 2019). Despite local government playing a very marginal role, at best, in the relationship between the United Kingdom and the European Union, thousands of local government representatives were voted out of office on voter sentiment primarily driven by this all-consuming national drama. Thus, while top leaders must shoulder the burden of increased focus, leaders at other levels must fight harder to be noticed and considered on their own terms.

Populism

Somewhat related to presidentialization in practical effect is *populism.* It is at once both easy to recognize and difficult to define. At its core, populism is a type of politics that reduces society into two groups – the 'elites' and the 'people' – and seeks to promote popular sovereignty while demonizing and defeating elites. It has been variously described as a political project, a style of leadership and a type of political theatre, and as such there is no common agreement on how to precisely define it (Mudde & Kaltwasser 2017: 5–8). Although some have termed it a political ideology, it is at best a 'thin ideology' that provides no real roadmap for policy, and populist rhetoric has been used by leaders and movements with political ideologies of all stripes (Stanley 2008). Some have described populism as inherently anti-pluralist and chauvinistic, seeking to promote 'the people' at the expense of minorities and 'outsiders' (Müller 2016). Populism may also be genuinely democratic in its nature or may have at its heart authoritarian intent, making it even harder to clearly define (de Beus 2009).

In political leadership, populism is a recurring technique and rhetorical device: many leaders will seek to present themselves as 'of the people' and stress their credentials and relatability as common citizens rather than elite functionaries. However, some will go beyond this and make populist appeals the core of their leadership style. Their rhetoric will turn to demonizing elites, and heralding themselves as patriotic outsiders and saviours. Populist leaders build highly personalized campaigns around themselves and position themselves as leaders of the people against mainstream politics (Mudde & Kaltwasser 2017: 43–74).

Often populism thrives in times of crisis, uncertainty or stagnation, or in the wake of exposed corruption or ineffectiveness by mainstream politicians. Precisely who 'the people' and 'the elite' are is often vague in populist rhetoric, and shifts to suit the purposes of its user. Populist leaders will often continue to use the same people-versus-elite rhetoric even while they are in office, redefining who the 'elite' are to suit their immediate political goals. Political opponents or other political institutions such as courts, legislatures or corporations are common targets (Mudde & Kaltwasser 2017: 13–14). This is in spite of the fact that many prominent populist leaders have come from the elite themselves. Millionaire businessmen (like H. Ross Perot and Donald Trump in the USA, Silvio Berlusconi in Italy), wealthy landholders (Jörg Haider in Austria), intelligentsia (Pim Fortuyn in the Netherlands, Pablo Iglesias Turrión in Spain) and experienced politicians (Rafeal Correa in Ecuador, Fernando Collor de Mello in Brazil) have all had success with populist-styled campaigns pitched against an 'elite'.

Many have observed a significant rise in the prevalence of populist rhetoric and candidates in the late twentieth and early twenty-first century. Cas Mudde offers several potential reasons for the rise. Some of these are the same factors that have led to the increasing personalization of democratic politics – intense media, voter and party focus on political leaders, as well as declining levels of voter partisanship and party loyalty. Others are demographic factors, like the rising education and urbanization of democracies, which see voters increasingly willing to challenge experts and elites in politics (Mudde 2004). Another popular strand of thinking has pointed to the huge changes wrought by globalization, free trade and deindustrialization in mature democracies as driving a rise in populist candidates who capitalize on economic marginalization and readily demonize a vaguely defined new global elite (Cox 2017; Rodrik 2018). Although many scholars have sought to address the issue of populism by calling for greater democracy and public participation in politics, analyses suggest that many populist voters are not especially interested in more democracy or class conflict, but more simply want leaders who will improve their circumstances and represent their interests and values (Mudde 2004: 557–560).

Whatever the cause, the effect has been clear: with rising public distrust of elites, politicians and government internationally – particularly in traditionally liberal democracies (see Clark et al. 2018: ch. 3) – there are significant openings for populist appeals that are being duly exploited by a wave of political newcomers.

Populism has often been criticized as bringing the worst out in democratic politics. Its appeal usually rests on irrational and emotive arguments and is used as a tool by leaders to manipulate public opinion and win electoral support, often in the absence of substantive solutions, policies or ideas. Moreover,

Case 10.1 The good populist?

Evo Morales

President of Bolivia, 2006–2019

Figure 10.1 Evo Morales in 2006

The case of Evo Morales offers insight into both the opportunities and dangers of populism in contemporary democratic politics. Born to an indigenous Aymara family in rural Bolivia, Morales spent his early career building a political movement around his country's most traditionally disenfranchised voices. Working in rural and agricultural communities in the provinces, his early cause was found in defending the rights of the ***cocaleros*** – coca growers – who were suppressed by a succession of right-wing governments backed by the United States who saw fighting coca production as critical to a global war on drugs. Yet coca is central to the cultural and religious practices of indigenous Bolivians, who have cultivated the plant for thousands of years. Morales began organizing farmers and indigenous communities against the government's coca policies.

Morales used the issue as a springboard into the traditional populist dichotomy between the elites and the people, seeing the actions against coca as driven by the wealthy, urban elite of Bolivia and the United States' engagement in a new global imperialism (Harten 2011: 74–77). As his protests and leadership rose in prominence, the scope of his platform and rhetoric widened, bringing together various groups traditionally less powerful in Bolivia's political system, including farmers, miners and indigenous groups. A succession of ever-larger political coalitions led by Morales resulted, eventually becoming the ***Movement for Socialism*** (MAS), a political instrument concentrating the power of grassroots movements around Bolivia (Harten 2011: ch.6). Though Morales's powerbase began on the political periphery, a series of social conflicts throughout the 1990s and early 2000s – including fights over water rights, natural gas resources, widespread economic inequality, indigenous marginalization and continuing conflict over coca production – catapulted Morales to national prominence (Brienen 2016). Morales put at the centre of his rhetoric the image of the 'beggar on a throne of gold' – the concept that despite Bolivia's great wealth in natural resources, the vast bulk of its people lived in severe poverty. He placed the blame for that disparity squarely at the feet of a wealthy urban elite, the traditional ruling class, and capitalist foreign interests (Brienen 2016: 85–86). Morales was credibly able to seize the mantle of the popular hero and the 'outsider' due to his humble background and long-standing work with social movements, but amplified it through his consciously 'rustic' way of speaking and his indigenous style of dress, while his movement at every turn sought to highlight its 'outsider' status and its consciously popular, rather than elite, origins.

The MAS became a political phenomenon that swept Morales into the presidency in 2005 in a watershed moment for people of indigenous origin in South America. Morales's government soon made good on its early promises, challenging traditional power structures in the nation. An ambitious economic program nationalized key industries and dramatically increased royalties on resource extraction, while using state subsidies to assist underdeveloped sectors of the economy and raise wages to combat poverty. Morales's government is widely regarded as highly successful in this regard – Bolivia's GDP grew on average at an impressive 4.8% during his years in power, while poverty rates were more than halved (Sarmiento 2019). Morales's government was also highly effective in many areas of social reform, including successful efforts to improve education, reduce illiteracy and expand access to better healthcare (see Farthing & Kohl 2014). The dramatic progress seen across the country in many areas of life led to Morales becoming one of the most popular leaders in the world, winning re-election handily in 2009 and 2014.

Because of his rhetoric and style of leadership, and the nature of the political movement he led, Morales has commonly been described as a ***populist*** politician (Philip & Panizza 2013: 68; Farthing & Kohl 2014: 16). And like most populists, the MAS movement became focused around the ideology and increasingly personalist leadership of Morales himself. The MAS and Morales became inseparable, causing leader and party alike unable to imagine one without the other. The illusion became dangerous as increasingly autocratic actions on the part of Morales were not checked by his followers or party, such as the construction of an elaborate presidential tower in La Paz in 2018 and repeated attempts to amend or bypass the Bolivian Constitution's term limits and seek indefinite re-election. Morales eventually lost sufficient support to lose his grasp on power after a contentious re-election in 2019, going into exile thereafter, leaving the MAS movement rudderless and a power vacuum in the country he'd helped transform (see Anderson 2020).

Morales is a seminal and transformative figure in modern Bolivian politics, and used populism as a successful political strategy to unseat entrenched urban and moneyed interests from power, uniting large swathes of the nation in a mission to address economic inequality and advance the well-being of the poorest. Yet in doing so, Morales' rule manifested many of the dangerous side-effects of populism, and an increasing tendency towards personalism that ultimately brought his government down, leaving behind a political movement that has struggled to adjust without its dynamic leading force and leaving questions as to the durability of the gains made.

there has long been a tendency for populism to trend towards authoritarian rule. Populist politics was at the core of the fascist movements in Germany and Italy, and authoritarian movements in Argentina, Venezuela and Peru, all of which handily won elections in democratic systems before rolling back democratic rights and consolidating the leader's power in the name of 'the people' (Germani 1978; Fritzsche 1990; Weyland 2013). In recent years, another trend has emerged in which leaders use the blunt force of populism to take power and roll back traditional liberal policies and democratic rights for the sake of decisive action against an 'other'. Viktor Orbán in Hungary against the threat of migration, the loss of national sovereignty within the European Union and the Coronavirus. Rodrigo Duterte in the Philippines against criminal syndicates and the drug trade. In 2018, Jair Bolsonaro's successful populist candidacy in Brazil was openly ambivalent about democracy, with Bolsonaro praising previous periods of dictatorship in Brazil (Phillips & Phillips 2018). Given this openness, it's even conceivable that his win suggests Brazilians are willing to accept a return to a more autocratic form of leadership if material improvement or desired policies are delivered.

Populism represents a dramatic tension at the core of democracy. On the one hand, populism is the very embodiment of democracy, since populist leaders and movements successfully capture public sentiment and act as a check on elite domination of politics. And yet on the other, populism usually centres around singular leaders who often embrace anti-democratic ideals and practices. Some have termed this style of politics *illiberal* democracy (see Zakaria 2007). Katherine Isbester, in a study of 10 Latin American democracies, exposes the paradox of the recent experiences there, in which despite the horrors of previous authoritarian regimes and slow but steady improvement in the economic conditions of these countries, the public has frequently been attracted to populist candidates, often at the expense of newly establish democratic norms (Isbester 2010). Recent experiences in Latin America (see Case 10.1) provide examples of populist leadership treading a fine line between democracy and autocracy.

Margaret Canovan describes the paradox as a tension between the 'redemptive' and the 'pragmatic' faces of democracy. On the pragmatic side, democracy is just a system of government designed to peacefully resolve debates and conflicts between competing points of view, allocate resources, manage complex problems, balance interests and limit power. Yet it has a redemptive side too – it is a forum for the hopes and dreams of the public, it is the affirmation that the people are the only source of legitimate power and authority, and it offers the romantic promise of making people's lives better and providing national salvation (Canovan 1999), something that all populist leaders seek to capitalize on (see Case 10.1). John Kane and Haig Patapan similarly conclude that there is an inherent, and unresolvable, tension at the heart of democratic leadership:

> The dynamic tension between the limited authority leaders are actually granted and the extensive authority they are expected to wield makes democratic leadership distinctively what it is: both

> the strongest and the weakest form of leadership. This democratic tension can be negotiated and managed by leaders...but never resolved. (Kane & Patapan 2012: 1)

Polarization

Political polarization is a phenomenon whereby political attitudes diverge and political parties, as well as the broader public, become progressively more doctrinaire in their views and behaviour. What results is the decline in the prevalence of 'moderates' and 'swing voters' as the electorate migrates towards the extremes of the political spectrum. The causes of this phenomenon are debated, but polarization has been widely observed internationally in recent decades (see Carothers & O'Donohue 2019).

Polarization has implications for every facet of political life, including the practice of political leadership. One obvious area of impact is negotiation – a key part of what leaders do is build coalitions and broker agreements amongst those who share power in order to make policy, pass legislation and so on (see Chapter 9). However, modern commentators have contended that zero-sum attitudes towards negotiation have become more dominant in contemporary politics. Voters and parties with increasingly polarized mindsets are likely to prefer hard-line politicians who cede little rather than those who actively seek effective compromise (Gutmann & Thompson 2010). Polarization diminishes or eliminates the zone of possible agreement (ZOPA) between parties to a negotiation – the more opposed their views and more dogmatic their beliefs, the harder it becomes to find areas of common ground. The purported result is the rise of 'gridlock', where government is hobbled by intractable intra-political disagreement and politics becomes stagnant and dysfunctional.

In the United States, where polarization has been closely studied in recent years, a decline in legislative productivity and an increase in legislative gridlock have been observed since the 1970s (e.g., Brownstein 2007). However, there are other comparable periods of low legislative productivity in US history, and moreover, the role and work that legislatures do evolves over time, making direct comparisons between eras challenging. Nor is there evidence that polarization, such as it is, leads to more extreme political legislation or systematically advantages a particular ideology. However, it is quite possible that increasing gridlock in legislatures and formal policy-making channels has fostered greater 'presidentialization' – either as legislative bodies fail to assert their prerogatives and executive branches fill the void, or as the executive branch actively works to bypass logjams through its own means (Lee 2015).

Polarization makes it difficult for leaders to play the role of compromisers too, even if they and their parties see its importance. Recent experience by political leaders who have sought to play the role seems to bear this out – Morgan Tsvangirai (Leader of Zimbabwe's Movement for Democratic Change) and Nick Clegg (Leader of the UK Liberal Democrats) are prominent examples of party leaders in recent decades who made hard but necessary compromises to allow workable government, only to be abandoned by voters at subsequent elections (Allison 2014; Jenkins 2014). It is often easier for leaders in contemporary politics to win support by engaging in grandstanding tactics (see Chapter 9) than it is to win support through painful compromise and hard choices. This may be a further reflection of the self-serving bias, insofar as voters themselves are far more convinced of their cause and the strength of their position than is realistic, and even if their leaders embrace the necessary reality of compromise, their supporters may see it as weakness or betrayal.

Contemporary political leadership exists in what has been described as a 'networked' world in which many political and policy actors operate independently. The increasing complexity of governance and density of actors and institutions means that stable government and workable policy solutions require compromise and collaborative leadership more than ever (Klijn 2014). Yet at the same time, the highly mediatized nature of modern politics and constant campaigning have helped create a 'drama democracy' that rewards theatrical grandstanding and performative authority on the part of leaders (Elchardus 2002). In this way rhetoric and negotiation, two essential tools in the persuasion toolbox for leadership, are not always compatible. The political leader who uses inflammatory rhetoric and grandstanding may surrender the opportunity for calm and reasoned behind-the-scenes negotiation later, as positions harden, and the public polarizes into camps. Ironically then, we need compromise and collaborative leadership more than ever in order to achieve change and coordinate the complex machinery of government to move forward towards goals, yet this need comes amidst a political environment in which playing the centrist and compromiser is ever more challenging.

The successful leaders of the twenty-first century, perhaps more than in previous eras, must find ways to manage their appearance 'frontstage' to survive in a polarized political environment, while working 'backstage' to achieve the collaborations and compromises necessary to effectively govern a fragmented political environment (Klijn 2014).

Democracy and leadership

Many of these trends keep us returning to one of the biggest challenges of contemporary political philosophy: how do we fit political leadership, one of our oldest political practices, into a modern liberal democracy, one of our newest? Kane and Patapan conclude it is one of the great unanswered questions of our time, and all we really have are a series of contradictions and paradoxical expectations around democratic leadership that seemingly foster growing public dissatisfaction with modern politics (Kane & Patapan 2014: 1–7).

Cast your eyes over any public poll of who the 'greatest' leaders of recent times were, or the most popular political biographies, and inarguably the public seems to favour heroic and individualist leader types like Winston Churchill, Charles De Gaulle and Indira Gandhi (Laing & Walter 2017: 211–212). Yet by contrast, more formal scholarship increasingly concludes that modern liberal democracies, with dispersed networks of power and responsibility, require us to shed the heroic leaders of the past and embrace consensus-making and collaborative leadership (Laing & Walter 2017: 214–217). Some of the most popular contemporary approaches to leadership, like 'servant leadership' (e.g., Greenleaf 1998) and 'authentic leadership' (e.g., Gardner et al. 2005), clash with the swashbuckling stereotype of the heroic leader. This conflict is inherent in our discussions of trends like populism and polarization – they are phenomena driven at least in part by the public itself, and yet may engender exactly the kind of leadership that will be inimical to the public good in the long term and threaten the democracy which produced it.

The problem is a serious one. Globally, trust in government and political leaders has plummeted (Edelman 2020). Polling reveals an across-the-board perception amongst voters of a 'crisis of leadership' in democracies from sub-Saharan Africa to North America (Shahid 2014). Whatever leadership our democratic systems are currently providing, clearly, it is not meeting public expectations.

So how does political leadership respond to this challenge? For some commentators, the answer has been to further weaken the power of elites and increase democracy (Coates 2013; Willis 2019). Deliberative democrats, for example, have long argued for a far greater degree of public participation in the decision-making of the state. Direct democratic experiments have proliferated in recent years as means of organizing policy and decision-making without the control of a leadership elite, and as a hopeful salve for polarization, disengagement and distrust in politics (see Chwalisz 2019).

Contemporary leadership theorists prescribe democratic and follower-focused leadership styles for the twenty-first century. 'Authentic' leaders and 'servant' leaders, for example, are two of the most popular new models of leadership that have arisen in recent years, and both emphasize the criticality of connectedness, awareness, receptiveness and other characteristics that help the leader understand and work constructively *with* their followers and to *empower* them to collectively achieve desired goals (see Northouse 2016: ch. 9–10). The heroic leadership style lionized in previous eras is increasingly thought to run counter to contemporary democratic and public values, and effective public leadership must be collaborative and collegial in order to work effectively in an intensely networked environment ('t Hart & Tummers 2019: 68–81).

Others, however, argue that the erosion of public trust and other problems are being *caused* by democratization rather than its absence. To take one example, the information revolution of the late twentieth century has dramatically democratized information access and the public discourse, profoundly changing the practice of politics in the process. And as political psychologist Shawn Rosenberg argues, this undermining of elite control over information has done little but leave the public increasingly distrustful, insecure and confused:

> The ever more democratic conditions of everyday life and the ever more democratic structuring of the public sphere, has undermined the essentially undemocratic power and authority of

> democratic elites to manage the structural weakness of democratic governance, a citizenry that lacks the cognitive and emotional capacities to think, feel and act in ways required. Instead in the increasingly open, free and equal sphere of public life characteristic of the contemporary western democracies like the United States, democratic elites are forced to compete with opponents, most significantly right wing populists, who offer a message that is intrinsically more comprehensible and satisfying to a recipient public hungry for meaning, security and direction. The probable result is clear. In this ever more democratic context, the authoritarian, nationalist vision of the right-wing populist is likely to triumph. (Rosenberg 2019; see also Brennan 2017)

These problems are likely only aggravated further by the rise of 'fake news' and 'narrowcasting', whereby an increasingly polarized public reinforces its own political biases and seeks leaders who confirm their views and can defeat the increasingly demonized 'other'. The rise of new populist strands of politics in both established and emerging democracies has brought this trend into sharp focus, with leaders like the Philippines' Rodrigo Duterte (Thompson 2017) and Hungary's Viktor Orbán (Krekó & Enyedi 2019). The rise of such leaders has been seen as evidence of democratic backsliding, as forms of autocratic politics come back into vogue in exchange for security, tough measures against 'others' and material improvements in people's lives (e.g., Wolf 2019). For some then, the answer to the question of what successful contemporary democratic leadership looks like is simply to water down the 'democratic' part.

Yet at the same time, some leaders have placed democratic and collaborative, follower-focused leadership at the core of their candidacies in recent decades to great success. Jacinda Ardern (Figure 10.2), elected Prime Minister of New Zealand in 2017, is a clear example of a twenty-first century public leader who has sought to embody democratic ideals and authentic leadership, earning widespread praise for her humane, open and honest handling of numerous national crises, her public commitment to inclusiveness and gender equality, and her ability to genuinely connect and get involved with her followers (Lester 2019; Lux 2020). Her style has triggered a wave of 'Jacindamania' and great acclaim both nationally and internationally. This style is thought to have been particularly effective during the Coronavirus pandemic – decisive action combined with Ardern's empathetic and authentic approach to communicating with the public throughout has made her one of the most popular leaders in New Zealand's history (Friedman 2020).

Yet style does not automatically lead to substance. The signature promise of Ardern's campaign and the central issue of the 2017 election – solving New Zealand's housing affordability crisis – was notably abandoned in late 2019 after the signature home-building project KiwiBuild had failed to make inroads into the problem. Indeed, though 2019 was touted as the 'year of delivery' for the Ardern government, commentators roundly concluded that relatively little was delivered (Edwards 2019).

Figure 10.2 Jacinda Ardern in 2019

In a heavily mediatized political sphere, though, leadership theatre is central. And indeed, this 'drama democracy' may provide a workable solution for leaders, who can act out the hero and everyman in the media to satiate the public desire for inspiration and direction, whilst being able to carefully manage the backstage in the far more consensual and collaborative manner that modern democratic systems require (Fischer 2003: 58–59; Klijn 2014: 411–412). In this sense, the good democratic leader is in fact a better actor – a leader who can act the strong leader for some crowds, authentic and consensual with others, and all the while take a measured and collaborative approach behind the scenes to build relationships and broker agreements in a fragmented political landscape.

Yet on the other hand, autocratic regimes have seized upon such tactics too, using an ever-wider array of sophisticated stratagems to maintain a veneer of democratic legitimacy whilst manipulating public opinion against democratic regimes elsewhere, blurring the lines (at least on the surface) between autocratic and democratic leadership (Frantz 2019). Some charismatic autocrats in the twenty-first century may be better at acting out the role of a 'democratic leader' than genuinely democratic leaders themselves, concealing an iron fist behind a velvet glove. For some, this might be enough – leaders like Singapore's Lee Kwan Yew (Case 4.3) straddle a grey zone between democracy and autocracy yet seemingly enjoy far stronger patterns of public support than those in purer democracies (Allison 2015).

In many ways, these paradoxes of contemporary leadership are just new manifestations of age-old debates about the place of leadership (see Chapters 3 and 4). We will never truly establish the 'proper' role of leaders in our political system – it is a debate each generation must have for itself. The ideological and stylistic clothing political leadership wears is a means, not an end, and as such must be calibrated in each era and society to suit the ends its followership means to accomplish.

Case 10.2 The image prevails

Benazir Bhutto

Prime Minister of Pakistan, 1988–1990; 1993–1996

Figure 10.3 Benazir Bhutto in 1995

Benazir Bhutto became an enduring symbol of Pakistan's struggle for democracy and freedom. In 1977 her father, after being re-elected as prime minister, was arrested in a military coup by Muhammad Zia-ul-Haq. Bhutto became a leading voice in her father's defence, defending him during a show trial and eventually being imprisoned herself with other members of her family (Bhatia 2008: 47). Refusing to leave Pakistan, she instead formed the Movement for the Restoration of Democracy and became a central figure in the political resistance against the Zia dictatorship, frequently imprisoned and subjected to severe treatment by the government (Khuhro & Soomro 2013). Going into exile for a period, Benazir would nevertheless return to Pakistan and became a symbol of the democratic aspirations of the country, and by the late 1980s was drawing millions to her speeches and appearances, despite frequent detainment by the authorities (Bhatia 2008: 21–22). Bhutto's profile continued to grow, attracting strong support from foreign leaders as an ardent fighter for freedom and democracy. In 1988, after the unexpected death of General Zia, free elections were called, and Benazir Bhutto's party won. After decades of fighting for the restoration of democracy, Bhutto had become the first female elected head of government of a predominantly Muslim nation, and in a nation enormously conservative on gender roles.

The image and the leader however became increasingly separated over the course of Bhutto's career. She carefully crafted a conservative female image domestically in Pakistan, agreeing to a traditional arranged marriage in 1987 as a nod to traditional sensibilities and to improve her political standing (Muñoz 2014: 56). She began wearing her iconic white head scarf as another concession to religious and gendered expectations in Pakistan (Stan 2007). Yet for Western audiences she promoted herself as a progressive icon of female empowerment, with her 1988 English-language autobiography offering hyperbolized and at times false accounts of her views and struggles (Allen 2016: 9–10). During her two terms as prime minister, her record on women's rights proved inconsistent, and many feminists later questioned her true dedication to the cause. Bhutto publicly campaigned against the Hudood ordinances, a series of draconian laws passed under the Zia regime that greatly restricted female freedoms, yet during her two terms she did not seek to repeal them. Though she made some concessions to women's rights by creating small quotas for female participation in government, there was little material, legal or socio-economic change to the status of women during her terms (Lichter 2009: 255–258).

"Benazir Bhutto has demonstrated that her skills of mass mobilization, regime confrontation, and manipulation of political elites are far superior to her managerial abilities. She has been effective and skillful as a leader of the opposition, but as prime minister she has yet to demonstrate a commitment to any progressive ideals" (Shafqat 1996: 655). Indeed, the progressive economic ideas of her father's party were quickly shed by Benazir, who assumed the finance ministry personally and adopted a mixed bag of policies that proved generally deleterious to the Pakistani economy (Shafqat 1996).

Similarly, her projected image as a champion of democracy, transparency and meritocratic government was undermined by her actions as Prime Minister and opposition leader. She declared herself leader of her party 'for life' in 1993 and intrigued to maintain undivided control over the political machine her father had built. In government, Bhutto gained a reputation for corruption, with some estimates valuing the embezzlement by her and her husband at over a billion dollars (Allen 2016: 114). Bhutto's regime engaged in lavish pet projects, including the construction of an enormous family mausoleum (Allen 2016: 109–116). Ultimately, both her governments were dismissed by presidential decree on the basis of corruption. In 1998 she went into self-imposed exile. Returning to Pakistan in 2007 after another period of military rule, she offered herself as a candidate once more in the 2008 elections, still enormously popular amongst the public, though she was assassinated at a political rally during the campaign.

Bhutto represents empowerment and change for millions of women across the Muslim world – her brave fight for democracy captured national and international imagination – and for many Pakistanis her election as leader was a turning point in the history of their nation (Stan 2007). A master of self-image, Bhutto crafted a version of herself for public consumption that achieved much more than her flawed leadership did in reality. "In her wake are the millions of Pakistani girls and women who look at her life, her determination, her perseverance in the face of all odds...they thrill to the idea, still radical in Pakistan 40 years after Ms. Bhutto began her political career, that gender doesn't have to stop them from achieving their dreams" (Shah 2014).

Symbolism

The American philosopher William James argued that the true issue of democracy was not who was necessarily most competent to lead the masses, but who was the best person to be their role model. His argument was that foremost the leader is a symbol, an embodiment of hopes and aspirations, and the society we live in is most profoundly affected by the cues it takes from its leaders (James 1907: 227–230; 1912: 318).

This aspect of political leadership does not fit neatly into any other section of this volume. It is not an explicit task of the leader, nor is it necessarily an essential part of how we understand them. But it is an incredibly important aspect of leader-follower relations, because fundamentally most followers in politics follow for something more than the vague promise of material benefit – they follow because they believe in what the leader represents. Their leader is a manifestation of their own vision for politics and society, and gives license to their beliefs, desires, words and actions.

In the twenty-first century, this aspect of political leadership is perhaps more salient than ever. As mass and social media spread the images and words of leaders to ever wider audiences, what leaders *say* and what they *do* have the potential to directly influence the public on an unprecedented scale.

In this light, it is unsurprising that political contests between leaders in the twenty-first century are often loaded with symbolic subtext. Social movements like #MeToo and Black Lives Matter have brought renewed scrutiny and accountability for public figures on gender and race, especially in a world in which political leadership, especially at the very top, is still strongly dominated by white men. And despite great strides in racial and gender equality in some sectors of society and profession, political leaders in nearly all nations do not yet come close enough to representing the demographic makeup of their constituencies.

It is often pioneering leaders who must themselves break ground and act as the symbolic vanguard. Evo Morales (Case 10.1) and Benazir Bhutto (Case 10.2) were watershed political figures not only (or perhaps not at all) because of their policies or ideologies, but because of *what* they represented for their societies. That symbolic influence can be particularly profound over children, for whom national political leaders are the first authority figures they learn of by name (Hess & Torney-Purta 2005: ch. 3). Ellen Johnson Sirleaf, first female president of Liberia, once relayed an experience she had speaking with a group of school children. In response to her question about what they wanted to be when they grew up, one young boy said he wanted to be the Vice President of Liberia. Surprised, Sirleaf asked him why he didn't want to President. The boy replied 'but being President is a woman's job!'

Yet the symbolic power of leaders touches all age groups. Barack Obama, who transcended hundreds of years of racial discrimination to become the first African American president of the United States, influenced how millions of Americans saw themselves, a fact likely reflected in the fact that after many years of stagnation, the ethnic diversity of people elected to the US Congress rose significantly in the wake of his victory (Pew Research Center 2019).

Indeed, it is the image of the leader that lives on far beyond their times. All most followers will ever see of their leader are images – they will never talk with or really know them, no matter how much they might feel they do. The image can be carefully crafted by the leader, but at a certain point the image breaks away from their control and takes on a life of its own, always at least a little detached from the reality it was once designed to present, and sometimes greatly so. Egyptian pharaohs had images of themselves carved in stone that radically distorted their appearance and associated the ruler with god-like qualities, and it is those images that remain on temple walls, while the real rulers behind them we barely know. Che Guevara's image blazons t-shirts and hats world-over, a symbol of rebellion and political counterculture now far exceeding the reach and success Guevara had as a leader within his lifetime. Leaders like Mohandas Gandhi, Abraham Lincoln, Winston Churchill and Martin Luther King Jr. have almost become impossible to objectively assess as their image looms so large in the public mind that any mention of their names invokes symbolic meaning and emotive responses that render sober analysis very challenging. Of course, most leaders will not achieve such status. But those that do continue to give their cues to the masses, and in doing so fulfil the recurring psychic need for heroes (see Campbell 1949).

Conclusion

If this overview has captured anything, it has hopefully captured the incredible complexity of political leadership, and the manifold ways in which this phenomenon might be gainfully approached. To try and understand how political leadership manifests in each moment may take us anywhere from evolutionary impulses evolved in our distant past to what a leader had for breakfast that morning. As stated at the outset, the perspectives and theories described in this volume (and countless more I haven't gotten to) are best thought of as tools in a very large toolbox. Any one of them is available at will to help us find answers, but it is hard for more than a couple of them to be used effectively at the same time. We must be content with being able to see just glimpses of the bigger picture at any given moment.

Much the same goes for the study of leaders themselves. Humans are complex. They live long and constantly changing lives that are hard to summarize. Robert Caro, one of the most acclaimed biographers of the twenty-first century, has spent almost four decades writing the most comprehensive account of the life and leadership of US President Lyndon Baines Johnson, in a project that now spans five volumes and more than 3,000 pages, and (as of 2020) is yet to be completed. It has taken almost a life's work to document and decrypt (as fully as we can ever hope) the rise and rule of just *one* political leader.

In trying to make sense of this complexity and be rigorous about how we study leadership, it is tempting just to focus on the concept of leadership in the abstract and the grand principles by which we desire our world to be run. To mistake the institutional structures and trappings of power and authority for leadership itself. To think of political leaders as incredibly capable, purpose-driven and cunning individuals. To assume that every word they say and every action they take are deliberate and part of a greater, carefully thought-out plan.

But we do well to remember that leadership is so complex precisely because this not the case – there is *always* an all-too-human wizard behind the political curtain. "Those concerned in government are still human beings. They retain their share of the ordinary traits of human nature…rarely can a person sink himself in to his political function; the best which most men attain to is the domination by public weal of their other desires" (Dewey 1927: 76). As much as they may attempt to present otherwise, political leaders are just as imperfect, unpredictable and frail as you or I. They exist in an environment of uncertainty and constant change, and they muddle their way through life as competently as they can, just as we do. They make mistakes, get emotional, give in to temptation, fall prey to ambition and self-interest, react irrationally, misinterpret situations, have bad days, and lie awake worrying at night just as we do.

This is a truth that may be discarded as glib, and yet it holds the key to understanding why – despite our attempts to tame it– political leadership is inevitably a messy affair. Our political institutions are the product of millennia of debate and discussion, all designed to find the best way to channel human energies into the forms of political leadership that are constructive for society. But whilst such institutions can incentivize and restrain behaviour, they cannot fundamentally alter human nature or completely control it. This reality is what provides us that ongoing link to our leaders of the past, because at its core it is a human drama that has been playing out since ancient times.

By the same token, our human character is what gives leadership its necessarily creative, unpredictable and even volatile nature – a nature that politics and society need to find new solutions to new problems, to create grand visions and inspire people, to destroy and rebuild, to innovate and change. That nature will always be a double-edged sword – our saviour in one moment, our tyrant in the next.

We will continue to struggle with it. Yet something deep within us continues to seek out the remarkable and heroic in our world, and to lead and be led to a glory just beyond our grasp.

Chapter Summary

- Presidentialization is a phenomenon whereby the top political leaders become relatively more powerful within their governments, parties and political systems. It also describes the ever-greater share of media attention given to national political leaders. It means leaders are increasingly central to the rhythms of modern politics.
- Populism is a style of adversarial politics in which the 'elites' of a society are construed as enemies of the 'people'. Leaders have long capitalized on this style in a variety of guises but populism is experiencing a resurgence in the twenty-first century. Though inherently democratic on some level, it

is often anti-democratic in its effects, and is perhaps heralding a twenty-first century shift towards more authoritarian political styles.

- Polarization is a process whereby individuals move towards the extremes of the political spectrum and abandon moderate positions. This makes compromise and broad leadership appeals much more challenging, and seems to incentivize a narrower brand of politics in which rhetoric and grandstanding by leaders become the norm.
- Twenty-first century democratic leadership finds itself caught between competing trends towards more traditional elements of strong, even authoritarian, leadership types on the one hand, and a push towards authenticity, empathy and citizen participation on the other. Widespread loss of trust in government indicates a growing scepticism of political authority in general, and greater pressure on modern political leaders to strike the right balance that can deliver in both the performative and substantive aspects of the role.
- Political leaders become symbols that have widespread but unpredictable power, and this power can endure well beyond a leader's term of office.
- Political leaders at their heart are still human, and subject to all the same foibles and follies all humans are. Though this understanding is often lost in the vaunted discussions of leadership, it is essential to comprehending its great power and yet paradoxical nature.

REFERENCES

Aarøe, Lene, Michael Bang Petersen, and Kevin Arceneaux. 2017. "The Behavioral Immune System Shapes Political Intuitions: Why and How Individual Differences in Disgust Sensitivity Underlie Opposition to Immigration." *American Political Science Review* 111(2): 277–294.

Abraham, Karl. 1915. "Amenhotep IV: Notes on the Psychoanalytic Interpretation of His Personality and on the Monotheistic Cult of Aton." *The Psychoanalytic Review* 2: 219–221.

Aburish, Said K. 2004. *Nasser: The Last Arab*. New York: Macmillan.

Abuza, Zachary. 2002. "The Politics of Reform in Vietnam, 1986–2000." In *Vietnam: Current Issues and Historical Background*, ed. V. Largo. Hauppauge: Nova Science.

Adams, John. 2003. *The Political Writings of John Adams: Representative Selections*. Indianapolis: Hackett Publishing.

Adams, Paul. 2015. "Greek MPs Approve Bailout Deal." *BBC World News*. https://www.bbc.com/news/world-europe-33925781

Adeney, Martin, and John Lloyd. 1988. *The Miners' Strike, 1984–85: Loss Without Limit*. London: Taylor & Francis.

Agamben, Giorgio. 2005. *State of Exception*. Chicago: University of Chicago Press.

Albertazzi, Daniele, and Duncan McDonnell. 2007. *Twenty-First Century Populism: The Spectre of Western European Democracy*. New York: Springer.

Alexander, Larry, and Michael Moore. 2016. "Deontological Ethics". In *Stanford Encyclopedia of Philosophy*, ed. Edward N. Zalta. https://plato.stanford.edu/archives/win2016/entries/ethics-deontological/

Alford, John R., Carolyn L. Funk, and John R. Hibbing. 2005. "Are Political Orientations Genetically Transmitted?" *American Political Science Review* 99(2): 153–167.

Allan, James P., and Lyle Scruggs. 2004. "Political Partisanship and Welfare State Reform in Advanced Industrial Societies." *American Journal of Political Science* 48(3): 496–512.

Allen, Brooke. 2016. *Benazir Bhutto: Favored Daughter*. New York: New Harvest.

Allen, Michael. 1984. "Elders, Chiefs, and Big Men: Authority Legitimation and Political Evolution in Melanesia." *American Ethnologist* 11(1): 20–41.

Allen, Mike et al. 2000. "Testing the Persuasiveness of Evidence: Combining Narrative and Statistical Forms." *Communication Research Reports* 17(4): 331–336.

Allison, Graham. 2015. "The Lee Kuan Yew Conundrum." *The Atlantic*. https://www.theatlantic.com/international/archive/2015/03/lee-kuan-yew-conundrum-democracy-singapore/388955/

Allison, Lincoln. 2009. "Power." In *The Concise Oxford Dictionary of Politics*, eds. Iain McLean and Alistair McMillan. Oxford: Oxford University Press.

Allison, Roy. 1985. *Finland's Relations with the Soviet Union, 1944–84*. Basingstoke: Macmillan.

Allison, Simon. 2014. "Morgan Tsvangirai Failed Zimbabwe, and Now He Must Go." *The Guardian*. http://www.theguardian.com/world/2014/apr/30/morgan-tsvangirai-zimbabwe-failed-must-go

Allred, Keith G., John S. Mallozzi, Fusako Matsui, and Christopher P. Raia. 1997. "The Influence of Anger and Compassion on Negotiation Performance." *Organizational Behavior and Human Decision Processes* 70(3): 175–187.

Almond, Gabriel, and Sidney Verba. 1963. *The Civic Culture: Political Attitudes and Democracy in Five Nations*. Thousand Oaks: SAGE.

Amossy, Ruth. 2001. "Ethos at the Crossroads of Disciplines: Rhetoric, Pragmatics, Sociology." *Poetics Today* 22(1): 1–23.

Anderson, Jon Lee. 2020. "The Fall of Evo Morales." *The New Yorker*. https://www.newyorker.com/magazine/2020/03/23/the-fall-of-evo-morales

Andeweg, Rudy B. 2000. "From Dutch Disease to Dutch Model? Consensus Government in Practice." *Parliamentary Affairs* 53(4): 697–709.

Andeweg, Rudy B., and Galen A. Irwin. 2014. *Governance and Politics of the Netherlands*. 4th ed. Basingstoke; New York: Red Globe Press.

Aquinas, Thomas. 1920. *The Summa Theologica of St. Thomas Aquinas*. New York: Benziger Brothers.

———. 1949. *De Regno Ad Regem Cypri*. Toronto: Pontifical Institute of Mediaeval Studies.

Arendt, Hannah. 1973. *The Origins of Totalitarianism*. New York: Harcourt, Brace, Jovanovich.

Artz, Benjamin, and Sarinda Taengnoi. 2016. "Do Women Prefer Female Bosses?" *Labour Economics* 42: 194–202.

Asch, Solomon. 1955. "Opinions and Social Pressure." *Scientific American* 193(5): 31–35.

Aschheim, Steven E. 1992. *The Nietzsche Legacy in Germany, 1890–1990*. Berkeley: University of California Press.

Ashraf, Ahmad. 1994. "Charisma, Theocracy, and Men of Power in Postrevolutionary Iran." In *The Politics of Social Transformation in Afghanistan, Iran, and Pakistan*, eds. Myron Weiner and Ali Banuazizi. Syracuse: Syracuse University Press.

Asserate, Asfa-Wossen. 2015. *King of Kings: The Triumph and Tragedy of Emperor Haile Selassie I of Ethiopia*. London: Haus.

Axford, Barrie, Peter Madgwick, and John Turner. 1992. "Image Management, Stunts and Dirty Tricks: The Marketing of Political Brands in Television Campaigns." *Media, Culture & Society* 14(4): 637–651.

Babcock, Linda, and George Loewenstein. 1997. "Explaining Bargaining Impasse: The Role of Self-Serving Biases." *Journal of Economic Perspectives* 11(1): 109–126.

Bachrach, Peter, and Morton S. Baratz. 1962. "Two Faces of Power." *The American Political Science Review* 56(4): 947–952.

Bailey, F.G. 2001. *Stratagems and Spoils: A Social Anthropology of Politics*. Boulder: Westview Press.

Bakunin, Mikhail. 1972. *Bakunin on Anarchy*, ed. Sam Dolgoff. New York: Vintage.

Banducci, Susan A., Jeffrey A. Karp, Michael Thrasher, and Colin Rallings. 2008. "Ballot Photographs as Cues in Low-Information Elections." *Political Psychology* 29(6): 903–17.

Bandura, Albert. 2002. "Selective Moral Disengagement in the Exercise of Moral Agency." *Journal of Moral Education* 31(2): 101–119.

Bandura, Albert. 2015. *Moral Disengagement: How People Do Harm and Live with Themselves*. New York: Worth.

Barber, James. 1992. *The Presidential Character*. Englewood Cliffs: Prentice Hall.

Barlow, Aaron. 2019. *The Manhattan Project and the Dropping of the Atomic Bomb: The Essential Reference Guide*. Santa Barbara: ABC-CLIO.

Barnhill, Anne. 2014. "What Is Manipulation?" In *Manipulation.* Oxford: Oxford University Press.

Barr, Michael D. 2014. *The Ruling Elite of Singapore: Networks of Power and Influence.* London: I.B. Tauris.

Barry, Bruce, Ingrid Smithey Fulmer, and Gerben A. Van Kleef. 2004. "I Laughed, I Cried, I Settled: The Role of Emotion in Negotiation." In *The Handbook of Negotiation and Culture.* Stanford: Stanford University Press, 71–94.

Bass, Bernard M. 1981. *Stogdill's Handbook of Leadership: A Survey of Theory and Research.* New York: Free Press.

Bass, Bernard M. 1990. *The Bass Handbook of Leadership: Theory, Research, and Managerial Applications.* 3rd ed. New York: Free Press.

Bastardoz, Nicolas, and Mark Van Vugt. 2019. "The Nature of Followership: Evolutionary Analysis and Review." *The Leadership Quarterly* 30(1): 81–95.

Bataille, Georges. 2015. *On Nietzsche.* Albany: SUNY Press.

Baumeister, Roy, Stuart Chesner, Pamela Senders, and Dianne Tice. 1988. "Who's in Charge Here? Group Leaders Do Lend Help in Emergencies." *Personality and Social Psychology Bulletin* 14(1): 17–22.

Baumgartner, Frank R., and Bryan D. Jones. 1993. *Agendas and Instability in American Politics.* Chicago: University of Chicago Press.

Bayles, Michael D. 1972. "A Concept of Coercion." In *Coercion.* Chicago: Aldine-Atherton.

Beetham, David. 2013. *The Legitimation of Power.* Basingstoke: Palgrave Macmillan.

Benacka, Elizabeth. 2017. *Rhetoric, Humor, and the Public Sphere: From Socrates to Stephen Colbert.* Lanham: Lexington Books.

Benczes, István. 2016. "From Goulash Communism to Goulash Populism: The Unwanted Legacy of Hungarian Reform Socialism." *Post-Communist Economies* 28(2): 146–166.

Bennett, David J., and Richard C. Jennings. 2011. *Successful Science Communication: Telling It Like It Is.* Cambridge: Cambridge University Press.

Bennis, Warren, and Burt Nanus. 1985. *Leaders: The Strategies for Taking Charge.* New York: Harper & Row.

Bennister, Mark. 2012. *Prime Ministers in Power: Political Leadership in Britain and Australia.* Basingstoke: Palgrave Macmillan.

Bennister, Mark, Ben Worthy, and Paul `t Hart. 2017. *The Leadership Capital Index: A New Perspective on Political Leadership.* Oxford: Oxford University Press.

Bentham, Jeremy. 1830. *Principles of Legislation.* Boston: Wells and Lilly.

Berghegger, Scott. 2009. "Sublime Inauthenticity: How Critical Is Truth in Autobiography?" *Inquiries Journal* 1(11).

Bernstein, Irwin S. 1970. "Primate Status Hierarchies." In *Primate Behavior*, ed. Leonard A. Rosenblum. Cambridge: Academic Press, 71–109.

Berry, Frances Stokes, and William D. Berry. 1992. "Tax Innovation in the States: Capitalizing on Political Opportunity." *American Journal of Political Science* 36(3): 715–742.

Bertsch, Gary K. 1977. "Ethnicity and Politics in Socialist Yugoslavia." *The Annals of the American Academy of Political and Social Science* 433: 88–99.

Bhatia, Shyam. 2008. *Goodbye Shahzadi: A Political Biography of Benazir Bhutto.* Mumbai: Lotus Collection.

Binder, Sarah A. 2004. *Stalemate: Causes and Consequences of Legislative Gridlock.* Washington, DC: Brookings Institution Press.

Bizzell, Patricia, and Bruce Herzberg. 1990. *The Rhetorical Tradition: Readings from Classical Times to the Present.* Boston: Bedford Books.

Bjerk, Paul. 2017. *Julius Nyerere.* Athens: Ohio University Press.

Blais, Andre, and William P. Cross. 2012. *Politics at the Centre: The Selection and Removal of Party Leaders in the Anglo Parliamentary Democracies.* Oxford: Oxford University Press.

Blanchard, Ken. 1985. *SLII: A Situational Approach to Managing People.* Escondido: Blanchard Training and Development.

Blanchard, Kenneth H., Drea Zigarmi, and Robert B. Nelson. 1993. "Situational Leadership After 25 Years: A Retrospective." *Journal of Leadership Studies.* 1(1): 21–36

Blank, Robert H. 2011. "Brain Sciences and Politics." In *Biology and Politics: Volume 9,* eds. Steven Peterson and Albert Somit. Bingley: Emerald Group.

Bligh, Michelle C., and Jeffrey C. Kohles. 2010. "Romance of Leadership." In *Encyclopedia of Group Processes & Intergroup Relations.* Thousand Oaks: SAGE, 718–719.

Blondel, Jean. 2018. "Elites or Leadership? Opposite or Complementary Paradigms?" In *The Palgrave Handbook of Political Elites,* eds. Heinrich Best and John Higley. London: Palgrave Macmillan.

Bodnick, Marc A. 1990. "'Going Public' Reconsidered: Reagan's 1981 Tax and Budget Cuts, and Revisionist Theories of Presidential Power." *Congress & the Presidency* 17(1): 13–28.

Boehm, Christopher. 2001. *Hierarchy in the Forest: The Evolution of Egalitarian Behavior.* Cambridge: Harvard University Press.

Boin, Arjen, Paul `t Hart, and Allan McConnell. 2009. "Crisis Exploitation: Political and Policy Impacts of Framing Contests." *Journal of European Public Policy* 16(1): 81–106.

Boin, Arjen, Paul `t Hart, Eric Stern, and Bengt Sundelius. 2005. *The Politics of Crisis Management: Public Leadership Under Pressure.* Cambridge: Cambridge University Press.

Boin, Arjen, Allan McConnell, and Paul `t Hart. 2008. *Governing After Crisis: The Politics of Investigation, Accountability and Learning.* Cambridge: Cambridge University Press.

Bono, Joyce E., and Timothy A. Judge. 2004. "Personality and Transformational and Transactional Leadership: A Meta-Analysis." *Journal of Applied Psychology* 89(5): 901–910.

Bornat, Joanna. 2008. "Biographical Methods." In *The SAGE Handbook of Social Research Methods,* eds. Pertti Alasuutari, Leonard Bickman, and Julia Brannen. Thousand Oaks: SAGE.

Bovens, Mark. 1998. *The Quest for Responsibility: Accountability and Citizenship in Complex Organisations.* Cambridge: Cambridge University Press.

Boyd, Douglas A. 1975. "Development of Egypt's Radio: 'Voice of the Arabs' Under Nasser." *Journalism Quarterly* 52(4): 645–653.

Brady, Christopher. 1997. "The Cabinet System and Management of the Suez Crisis." *Contemporary British History* 11(2): 65–93.

Brady, Christopher, and Peter Catterall. 1997. "Managing the Core Executive." *Public Administration* 75(3): 509–529.

Bravata, Dena et al. 2020. "Prevalence, Predictors, and Treatment of Impostor Syndrome: A Systematic Review." *Journal of General Internal Medicine* 35(4): 1252–1275.

Brazeal, Gregory. 2009. Against Gridlock: The Viability of Interest-Based Legislative Negotiation. *Harvard Law & Policy Review Online,* 3(1): 1–14.

Breasted, James Henry. 1908. *A History of the Ancient Egyptians.* London: Smith, Elder & Company.

Brennan, Jason. 2017. *Against Democracy: New Preface*. Princeton: Princeton University Press.

Brett, Judith. 2014. *Robert Menzies' Forgotten People*. Melbourne: Melbourne University Publishing.

Brienen, Marten. 2016. "A Populism of Indignities: Bolivian Populism Under Evo Morales." *The Brown Journal of World Affairs* 23(1): 77–93.

Brill, Steven. 2015. *America's Bitter Pill: Money, Politics, Backroom Deals, and the Fight to Fix Our Broken Healthcare System*. New York: Random House.

Brooker, Paul. 2013. *Non-democratic Regimes*. London: Red Globe Press.

Brownstein, Ronald. 2007. *The Second Civil War: How Extreme Partisanship Has Paralyzed Washington and Polarized America*. New York: Penguin.

Buchanan, Allen. 2002. "Political Legitimacy and Democracy." *Ethics* 112(4): 689–719.

Buckley, Stephen. 2006. *The Prime Minister and Cabinet*. Edinburgh: Edinburgh University Press.

Bueno de Mesquita, Bruce, and Alastair Smith. 2012. *The Dictator's Handbook: Why Bad Behavior Is Almost Always Good Politics*. New York: PublicAffairs.

Bueno de Mesquita, Bruce, Alastair Smith, Randolph M. Siverson, and James D. Morrow. 2004. *The Logic of Political Survival*. Cambridge: The MIT Press.

Bufe, Chaz. 1998. *A Future Worth Living: Thoughts on Getting There*. Tucson: See Sharp Press.

Bunce, Valerie, and Echols John M. 1978. "Power and Policy in Communist Systems: The Problem of 'Incrementalism'." *The Journal of Politics* 40(4): 911–932.

Burchell, Jon. 2002. *The Evolution of Green Politics: Development and Change Within European Green Parties*. London: Routledge.

Burke, Edmund. 1899. *The Works of the Right Honourable Edmund Burke, Volume 2*. London: George Bell and Sons.

Burke, Kenneth. 1969. *A Rhetoric of Motives*. Berkeley: University of California Press.

Burkett, Elinor. 2008. *Golda*. New York: Harper.

Burns, James MacGregor. 1978. *Leadership*. New York: Harper & Row.

———. 2009. *Running Alone: Presidential Leadership from JFK to Bush II*. New York: Basic Books.

Byman, Daniel, and Kenneth M. Pollack. 2001. "Let Us Now Praise Great Men: Bringing the Statesman Back In." *International Security* 25(4): 107–146.

Cahn, Zachary, and Emily M. Johnston. 2018. "Clintoncare and Obamacare: Lessons for Gridlock Theory." *Congress & the Presidency* 45(3): 225–253.

Callander, Steven. 2008. "Political Motivations." *The Review of Economic Studies* 75(3): 671–697.

Calvert, Randall L. 1992. "Leadership and Its Basis in Problems of Social Coordination." *International Political Science Review* 13(1): 7–24.

Cameron, Esther, and Mike Green. 2017. *Essential Leadership: Develop Your Leadership Qualities Through Theory and Practice*. London: Kogan Page.

Campbell, Joseph. 1949. *The Hero with a Thousand Faces*. New York: Pantheon Books.

Campbell, Rosie, and Oliver Heath. 2017. "Do Women Vote for Women Candidates? Attitudes Toward Descriptive Representation and Voting Behavior in the 2010 British Election." *Politics & Gender* 13(2): 209–231.

Campus, Donatella. 2010. "Mediatization and Personalization of Politics in Italy and France: The Cases of Berlusconi and Sarkozy." *The International Journal of Press/Politics* 15(2): 219–235.

Canes-Wrone, Brandice. 2001. "The President's Legislative Influence from Public Appeals." *American Journal of Political Science* 45(2): 313–329.

Canovan, Margaret. 1999. "Trust the People! Populism and the Two Faces of Democracy." *Political Studies* 47(1): 2–16.

———. 2004. "The Leader and the Masses: Hannah Arendt on Totalitarianism and Dictatorship." In *Dictatorship in History and Theory Bonapartism, Caesarism, and Totalitarianism*. Cambridge: Cambridge University Press.

Cap, Piotr. 2016. *The Language of Fear: Communicating Threat in Public Discourse*. London: Palgrave Macmillan.

Carbert, Louise. 2009. "A Political Economic Analysis of Women's Political Leadership." In *The Ashgate Research Companion to Political Leadership*, eds. Joseph Masciulli, Mikhail A. Molchanov, and W. Andy Knight. Farnham: Ashgate.

Carlyle, Thomas. 1849. *On Heroes, Hero-Worship, and the Heroic in History: Six Lectures*. London: James Fraser.

Carmichael, D.J.C. 1982. "Of Beasts, Gods, and Civilized Men: The Justification of Terrorism and of Counterterrorist Measures." *Terrorism* 6(1–2): 1–26.

Carmines, Edward G., and Matthew Fowler. 2017. "The Temptation of Executive Authority: How Increased Polarization and the Decline in Legislative Capacity Have Contributed to the Expansion of Presidential Power." *Indiana Journal of Global Legal Studies* 24(2): 369–398.

Carnevale, Peter J.D., and Alice M. Isen. 1986. "The Influence of Positive Affect and Visual Access on the Discovery of Integrative Solutions in Bilateral Negotiation." *Organizational Behavior and Human Decision Processes* 37(1): 1–13.

Caro, Robert. 2012. *The Years of Lyndon Johnson: The Passage of Power*. New York: Vintage.

Carothers, Thomas, and Andrew O'Donohue. 2019. *Democracies Divided: The Global Challenge of Political Polarization*. Washington, DC: Brookings Institution Press.

Carroll, Susan. 1984. "Feminist Scholarship on Political Leadership." In *Leadership: Multidisciplinary Perspectives*, ed. Barbara Kellerman. Englewood Cliffs: Prentice Hall.

Cartwright, Nancy, and Jeremy Hardie. 2012. *Evidence-Based Policy: A Practical Guide to Doing It Better*. Oxford: Oxford University Press.

Cassani, Andrea. 2017. "Social Services to Claim Legitimacy: Comparing Autocracies' Performance." *Contemporary Politics* 23(3): 348–368.

Cassese, Erin C. 2019. "Partisan Dehumanization in American Politics." *Political Behavior*. doi:https://doi.org/10.1007/s11109-019-09545-w

Castle, Stephen. 2019. "A Brexit Backlash in Local Elections: Main Parties Lose Seats." *The New York Times*. https://www.nytimes.com/2019/05/03/world/europe/uk-local-elections.html

Catalyst. 2007. *The Double-Bind Dilemma for Women in Leadership: Damned If You Do, Doomed If You Don't*. New York: Catalyst.

Cato. 1787. "Letter V." *New York Journal*, November 22.

Cawthorn, David. 2017. *Philosophical Foundations of Leadership*. London: Routledge.

Chan, Joseph. 2007. "Democracy and Meritocracy: Toward a Confucian Perspective." *Journal of Chinese Philosophy* 34(2): 179–193.

Chan, Joseph, and Elton Chan. 2014. "Confucianism." In *The Oxford Handbook of Political Leadership*, eds. R.A.W. Rhodes and Paul 't Hart. Oxford: Oxford University Press.

Chandra, Kanchan. 2016. *Democratic Dynasties: State, Party and Family in Contemporary Indian Politics*. Cambridge: Cambridge University Press.

Chang, Jung. 2013. *Empress Dowager Cixi*. New York: Knopf Doubleday.

Charteris-Black, Jonathan. 2018. *Analysing Political Speeches*. London: Red Globe Press.

Chen, Shyh-Wei. 2011. "Current Account Deficits and Sustainability: Evidence from the OECD Countries." *Economic Modelling* 28(4): 1455–1464.

Chhokar, Jagdeep S., Felix Brodbeck, and Robert J. House. 2007. *Culture and Leadership Across the World: The GLOBE Book of In-Depth Studies of 25 Societies*. Mahwah: Lawrence Erlbaum Associates.

Christiansen, Peter Munk, Birgitta Niklasson, and Patrik Öhberg. 2016. "Does Politics Crowd Out Professional Competence? The Organisation of Ministerial Advice in Denmark and Sweden." *West European Politics* 39(6): 1230–1250.

Churchman, David. 1995. *Negotiation: Process, Tactics, Theory*. Lanham: University Press of America.

Chwalisz, Claudia. 2019. "A New Wave of Deliberative Democracy." *Carnegie Europe*. https://carnegieeurope.eu/2019/11/26/new-wave-of-deliberative-democracy-pub-80422

Clance, Pauline, and Suzanne Imes. 1976. "The Imposter Phenomenon in High Achieving Women: Dynamics and Therapeutic Intervention." *Psychotherapy: Theory, Research & Practice* 15(3): 241–247.

Clarke, Nick, Will Jennings, Jonathan Moss, and Gerry Stoker. 2018. *The Good Politician: Folk Theories, Political Interaction, and the Rise of Anti-Politics*. Cambridge: Cambridge University Press.

Close, David. 1999. *Nicaragua: The Chamorro Years*. Boulder: Lynne Rienner.

Coad, Malcolm. 2006. "Obituary: Augusto Pinochet." *The Guardian*, December 11.

Coates, David. 2016. "Reflections on the Obama Presidency: The Politics of Gridlock." *HuffPost*. https://www.huffpost.com/entry/reflections-on-the-obama_b_13530962

Coates, Ta-Nehisi. 2013. "The Answer to the Crisis in Democracy Is More Democracy." *The Atlantic*. https://www.theatlantic.com/politics/archive/2013/11/the-answer-to-the-crisis-in-democracy-is-more-democracy/281850/

Cobb, Julia Symmes, and Nicholas Casey. 2016. "Colombia Vote Overturns Deal to End Its War." *The New York Times*, October 3.

Cocks, Geoffrey. 1986. "Contributions of Psychohistory to Understanding Politics." In *Political Psychology*, ed. Margaret G. Hermann. New York: Psychology Press.

Cohen, Abner. 2016 *Two-Dimensional Man: An Essay on the Anthropology of Power and Symbolism in Complex Society*. Abingdon: Routledge.

Cohen, Michael D., James G. March, and Johan P. Olsen. 1972. "A Garbage Can Model of Organizational Choice." *Administrative Science Quarterly* 17(1): 1–25.

Coicaud, Jean-Marc. 2002. *Legitimacy and Politics: A Contribution to the Study of Political Right and Political Responsibility*. Cambridge: Cambridge University Press.

Cole, Alistair. 1994. *Francois Mitterrand: A Study in Political Leadership*. Abingdon. Routledge.

Compton, Robert W. 2000. *East Asian Democratization: Impact of Globalization, Culture, and Economy*. Westport: Greenwood.

Confucius. 1885. *The Sacred Books of China: The Texts of Confucianism*. Oxford: Oxford University Press.

Connolly, Terry, Hal R. Arkes, and Kenneth R. Hammond. 2003. *Judgment and Decision Making: An Interdisciplinary Reader*. Cambridge: Cambridge University Press.

Copland, Ian. 1991. "The Princely States, the Muslim League, and the Partition of India in 1947." *The International History Review* 13(1): 38–69.

———. 2002. *The Princes of India in the Endgame of Empire, 1917–1947*. Cambridge: Cambridge University Press.

Council on Foreign Relations. 2016. "Who Is Bashar Al-Assad?" https://www.cfr.org/event/who-bashar-al-assad

Courtney, John C. 1995. *Do Conventions Matter?: Choosing National Party Leaders in Canada*. Montreal: McGill-Queen's Press.

Cox, Michael. 2017. "The Rise of Populism and the Crisis of Globalisation: Brexit, Trump and Beyond." *Irish Studies in International Affairs* 28: 9–17.

Cronin, Thomas E., and Michael A. Genovese. 2012. *Leadership Matters: Unleashing the Power of Paradox*. Abingdon: Routledge.

Cuevillas, Fernando N.A. 1992. "A Case for Caudillaje and Juan Peron." In *Caudillos: Dictators in Spanish America*. Norman: University of Oklahoma Press.

Dae Jung, Kim. 1994. "Is Culture Destiny? The Myth of Asia's Anti-Democratic Values." *Foreign Affairs*, November/December.

Dalton, Patricio S., and Sayantan Ghosal. 2018. "Self-Confidence, Overconfidence and Prenatal Testosterone Exposure: Evidence from the Lab." *Frontiers in Behavioral Neuroscience* 12: 1–9.

Daly, Mary. 1985. *Beyond God the Father: Toward a Philosophy of Women's Liberation*. 5th ed. Boston: Beacon Press.

Daragahi, Borzou. 2018. "Erdogan Is Failing Economics 101." *Foreign Policy*. https://foreignpolicy.com/2018/05/25/erdogan-is-a-mad-economist-and-turkey-is-his-laboratory/

Darch, Colin, and David Hedges. 2011. "Samora Machel: The Beira Speech." *African Yearbook of Rhetoric* 2(3): 67–83.

———. 2013. "Political Rhetoric in the Transition to Mozambican Independence: Samora Machel in Beira, June 1975." *Kronos* 39(1): 10–19.

Daum, Courtenay W. 2010. "Women as Leaders in Congress." In *Gender and Women's Leadership: A Reference Handbook*, ed. Karen O'Connor. Thousand Oaks: SAGE.

Davies, Christian. 2018. "Hostile Takeover: How Law and Justice Captured Poland's Courts." *Freedom House*. https://freedomhouse.org/report/analytical-brief/2018/hostile-takeover-how-law-and-justice-captured-polands-courts

Davies, James Chowning. 1986. "Roots of Political Behavior." In *Political Psychology*, ed. Margaret G. Hermann. San Francisco: Jossey-Bass.

De Beus, Jos. 2009. *Populist Leadership*. Oxford: Oxford University Press.

De Boef, Suzanna, and Paul M. Kellstedt. 2004. "The Political (and Economic) Origins of Consumer Confidence." *American Journal of Political Science* 48(4): 633–649.

De Castella, Krista, Craig McGarty, and Luke Musgrove. 2009. "Fear Appeals in Political Rhetoric About Terrorism: An Analysis of Speeches by Australian Prime Minister Howard." *Political Psychology* 30(1): 1–26.

De Neve, Jan-Emmanuel et al. 2013. "Born to Lead? A Twin Design and Genetic Association Study of Leadership Role Occupancy." *The Leadership Quarterly* 24(1): 45–60.

Dealy, Glen Caudill. 1992. "The Public Man." In *Caudillos: Dictators in Spanish America*, ed. Hugh M. Hamill. Norman: University of Oklahoma Press.

DeLuca, Tom. 1995. *The Two Faces of Political Apathy*. Philadelphia: Temple University Press.

van der Dennen, Johan M.G. 2011. "The Biopolitics of Primates." In *Biology and Politics: Volume 9*, eds. Steven Peterson and Albert Somit. Bingley: Emerald Group, 53–96.

DeVore, Irven. 1965. *Primate Behaviour: Field Studies of Monkeys and Apes*. New York: Holt, Rinehart & Winston.

Dewey, John. 1927. *The Public and Its Problems*. New York: Henry Holt.

Dinan, Desmond. 2017. "Leadership in the European Council: An Assessment of Herman Van Rompuy's Presidency." *Journal of European Integration* 39(2): 157–173.

Dixson, Alan, T. Bossi, and E.J. Wickings. 1993. "Male Dominance and Genetically Determined Reproductive Success in the Mandrill." *Primates* 34(4): 525–532.

Djilas, Milovan. 1957. *The New Class: An Analysis of the Communist System*. New York: Harcourt Brace Jovanovich.

Dobbins, Gregory, and Jeanne Russell. 1986. "Self-Serving Biases in Leadership: A Laboratory Experiment." *Journal of Management* 12(4): 475–483.

Dobbs, Michael, K.S. Karol, and Dessa Trevisan. 2013. *Poland, Solidarity, Walesa*. Amsterdam: Elsevier.

Dodd, Lawrence. 2015. *Coalitions in Parliamentary Government*. Princeton: Princeton University Press.

Dolan, Julie. 2010. "Women as Leaders in Executive Service." In *Gender and Women's Leadership: A Reference Handbook*, ed. Karen O'Connor. Thousand Oaks: SAGE.

Döring, Herbert. 1995. "Time as a Scarce Resource: Government Control of the Agenda." In *Parliaments and Majority Rule in Western Europe*, ed. Herbert Döring. Frankfurt: Campus.

Douglas, Tommy. 1970. "On His Legacy." Speech to the New Democratic Party, Prince Albert, CA.

Dowding, Keith M. 1996. *Power*. Minneapolis: University of Minnesota Press.

———. 2006. "Three-Dimensional Power: A Discussion of Steven Lukes' Power: A Radical View." *Political Studies Review* 4(2): 136–145.

———. 2011. *Encyclopedia of Power*. Thousand Oaks: SAGE.

———. 2016. *The Philosophy and Methods of Political Science*. London: Red Globe Press.

Downie, R.S. 1969. "Collective Responsibility." *Philosophy* 44(167): 66–69.

Drew, Elizabeth. 2015. "Richard Nixon Was Not Misunderstood." *The Atlantic*. https://www.theatlantic.com/politics/archive/2015/07/revisionist-histories-richard-nixon/397319/

Druckman, James, Erik Peterson, and Rune Slothuus. 2013. "How Elite Partisan Polarization Affects Public Opinion Formation." *The American Political Science Review* 107(1): 57–79.

Drummond, Jocelyn, Qian Zhang, and Victoria Lawson. 2016. *Who Runs Our Cities? The Political Gender Gap in the Top 100 U.S. Cities*. New York: CUNY Institute for State & Local Governance.

Dukalskis, Alexander, and Johannes Gerschewski. 2017. "What Autocracies Say (and What Citizens Hear): Proposing Four Mechanisms of Autocratic Legitimation." *Contemporary Politics* 23(3): 251–268.

Dumm, Thomas L. 1999. *A Politics of the Ordinary*. New York: NYU Press.

Dundas, Carl W. 2012. *Close Elections and Political Succession in the African Union*. Bloomington: Author House.

Dunleavy, Patrick, and R.A.W. Rhodes. 1990. "Core Executive Studies in Britain." *Public Administration* 68(1): 3–28.

Eagly, Alice H., and Linda L. Carli. 2007. *Through the Labyrinth: The Truth About How Women Become Leaders*. Boston: Harvard Business Press.

Eagly, Alice H., and Blair T. Johnson. 1990. "Gender and Leadership Style: A Meta-Analysis." *Psychological bulletin* 108(2): 233–256.

Eagly, Alice H., and Steven J. Karau. 2002. "Role Congruity Theory of Prejudice Toward Female Leaders." *Psychological Review* 109(3): 573–598.

Easton, David. 1958. "The Perception of Authority and Political Change." In *Authority*, ed. Carl J. Friedrich. Cambridge: Harvard University Press.

Edelman Insights. 2020. *2020 Edelman Trust Barometer*. New York: Edelmen Insights. https://www.edelman.com/trustbarometer

Edmundson, William A. 1998. "Legitimate Authority Without Political Obligation." *Law and Philosophy* 17(1): 43–60.

Edwards, Bryce. 2019. "New Zealand's Year of Style Over Substance." *The Guardian*. https://www.theguardian.com/world/2019/dec/31/new-zealands-year-of-style-over-substance

Eisenegger, Christoph et al. 2017. "Testosterone and Androgen Receptor Gene Polymorphism Are Associated with Confidence and Competitiveness in Men." *Hormones and Behavior* 92: 93–102.

El Amine, Loubna. 2015. *Classical Confucian Political Thought: A New Interpretation*. Princeton: Princeton University Press.

Elchardus, M. 2002. *De Dramademocratie*. Tielt: Lannoo Uitgeverij.

Elcock, Howard. 2001. *Political Leadership*. Cheltenham: Edward Elgar.

Elgie, Robert. 2011. *Semi-Presidentialism: Sub-Types and Democratic Performance*. Oxford: Oxford University Press.

———. 2018. *Political Leadership: A Pragmatic Institutionalist Approach*. Basingstoke: Palgrave Macmillan.

Eller, Cynthia. 2001. *The Myth of Matriarchal Prehistory: Why an Invented Past Won't Give Women a Future*. Boston: Beacon Press.

Elson, Robert Edward. 2001. *Suharto: A Political Biography*. Cambridge: Cambridge University Press.

Elstein, David. 2010. "Why Early Confucianism Cannot Generate Democracy." *Dao* 9(4): 427–443.

Ergas, Zaki. 1980. "Why Did the Ujamaa Village Policy Fail? – Towards a Global Analysis." *The Journal of Modern African Studies* 18(3): 387–410.

van Esch, F.A.W.J. 2017. "The Paradoxes of Legitimate EU Leadership. An Analysis of the Multi-Level Leadership of Angela Merkel and Alexis Tsipras During the Euro Crisis." *Journal of European Integration* 39(2): 223–237.

Eshbaugh-Soha, Matthew. 2016. *Going Public and Presidential Leadership*. Oxford: Oxford University Press. http://oxfordre.com/view/10.1093/acrefore/9780190228637.001.0001/acrefore-9780190228637-e-57

Esposito, John. 1997. *Political Islam: Revolution, Radicalism, or Reform*. Boulder: Lynne Rienner.

Eswaran, Mukesh. 2014. *Why Gender Matters in Economics*. Princeton: Princeton University Press.

Esser, Frank, and Jesper Strömbäck. 2014. *Mediatization of Politics: Understanding the Transformation of Western Democracies*. Basingstoke: Palgrave Macmillan.

Etzioni-Halevy, Eva. 1997. *Classes and Elites in Democracy and Democratization: A Collection of Readings*. New York: Garland.

Ezrow, Natasha M., and Erica Frantz. 2011. *Dictators and Dictatorships: Understanding Authoritarian Regimes and Their Leaders*. New York: Continuum.

Fan, Ziying, Wei Xiong, and Li-An Zhou. 2016. "Information Distortion in Hierarchical Organizations: A Study of China's Great Famine." Fordham University. Unpublished Working Paper. https://wxiong.mycpanel.princeton.edu/papers/Famine.pdf

Farrell, John A. 2017. *Richard Nixon: The Life*. New York: Knopf Doubleday Publishing Group.

Farthing, Linda C., and Benjamin H. Kohl. 2014. *Evo's Bolivia: Continuity and Change.* Austin: University of Texas Press.

Felfe, Jörg, and Lars-Eric Petersen. 2007. "Romance of Leadership and Management Decision Making." *European Journal of Work and Organizational Psychology* 16(1): 1–24.

Fels, Anna. 2005. *Necessary Dreams: Ambition in Women's Changing Lives.* New York: Anchor Books.

Ferguson, Will. 1999. *Bastards & Boneheads: Canada's Glorious Leaders, Past and Present.* Vancouver: Douglas & McIntyre.

Ferraro, Geraldine, and Linda Bird Francke. 2004. *Ferraro: My Story.* Evanston: Northwestern University Press.

Ferree, Myra Marx. 2006. "Angela Merkel: What Does It Mean to Run as a Woman?" *German Politics & Society* 24(1 (78)): 93–107.

Festinger, Leon. 1957. *A Theory of Cognitive Dissonance.* Stanford: Stanford University Press.

Fiedler, Fred Edward. 1967. *A Theory of Leadership Effectiveness.* New York: McGraw-Hill.

Fiers, Stefan, and Andre Krouwel. 2005. "The Low Countries: From 'Prime Minister' to President-Minister." In *The Presidentialization of Politics: A Comparative Study of Modern Democracies*, eds. Thomas Poguntke and Paul D. Webb. Oxford: Oxford University Press.

Figes, Orlando. 2017. *A People's Tragedy: The Russian Revolution.* New York: Random House.

Finer, S.E. 1962. *The Man on Horseback: The Role of the Military in Politics.* London: Pall Mall.

Fischer, Frank. 2003. *Reframing Public Policy: Discursive Politics and Deliberative Practices.* Oxford: Oxford University Press.

Fisher, Roger, William Ury, and Bruce Patton. 1991. *Getting to Yes: Negotiating Agreement Without Giving In.* New York: Houghton Mifflin Harcourt.

Foley, Michael. 2013. *Political Leadership: Themes, Contexts, and Critiques.* Oxford: Oxford University Press.

Foot, Philippa. 1978. *Virtues and Vices and Other Essays in Moral Philosophy.* Berkeley: University of California Press.

Forero, Juan. 2006. "The Fashion of the Populist." *The New York Times.* https://www.nytimes.com/2006/02/02/fashion/thursdaystyles/the-fashion-of-the-populist.html

Forsyth, Donelson R. 2009. *Group Dynamics.* Boston: Cengage Learning.

Fortes, Meyer, and E.E. Evans-Pritchard. 1940. *African Political Systems.* Oxford: Oxford University Press.

Fowler, Linda L., and Jennifer L. Lawless. 2009. "Looking for Sex in All the Wrong Places: Press Coverage and the Electoral Fortunes of Gubernatorial Candidates." *Perspectives on Politics* 7(3): 519–536.

Fox, Richard L., and Jennifer L. Lawless. 2005. "To Run or Not to Run for Office: Explaining Nascent Political Ambition." *American Journal of Political Science* 49(3): 642–659.

France, Peter, and William St Clair. 2004. *Mapping Lives: The Uses of Biography.* Oxford: Oxford University Press.

Frantz, Erica. 2019. "The Evolution of the Strongman." *Foreign Policy.* https://foreignpolicy.com/2019/03/11/the-evolution-of-the-strongman/

Freeman, Jo. 1972. "The Tyranny of Structurelessness." *Berkeley Journal of Sociology* 17: 151–164.

French, John R., and Bertram Raven. 1959. "The Bases of Social Power." In *Studies in Social Power*, ed. Dorwin Cartwright. Ann Arbor: University of Michigan Press.

Fried, Morton H. 1967. *The Evolution of Political Society: An Essay in Political Anthropology*. New York: Random House.

Friedman, Uri. 2020. "New Zealand's Prime Minister May Be the Most Effective Leader on the Planet." *The Atlanti*. https://www.theatlantic.com/politics/archive/2020/04/jacinda-ardern-new-zealand-leadership-coronavirus/610237/

Fritzsche, Peter. 1990. *Rehearsals for Fascism: Populism and Political Mobilization in Weimar Germany*. Oxford: Oxford University Press.

Fromm, Erich. 1941. *Escape from Freedom*. New York: Farrar & Rinehart.

Fukuyama, Francis. 2006. *The End of History and the Last Man*. New York: Free Press.

Fulton, Sarah A. 2014. "When Gender Matters: Macro-Dynamics and Micro-Mechanisms." *Political Behavior* 36(3): 605–630.

Gabriel, Trip. 2019. "Virginia's Legislature Is Up for Grabs. It's a Referendum on Trump." *The New York Times*. https://www.nytimes.com/2019/11/04/us/politics/virginia-elections.html

Gains, Francesca. 2014. "Observational Analysis." In *The Oxford Handbook of Political Leadership*, eds. R.A.W. Rhodes and Paul `t Hart. Oxford: Oxford University Press.

Gardner, John W. 1990. *On Leadership*. New York: Free Press.

Gardner, William, B.J. Avolio, and Fred O. Walumbwa. 2005. *Authentic Leadership Theory and Practice: Origins, Effects and Development*. Bingley: Emerald Group.

Garzia, Diego. 2014. *Personalization of Politics and Electoral Change*. Basingstoke: Palgrave Macmillan.

Gaus, Gerald F. 2011. *The Order of Public Reason*. Cambridge: Cambridge University Press.

Geddes, Barbara, Joseph Wright, and Erica Frantz. 2018. *How Dictatorships Work: Power, Personalization, and Collapse*. Cambridge: Cambridge University Press.

Geertz, Clifford. 1973. *The Interpretation of Cultures*. New York: Basic Books.

George, Alexander L. 1968. "Power as a Compensatory Value for Political Leaders." *Journal of Social Issues* 24(3): 29–49.

George, Alexander L., and Juliette L. George. 1964. *Woodrow Wilson and Colonel House: A Personality Study*. New York: Dover Publications.

Germani, Gino. 1978. *Authoritarianism, Fascism, and National Populism*. New Brunswick: Transaction Publishers.

George, Cherian. 2007. "Consolidating Authoritarian Rule: Calibrated Coercion in Singapore." *The Pacific Review* 20(2): 127–145.

Ghaemi, Nassir. 2011. *A First-Rate Madness: Uncovering the Links Between Leadership and Mental Illness*. London: Penguin.

Gilens, Martin, and Benjamin I. Page. 2014. "Testing Theories of American Politics: Elites, Interest Groups, and Average Citizens." *Perspectives on Politics* 12(3): 564–581.

Gill, Roger. 2011. *Theory and Practice of Leadership*. Thousand Oaks: SAGE.

Gillespie, Andra. 2018. "Trump and the Limits of Transactional Politics." *CNN*. https://www.cnn.com/2018/01/18/opinions/trump-transactional-politics-problem-gillespie-opinion/index.html

Giorgini, Giovanni. 2013. "Five Hundred Years of Italian Scholarship on Machiavelli's Prince." *The Review of Politics* 75(4): 625–640.

Glenn, Paul F. 2001. "Nietzsche's Napoleon: The Higher Man as Political Actor." *The Review of Politics* 63(1): 129–158.

Goldberg, Steven. 1973. *The Inevitability of Patriarchy*. New York: William Morrow & Company.

———. 1999. *Why Men Rule: A Theory of Male Dominance*. Chicago: Open Court.

Goldsmith, Mike, and Helge Larsen. 2004. "Local Political Leadership: Nordic Style." *International Journal of Urban and Regional Research* 28(1): 121–133.

Gorenberg, Gershom. 2007. *The Accidental Empire: Israel and the Birth of the Settlements, 1967–1977*. New York: Macmillan.

Gorr, Michael. 1986. "Toward a Theory of Coercion." *Canadian Journal of Philosophy* 16(3): 383–405.

Gough, Roger. 2006. *A Good Comrade: János Kádár, Communism and Hungary*. London: I.B. Tauris.

Greenberg, David. 2017. "Was Obama a Transformational President?" *POLITICO Magazine*. https://www.politico.com/magazine/story/2017/01/barack-obama-president-legacy-transformational-transactional-214672

Greenleaf, Robert K. 1998. *The Power of Servant-Leadership*. San Francisco: Berrett-Koehler.

Greenstein, Fred I. 2004. "Can Personality and Politics Be Studied Systemically?" In *Political Psychology*, eds. John T. Jost and Jim Sidanius. New York: Psychology Press.

Grint, Keith, Owain Smolovic Jones, and Clare Holt. 2017. "What Is Leadership: Person, Result, Position or Process, or All or None of These?" In *The Routledge Companion to Leadership*, eds. John Storey et al. New York: Routledge.

Grossback, Lawrence J., David A.M. Peterson, and James A. Stimson. 2012. *Mandate Politics*. Cambridge: Cambridge University Press.

Gubler, Joshua R., and Nathan P. Kalmoe. 2015. "Violent Rhetoric in Protracted Group Conflicts: Experimental Evidence from Israel and India." *Political Research Quarterly* 68(4): 651–664.

Gustainis, J. Justin. 1990. "Demagoguery and Political Rhetoric: A Review of the Literature." *Rhetoric Society Quarterly* 20(2): 155–161.

Gutmann, Amy, and Dennis Thompson. 2010. "The Mindsets of Political Compromise." *Perspectives on Politics* 8(4): 1125–1143.

Gutting, Gary, and Jeff McMahan. 2015. "Can Torture Ever Be Moral?" *New York Times*. https://opinionator.blogs.nytimes.com/2015/01/26/can-torture-ever-be-moral/

Habibi, Nader. 2016. "How Will Turkey's Failed Coup and Massive Purge Affect Its Economic Future?" *The Conversation*. http://theconversation.com/how-will-turkeys-failed-coup-and-massive-purge-affect-its-economic-future-62947

Hadenius, Axel, and Jan Teorell. 2007. "Pathways from Authoritarianism." *Journal of Democracy* 18(1): 143–157.

Hall, Peter A., and Rosemary C.R. Taylor. 1996. "Political Science and the Three New Institutionalisms." *Political Studies* 44: 936–957.

Hallerberg, Mark. 2010. "Empirical Applications of Veto Player Analysis and Institutional Effectiveness." In *Reform Processes and Policy Change: Veto Players and Decision-Making in Modern Democracies*, eds. Thomas König, Marc Debus and George Tsebelis. New York: Springer.

Hamblin, Robert. 1958. "Leadership and Crises." *Sociometry* 21: 322–335.

Hampshire, Stuart. 1978. *Public and Private Morality*. Cambridge: Cambridge University Press.

Hampton, Jean. 1998. *Political Philosophy*. Boulder: Westview Press.

Hannagan, Rebecca J. 2011. "From Genes to Politics." In *Biology and Politics: Volume 9*, eds. Steven Peterson and Albert Somit. Bingley: Emerald Group, 139–158.

Harris, Abram L. 1964. "John Stuart Mill: Servant of the East India Company." *The Canadian Journal of Economics and Political Science* 30(2): 185–202.

Harsch, Ernest. 2014. *Thomas Sankara: An African Revolutionary*. Athens: Ohio University Press.

`t Hart, Paul. 1994. *Groupthink in Government: A Study of Small Groups and Policy Failure*. Baltimore: Johns Hopkins University Press.

`t Hart, Paul, and Lars Tummers. 2019. *Understanding Public Leadership*. 2nd ed. London: Red Globe Press.

Hartcher, Peter. 2017. "'If He Just Had Guts': Focus Groups Savage Malcolm Turnbull as a Do-Nothing PM." *The Sydney Morning Herald*. https://www.smh.com.au/politics/federal/if-he-just-had-guts-focus-groups-savage-malcolm-turnbull-as-a-donothing-pm-20170806-gxqcvo.html

Harten, Sven. 2011. *The Rise of Evo Morales and the MAS*. London: Zed Books.

Hartley, Ray. 2016. "Zuma's Rise and Fall." *The Independent*. http://www.independent.co.uk/news/world/jacob-zuma-the-rise-and-near-fall-of-south-africa-s-president-a7083701.html

Haslam, S. Alexander, Stephen D. Reicher, and Michael J. Platow. 2011. *The New Psychology of Leadership: Identity, Influence and Power*. New York: Psychology Press.

Haslam, S. Alexander, and Stephen D. Reicher. 2012. "Contesting the 'Nature' of Conformity: What Milgram and Zimbardo's Studies Really Show." *PLOS Biology* 10(11): 1–4.

Hassan, Hamdy A. 2009. "The Comoros and the Crisis of Building a National State." *Contemporary Arab Affairs* 2(2): 229–239.

van Haute, Emilie. 2016. *Green Parties in Europe*. Abingdon: Routledge.

Heazle, Michael, and John Kane. 2015. *Policy Legitimacy, Science and Political Authority: Knowledge and Action in Liberal Democracies*. Abingdon: Routledge.

Hedges, Jill. 2017. *Evita: The Life of Eva Perón*. London: I.B. Tauris.

Heffernan, Richard. 2003. "Prime Ministerial Predominance? Core Executive Politics in the UK." *The British Journal of Politics and International Relations* 5(3): 347–372.

———. 2005. "Exploring (and Explaining) the British Prime Minister." *The British Journal of Politics and International Relations* 7(4): 605–620.

Heifetz, Ronald. 1994. *Leadership Without Easy Answers*. Cambridge: Harvard University Press.

Helms, Ludger. 2005. *Presidents, Prime Ministers and Chancellors – Executive Leadership in Western Democracies*. London: Palgrave Macmillan.

———. 2012. *Comparative Political Leadership*. London: Palgrave Macmillan.

———. 2014. "Institutional Analysis." In *The Oxford Handbook of Political Leadership*, eds. R.A.W. Rhodes and Paul `t Hart. Oxford: Oxford University Press.

Hendriks, Frank, and Niels Karsten. 2014. "Theory of Democratic Leadership." In *Oxford Handbook of Political Leadership*, eds. R.A.W. Rhodes and Paul `t Hart. Oxford: Oxford University Press.

Hendriks, Frank. 2018. "Polder Politics in the Netherlands: The 'Viscous State' Revisited." In *Polder Politics: The Re-Invention of Consensus Democracy in the Netherlands*, eds. Frank Hendriks and Theo A.J. Toonen. Abingdon: Routledge.

Hermann, Margaret G. 1988. "Hafez Al-Assad, President of Syria: A Leadership Profile." In *Leadership and Negotiation: A New Look at the Middle East*, eds. Barbara Kellerman and Jeffrey Rubin. New York: Praeger.

———. 2002. *Assessing Leadership Style: A Trait Analysis*. Slingerlands: Social Science Automation.

———. 2003. "Saddam Hussein's Leadership Style." In *The Psychological Assessment of Political Leaders: With Profiles of Saddam Hussein and Bill Clinton*, ed. Jerrold M. Post. Ann Arbor: University of Michigan Press.

Hermann, Margaret G., Thomas Preston, Baghat Korany, and Timothy M. Shaw. 2001. "Who Leads Matters: The Effects of Powerful Individuals." *International Studies Review* 3(2): 83–131.

Herrick, James A. 2017. *The History and Theory of Rhetoric: An Introduction*. London: Routledge.

Herrnson, Paul S., J. Celeste Lay, and Atiya Kai Stokes. 2003. "Women Running 'as Women': Candidate Gender, Campaign Issues, and Voter-Targeting Strategies." *The Journal of Politics* 65(1): 244–255.

Hess, Robert Daniel, and Judith V. Torney-Purta. 2005. *The Development of Political Attitudes in Children*. New Brunswick: Transaction Publishers.

Higham, Nick. 2014. "Archives Reveal Pits Closure Plan." *BBC News*. https://www.bbc.com/news/uk-25549596

Hill, Thomas E. 1980. "Humanity as an End in Itself." *Ethics* 91(1): 84–99.

Hobbes, Thomas. 1996. *Hobbes: Leviathan*, ed. Richard Tuck. Cambridge: Cambridge University Press.

Hoffman, Brian, David Woehr, Robyn Maldagen-Youngjohn, and Brian Lyons. 2011. "Great Man or Great Myth? A Quantitative Review of the Relationship Between Individual Differences and Leader Effectiveness." *Journal of Occupational and Organizational Psychology* 84(2): 347–381.

Hofstede, Geert. 2011. "Dimensionalizing Cultures: The Hofstede Model in Context." *Online Readings in Psychology and Culture* 2(1).

Hogg, Michael A. 2001. "A Social Identity Theory of Leadership." *Personality and Social Psychology Review* 5(3): 184–200.

Hollis, Martin. 1996. *Reason in Action: Essay in the Philosophy of Social Science*. Cambridge: Cambridge University Press.

Holman, Mirya R. 2016. "Gender, Political Rhetoric, and Moral Metaphors in State of the City Addresses." *Urban Affairs Review* 52(4): 501–530.

Holmberg, Ingalill, and Staffan Åkerblom. 2004. "'Primes Inter Pares': Leadership and Culture in Sweden." In *Managerial Cultures of the World: A GLOBE Report of In-Depth Studies of the Cultures of 25 Countries*, eds. Jagdeep S. Chhokar, Felix Brodbeck, and Robert J. House. Mahwah: Lawrence Erlbaum Associates.

Holsti, Ole R., and James Rosenau. 1981. "The Foreign Policy Beliefs of Women in Leadership Positions." *The Journal of Politics* 43(2): 326–347.

Hopkins, Daniel J. 2018. *The Increasingly United States: How and Why American Political Behavior Nationalized*. Chicago: University of Chicago Press.

Hoppe, Michael, and Rabi S. Bhagat. 2004. "Leadership in the United States of America: The Leader as Cultural Hero." In *Managerial Cultures of the World: A GLOBE Report of In-Depth Studies of the Cultures of 25 Countries*, eds. Jagdeep S. Chhokar, Felix Brodbeck, and Robert J. House. Mahwah: Lawrence Erlbaum Associates.

Horesh, Niv. 2015. "The West Is Blind to the Appeal of China's Model of Authoritarian Capitalism." *Business Insider*. https://www.businessinsider.com/the-west-is-blind-to-the-appeal-of-chinas-model-of-authoritarian-capitalism-2015-7

Houghton, David Patrick. 2015. *Political Psychology: Situations, Individuals, and Cases*. 2nd ed. New York: Routledge.

House, Robert J. 1996. "Path-Goal Theory of Leadership: Lessons, Legacy, and a Reformulated Theory." *The Leadership Quarterly* 7(3): 323–352.

House, Robert J., Paul J. Hanges, Mansour Javidan, Peter W. Dorfman and Vipin Gupta. 2004. *Culture, Leadership, and Organizations: The GLOBE Study of 62 Societies*. Thousand Oaks: SAGE.

Howlett, Michael, and M. Ramesh. 2003. *Studying Public Policy: Policy Cycles and Policy Subsystems*. Oxford: Oxford University Press.

Huddy, Leonie, and Nayda Terkildsen. 1993. "Gender Stereotypes and the Perception of Male and Female Candidates." *American Journal of Political Science* 37(1): 119–147.

Hudson, Kimberly A. 2010. "Negotiating." In *Political and Civic Leadership: A Reference Handbook*. Thousand Oaks: SAGE, 726–733.

Huemer, Michael. 2012. *The Problem of Political Authority: An Examination of the Right to Coerce and the Duty to Obey*. Basingstoke: Palgrave Macmillan.

Hursthouse, Rosalind. 1999. *On Virtue Ethics*. Oxford: Oxford University Press.

Hussain, Zakir. 2014. "Growing Nostalgia in Indonesia for Life Under Suharto." *The Jakarta Post*. https://www.thejakartapost.com/news/2014/01/29/growing-nostalgia-indonesia-life-under-suharto.html

Hyman, Gerald. 2015. "Lee Kuan Yew's Enigma: Authoritarian Yet a Kind of Democrat." *Center for Strategic and International Studies*. https://www.csis.org/analysis/lee-kuan-yew%E2%80%99s-enigma-authoritarian-yet-kind-democrat

Ingersoll, Ralph. 1940. *Report on England, November 1940*. New York: Simon & Schuster.

International Parliamentary Union. 2019a. "Women in Parliaments: World and Regional Averages." *Women in Parliaments: World and Regional Averages*. http://archive.ipu.org/wmn-e/world.htm. December 9, 2019.

———. 2019b. "Women in Parliaments: World Classification." *Women in Parliaments: World Classification*. http://archive.ipu.org/wmn-e/classif.htm

Irwin, Neil. 2017. "Presidents Have Less Power Over the Economy Than You Might Think." *The New York Times*. https://www.nytimes.com/2017/01/17/upshot/presidents-have-less-power-over-the-economy-than-you-might-think.html

Isbester, Katherine. 2010. *The Paradox of Democracy in Latin America*. Toronto: University of Toronto Press.

Jackson, Robert H., and Carl Gustav Rosberg. 1982. *Personal Rule in Black Africa: Prince, Autocrat, Prophet, Tyrant*. Berkeley: University of California Press.

Jackson, Gregory. 2010. "Actors and Institutions." In *The Oxford Handbook of Comparative Institutional Analysis*, eds. Glenn Morgan, John Campbell, Colin Crouch, Ove Kaj Pedersen and Richard Whitley. Oxford: Oxford University Press.

James, Simon. 1995. "Relations Between Prime Minister and Cabinet: From Wilson to Thatcher." In *Prime Minister, Cabinet and Core Executive*, eds. R.A.W. Rhodes and Patrick Dunleavy. Basingstoke: Macmillan, 76–87.

James, William. 1907. *The Will to Believe and Other Essays in Popular Philosophy*. New York: Longmans, Green and Co.

———. 1912. *Memories and Studies*. New York: Longmans, Green and Co.

Janis, Irving. 1972. *Victims of Groupthink: A Psychological Study of Foreign-Policy Decisions and Fiascoes*. Boston: Houghton Mifflin.

Jankowski, James P. 2002. *Nasser's Egypt, Arab Nationalism, and the United Arab Republic*. Boulder: Lynne Rienner.

Jann, Werner, and Kai Weigrich. 2017. "Theories of the Policy Cycle." In *Handbook of Public Policy Analysis: Theory, Politics, and Methods*, eds. Frank Fischer, Gerald J. Miller, and Mara S. Sidney. Abingdon: Routledge.

Jelonek, Adam. 2005. "Political Culture and Its Impact to the Contemporary Regimes of East Asia." *Polish Sociological Review* 150: 179–195.

Jenkins, Ryan. 2013. *The Thin Line Between Propaganda and Persuasion*. Carbondale: SIU Press.

Jenkins, Simon. 2014. "Nick Clegg Is Paying the Price for Being King of Compromise." *The Guardian*. https://www.theguardian.com/commentisfree/2014/may/28/nick-clegg-king-of-compromise-lib-dems-eu-election

Jensen, Nathan M., and Edmund J. Malesky. 2018. *Incentives to Pander: How Politicians Use Corporate Welfare for Political Gain*. Cambridge: Cambridge University Press.

Jiang, Junyan, and Jeremy Wallace. 2017. *Informal Institutions and Authoritarian Information Systems: Theory and Evidence from China*. Rochester: Social Science Research Network. https://papers.ssrn.com/abstract=2992165

Johnson, Dominic, and James H. Fowler. 2011. "The Evolution of Overconfidence." *Nature* 477(7364): 317–320.

Johnson, Ralph A. 1993. *Negotiation Basics: Concepts, Skills, and Exercises*. Thousand Oak: SAGE.

Johnson, Stefanie K., Susan Elaine Murphy, Selamawit Zewdie, and Rebecca J. Reichard. 2008. "The Strong, Sensitive Type: Effects of Gender Stereotypes and Leadership Prototypes on the Evaluation of Male and Female Leaders." *Organizational Behavior and Human Decision Processes* 106(1): 39–60.

Jokinen, Tom. 2013. "The Biographer as a Fool in Love." *Hazlitt*. https://hazlitt.net/feature/biographer-fool-love

Jones, Jennifer J. 2016. "Talk 'Like a Man': The Linguistic Styles of Hillary Clinton, 1992–2013." *Perspectives on Politics* 14(3): 625–642.

Jones, Toby. 2011. *Desert Kingdom*. Cambridge: Harvard University Press.

Joppien, Charlotte. 2017. *Municipal Politics in Turkey: Local Government and Party Organisation*. London: Routledge.

Jost, John T., and Jim Sidanius. 2004. *Political Psychology*. New York: Psychology Press.

Judge, Timothy A., and Joyce E. Bono. 2000. "Five-Factor Model of Personality and Transformational Leadership." *Journal of Applied Psychology* 85(5): 751–765.

Judge, Timothy A., Joyce E. Bono, Remus Ilies, and Megan W. Gerhardt. 2002. "Personality and Leadership: A Qualitative and Quantitative Review." *The Journal of Applied Psychology* 87(4): 765–780.

Judge, Timothy A., Ronald F. Piccolo, and Tomek Kosalka. 2009. "The Bright and Dark Sides of Leader Traits: A Review and Theoretical Extension of the Leader Trait Paradigm." *The Leadership Quarterly* 20(6): 855–875.

Judge, Timothy A., and Robert Hogan. 2015. "Fitness, Adaptation, and Survival: The Role of Socio-Anthropic Characteristics, Personality, and Intelligence in Work Behavior." In *The Biological Foundations of Organizational Behavior*, eds. Stephen M. Colarelli and Richard D. Arvey. Chicago: University of Chicago Press.

Jung, C.G. 1981. *The Archetypes and the Collective Unconscious*. 2nd ed. Princeton: Princeton University Press.

Kaarbo, Juliet. 2012. *Coalition Politics and Cabinet Decision Making: A Comparative Analysis of Foreign Policy Choices*. Ann Arbor: University of Michigan Press.

Kabasakal, Hayat, and Muzaffer Bodur. 2007. "Leadership and Culture in Turkey: A Multifaceted Phenomenon." In *Culture and Leadership Across the World: The Globe Book of In-Depth Studies of 25 Societies*. Mahwah: Lawrence Erlbaum Associates.

Kahn, Kim Fridkin. 1994. "The Distorted Mirror: Press Coverage of Women Candidates for Statewide Office." *The Journal of Politics* 56(1): 154–173.

Kahneman, Daniel, Paul Slovic, and Amos Tversky. 1982. *Judgment Under Uncertainty: Heuristics and Biases*. Cambridge: Cambridge University Press.

Kahneman, Daniel, and Amos Tversky. 1979. "Prospect Theory: An Analysis of Decision Under Risk." *Econometrica* 47(2): 263–291.

Kalmoe, Nathan P. 2014. "Fueling the Fire: Violent Metaphors, Trait Aggression, and Support for Political Violence." *Political Communication* 31(4): 545–563.

Kampwirth, Karen. 1996. "The Mother of the Nicaraguans: Dona Violeta and the UNO's Gender Agenda." *Latin American Perspectives* 23(1): 67–86.

Kandeh, Jimmy. 2004. *Coups from Below: Armed Subalterns and State Power in West Africa*. New York: Palgrave Macmillan.

Kane, John. 2001. *The Politics of Moral Capital*. Cambridge: Cambridge University Press.

Kane, John, and Haig Patapan. 2012. *The Democratic Leader: How Democracy Defines, Empowers and Limits Its Leaders*. Oxford: Oxford University Press.

———. 2014. *Good Democratic Leadership: On Prudence and Judgment in Modern Democracies*. Oxford: Oxford University Press.

Kant, Immanuel. 1993. *Grounding for the Metaphysics of Morals*. 3rd ed. Indianapolis: Hackett.

Kapoor, Rajesh. 2011. *Japanese (Re)Militarization and Asia*. New Delhi: Pentagon Press.

Kay, Katty, and Claire Shipman. 2014. *The Confidence Code: The Science and Art of Self-Assurance – What Women Should Know*. New York: HarperBusiness.

Keane, John. 2009. *The Life and Death of Democracy*. London: Simon and Schuster.

Kearns Goodwin, Doris. 2006. *Team of Rivals: The Political Genius of Abraham Lincoln*. New York: Simon & Schuster.

Kebede, Messay. 2006. *The Roots and Fallouts of Haile Selassie's Educational Policy*. UNESCO. https://unesdoc.unesco.org/ark:/48223/pf0000147348

Kelly, Paul. 2014. *Triumph and Demise: The Broken Promise of a Labor Generation*. Melbourne: Melbourne University Publishing.

Kepplinger, Hans Mathias. 2002. "Mediatization of Politics: Theory and Data." *Journal of Communication* 52(4): 972–986.

Kernell, Samuel H. 2007. *Going Public: New Strategies of Presidential Leadership*. Washington, DC: CQ Press.

Kertzer, David I. 1988. *Ritual, Politics, and Power*. New Haven: Yale University Press.

Key, V.O. 1961. *Public Opinion and American Democracy*. New York: Alfred A. Knopf.

Khaldūn, Ibn. 1989. *The Muqaddimah*, ed. N.J. Dawood. Princeton: Princeton University Press.

Khuhro, Amir Ahmed, and Ali Nawaz Soomro. 2013. "The Role of Benazir Bhutto in the Movement for the Restoration of Democracy: An Analysis." *International Journal of Social Science and Humanity* 3(3): 274–277.

King, Anthony Stephen, and Robert J. Wybrow. 2001. *British Political Opinion, 1937–2000: The Gallup Polls*. London: Politcos.

King, Gary, Robert O. Keohane, and Sidney Verba. 1994. *Designing Social Inquiry: Scientific Inference in Qualitative Research*. Princeton: Princeton University Press.

Kingdon, John. 1995. *Agendas, Alternatives, and Public Policies*. 2nd ed. Boston: Addison-Wesley.

Kirkpatrick, Shelley, and Edwin A. Locke. 1991. "Leadership: Do Traits Matter?" *Academy of Management Executive* 5(2): 48–60.

Kjeldsen, Jens E., Amos Kiewe, Marie Lund, and Jette Barnholdt Hansen. 2019. *Speechwriting in Theory and Practice*. New York: Springer.

Klagsbrun, Francine. 2019. *Lioness: Golda Meir and the Nation of Israel*. New York: Knopf Doubleday.

Klein, Pieter. 1998. *Wim Kok: Het Taaie Gevecht van een Polderjongen*. Amsterdam: Prometheus.

Klijn, Erik-Hans. 2014. "Political Leadership in Networks." In *The Oxford Handbook of Political Leadership*, eds. R.A.W. Rhodes and Paul `t Hart. Oxford: Oxford University Press.

Klofstad, Casey A. 2015. "Candidate Voice Pitch Influences Election Outcomes." *Political Psychology* 37(5): 725–738.

Klor, Esteban, and Efraim Benmelech. 2018. "What Explains the Flow of Foreign Fighters to ISIS?" *Terrorism & Political Violence* 30: 1–24.

Klosko, George. 2006. *The Development of Plato's Political Theory*. Oxford: Oxford University Press.

Knight, W. Andy. 2009. "Distinguishing and Unifying Visionary Leadership and Mechanical Management." In *The Ashgate Research Companion to Political Leadership*, eds. Joseph Masciulli, Mikhail A. Molchanov, and W. Andy Knight. Farnham: Ashgate.

Kochanek, Stanley A., and Robert L. Hardgrave. 2008. *India: Government and Politics in a Developing Nation*. Boston: Thomson Wadsworth.

Koh, David. 2001. "The Politics of a Divided Party and Parkinson's State in Vietnam." *Contemporary Southeast Asia* 23(3): 533–551.

Kollander, Patricia. 1995. *Frederick III: Germany's Liberal Emperor*. Santa Barbara: Greenwood.

Kopecký, Petr. 2004. "Power to the Executive! The Changing Executive–Legislative Relations in Eastern Europe." *The Journal of Legislative Studies* 10(2–3): 142–153.

Kopfman, Jenifer E., Sandi W. Smith, James K. Ah Yun, and Annemarie Hodges. 1998. "Affective and Cognitive Reactions to Narrative Versus Statistical Evidence Organ Donation Messages." *Journal of Applied Communication Research* 26: 279–300.

Korab-Karpowicz, W. Julian. 2018. "Political Realism in International Relations." In *Stanford Encyclopedia of Philosophy*, ed. Edward N. Zalta. https://plato.stanford.edu/entries/realism-intl-relations/

Kort, Michael G. 2019. *The Soviet Colossus: History and Aftermath*. New York: Routledge.

Kotter, John P. 1990. *Force for Change: How Leadership Differs from Management*. New York: Free Press.

Kouzes, James M., and Barry Z. Posner. 2011. *Credibility: How Leaders Gain and Lose It, Why People Demand It*. San Francisco: John Wiley & Sons.

Krekó, Péter, and Zsolt Enyedi. 2019 "Explaining Eastern Europe: Orbán's Laboratory of Illiberalism." *Journal of Democracy* 29(3): 39–51.

Krishna, Balraj. 2007. *India's Bismarck, Sardar Vallabhbhai Patel*. Mumbai: Indus Source.

Kumar, Arun, and Rachana Sharma. 2000. *Principles of Business Management*. New Delhi: Atlantic.

Kuromiya, Hiroaki. 2013. *Stalin*. Abingdon: Routledge.

Kurtz, Donald V. 2001. *Political Anthropology: Paradigms and Power*. Boulder: Westview.

Kuyper, Jonathan W. 2012. "Deliberative Democracy and the Neglected Dimension of Leadership." *Journal of Public Deliberation* 8(1): 34.

Lacouture, Jean, and Simonne Lacouture. 1958. *Egypt in Transition*. New York: Criterion Books.

Lagarde, Christine. 2019. "Angela Merkel – Striking the Right Note on Leadership." Presented at the HHL Leipzig Graduate School of Management, Leipzig. https://www.imf.org/en/News/Articles/2019/08/31/sp083119-Angela-Merkel-Striking-the-Right-Note-on-Leadership

Laing, Matthew. 2012. "Towards a Pragmatic Presidency? Exploring the Waning of Political Time." *Polity* 44(2): 234–259.

Laing, Matthew, and Brendan McCaffrie. 2017. "The Impossible Leadership Situation? Analyzing Success for Disjunctive Presidents." *Presidential Studies Quarterly* 47(2): 255–276.

Laing, Matthew, and James Walter. 2017. "Great Expectations and Great Limitations: Walking the Tightrope of Political Leadership in the Twenty-First Century." In *The Routledge Companion to Leadership*, eds. John Storey, Jean Hartley, Jean-Louis Denis, Paul 't Hart, and Dave Ulrich. New York: Routledge.

Lambers, William. 2006. *Nuclear Weapons*. Cincinnati: Lambers Publications.

Landtsheer, Christ'l De, Philippe De Vries, and Dieter Vertessen. 2008. "Political Impression Management: How Metaphors, Sound Bites, Appearance Effectiveness, and Personality Traits Can Win Elections." *Journal of Political Marketing* 7(3–4): 217–238.

Lapavitsas, Costas. 2016. "One Year on, Syriza Has Sold Its Soul for Power." *The Guardian*. https://www.theguardian.com/commentisfree/2016/jan/25/one-year-on-syriza-radicalism-power-euro-alexis-tsipras

Lasswell, Harold. 1948. *Power and Personality*. Berkeley: University of California Press.

———. 1962. *The Future of Political Science*. Abingdon: Routledge.

Laver, Michael, and Norman Schofield. 1998. *Multiparty Government: The Politics of Coalition in Europe*. Ann Arbor: University of Michigan Press.

Lawless, Jennifer L. 2010. "Women's Political Ambition." In *Gender and Women's Leadership: A Reference Handbook*, ed. Karen O'Connor. Thousand Oaks: SAGE.

Lawless, Jennifer L., and Richard L. Fox. 2010. *It Still Takes A Candidate: Why Women Don't Run for Office*. New York: Cambridge University Press.

Lawson, Nigel, and Robert Armstrong. 1994. "Cabinet Government in the Thatcher Years." *Contemporary Record* 8(3): 440–452.

Lax, David A., and James K. Sebenius. 2006. *3-D Negotiation*. Boston: Harvard Business Press.

LeBor, Adam. 2012. *Milosevic: A Biography*. London: Bloomsbury.

Lecy, Jesse D., Ines A. Mergel, and Hans Peter Schmitz. 2014. "Networks in Public Administration: Current Scholarship in Review." *Public Management Review* 16(5): 643–665.

Lee, Frances E. 2015. "How Party Polarization Affects Governance." *Annual Review of Political Science* 18(1): 261–282.

Lemire, Jonathan. 2018. "How Trump Has Rewritten the Rules of the Presidency." *PBS NewsHour*. https://www.pbs.org/newshour/politics/how-trump-has-rewritten-the-rules-of-the-presidency

Lepore, Jill. 2015. "Are Polls Ruining Democracy?" *The New Yorker*. https://www.newyorker.com/magazine/2015/11/16/politics-and-the-new-machine

Lerner, Gerda. 1986. *The Creation of Patriarchy*. Oxford: Oxford University Press.

Lester, Amelia. 2019. "The Roots of Jacinda Ardern's Extraordinary Leadership After Christchurch." *The New Yorker*. https://www.newyorker.com/culture/culture-desk/what-jacinda-arderns-leadership-means-to-new-zealand-and-to-the-world

Letts, Marcus. 2009. *Obama's Discourse of "Hope": Making Rhetoric Work Politically*. University of Bristol: SPAIS. http://www.bris.ac.uk/media-library/sites/spais/migrated/documents/letts0409.pdf

Levin, Kelly, Benjamin Cashore, Steven Bernstein, and Graeme Auld. 2012. "Overcoming the Tragedy of Super Wicked Problems: Constraining Our Future Selves to Ameliorate Global Climate Change." *Policy Sciences* 45(2): 123–152.

Levin, Michael. 1997. "Natural Subordination, Aristotle On." *Philosophy* 72(280): 241–257.

Levitsky, Steven, and Lucan A. Way. 2010. *Competitive Authoritarianism: Hybrid Regimes After the Cold War*. Cambridge: Cambridge University Press.

Levy, Jack S. 2018. "Political Decision-Making." In *Political Psychology: A Social Psychological Approach*, eds. Christopher J. Hewer and Evanthia Lyons. Hoboken: John Wiley & Sons.

Lewellen, Ted C. 2003. *Political Anthropology: An Introduction*. Westport: Praeger.

Lewicki, Roy, and Joseph August Litterer. 1985. *Negotiation*. Homewood: R.D. Irwin.

Lewicki, Roy, and John Minton. 2003. *Essentials of Negotiation*. 3rd ed. Boston: McGraw-Hill.

Lewin, Leif. 1991. *Self-Interest and Public Interest in Western Politics*. Oxford: Oxford University Press.

Lichter, Ida. 2009. *Muslim Women Reformers: Inspiring Voices Against Oppression*. Amherst: Prometheus Books.

Lidén, Gustav. 2014. "Theories of Dictatorships: Sub-Types and Explanations." *Studies of Transition States and Societies* 6(1): 50–67.

Liden, Robert C. 1985. "Female Perceptions of Female and Male Managerial Behavior." *Sex Roles* 12(3): 421–432.

Lijphart, Arend. 1984. *Democracies: Patterns of Majoritarian and Consensus Government in Twenty-One Countries*. New Haven: Yale University Press.

———. 2012. *Patterns of Democracy*. New Haven: Yale University Press.

Lindblom, Charles E. 1959. "The Science of 'Muddling Through'." *Public Administration Review* 19(2): 79–88.

Lipman-Blumen, Jean. 1984. *Gender Roles and Power*. Upper Saddle River: Prentice-Hall.

———. 2005. *The Allure of Toxic Leaders: Why We Follow Destructive Bosses and Corrupt Politicians – And How We Can Survive Them*. New York: Oxford University Press.

Lippmann, Walter. 1922. *Public Opinion*. New York: Harcourt Brace.

———. 1925. *The Phantom Public*. New York: Harcourt Brace.

Listhaug, Ola, and Tor Georg Jakobsen. 2018. "Foundations of Political Trust." In *The Oxford Handbook of Social and Political Trust*, ed. Eric M. Uslaner. Oxford: Oxford University Press.

Little, Graham. 1985. *Political Ensembles: A Psychosocial Approach to Politics and Leadership*. Oxford: Oxford University Press.

Lo, Min-Tzu et al. 2017. "Genome-Wide Analyses for Personality Traits Identify Six Genomic Loci and Show Correlations with Psychiatric Disorders." *Nature Genetics* 49(1): 152–156.

Locke, John. 1821. *Two Treatises of Government*. London: Whitmore and Fenn.

———. 1980. *Second Treatise of Government*. Indianapolis: Hackett.

Lodge, Milton, and Charles S. Taber. 2005. "The Automaticity of Affect for Political Leaders, Groups, and Issues: An Experimental Test of the Hot Cognition Hypothesis." *Political Psychology* 26(3): 455–482.

Londregan, John B., and Keith T. Poole. 1990. "Poverty, the Coup Trap, and the Seizure of Executive Power." *World Politics* 42(2): 151–183.

Lord, Carnes. 2003. *The Modern Prince: What Leaders Need to Know Now*. New Haven: Yale University Press.

Losco, Joseph. 2017. "Public Administration and the Life Sciences: Pathways Forward." In *Handbook of Biology and Politics*, eds. Steven Peterson and Albert Somit. Cheltenham: Edward Elgar.

Ludwig, Arnold M. 2002. *King of the Mountain: The Nature of Political Leadership*. Lexington: University of Kentucky Press.

Lukes, Stephen. 2005. *Power: A Radical View*. 2nd ed. London: Red Globe Press.

Lussier, Danielle N. 2010. "From Solidarity to Division: An Analysis of Lech Wałęsa's Transition to Constituted Leadership." *The Leadership Quarterly* 21(5): 703–715.

Lux, Andrei Alexander. 2020 "Open, Honest and Effective: What Makes Jacinda Ardern an Authentic Leader." *The Conversation*. http://theconversation.com/open-honest-and-effective-what-makes-jacinda-ardern-an-authentic-leader-132513

Lynch, John. 1992. *Caudillos in Spanish America, 1800–1850*. Oxford: Clarendon Press.

Lyons, Martyn. 1994. *Napoleon Bonaparte and the Legacy of the French Revolution*. New York: Macmillan Education.

MacDonogh, Giles. 2001. *Frederick the Great: A Life in Deed and Letters*. New York: St. Martin's.

Machiavelli, Niccolo. 1999. *Machiavelli: The Chief Works and Others*. Durham: Duke University Press.

Mackie, Jamie. 2010. "Patrimonialism: The New Order and Beyond." In *Soeharto's New Order and Its Legacy: Essays in Honour of Harold Crouch*, eds. Edward Aspinall and Greg Fealy. Canberra: ANU E-Press.

Mackinac Center for Public Policy. 2019. "The Overton Window." http://www.mackinac.org/OvertonWindow (May 29, 2020).

Madsen, Douglas, and Peter G. Snow. 1991. *The Charismatic Bond: Political Behavior in Time of Crisis*. Cambridge: Harvard University Press.

Maestas, Cherie. 2000. "Professional Legislatures and Ambitious Politicians: Policy Responsiveness of State Institutions." *Legislative Studies Quarterly* 25(4): 663–690.

Mahoney, James, and Kathleen Thelen. 2010. "A Theory of Gradual Institutional Change: Ambiguity, Agency and Power." In *Explaining Institutional Change*. Cambridge: Cambridge University Press.

Mancini, Paolo. 2011. *Between Commodification and Lifestyle Politics Does Silvio Berlusconi Provide a New Model of Politics for the Twenty-First Century?* Oxford: Reuters Institute for the Study of Journalism.

Mann, Richard D. 1959. "A Review of the Relationships Between Personality and Performance in Small Groups." *Psychological Bulletin* 56(4): 241–270.

Mansbridge, Jane, and Cathie Jo Martin. 2016. *Political Negotiation: A Handbook*. Washington, DC: Brookings Institution Press.

March, James G. 1994. *Primer on Decision Making: How Decisions Happen*. New York: Free Press.

March, James G., and Johan P. Olsen. 2008. "Elaborating the 'New Institutionalism'." In *The Oxford Handbook of Political Institutions*, eds. Sarah A. Binder, R.A.W. Rhodes, and Bert A. Rockman. Oxford: Oxford University Press.

Marcus, G.E. 2000. "Emotions in Politics." *Annual Review of Political Science* 3(1): 221–250.

Marcus, George, W. Russell Neuman, and Michael Mackuen. 2000. *Affective Intelligence and Political Judgment.* Chicago: University of Chicago Press.

Marcus, Harold G. 1994. *A History of Ethiopia*. Berkeley: University of California Press.

Marsh, David, Paul 't Hart, and Karen Tindall. 2010. "Celebrity Politics: The Politics of the Late Modernity?" *Political Studies Review* 8(3): 322–340.

Marshall, Monty, and Gabrielle Elzinga-Marshall. 2017. *Global Report 2017: Conflict, Governance and State Fragility*. Vienna: Center of Systemic Peace.

Martin, Guy. 1987. "Ideology and Praxis in Thomas Sankara's Populist Revolution of 4 August 1983 in Burkina Faso." *African Issues* 15: 77–90.

Martin, James. 2014. *Politics and Rhetoric: A Critical Introduction*. London: Routledge.

Martin, Lanny W. 2004. "The Government Agenda in Parliamentary Democracies." *American Journal of Political Science* 48(3): 445–461.

Masciulli, Joseph, and W. Andy Knight. 2009. "Conceptions of Global Leadership for Contextually Intelligent, Innovatively Adaptive Political Leaders." In *The Ashgate Research Companion to Political Leadership*, eds. Joseph Masciulli, Mikhail A. Molchanov, and W. Andy Knight. Farnham: Ashgate.

Maslow, Abraham. 1954. *Motivation and Personality*. New York: Harper.

Mason, Lilliana. 2018. *Uncivil Agreement: How Politics Became Our Identity*. Chicago: University of Chicago Press.

Massicard, Elise, and Nicole Watts. 2013. *Negotiating Political Power in Turkey: Breaking Up the Party*. Abingdon: Routledge.

Matthews, Gerald, Ian J. Deary, and Martha C. Whiteman. 2009. *Personality Traits*. 3rd ed. Cambridge: Cambridge University Press.

May, Ernest R. 1975. *"Lessons" of the Past: The Use and Misuse of History in American Foreign Policy*. Oxford: Oxford University Press.

May, Rollo. 1972. *Power and Innocence: A Search for the Sources of Violence*. New York: W.W. Norton.

Mazraani, Nathalie. 2013. *Aspects of Language Variation in Arabic Political Speech-Making*. Abingdon: Routledge.

McAdam, Doug, John D. McCarthy, and Mayer N. Zald, eds. 1996. *Comparative Perspectives on Social Movements: Political Opportunities, Mobilizing Structures, and Cultural Framings*. Cambridge: Cambridge University Press.

McAdams, Dan P. 2017. "The Appeal of the Primal Leader: Human Evolution and Donald J. Trump." *Evolutionary Studies in Imaginative Culture* 1(2): 1–13.

McAllister, Ian. 2007. "The Personalization of Politics." In *The Oxford Handbook of Political Behavior*, eds. Russell J. Dalton and Hans-Dieter Klingemann. Oxford: Oxford University Press.

McAuley, Ian. 2014. "Rudd Humbled, but Real Lessons of Insulation Scheme Go Unlearned." *The Conversation*. http://theconversation.com/rudd-humbled-but-real-lessons-of-insulation-scheme-go-unlearned-26711

McCombs, Maxwell E., and Donald L. Shaw. 1972. "The Agenda-Setting Function of Mass Media." *The Public Opinion Quarterly* 36(2): 176–187.

McConnell, Allan. 2018. "Rethinking Wicked Problems as Political Problems and Policy Problems." *Policy & Politics* 46(1): 165–180.

McDermott, Rose. 2001. *Risk-Taking in International Politics: Prospect Theory in American Foreign Policy*. Ann Arbor: University of Michigan Press.

McGlen, Nancy E., and Meredith Reid Sarkees. 1993. *Women in Foreign Policy: The Insiders*. New York: Routledge.

McGraw, Kathleen M. 1998. "Manipulating Public Opinion with Moral Justification." *The Annals of the American Academy of Political and Social Science* 560: 129–142.

McGraw, Kathleen M., Samuel Best, and Richard Timpone. 1995. "'What They Say or What They Do?' The Impact of Elite Explanation and Policy Outcomes on Public Opinion." *American Journal of Political Science* 39(1): 53–74.

McGrory, Mary. 1963. "Polite, Happy, Helpful: The Real Hero Was the Crowd." *Boston Globe* August 29.

McGuire, William J. 2004. "The Poly-Psy Relationship: Three Phases of a Long Affair." In *Political Psychology*, eds. John T. Jost and Sidanius, Jim. New York: Psychology Press.

McLynn, Frank. 2009. *Marcus Aurelius: A Life*. Cambridge: Da Capo.

McMillan, M.E. 2013. *Fathers and Sons: The Rise and Fall of Political Dynasty in the Middle East*. Basingstoke: Palgrave Macmillan.

Meegan, Daniel V. 2010. "Zero-Sum Bias: Perceived Competition Despite Unlimited Resources." *Frontiers in Psychology* 1: 191.

Meindl, James R., Sanford B. Ehrlich, and Janet M. Dukerich. 1985. "The Romance of Leadership." *Administrative Science Quarterly* 30(1): 78–102.

Menon, V.P. 1955. *The Story of the Integration of the Indian States*. Bangalore: Longmans, Green and Co.

Meredith, Martin. 2002. *Our Votes, Our Guns: Robert Mugabe and the Tragedy of Zimbabwe*. New York: PublicAffairs.

Merolla, Jennifer L., and Elizabeth J. Zechmeister. 2011. "The Nature, Determinants, and Consequences of Chávez's Charisma: Evidence from a Study of Venezuelan Public Opinion." *Comparative Political Studies* 44(1): 28–54.

Metoyer, Cynthia Chavez. 2000. *Women and the State in Post-Sandinista Nicaragua*. Boulder: Lynne Rienner.

Meyer, David S. 2004. "Protest and Political Opportunities." *Annual Review of Sociology* 30: 125–145.

Michels, Robert. 1911. *Political Parties: A Sociological Study of the Oligarchical Tendencies of Modern Democracy*. Leipzig: Werner Klinkhardt.

Milekic, Sven. 2016. "Croatia's Ex-PM Was Doomed from Start, Experts Say." *Balkan Insight*. https://balkaninsight.com/2016/06/23/ex-croatian-pm-s-success-doomed-from-start-06-22-2016/

Milgram, Stanley. 1974. *Obedience to Authority*. New York: Harper & Row.

Mill, John Stuart. 1863. *On Liberty*. 2nd ed. Boston: Ticknor and Fields.

Millard, Frances. 2000. "Presidents and Democratization in Poland: The Roles of Lech Wałesa and Aleksander Kwaśniewski in Building a New Polity." *Journal of Communist Studies and Transition Politics* 16(3): 39–62.

Miller, Chris. 2007. "Authority." In *Leadership: The Key Concepts*, eds. Antonio Marturano and Jonathan Gosling. London: Routledge.

Millett, Kate. 1970. *Sexual Politics*. London: Rupert Hart-Davis.

Mills, C. Wright. 1956. *The Power Elite*. New York: Oxford University Press.

Mintz, Alex, and Carly Wayne. 2016. *The Polythink Syndrome: U.S. Foreign Policy Decisions on 9/11, Afghanistan, Iraq, Iran, Syria, and ISIS.* Stanford: Stanford University Press.

Mitchell, Alison. 1998. "Impeachment: The Overview." *The New York Times*, December 20.

Mithen, Steven. 2012. *Thirst: For Water and Power in the Ancient World.* Cambridge: Harvard University Press.

Molavi, Afshin. 2005. *The Soul of Iran: A Nation's Struggle for Freedom.* New York: W.W. Norton.

Montesquieu, Charles Baron De. 2011. *The Spirit of Laws.* New York: Cosimo Classics.

Moodian, Michael A. 2008. *Contemporary Leadership and Intercultural Competence: Exploring the Cross-Cultural Dynamics Within Organizations.* Thousand Oaks: SAGE.

Moore, Charles. 2016. *Margaret Thatcher: At Her Zenith: In London, Washington and Moscow.* New York: Knopf Doubleday.

Moritz, Robin F.A., and Elke Hillesheim. 1985. "Inheritance of Dominance in Honeybees." *Behavioral Ecology and Sociobiology* 17(1): 87–89.

Morray, Joseph P. 1997. *Grand Disillusion: François Mitterrand and the French Left.* Santa Barbara: Greenwood Publishing Group.

Morris, Dick. 1999. *The New Prince.* New York: St. Martin's.

Muckelbauer, John. 2008. *The Future of Invention: Rhetoric, Postmodernism, and the Problem of Change.* New York: SUNY Press.

Mudde, Cas. 2004. "The Populist Zeitgeist." *Government and Opposition* 39(4): 541–563.

Mudde, Cas, and Cristobal Rovira Kaltwasser. 2017. *Populism: A Very Short Introduction.* New York: Oxford University Press.

Mulgan, Richard. 2008. "How Much Responsiveness Is Too Much or Too Little?" *Australian Journal of Public Administration* 67(3): 345–356.

Mullainathan, Sendhil, and Ebonya Washington. 2009. "Sticking with Your Vote: Cognitive Dissonance and Political Attitudes." *American Economic Journal: Applied Economics* 1(1): 86–111.

Müller, Jan-Werner. 2016. *What Is Populism?* Philadelphia: University of Pennsylvania Press.

Munir, Kamal, and Natalya Naqvi. 2017. "Privatization in the Land of Believers: The Political Economy of Privatization in Pakistan." *Modern Asian Studies* 51(6): 1695–1726.

Muñoz, Heraldo. 2014. *Getting Away with Murder: Benazir Bhutto's Assassination and the Politics of Pakistan.* New York: W.W. Norton.

Murphy, F.C. et al. 2001. "Decision-Making Cognition in Mania and Depression." *Psychological Medicine* 31(4): 679–693.

Murray, Greg R., and J. David Schmitz. 2011. "Caveman Politics: Evolutionary Leadership Preferences and Physical Stature." *Social Science Quarterly* 92(5): 1215–1235.

Mwakikagile, Godfrey. 2006. *Tanzania Under Mwalimu Nyerere: Reflections on an African Statesman.* Dar es Salaam: New Africa Press.

Nabi, Robin. 2002. "Discrete Emotions and Persuasion." In *The Persuasion Handbook: Developments in Theory and Practice*, eds. James Prince Dillard and Michael Pfau. Thousand Oaks: SAGE.

Nadeau, Richard, Michael S. Lewis-Beck, and Éric Bélanger. 2013. "Economics and Elections Revisited." *Comparative Political Studies* 46(5): 551–573.

Narayanan, Jayanth, and Smrithi Prasad. 2015. "Neurobiological Systems: Implications for Organizational Behavior." In *The Biological Foundations of Organizational Behavior*, eds. Stephen M. Colarelli and Richard D. Arvey. Chicago: University of Chicago Press.

Nass, Clifford I. 1986. "Bureaucracy, Technical Expertise, and Professionals: A Weberian Approach." *Sociological Theory* 4(1): 61–70.

Natten, Donna Van. 2020. *The Body Language of Politics: Decide Who Is Lying, Who Is Sincere, and How You'll Vote.* New York: Simon and Schuster.

Neely, Mark E. Neely. 1992. *The Fate of Liberty: Abraham Lincoln and Civil Liberties.* Oxford: Oxford University Press.

Nelson, Michael. 2015. *Guide to the Presidency.* Abingdon: Routledge.

Netelenbos, Benno. 2016. *Political Legitimacy Beyond Weber: An Analytical Framework.* London: Palgrave Macmillan.

Neuman, W. Russell. 1986. *The Paradox of Mass Politics: Knowledge and Opinion in the American Electorate.* Cambridge: Harvard University Press.

Ng, Yee-Fui. 2018. *The Rise of Political Advisors in the Westminster System.* Abingdon: Routledge.

Nickerson, Raymond S. 1998. "Confirmation Bias: A Ubiquitous Phenomenon in Many Guises." *Review of General Psychology* 2(2): 175–220.

Nietzsche, Friedrich. 1974. *The Gay Science: With a Prelude in Rhymes and an Appendix of Songs.* New York: Vintage.

———. 2008a. *Beyond Good and Evil.* Oxford: Oxford University Press.

———. 2008b. *Thus Spoke Zarathustra.* Oxford: Oxford University Press.

Nijstad, Bernard A. 2009. *Group Performance.* New York: Psychology Press.

Nixon, Richard M. 1974. "Farwell Address to Whitehouse Staff." Speech at the White House, Washington, DC.

Northouse, Peter G. 2016. *Leadership: Theory and Practice.* 7th ed. Thousand Oaks: SAGE.

Nozick, Robert. 1969. "Coercion." In *Philosophy, Science, and Method: Essays in Honor of Ernest Nage,* eds. Sidney Morgenbesser, Patrick Suppes, and Morton White. New York: St Martin's.

Nugent, Neill. 2017. *The Government and Politics of the European Union.* 8th ed. London: Red Globe Press.

Nussbaum, Martha. 1997. "Is Nietzsche a Political Thinker?" *International Journal of Philosophical Studies* 5(1): 1–13.

Nye, Joseph. 2008. *The Powers to Lead.* Oxford: Oxford University Press.

Oakley, Vern. 2017. *Leadership in Focus: Bringing Out Your Best on Camera.* Austin: Greenleaf Book Group.

Oberdiek, Hans. 1986. "Clean and Dirty Hands in Politics." *International Journal of Moral and Social Studies* 1(1): 41–61.

Oberlander, Jonathan. 2010. "Long Time Coming: Why Health Reform Finally Passed." *Health Affairs* 29(6): 1112–1116.

———. 2019. "Sitting in Limbo—Obamacare Under Divided Government." *New England Journal of Medicine* 380(26): 2485–2487.

O'Brien, Patrick K. 1998. "Political Biography: A Polemical Review of the Genre." *Biography* 21(1): 50–57.

O'Keefe, Daniel J. 2000. "Guilt and Social Influence." *Annals of the International Communication Association* 23(1): 67–101.

Okin, Susan Moller. 1991. *Justice, Gender, and the Family.* New York: Basic Books.

Olson, Mancur. 1965. *The Logic of Collective Action.* Cambridge: Harvard University Press.

O'Neil, Patrick H., Karl Fields, and Don Share. 2015. *Cases in Comparative Politics.* 5th ed. New York: W. W. Norton & Company.

O'Shea, Owen. 2012. *Heirs to the Kingdom: Kerry's Political Dynasties*. Dublin: O'Brien Press.

Ottaway, David, and Marina Ottaway. 1970. *Algeria: The Politics of a Socialist Revolution*. Berkeley: University of California Press.

Overholt, Thomas W. 1974. "The Ghost Dance of 1890 and the Nature of the Prophetic Process." *Ethnohistory* 21(1): 37–63.

Owen, David. 2008. *In Sickness and in Power: Illnesses in Heads of Government During the Last 100 Years*. Westport: Praeger.

Owen, David, and Jonathan Davidson. 2009. "Hubris Syndrome: An Acquired Personality Disorder? A Study of US Presidents and UK Prime Ministers Over the Last 100 Years." *Brain* 132(5): 1396–1406.

Padró i Miquel, Gerard, and James M. Snyder. 2006. "Legislative Effectiveness and Legislative Careers." *Legislative Studies Quarterly* 31(3): 347–381.

Page, Joseph. 1983. *Peron: A Biography*. New York: Random House.

Pal, Joyojeet, Priyank Chandra, and V.G. Vinod Vydiswaran. 2016. "Twitter and the Rebranding of Narendra Modi." *Economic & Political Weekly* 51(8): 52–60.

Pareto, Vilfredo. 1935. *The Mind and Society*. New York: Harcourt Brace.

Parkinson, Cyril Northcote. 1958. *Parkinson's Law or the Pursuit of Progress*. London: Penguin.

Parton, James. 1860. *Life of Andrew Jackson*. New York: Mason Brothers.

Paschen, Michael, and Erich Dihsmaier. 2014. *The Psychology of Human Leadership: How to Develop Charisma and Authority*. Heidelberg: Springer.

Pasquino, Pasquale. 1998. "Locke on King's Prerogative." *Political Theory* 26(2): 198–208.

Passarelli, Gianluca. 2015. *The Presidentialization of Political Parties: Organizations, Institutions and Leaders*. Basingstoke: Palgrave Macmillan.

Pateman, Carole. 1988. *The Sexual Contract*. Stanford: Stanford University Press.

Pauwels, Teun. 2014. *Populism in Western Europe Comparing Belgium, Germany and The Netherlands*. London: Routledge.

Peake, Jeffrey S., and Matthew Eshbaugh-Soha. 2008. "The Agenda-Setting Impact of Major Presidential TV Addresses." *Political Communication* 25(2): 113–137.

Pearce, Susan C. 2010. "Gender and Power." In *Political and Civic Leadership: A Reference Handbook*, ed. Richard A. Couto. Thousand Oaks: SAGE.

Persky, Joseph. 1995. "Retrospectives: The Ethology of Homo Economicus." *The Journal of Economic Perspectives* 9(2): 221–231.

Peter, Fabienne. 2008. *Democratic Legitimacy*. New York: Routledge.

Peters, B. Guy. 2018. "The Challenge of Policy Coordination." *Policy Design and Practice* 1(1): 1–11.

Pew Research Center. 2015a. *Beyond Distrust: How Americans View Their Government*. Washington: Pew Research Center. https://www.people-press.org/2015/11/23/beyond-distrust-how-americans-view-their-government/

———. 2015b. *Women and Leadership: Public Says Women Are Equally Qualified, but Barriers Persist*. Washington: Pew Research Center.

———. 2018. "Men, Women Differ on What's Essential in a Political or Business Leader." *Pew Research Center*. https://www.pewresearch.org/fact-tank/2018/09/20/men-women-differ-over-some-qualities-they-see-as-essential-for-political-and-business-leadership/

———. 2019. "For the Fifth Time in a Row, the New Congress Is the Most Racially and Ethnically Diverse Ever." *Pew Research Center*. https://www.pewresearch.org/

fact-tank/2019/02/08/for-the-fifth-time-in-a-row-the-new-congress-is-the-most-racially-and-ethnically-diverse-ever/

Pfiffner, James P. 1999. *The Managerial Presidency*. College Station: Texas A&M University Press.

Philip, George, and Francisco Panizza. 2013. *The Triumph of Politics*. Cambridge: Polity.

Phillips, Jim. 2014. "Containing, Isolating, and Defeating the Miners: The UK Cabinet Ministerial Group on Coal and the Three Phases of the 1984–85 Strike." *Historical Studies in International Relations* 35: 117–141.

Phillips, Tom, and Dom Phillips. 2018. "Jair Bolsonaro on Brink of Victory in Brazil as Fears for Democracy Grow." *The Guardian*. https://www.theguardian.com/world/2018/oct/28/jair-bolsonaro-on-brink-of-victory-in-brazil-as-fears-for-democracy-grow

Pierson, Paul. 2004. *Politics in Time: History, Institutions, and Social Analysis*. Princeton: Princeton University Press.

Pitkin, Hanna. 1965. "Obligation and Consent." *The American Political Science Review* 59(4): 990–999.

de Pizan, Christine. 2018. *The Book of the City of Ladies and Other Writings*, eds. Sophie Bourgault and Rebecca Kingston. Indianapolis: Hackett.

Plato. 1892. *The Dialogues of Plato, Volume 3*. 3rd ed. Oxford: Oxford University Press.

Plutarch. 1906. *Plutarch's Lives, Volume 3*. London: George Bell and Sons.

Plutarch. 1918. *Plutarch's Lives, Vol. VI*. London: William Heinemann.

Poel, Ibo van de, Lambèr Royakkers, and Sjoerd D. Zwart. 2015. *Moral Responsibility and the Problem of Many Hands*. London: Routledge.

Poguntke, Thomas, and Paul D. Webb. 2005. *The Presidentialization of Politics: A Comparative Study of Modern Democracies*. Oxford: Oxford University Press.

Polanyi, Karl. 2001. *The Great Transformation: The Political and Economic Origins of Our Time*. Boston: Beacon.

Pope, Maurice. 1988. "Thucydides and Democracy." *Historia: Zeitschrift für Alte Geschichte* 37(3): 276–296.

Popper, Karl. 1971. *The Open Society and Its Enemies: The Spell of Plato*. Princeton: Princeton University Press.

———. 2014. *Conjectures and Refutations: The Growth of Scientific Knowledge*. Abingdon: Routledge.

Post, Jerrold M. 1987. "Review of the Immortal Atatürk: A Psychobiography." *Political Psychology* 8(4): 673–676.

———. 2003. "Saddam Hussein of Iraq: A Political Psychology Profile." In *The Psychological Assessment of Political Leaders: With Profiles of Saddam Hussein and Bill Clinton*, ed. Jerrold M. Post. Ann Arbor: University of Michigan Press.

Power, R.A., and Michael Pluess. 2015. "Heritability Estimates of the Big Five Personality Traits Based on Common Genetic Variants." *Translational Psychiatry* 5(7): e604.

Powers, Charles T. 1989. "Ex-Hungarian Leader Janos Kadar Dead at 77." *Los Angeles Times*, July 7.

Pratt, Cranford. 1976. *The Critical Phase in Tanzania, 1945–1968: Nyerere and the Emergence of a Socialist Strategy*. Cambridge: Cambridge University Press.

Pressman, Jeffrey L., and Aaron Wildavsky. 1984. *Implementation: How Great Expectations in Washington Are Dashed in Oakland*. Berkeley: University of California Press.

Preston, Thomas. 2001. *The President and His Inner Circle: Leadership Style and the Advisory Process in Foreign Affairs*. New York: Columbia University Press.

Price, Michael E., and Mark Van Vugt. 2014. "The Evolution of Leader-Follower Reciprocity: The Theory of Service-for-Prestige." *Frontiers in Human Neuroscience* 8: 363.

Przeworski, Adam, and Fernando Limongi. 1993. "Political Regimes and Economic Growth." *Journal of Economic Perspectives* 7(3): 51–69.

Quattrone, George A., and Amos Tversky. 1988. "Contrasting Rational and Psychological Analyses of Political Choice." *American Political Science Review* 82(3): 719–736.

Quimpo, Nathan Gilbert. 2015. "Can the Philippines' Wild Oligarchy Be Tamed?" In *Routledge Handbook of Southeast Asian Democratization*. London: Routledge.

Quong, Jonathan. 2011. *Liberalism Without Perfection*. Oxford: Oxford University Press.

Raelin, Joe. 2011. "From Leadership-as-Practice to Leaderful Practice." *Leadership* 7(2): 195–211.

Raiffa, Howard. 2002. *Negotiation Analysis: The Science and Art of Collaborative Decision Making*. Cambridge: Harvard University Press.

Raikes, P.L. 1975. "Ujamaa and Rural Socialism." *Review of African Political Economy* 2(3): 33–52.

Rakel, Eva Patricia. 2009. "The Political Elite in the Islamic Republic of Iran: From Khomeini to Ahmadinejad." *Comparative Studies of South Asia, Africa and the Middle East* 29(1): 105–125.

Ranta, Ronald. 2015. *Political Decision Making and Non-Decisions: The Case of Israel and the Occupied Territories*. Basingstoke: Palgrave Macmillan.

Raspberry, William. 1985. "The Real Reason Mondale Lost." *Washington Post*, February 20.

Rauch, Jonathan. 2016. "How American Politics Went Insane." *The Atlantic*. https://www.theatlantic.com/magazine/archive/2016/07/how-american-politics-went-insane/485570/

Rawls, John. 1993. *Political Liberalism*. New York: Columbia University Press.

———. 1995. "Political Liberalism: Reply to Habermas." *The Journal of Philosophy* 92(3): 132–180.

Rawls, John. 2001. *Justice as Fairness: A Restatement*. Cambridge: Cambridge University Press.

Raz, Joseph. 1988. *The Morality of Freedom*. Oxford: Oxford University Press.

Reddy, P.S., and S.N. Mishra. 2004. *Sardar Vallabhbhai Patel, the Nation Builder*. New Delhi: Indian Institute of Public Administration.

Redei, Lorinc. 2014. "Weak and Weaker." *Foreign Affairs*. https://www.foreignaffairs.com/articles/europe/2014-09-04/weak-and-weaker

Reich, Wilhelm. 1972. *Character Analysis*. New York: Farrar, Straus and Giroux.

Reno, William. 1997. "Sovereignty and Personal Rule in Zaire." *African Studies Quarterly* 1(3): 39–64.

Renshon, Stanley. 2014. "Psychoanalytic Theories." In *The Oxford Handbook of Political Leadership*, eds. R.A.W. Rhodes and Paul 't Hart. Oxford: Oxford University Press.

Reynolds, Nedra. 1993. "Ethos as Location: New Sites for Understanding Discursive Authority." *Rhetoric Review* 11(2): 325–338.

Reynolds, Rodney, and J. Lynn Reynolds. 2002. "Evidence." In *The Persuasion Handbook: Developments in Theory and Practice*, eds. James Price Dillard and Michael Pfau. Thousand Oaks: SAGE.

Reynolds, Vernon, Vincent Falger, and Ian Vine. 1987. *The Sociobiology of Ethnocentrism: Evolutionary Dimensions of Xenophobia, Discrimination, Racism, and Nationalism*. Athens: University of Georgia Press.

Rhodes, R.A.W., John Wanna, and Patrick Weller. 2009. *Comparing Westminster*. Oxford: Oxford University Press.

Rhodes, Richard. 2012. *The Making of the Atomic Bomb*. New York: Simon & Schuster.

Rich, Adrienne. 1995. *Of Woman Born: Motherhood as Experience and Institution*. New York: W.W. Norton.

van der Rijt, Jan-Willem. 2011. "Coercion, Analytic." In *Encyclopedia of Power*, ed. Keith Dowding. Thousand Oaks: SAGE.

Riker, William H. 1986. *The Art of Political Manipulation*. New Haven: Yale University Press.

Rinke, Eike Mark. 2016. "The Impact of Sound-Bite Journalism on Public Argument." *Journal of Communication* 66(4): 625–645.

Rittel, Horst W.J., and Melvin M. Webber. 1973. "Dilemmas in a General Theory of Planning." *Policy Sciences* 4(2): 155–169.

Robin, Corey. 2004. *Fear: The History of a Political Idea*. Oxford: Oxford University Press.

Rodrik, Dani. 2018. "Populism and the Economics of Globalization." *Journal of International Business Policy* 1(1–2): 12–33.

Rodzinski, Witold. 2017. *A History of China*. Oxford: Pergamon.

Rogers, Mary Beth. 1998. *Barbara Jordan: American Hero*. New York: Bantam.

Rosar, Ulrich, Markus Klein, and Tilo Beckers. 2012. "Magic Mayors: Predicting Electoral Success from Candidates' Physical Attractiveness Under the Conditions of a Presidential Electoral System." *German Politics* 21(4): 372–391.

Rose, Richard. 1976. *Managing Presidential Objectives*. New York: Free Press.

Rose, Richard, and Phillip L. Davies. 1994. *Inheritance in Public Policy: Change Without Choice in Britain*. New Haven: Yale University Press.

Rosenberg, Shawn. 2019. "Democracy Devouring Itself: The Rise of the Incompetent Citizen and the Appeal of Right Wing Populism." In *Psychology of Political and Everyday Extremisms*, eds. Domenico Uhng Hur and Jose Manuel Sabucedo. Forthcoming. https://escholarship.org/uc/item/8806z01m#main

Rosener, Judy B. 1995. "Ways Women Lead." In *The Leader's Companion*, ed. Thomas J. Wren. New York: Free Press.

Rostboll, Christian, and Theresa Scavenius. 2017. *Compromise and Disagreement in Contemporary Political Theory*. Abingdon: Routledge.

Rousseau, Jean-Jacques. 1947. *The Social Contract*. New York: Hafner.

Rowell, T. 1969. "Long-Term Changes in a Population of Ugandan Baboons." *Folia Primatologica; International Journal of Primatology* 11(4): 241–254.

Ruscio, Kenneth P. 2004. *The Leadership Dilemma in Modern Democracy*. Cheltenham: Edward Elgar.

Rush, Myron. 1974. *How Communist States Change Their Rulers*. Ithaca: Cornell University Press.

Russell, Bertrand. 1938. *Power: A New Social Analysis*. London: George Allen & Unwin.

Saalfeld, Thomas. 2010. "Veto Players, Agenda Control and Cabinet Stability in 17 European Parliaments, 1945–1999." In *Reform Processes and Policy Change: Veto Players and Decision-Making in Modern Democracies*, eds. Thomas König, Marc Debus and George Tsebelis. New York: Springer.

Sabatier, Paul. 2007. *Theories of the Policy Process*. Boulder: Westview Press.

Sabatier, Paul, and Daniel Mazmanian. 1979. "The Conditions of Effective Implementation: A Guide to Accomplishing Policy Objectives." *Policy Analysis* 5(4): 481–504.

Sabatier, Paul, and Christopher Weible. 2014. *Theories of the Policy Process*. 3rd ed. Boulder: Westview.

Sabine, George. 1937. *A History of Political Theory*. New York: Holt, Rinehart & Winston.

Sadler-Smith, Eugene, Vita Akstinaite, Graham Robinson, and Tim Wray. 2017. "Hubristic Leadership: A Review." *Leadership* 13(5): 525–548.

Safire, William. 2008. *Safire's Political Dictionary*. Oxford: Oxford University Press.

Sahlins, Marshall D. 1963. "Poor Man, Rich Man, Big-Man, Chief: Political Types in Melanesia and Polynesia." *Comparative Studies in Society and History* 5(3): 285–303.

Saint-Germain, Michelle A. 2013. "Women in Power in Nicaragua: Myth and Reality." In *Women as Political Leaders*. London: Routledge, 128–161.

Salmond, Kimberlee, and Paula Fleshman. 2010. "The Development of Children's Perceptions of Leadership." In *Gender and Women's Leadership: A Reference Handbook*, ed. Karen O'Connor. Thousand Oaks: SAGE.

Salovaara, Perttu, and Ralph Bathurst. 2016. "Power-With Leadership Practices: An Unfinished Business." *Leadership* 14(2): 179–202.

Samons, Loren J. 2007. *What's Wrong with Democracy? From Athenian Practice to American Worship*. Berkeley: University of California Press.

Samuels, David J., and Matthew S. Shugart. 2010. *Presidents, Parties, and Prime Ministers: How the Separation of Powers Affects Party Organization and Behavior*. Cambridge: Cambridge University Press.

Sanday, Peggy Reeves. 1981. *Female Power and Male Dominance: On the Origins of Sexual Inequality*. Cambridge: Cambridge University Press.

Sandbrook, Jeremy. 2016. "10 Most Corrupt World Leaders of Recent History." *Integritas 360*. https://integritas360.org/2016/07/10-most-corrupt-world-leaders/

Sarmiento, Isabella. (2019) "How Evo Morales Made Bolivia A Better Place ... Before He Fled The Country." *NPR.org*. https://www.npr.org/sections/goatsandsoda/2019/11/26/781199250/how-evo-morales-made-bolivia-a-better-place-before-he-was-forced-to-flee

Sartori, Giovanni. 2005. *Parties and Party Systems: A Framework for Analysis*. London: ECPR Press.

Scharpf, Fritz W. 1997. *Games Real Actors Play: Actor-Centered Institutionalism in Policy Research*. Boulder: Westview.

Schauer, Frederick. 2000. "Can Public Figures Have Private Lives?" *Social Philosophy and Policy* 17(2): 293–309.

Schedler, Andreas. 2006. *Electoral Authoritarianism: The Dynamics of Unfree Competition*. Boulder: Lynne Rienner.

Scheina, Robert L. 2003. *Latin America's Wars Volume I: The Age of the Caudillo, 1791–1899*. Washington: Potomac Books.

Schelling, Thomas C. 1980. *The Strategy of Conflict*. Cambridge: Harvard University Press.

Schjelderup-Ebbe, Thorleif. 1922. "Beiträge Zur Sozialpsychologie Des Haushuhns." *Zeitschrift für Psychologie* 88: 225–252.

Schneewind, J.B. 1990. "The Misfortunes of Virtue." *Ethics* 101(1): 42–63.

Schofield, Philip. 2006. *Utility and Democracy: The Political Thought of Jeremy Bentham*. Oxford: Oxford University Press.

Schuettinger, Robert L., and Eamonn F. Butler. 2009. *Forty Centuries of Wage and Price Controls: How Not to Fight Inflation*. Thornwood: Caroline House.

Schumacher, Gijs, and Nathalie Giger. 2017. "Who Leads the Party? On Membership Size, Selectorates and Party Oligarchy." *Political Studies* 65(1): 162–181.

Schumpeter, Joseph. 1942. *Capitalism, Socialism, and Democracy*. New York: Harper.

Seaton, S. Lee, and Henri J.M. Claessen, eds. 1979. *Political Anthropology: The State of the Art*. Berlin: Mouton de Gruyter.

Sedigh, Shahrzad, and Alex Muganda. 1999. "The Fight Against Corruption in Tanzania." In *Curbing Corruption: Toward a Model for Building National Integrity*, eds. Rick Stapenhurst and Sahr John Kpundeh. Washington, DC: World Bank Publications.

Seibert, Scott, and Maria Kraimer. 2001. "The Five-Factor Model of Personality and Career Success." *Journal of Vocational Behavior* 58(1): 1–21.

Seldon, Anthony. 2019. *May at 10*. London: Biteback.

Sell, Louis. 2002. *Slobodan Milosevic and the Destruction of Yugoslavia*. Durham; London: Duke University Press.

Sergi, Viviane, Jean-Louis Denis, and Ann Langley. 2016. "Beyond the Hero-Leader: Leadership by Collectives." In *The Routledge Companion to Leadership*, eds. John Storey et al. New York: Routledge.

Service, Elman Rogers. 1975. *Origins of the State and Civilization: The Process of Cultural Evolution*. New York: W.W. Norton.

Shafqat, Saeed. 1996. "Pakistan under Benazir Bhutto." *Asian Survey* 36(7): 655–672.

Shah, Bina. 2014. "The Legacy of Benazir Bhutto." *The New York Times*. https://www.nytimes.com/2014/12/27/opinion/the-legacy-of-benazir-bhutto.html

Shahid, Shiza. 2014. *Lack of Leadership*. Davos: World Economic Forum. http://reports.weforum.org/outlook-global-agenda-2015/top-10-trends-of-2015/3-lack-of-leadership/

Shaw, Julia. 2016. *The Memory Illusion: Remembering, Forgetting, and the Science of False Memory*. New York: Random House.

Shugart, Matthew Soberg, and John M. Carey. 1992. *Presidents and Assemblies: Constitutional Design and Electoral Dynamics*. Cambridge: Cambridge University Press.

Siavelis, Peter M., and Bonnie N. Field. 2015. "The Presidentialization of Parties in Chile." In *The Presidentialization of Political Parties*, ed. Gianluca Passarelli. Basingstoke: Palgrave Macmillan, 26–48.

Silbey, David J. 2012. *The Boxer Rebellion and the Great Game in China: A History*. New York: Farrar, Straus and Giroux.

Silva, Eduardo. 2014. "Authoritarianism, Democracy and Development." In *Latin America Transformed*, eds. Robert N. Gwynne and Kay Cristobal. London: Routledge.

Simeone, Jim. 2010. "Political Culture." In *Political and Civic Leadership: A Reference Handbook*. Thousand Oaks: SAGE.

Simmel, Georg. 1964. *The Sociology of Georg Simmel*. New York: Free Press.

Simon, Herbert A. 1985. "Human Nature in Politics: The Dialogue of Psychology with Political Science." *The American Political Science Review* 79(2): 293–304.

———. 1997. *Administrative Behavior*. 4th ed. New York: Free Press.

Sinclair, Barbara. 2014. "The Offered Hand and the Veto Fist: George Bush, Congress, and Domestic Policy Making." In *41: Inside the Presidency of George H.W. Bush*, eds. Michael Nelson and Barbara A. Perry. Ithaca: Cornell University Press.

Sinott-Armstrong, Walter. 2019. "Consequentialism." In *The Stanford Encyclopedia of Philosophy*, ed. Edward N. Zalta. Stanford: Stanford University. https://plato.stanford.edu/archives/sum2019/entries/consequentialism/

Sipiora, Phillip, and James S. Baumlin. 2012. *Rhetoric and Kairos: Essays in History, Theory, and Praxis*. New York: SUNY Press.

Sjoberg, Laura. 2014. "Feminism." In *The Oxford Handbook of Political Leadership*, eds. R.A.W. Rhodes and Paul 't Hart. Oxford: Oxford University Press.

Skard, Torild. 2014. *Women of Power: Half a Century of Female Presidents and Prime Ministers Worldwide*. Bristol: Policy Press.

Skowronek, Stephen. 1997. *The Politics Presidents Make: Leadership from John Adams to Bill Clinton, Revised Edition*. Cambridge: Belknap.

Smith, David Livingstone. 2007. *Why We Lie: The Evolutionary Roots of Deception and the Unconscious Mind*. New York: St. Martin's Griffin.

Smith, Philip. 2000. "Culture and Charisma: Outline of a Theory." *Acta Sociologica* 43(2): 101–111.

Soest, Christian von, and Julia Grauvogel. 2017. "Identity, Procedures and Performance: How Authoritarian Regimes Legitimize Their Rule." *Contemporary Politics* 23(3): 287–305.

Solomon, Steven. 2011. *Water: The Epic Struggle for Wealth, Power, and Civilization*. New York: HarperCollins.

Somit, Albert. 1968. "Toward a More Biologically-Oriented Political Science: Ethology and Psychopharmacology." *Midwest Journal of Political Science* 12(4): 550–567.

Sorokowski, Piotr. 2010. "Politicians' Estimated Height as an Indicator of Their Popularity." *European Journal of Social Psychology* 40(7): 1302–1309.

Spence, Jonathan D. 1990. *The Search for Modern China*. New York: W.W. Norton.

Spencer, Herbert. 1880. *The Study of Sociology*. London: Williams and Norgate.

Spitaletta, Jason. 2014. "Approach 3: Leadership Trait Analysis." In *A Multi-Disciplinary, Multi-Method Approach to Leader Assessment at a Distance: The Case of Bashar al-Assad*, eds. Hriar Cabayan and Nicholas Wright. Washington, DC: US Department of Defense.

Stan, Adele M. 2007. "Benazir Bhutto: An Imperfect Feminist." *The American Prospect*. https://prospect.org/article/benazir-bhutto-imperfect-feminist

Stanley, Ben. 2008. "The Thin Ideology of Populism." *Journal of Political Ideologies* 13(1): 95–110.

Stanyer, James. 2007. *Modern Political Communications: Mediated Politics in Uncertain Terms*. Cambridge: Polity.

Stead, Valerie, and Carole Elliott. 2009. *Women's Leadership*. London: Palgrave Macmillan.

Stehr, Steven D. 1997. "Top Bureaucrats and the Distribution of Influence in Reagan's Executive Branch." *Public Administration Review* 57(1): 75–82.

Stevens, Daniel. 2019. "Satisficing in Political Decision Making." In *The Oxford Encyclopedia of Political Decision Making*, ed. Daniel Redlawsk. Oxford: Oxford University Press.

Stevens, Evelyn P. 1973. *Marianismo: The Other Face of Machismo in Latin America*. Pittsburgh: University of Pittsburgh Press.

Stiff, James B., and Paul A. Mongeau. 2016. *Persuasive Communication*. New York: Guildford.

Stogdill, Ralph M. 1948. "Personal Factors Associated with Leadership: A Survey of the Literature." *The Journal of Psychology* 25(1): 35–71.

Stogdill, Ralph Melvin. 1974. *Handbook of Leadership: A Survey of Theory and Research*. New York: Free Press.

Stokes, Bruce. 2015. "70 Years After Hiroshima, Opinions Have Shifted on Use of Atomic Bomb." *Pew Research Center*. https://www.pewresearch.org/fact-tank/2015/08/04/70-years-after-hiroshima-opinions-have-shifted-on-use-of-atomic-bomb/

Stone, Deborah. 2012. *Policy Paradox: The Art of Political Decision Making*. New York: W.W. Norton.

Stone, Martin. 1997. *The Agony of Algeria*. New York: Columbia University Press.

Strachey, Lytton. 1918. *Eminent Victorians*. New York: Harcourt Brace.

Streeck, Wolfgang, and Kathleen Ann Thelen. 2005. *Beyond Continuity: Institutional Change in Advanced Political Economies*. Oxford: Oxford University Press.

Strøm, Kaare, and Wolfgang C. Müller. 1999. "The Keys to Togetherness: Coalition Agreements in Parliamentary Democracies." *The Journal of Legislative Studies* 5(3–4): 255–282.

Stutje, Jan Willem. 2012. *Charismatic Leadership and Social Movements: The Revolutionary Power of Ordinary Men and Women*. New York: Berghahn.

Sutin, Angelina R., Paul T. Costa, Richard Miech, and William W. Eaton. 2009. "Personality and Career Success: Concurrent and Longitudinal Relations." *European Journal of Personality* 23(2): 71–84.

Svenson, Ola, and A.J. Maule. 1993. *Time Pressure and Stress in Human Judgment and Decision Making*. New York: Springer.

Sverdlik, Steven. 1987. "Collective Responsibility." *Philosophical Studies: An International Journal for Philosophy in the Analytic Tradition* 51(1): 61–76.

Svolik, Milan W. 2009. "Power Sharing and Leadership Dynamics in Authoritarian Regimes." *American Journal of Political Science* 53(2): 477–494.

Swain, Nigel. 1992. *Hungary: The Rise and Fall of Feasible Socialism*. London: Verso.

Swinkels, Marij, Sabine van Zuydam, and Femke Van Esch. 2017. *Modern Prime-Ministerial Leadership in the Netherlands: Consensus or Confrontation?* Oxford: Oxford University Press.

Sykes, Patricia. 2014. "Does Gender Matter?" In *The Oxford Handbook of Political Leadership*, eds. R.A.W. Rhodes and Paul 't Hart. Oxford: Oxford University Press.

Taber, Charles S., and Milton Lodge. 2006. "Motivated Skepticism in the Evaluation of Political Beliefs." *American Journal of Political Science* 50(3): 755–769.

Taleb, Nassim Nicholas. 2007. *The Black Swan: The Impact of the Highly Improbable*. New York: Random House.

Tan, Eugene K. 2010. "The Evolving Social Compact and the Transformation of Singapore." In *Management of Success: Singapore Revisited*, ed. Terence Chong. Singapore: Institute of Southeast Asian Studies.

Tan, Kenneth. 2016. *Governing Global-City Singapore: Legacies and Futures After Lee Kuan Yew*. Abingdon: Routledge

Tarallo, Fernando. 2009. "Major Sociolinguistic Patterns in Brazilian Portuguese." *International Journal of the Sociology of Language* 89(1): 9–24.

Taras, Raymond. 1989. *Leadership Change in Communist States*. Boston: Unwin Hyman.

Tarrow, Sidney G. 2011. *Power in Movement: Social Movements and Contentious Politics*. Cambridge: Cambridge University Press.

Taub, Amanda. 2020. "Why Are Women-Led Nations Doing Better with Covid-19?" *New York Times*. https://www.nytimes.com/2020/05/15/world/coronavirus-women-leaders.html

Tavits, Margit. 2007. "Principle vs. Pragmatism: Policy Shifts and Political Competition." *American Journal of Political Science* 51(1): 151–165.

Taylor, Robert. 1993. *The Trade Union Question in British Politics: Government and Unions Since 1945*. Hoboken: Wiley-Blackwell.

Teehankee, Julio C. 2012. "Clientelism and Party Politics in the Philippines." In *Party Politics in Southeast Asia: Clientelism and Electoral Competition in Indonesia, Thailand and the Philippines*, eds. Dirk Tomsa and Andreas Ufen. London: Routledge.

The Economist. 2016. "Tired of Syriza, Greece Embraces a Mainstream Party." *The Economist*. https://www.economist.com/europe/2016/12/01/tired-of-syriza-greece-embraces-a-mainstream-party

———. 2018. "Why Colombians Distrust the FARC Peace Deal." *The Economist*. https://www.economist.com/the-economist-explains/2018/05/24/why-colombians-distrust-the-farc-peace-deal

Theakston, Kevin. 2013. "Evaluating Prime-Ministerial Performance: The British Experience." In *Understanding Prime-Ministerial Performance: Comparative Perspectives*, eds. Paul Strangio, Paul 't Hart, and James Walter. Oxford: Oxford University Press.

Thomas, Evan. 2015. *Being Nixon: A Man Divided*. New York: Random House.

Thompson, C. Bradley. 1995. "John Adams's Machiavellian Moment." *The Review of Politics* 57(3): 389–417.

Thompson, Dennis. 1980. "Moral Responsibility of Public Officials: The Problem of Many Hands." *American Political Science Review* 74(4): 905–916.

———. 1987. *Political Ethics and Public Office*. Cambridge: Harvard University Press.

Thompson, Leigh L. 2007. *The Truth About Negotiations*. Upper Saddle River: Pearson.

Thompson, Mark. 1999. *Forging War: The Media in Serbia, Croatia, Bosnia, and Hercegovina*. Bloomington: Indiana University Press.

Thompson, Mark R. 2017. "Bloodied Democracy: Duterte and the Death of Liberal Reformism in the Philippines." *Journal of Current Southeast Asian Affairs* 35(3): 39–68.

Thorson, Thomas Landon. 1970. *Biopolitics*. Austin: Holt McDougal.

Tömmel, Ingeborg. 2017. "The Standing President of the European Council: Intergovernmental or Supranational Leadership?" *Journal of European Integration* 39(2): 175–189.

Truman, Harry. 1948. "Address in Milwaukee, Wisconsin." Speech at Botcherr Field, Milwaukee. https://www.presidency.ucsb.edu/documents/address-milwaukee-wisconsin

Tsebelis, George. 1995. "Decision Making in Political Systems: Veto Players in Presidentialism, Parliamentarism, Multicameralism and Multipartyism." *British Journal of Political Science* 25(3): 289–325.

———. 2011. *Veto Players: How Political Institutions Work*. Princeton: Princeton University Press.

Tsebelis, George, and Xenophon Yataganas. 2002. "Veto Players and Decision-Making in the EU After Nice: Policy Stability and Bureaucratic/Judicial Discretion." *Journal of Common Market Studies* 40(2): 283–307.

Tucker, Robert C. 1995. *Politics as Leadership*. Columbia: University of Missouri Press.

Tullock, Gordon. 1987. *Autocracy*. Dordrecht: Springer Science & Business Media.

Turan, Keith. 2003. "McNamara's Complexities Are Revealed in 'Fog of War'." *Los Angeles Times*. https://www.latimes.com/archives/la-xpm-2003-dec-19-et-fog19-story.html

Uhr, John. 2011. "Persuasion." In *Encyclopedia of Power*, ed. Keith Dowding. Thousand Oaks: SAGE.

Vallentyne, Peter. 1987. "Prohibition Dilemmas and Deontic Logic." *Logique et Analyse* 30(117/118): 113–122.

Van Vugt, Mark, and David De Cremer. 1999. "Leadership in Social Dilemmas: The Effects of Group Identification on Collective Actions to Provide Public Goods." *Journal of Personality and Social Psychology* 76(4): 587–599.

Van Vugt, Mark, Robert Hogan, and Robert B. Kaiser. 2008. "Leadership, Followership, and Evolution: Some Lessons from the Past." *The American Psychologist* 63(3): 182–196.

Van Vugt, Mark, Sarah F. Jepson, Claire M. Hart, and David De Cremer. 2004. "Autocratic Leadership in Social Dilemmas: A Threat to Group Stability." *Journal of Experimental Social Psychology* 40(1): 1–13.

Vatikiotis, Michael R.J. 1998. *Indonesian Politics Under Suharto: The Rise and Fall of the New Order*. Abingdon: Routledge.

te Velde, Henk. 2002. *Stijlen van Leiderschap: Persoon en Politiek van Thorbecke tot Den Uyl*. Amsterdam: Uitgeverij Wereldbibliotheek.

Verbeek, Bert Jan. 1994. "Do Individual and Group Beliefs Matter? British Decision-Making During the 1956 Suez Crisis." *Cooperation and Conflict* 29(4): 307–332.

Verzichelli, Luca. 2018. "Elite Circulation and Stability." In *The Palgrave Handbook of Political Elites*, eds. Heinrich Best and John Higley. London: Palgrave Macmillan.

Vetter, Lisa Pace. 2010. "Overview: Feminist Theories of Leadership." In *Gender and Women's Leadership: A Reference Handbook*, ed. Karen O'Connor. Thousand Oaks: SAGE.

Vis, Barbara. 2019. "Heuristics and Political Elites' Judgment and Decision-Making." *Political Studies Review* 17(1): 41–52.

Vis, Barbara, and Kees van Kersbergen. 2007. "Why and How Do Political Actors Pursue Risky Reforms?" *Journal of Theoretical Politics* 19(2): 153–172.

Volkan, Vamık D., and Norman Itzkowitz. 1984. *The Immortal Atatürk: A Psychobiography*. Chicago: University of Chicago Press.

Vroom, Victor, and Philip Yetton. 1973. *Leadership and Decision-Making*. Pittsburgh: University of Pittsburgh Press.

van Vugt, Mark, and Anjana Ahuja. 2011. *Selected: Why Some People Lead, Why Others Follow, and Why It Matters*. Toronto: Random House.

Waldron, Jeremy. 1987. "Theoretical Foundations of Liberalism." *The Philosophical Quarterly* 37(147): 127–150.

Walgrave, Stefaan, and Peter Van Aelst. 2016. "Political Agenda Setting and the Mass Media." In *Oxford Research Encyclopedia of Politics*. Oxford: Oxford University Press.

Wallas, Graham. 1908. *Human Nature in Politics*. London: Archibald Constable.

Walter, James. 2014. "Biographical Analysis". In *The Oxford Handbook of Political Leadership*, eds. R.A.W. Rhodes and Paul `t Hart. Oxford: Oxford University Press.

Walton, Richard., and Robert B. McKersie. 1991. *A Behavioral Theory of Labor Negotiations: An Analysis of a Social Interaction System*. Ithaca: Cornell University Press.

Walzer, Michael. 1973. "Political Action: The Problem of Dirty Hands." *Philosophy & Public Affairs* 2(2): 160–180.

———. 2006. *Just and Unjust Wars: A Moral Argument with Historical Illustrations*. 4th ed. New York: Basic Books.

Wang, Yanwen, Michael Lewis, and David A. Schweidel. 2018. "A Border Strategy Analysis of Ad Source and Message Tone in Senatorial Campaigns." *Marketing Science* 37(3): 333–355.

Ward, Ashley, and Mike Webster. 2016. *Sociality: The Behaviour of Group-Living Animals*. Basel: Springer.

Warren, Mark. 1985. "Nietzsche and Political Philosophy." *Political Theory* 13(2): 183–212.

Warwick, Paul. 1992. "Ideological Diversity and Government Survival in Western European Parliamentary Democracies." *Comparative Political Studies* 25(3): 332–361.

Washington Post. 2010. *Landmark: The Inside Story of America's New Health-Care Law and What It Means for Us All.* Washington, DC: Thorndike Press.

Watkins, Tracy. 2017. "Bill English Ran the Campaign of His Life – But It Just Wasn't Enough." *Stuff.* https://www.stuff.co.nz/national/politics/opinion/98015573/bill-english-ran-the-campaign-of-his-life%2D%2Dbut-it-just-wasnt-enough

Wattenberg, Martin. 2013. *The Rise of Candidate-Centered Politics.* Cambridge: Harvard University Press.

Weaver, R. Kent. 1986. "The Politics of Blame Avoidance." *Journal of Public Policy* 6(4): 371–398.

Weber, Max. 1958. "The Three Types of Legitimate Rule." *Berkeley Publications in Society and Institutions* 4(1): 1–11.

———. 1964. *The Theory of Social and Economic Organization.* ed. Talcott Parson. New York: Free Press.

Weinberg, Ashley. 2011. *The Psychology of Politicians.* Cambridge: Cambridge University Press.

Weintraub, Walter. 2003. "General Personality Traits and Ego Defenses." In *The Psychological Assessment of Political Leaders: With Profiles of Saddam Hussein and Bill Clinton*, ed. Jerrold M. Post. Ann Arbor: University of Michigan Press.

Weissberg, Robert. 2001. *Why Policymakers Should Ignore Public Opinion Polls.* Washington, DC: Cato Institute. https://www.cato.org/publications/policy-analysis/why-policymakers-should-ignore-public-opinion-polls

Weller, Patrick. 2007. *Cabinet Government in Australia, 1901–2006: Practice, Principles, Performance.* Sydney: UNSW Press.

Weyland, Kurt. 1996. "Risk Taking in Latin American Economic Restructuring: Lessons from Prospect Theory." *International Studies Quarterly* 40(2): 185–207.

———. 2003. "Economic Voting Reconsidered: Crisis and Charisma in the Election of Hugo Chávez." *Comparative Political Studies* 36(7): 822–848.

Weyland, Kurt. 2013. "Latin America's Authoritarian Drift: The Threat from the Populist Left." *Journal of Democracy* 24(3): 18–32.

White, Ronald F. 2017"Political Behavior and Biology: Evolutionary Leadership and Followership." In *Handbook of Biology and Politics*, eds. Steven Peterson and Albert Somit. Cheltenham: Edward Elgar.

Whyte, Max. 2008. "The Uses and Abuses of Nietzsche in the Third Reich: Alfred Baeumler's 'Heroic Realism'." *Journal of Contemporary History* 43(2): 171–194.

Wigington, John T. 1992. *Syria's Negotiations with Israel.* Washington, DC: Industrial College of the Armed Forces.

Wildavsky, Aaron B. 2006. *Cultural Analysis: Politics, Public Law, and Administration.* New Brunswick: Transaction.

Willhoite, Fred H. 1976. "Primates and Political Authority: A Biobehavioral Perspective." *American Political Science Review* 70(4): 1110–1126.

Willis, Rebecca. 2019. "To Tackle the Climate Crisis We Need More Democracy, Not Less." *The Conversation.* http://theconversation.com/to-tackle-the-climate-crisis-we-need-more-democracy-not-less-119265

Willner, Ann Ruth. 1984. *The Spellbinders: Charismatic Political Leadership.* New Haven: Yale University Press.

Wilson, Edward O. 2000. *Sociobiology: The New Synthesis*. 25th Anniversary. Cambridge: Harvard University Press.

Wilson, James Q. 1995. *The Moral Sense*. New York: Free Press.

Winter, David G. 1987. "Leader Appeal, Leader Performance, and the Motive Profiles of Leaders and Followers: A Study of American Presidents and Elections." *Journal of Personality and Social Psychology* 52(1): 196–202.

———. 1991. "Measuring Personality at a Distance: Development of an Integrated System for Scoring Motives in Running Text." In *Perspectives in Personality: Approaches to Understanding Lives*, eds. A.J. Stewart, J.M. Healy, Jr., and Daniel Ozer. London: Jessica Kingsley.

———. 2003. "Motivations and Mediation of Self-Other Relationships." In *The Psychological Assessment of Political Leaders: With Profiles of Saddam Hussein and Bill Clinton*, ed. Jerrold M. Post. Ann Arbor: University of Michigan Press.

———. 2005. "Things I've Learned About Personality from Studying Political Leaders at a Distance." *Journal of Personality* 73(3): 557–584.

Winterton, Jonathan, and Ruth Winterton. 1989. *Coal, Crisis and Conflict: The 1984–85 Miners' Strike in Yorkshire*. Manchester: Manchester University Press.

Wintrobe, Ronald. 2000. *The Political Economy of Dictatorship*. Cambridge: Cambridge University Press.

Wittman, Donald. 1983. "Candidate Motivation: A Synthesis of Alternative Theories." *American Political Science Review* 77(1): 142–157.

Wolf, Martin. 2019. "The Rise of the Populist Authoritarians." *Financial Times*. https://www.ft.com/content/4faf6c4e-1d84-11e9-b2f7-97e4dbd3580d

Wolff, Robert Paul. 1998. *In Defense of Anarchism*. Berkeley: University of California Press.

Wolpert, Stanley A. 2009. *Shameful Flight: The Last Years of the British Empire in India*. Oxford: Oxford University Press.

Woodward, Bob. 1994. *The Agenda*. New York: Simon & Schuster.

Wren, Thomas J., and Marc J. Swatez. 1995. "The Historical and Contemporary Contexts of Leadership." In *The Leader's Companion: Insights on Leadership Through the Ages*, ed. Thomas J. Wren. New York: Free Press.

Wrong, Dennis H. 2004. *Power: Its Forms, Bases and Uses*. 4th ed. New Brunswick: Transaction.

Wyke, Maria. 2008. *Julius Caesar in Western Culture*. Malden: Blackwell.

Zaccaro, Stephen J., Cary Kemp, and Paige Bader. 2004. "Leader Traits and Attributes." In *The Nature of Leadership*, eds. John Antonakis, Anna Cianciolo, and Robert J. Sternberg. Thousand Oaks: SAGE.

Zagacki, Kenneth S., and Patrick A. Boleyn-Fitzgerald. 2006. "Rhetoric and Anger." *Philosophy & Rhetoric* 39(4): 290–309.

Zajonc, R.B. 1980. "Feeling and Thinking: Preferences Need No Inferences." *American Psychologist* 35(2): 151–175.

Zakaria, Fareed. 2007. *The Future of Freedom: Illiberal Democracy at Home and Abroad*. New York: W.W. Norton.

Zamir, Eyal, and Barak Medina. 2010. *Law, Economics and Morality*. Oxford: Oxford University Press.

Zartman, I. William. 1988. "Common Elements in the Analysis of the Negotiation Process." *Negotiation Journal* 4(1): 31–43.

Zhang, Shanruo Ning. 2016. *Confucianism in Contemporary Chinese Politics: An Actionable Account of Authoritarian Political Culture*. Lanham: Lexington Books.

Zimbardo, Philip G. 2008. *The Lucifer Effect: Understanding How Good People Turn Evil*. New York: Random House.

Zimmermann, Warren. 1999. *Origins of a Catastrophe: Yugoslavia and Its Destroyers*. New York: Times Books.

Zinsmeister, Karl. 2018. "15 Years Later, Iraq Is a Modest Success." *Wall Street Journal*. https://www.wsj.com/articles/15-years-later-iraq-is-a-modest-success-1523219424

Zubek, Voytek. 2007. "The Eclipse of Walesa's Political Career." *Europe-Asia Studies* 49: 107–124.

Zukin, Cliff et al. 2006. *A New Engagement? Political Participation, Civic Life, and the Changing American Citizen*. Oxford: Oxford University Press.

van Zuydam, Sabine. 2018. *The Credibility Challenge of Political Leaders*. Tilburg: Tilburg University.

INDEX

A

Abraham, Karl, 131
absolutism, 54, 55–6, 57–8, 60, 90
accountability, 69–71, 178, 212, 224
Adams, John, 54, 65, 144
agenda-setting, 15, 25–6, 83, 194–5, 217–18, 219
al-Assad, Bashar, 150–1
al-Assad, Hafez, 150–1
Albright, Madeline, 124
Alexander the Great, 3, 130
Amenhotep IV, 131
anarchism, 61–2
anocracies, 77, 88, 98–9, 243
Aquinas, Thomas, 56–7, 176
Ardern, Jacinda, 242–3
Arendt, Hannah, 34, 61, 160–1
Aristotle, 41, 108, 110, 207, 210
Arroyo, Gloria, 123
Atatürk, Mustafa Kemal, 134–5
Attlee, Clement, 109, 147
Aurelius, Marcus, 56
authoritarianism *see* autocracies
authority
  and anarchism, 61
  charismatic, 30, 34–5, 37, 38, 89, 160
  competent, 30, 32–3, 36
  credibility of, 38–9, 40
  definitions of, 27, 30
  development of, 111–12
  and gender, 120–2
  and history, 166–70
  ideational-moral, 30, 33–4, 36–7, 63
  legal-rational, 30–1, 37, 63, 88, 92
  legitimacy of, 38, 39–40, 49–50, 52, 61, 87–8
  obedience to, 42, 211
  and public approval, 95, 97, 166–7
  sources of, 27–38, 160, 193
  traditional, 30, 31–2, 37, 111–12
autobiography, 132
autocracies
  benefits of, 57–8, 112
  classifications of, 78–9
  and collective action, 41
  and corruption, 92, 99
  definition of, 77
  and elites, 44–5, 86–9, 90–1, 171
  and followers, 160–1, 243
  and governance, 89–93, 112
  and populism, 234–5, 238
  and separation of power, 77
Aziz, Shaukat, 204

B

Bailey, F.G., 113
Bakunin, Mikhail, 61
Bandura, Albert, 70–71
Barber, James David, 141–4
bargaining *see* negotiation
BATNA, 222, 224
Beetham, David, 40, 49
Ben Bella, Ahmed, 185–6
benevolent dictator, 55, 61
Bentham, Jeremy, 50–1
Bentsen, Lloyd, 212
Berlusconi, Silvio, 64, 235
Bhutto, Benazir, 124, 244–5, 246
biography, 130–3
biopolitics, 102–110
Blair, Tony, 51
Bolívar, Simón, 116–17
Bolsonaro, Jair, 238
Bonaparte, Louis-Napoleon, 76
Bonaparte, Napoleon, 60, 133, 141, 207
bounded rationality, 184
brinkmanship, 227
Buchanan, James, 157–8
budgets, 24, 83, 86, 171
bureaucracies
  capacity of, 200–1, 204
  leading, 14, 44–5, 69, 90–1, 159, 171–2
  power of, 45, 94, 192–3, 195–6
  role of, 69, 179, 182, 195–6

Burke, Edmund, 96, 211
Burns, James MacGregor, 3, 10, 148
Bush, George H.W., 95
Bush, George W., 51, 170

C

cabinets
    agenda-setting, 26, 194–5
    appointment of, 80–1
    decision-making, 69, 191–2, 196–8, 203–4
    leading, 13, 14, 26, 85–6, 159, 195, 197–8
    longevity of, 82–3
    multi-party, 85–6
    specialization within, 186, 191
    See also executive government
Caesar, Julius, 54, 59, 133
campaigning, 5, 14, 94, 160, 212, 218–19, 232, 235, 240
Campbell, Joseph, 114, 117
Campbell, Kim, 124–5, 213
Canovan, Margaret, 238
Carlyle, Thomas, 156
categorial imperative, 66–7
caudillo, 37, 116–17, 118
Chamorro, Violetta, 124, 126–7
charisma, 30, 34–5, 38, 94–5, 111, 114, 116–17, 139, 160, 164, 191, 220–1, 243
Chávez, Hugo, 35, 38, 46, 117
Chernyshevsky, Nikolay, 133
Chulalongkorn, 166
Churchill, Winston, 109, 131, 211, 240, 247
civil service, the *see* bureaucracies
Cixi, 168–9
Claudius, 131
Clegg, Nick, 239–40
Clinton, Bill, 71, 95, 194
Clinton, Hillary, 5
coercion, 10–11, 23, 28–9, 50, 67, 225, 227
cognitive biases, 105, 132, 186, 187, 223, 226
cognitive dissonance, 71, 186
collective action problem, 41
collective decisions *see* decision-making
collective leadership, 8–9, 69–70, 93, 161, 197–8, 240, 241
Columbus, Christopher, 26–7
communication *see* rhetoric
Confucius, 63–4, 71
consequentialism, 50–1, 65–6, 72
context
    decision-making, 25–6
    institutional, 170–6
    and leadership tasks, 159–60
    and leadership traits, 158
    leaders shaping, 172–3, 174–5
    and legitimacy, 49, 74
    levels of, 157–8
    and opportunity, 4, 164–70
    and personality, 147–8, 149–51
    shaping leaders, 156
    understanding, 17, 165, 176
credibility, 38–9, 40–1, 212, 218–19, 225–6
crises, 34–5, 54, 105, 147, 159–60, 166, 167, 188–9, 218–19, 227, 235
culture
    civic, 114–15, 118
    and globalization, 119
    and language, 212–13, 215
    political, 114–19

D

Da Silva, Lula, 215
Davies, James, 137–8
decision-making
    and advice, 92, 192, 196–7
    biases in, 186–9
    challenges of, 178–9, 182, 183–7
    cognitive complexity, 149–51, 152–3, 193–4
    collective, 43, 69, 84–5, 164, 191–4, 196–8
    and crises, 105, 187–91
    and democracy, 93, 95–7, 241
    and emotion, 187, 190, 191
    evolution of, 105, 108
    and expertise, 185–6, 194, 195–6
    and information, 92, 182, 183, 184–7, 191
    and learning, 153, 185
    and non-decisions, 180–1
    participation in, 95–6, 192, 198, 204
    rationality of, 183–191
    and risk, 187, 207
    stages of, 182–3
    structures, 191–3, 197–8

Decius, 38
De Gaulle, Charles, 211, 240
democracy
  classifications of, 80–1
  culture of, 114–15, 118
  definition of, 77, 79
  deliberative, 241
  and elites, 86–9, 171, 234–5, 241–3
  and governance, 93–9, 112
  and leadership, 16, 61–2, 63, 79, 84–5, 95–6, 240–3
  and legitimacy, 95–7, 98–9
  monitory, 212
  paradoxes of, 238–9, 240
  and populism, 235–9, 241, 242–3
  as restraint on rule, 50, 79, 93–7
  and separation of power, 77
deontology, 66–7, 72–3
De Pizan, Christine, 122
despotism *see* tyranny
determinism, 128, 176
De Tocqueville, Alexis, 41
Dewey, Thomas, 9, 95–6
dictatorships *see* autocracies
Đilas, Milovan, 46
dirty hands problem, 67–9
distributed leadership, 8–9, 161, 199, 201, 240
double bind, the, 123
Douglas, Tommy, 211
Dowding, Keith, 22, 27, 32
Döring, Herbert, 83
Dumm, Thomas, 64
Duterte, Rodrigo, 238, 242
dynasties, 56, 108

E
Edel, Leon, 132
Eden, Anthony, 188–190, 197
elections, 40, 123, 124
elites, 42–6, 56, 71, 86–9, 99, 179, 201, 234–5
English, Bill, 35
Erdoğan, Recep Tayyip, 89
ethics
  character, 63–4
  consequentialist, 65–7, 72
  deontological, 66–7, 72–3
  and followers, 68–9, 71, 122
  and leadership, 62–73, 142–3, 187
ethos, 211–13
evolution
  and dominance, 103–4, 109
  and egalitarianism, 105
  and gender, 121–2
  and leadership traits 108–10
  of political systems, 110–12, 117
  and xenophobia, 106–7
evolutionary leadership theory, 104–5
executive government
  appointments to, 193, 196–7
  core executive, 192–3, 196
  leader domination of, 82–4, 85–6, 172, 192–3, 198, 232–4
  leading, 179–80, 193–4, 195–9, 202
  managing, 159–60, 163
  ministers of, 191, 196–7
  styles of, 193
  systems of, 58–9, 77, 80–1

F
false consciousness, 26
Fascism, 60, 78–9
Fayol, Henri, 11
feminism, 8, 102, 120–2, 127, 244–5
Ferraro, Geraldine, 124
Fiedler, Fred, 159–160
five factor model, 145–7
Follett, Mary Parker, 120
followers
  and apathy, 41
  and compromise, 226, 227, 239–40
  and crises, 105, 218, 219
  cultural expectations, 114–19
  evolved behaviours of, 104–8, 109–10
  gendered expectations, 121–3, 244–5
  and identity, 35, 139, 216–17, 246–7
  interests of, 8–10, 15–16, 23–6, 46, 104, 111–12, 113–14
  and morality, 68–9, 71
  needs of, 38, 42, 139, 158–61, 191, 247
  power of, 22–3, 38–9, 40, 46, 49–50
  psychology of, 34–5, 42, 43, 114, 136, 139, 217
  and trust, 33, 211–13, 235, 241–2
Fortuyn, Pim, 85, 235
Foucault, Michael, 61
Freud, Sigmund, 31, 131, 140
Friedrich III, 156

Fromm, Erich, 42
Fukuyama, Francis, 79

G
Gandhi, Indira, 124, 240
garbage can model, 203–4
Geertz, Clifford, 102
gender
 and ambition, 121–2
 and dominance, 120
 and language, 212–13
 and leadership, 102, 119–28, 246
 and leadership style, 122–7, 244–5
 and media bias, 123, 213
 and power, 102, 120
George, Alexander, 137
Gephardt, Dick, 71
Ghaemi, Nassir, 147
Gilgamesh, 1–2
Gillard, Julia, 94
going public, 225
Goldberg, Steven, 121
Gordon, Charles, 131
groupthink, 196–7
Guevara, Che, 247

H
Habermas, Jürgen, 67
Hamilton, Alexander, 59
Hatshepsut, 120
Heifetz, Roland, 159–60
Hermann, Margaret, 149–51, 153
heuristics, 6, 22, 183, 186
Hitler, Adolf, 10, 131–2
Hobbes, Thomas, 57–8
Hofstede, Geert, 115
Hoover, Herbert, 167
House, Robert, 160
hubris, 105, 152–3, 191
Hughes, Billy, 198
Hussein, Saddam, 51, 152–3
Hutcheson, Francis, 50

I
incrementalism, 203
inducement, 24, 29, 207
inferiority complex, 137, 152
inner circles, 23, 24, 192–4, 195–8
institutionalism, 132–3, 170–176
Isbester, Katherine, 238

J
Jackson, Andrew, 17, 167
James, William, 61, 246
Janis, Irving, 197
Johnson, Lyndon, 30, 149, 194, 247
Jordan, Barbara, 209
Jung, Carl, 114

K
Kádár, János, 174–5
kairos, 213
Kane, John, 9, 238, 240
Kant, Immanuel, 66–7, 71
Kekkonen, Urho, 32–3
Kennedy, John F., 30, 139, 143, 144, 149
Keynes, John Maynard, 166–7
Khaldūn, Ibn, 56–7
Khomeini, Ruhollah, 35
Kingdon, John, 165, 195–6
King, Martin Luther, 213, 247
Kok, Wim, 84–5
Kotter, John, 11

L
Lasswell, Harold, 130, 136
leaders
 as agents of change, 60–1, 94, 165–6, 167–71, 202
 character of, 63–4, 141
 and elites, 44–5, 46, 86–9, 168–9
 historical assessment of, 17, 54–5, 156–8, 169
 and media, 97, 212, 232–4
 motivations of, 16, 60, 110, 121–2, 132, 134–5, 136–9, 148–9, 152
 and political parties, 13–14, 113, 171–2
 and public image, 39, 64, 232–3
 as representatives, 68–9, 96, 139
 responsibility of, 69–71, 73
 restraints upon, 56, 57, 58–9, 96, 164–70, 171–6
 role of, 54–62, 94, 95–6, 178–9, 195
 self-interest of, 16, 51, 58
 and social identity, 139
 as symbols, 2, 9, 35, 113–14, 117, 127, 244–7
leadership
 and anarchy, 8, 61–2
 in animals, 103–4

authentic, 241, 242
collaborative, 79, 84–5, 86, 120, 115, 125, 164, 197, 240–3
and compromise, 225–7, 239–40
and crises, 34–5, 54, 55, 105, 147, 166, 167, 218
and culture, 110, 114–19
definitions of, 8–10, 12–14
and family, 121, 134–5, 136
heroic, 114, 156, 240–1
and history, 4, 54–5, 156–8, 166–71
and human nature, 3, 57, 59, 60, 106–8, 248
and law, 55, 56, 57, 65
and management, 11–12, 159–60
and morality, 4, 11, 16–17, 18–19, 60, 63–73
paradoxes of, 4, 67, 166, 184, 243, 248
performative, 64, 233–4, 240, 243
and pragmatism, 113
and stability, 57, 65, 99, 169
style, 148–51, 193–4, 198
succession, 89
traits, 108–10, 115, 118, 122–3, 130–1
and tyranny, 57–9

Lee Kuan Yew, 98–9, 243

legislatures
checks on, 58, 80–1, 172
and going public, 225, 233
and gridlock, 93–4, 239
leading, 13, 79, 83–4, 164, 218
and negotiation, 224–5
relative power of, 80–1, 171–2, 233
women in, 119–20

legitimacy, 31, 38, 39–40, 49–54, 61, 95–7, 243

Lenin, Vladimir, 133

Lijphart, Arend, 82

Lincoln, Abraham, 11, 147, 167, 247

Lindblom, Charles, 203

Lippmann, Walter, 9, 95–6

Little, Graham, 217

Locke, John, 50, 51–3, 58, 120

logos, 208–9

Lord, Carnes, 62

Lukes, Stephen, 25

Lumumba, Patrice, 216–17

M

Machel, Samora, 214–15

Machiavelli, Niccolò, 64–5, 122

Macmillan, Harold, 195

Madison, James, 59, 144

management, 11–12, 104, 120, 158–9, 161

mandates, 40, 167, 222

Mandela, Nelson, 206

manipulation, 25–6, 29, 198

many hands problem, 69–70, 73

March, James, 185, 203

Marcon, Emmanuel, 233

Maslow, James, 137

Mauroy, Pierre, 164

May, Rollo, 22

May, Theresa, 97

Mead, Margaret, 110

media
democratic role, 97, 194, 212
influence on leaders, 96, 125, 136, 142–3, 217, 232–4, 240
influence on public opinion, 29, 64, 157, 217, 240
influence on rhetoric, 199, 207, 213, 214–15, 240
social, 232–3, 246

Meir, Golda, 124, 180–1

Mencius, 63

Menon, V.P., 228–9

Menzies, Robert, 217

meritocracy, 43, 55, 99

Merkel, Angela, 123, 124

Michels, Robert, 43

Milgram, Stanley, 42

Millet, Kate, 102, 121

Mill, John Stuart, 50–1

Milošević, Slobodan, 106–7

mismatch hypothesis, 108, 186

Mitterrand, Francois, 164

Modi, Narendra, 233

Mollet, Guy, 188–90

monarchy *see* autocracies

Mondale, Walter, 209

Montesquieu, Baron de, 58–9, 76

moral authority, 30, 33–4, 39, 57, 63–4

moral disengagement, 70–1, 73

Morales, Evo, 215, 236–7, 246

morality *see* ethics

Morris, Dick, 97

Mudde, Cas, 235

Mugabe, Robert, 218
Mulroney, Brian, 123–4
Murray, Henry, 131–2
Mussolini, Benito, 141, 215

N

Nasser, Gamal Abdel, 188–90, 220–1
negotiation
  and bias, 226
  challenges in, 64, 83, 226–7, 239
  definition of, 222–3
  and emotion, 224
  need for, 81, 86, 147, 219, 222
  and power, 96, 125, 147
  satisficing in, 202
  tactics, 148, 159–60, 223–6
  types of, 222–3
Nehru, Jawaharlal, 176, 211
network leadership *see* distributed leadership
Nietzsche, Friedrich, 60–1
Nixon, Richard, 142–3, 144, 209
non-decisions, 180–1
Northouse, Peter, 8
Nyerere, Julius, 200–1

O

Obama, Barack, 93–4, 148–9, 170, 174, 219, 222, 246
Okin, Susan Moller, 121
Olson, Mancur, 41
opportunity structure, 165–6
Orbán, Viktor, 238, 242
Orešković, Tihomir, 14
Overton, Joseph, 164–5

P

Pareto, Vilfredo, 43
Parkinson, Cyril, 198
parliaments *see* legislatures
Patapan, Haig, 238, 240
Patel, Vallabhbhai, 228–9
Pateman, Carole, 120
path dependency, 173, 181
pathos, 209–11
patriarchy *see* feminism; gender
Perón, Juan and Eva, 36–7
personality
  agreeableness, 145–7
  ambition, 59, 121–2, 131, 138–9, 144
  confidence, 145, 186, 191, 221, 226
  contradictions in, 142–3
  depression, 187
  development, 134–5, 140–4
  extraversion, 145–6, 147
  and leadership style, 148–9
  narcissism, 131–2, 135, 140–1, 152–3
  traits, 108–10, 115, 118, 122–3, 130–1, 144–8
philosopher king, 55–6
Pinochet, Augusto, 215
Plato, 41, 55–6
Plutarch, 54, 130–1
polarization, 239–40, 241
policy
  agendas, 194–5, 203–4
  capacity, 89, 92, 200–1
  challenges for, 179, 182, 183–7, 199
  definition of, 179
  evaluation, 182, 202
  experimentation, 172, 175, 203, 204
  and gender, 124, 127, 244–5
  implementation, 14, 165, 179, 182, 199–201, 222
  moral responsibility, 69–70
  options, 164–5, 175, 179, 184–5, 191, 195–6, 199, 202–4
  paradigms, 166–7
  problem types, 159–60
  process, 182–3, 194–9, 202–4, 222
  stability, 165–6, 203
political advisers, 196
political anthropology, 110–14, 121, 179
political apathy, 41
political blame, 69–70, 187, 224
  See also accountability
political communication *see* rhetoric
political economy, 111–12
political gridlock, 93–4, 239
political obligation, 49–50
political parties
  competition between, 113
  leader domination of, 172, 232–4
  leading, 13–14, 113, 167, 171–2, 180–1, 201, 222, 237
  member input, 172, 203
  member values, 161, 164, 203
  multi-party systems, 80, 83, 84–5
  one-party systems, 78, 86–7, 88, 92–3
  platforms, 194–5

structures, 198, 237
two-party systems, 80, 83
politicians *see* leaders
polythink, 197
Popper, Karl, 56
populism, 62, 116, 234–9, 241
power
and authority, 22
checks on, 57, 58–9
definitions of, 21–2
faces of, 25
feminist perspectives of, 120–1
as motivation, 136–7, 138–9, 140–1, 144, 148–9, 152–3, 193
and persuasion, 21, 24–5
sharing, 164
use by leaders, 28–9, 65, 160, 193
will to, 60
presidentialism, 81
presidentialization, 232–4, 239
Preston, Thomas, 193–4
propaganda, 26, 218
prospect theory, 187
prudence, 16, 18–19, 176
psychoanalysis, 140–4, 152
psychobiography, 131–2, 134–5
psychology
archetypes, 114
of emotion, 141, 144, 187
of followers, 139
hierarchy of needs, 137–8
motivations, 136–9
political, 133–54
and sexuality, 140–1
of the unconscious, 140
psychosis, 131, 147
public consent, 49, 51–3, 58, 63
public good, the *see* public interest
public image, 39, 64
public interest, the, 9, 15, 52–3, 63, 64, 88, 95
public reason, 53–4
public will, 52, 56
punctuated equilibrium, 165–6

Q
Quayle, Dan, 212
Quintilian, 213

R
Raiffa, Howard, 226–7
Rankin, Jeannette, 68–9
rational choice model, 183–4
Rawls, John, 49, 53–4, 67
Reagan, Ronald, 124, 144, 167, 209
realpolitik, 65
Reich, William, 140
Renshon, Stanley, 137
revolutions, 87–8
rhetoric
and audiences, 208, 213, 214
and body language, 215
canons of, 213–16
definition of, 206–7
and emotion, 26, 208, 209–11, 221
and evidence, 208–9
and gender, 212–13
and moment, 213
and negotiation, 224–5
populist, 234–5
and symbolism, 113–14, 215
techniques of, 207–16, 220–1
uses of, 216–19
Rice, Condoleezza, 124
role congruity theory, 123
romance of leadership, 157
Roosevelt, Franklin Delano, 167, 234
Rosenberg, Shaun, 241–2
Rousseau, Jean-Jacques, 51–3, 58, 76
Rudd, Kevin, 12, 69–70
Ruscio, Kenneth, 79
Russell, Bertrand, 21

S
Sahlins, Marshall, 111–12
Sankara, Thomas, 90–1
Santos, Juan Manuel, 96–7
Sartori, Giovanni, 82
satisficing, 202–3
Scargill, Arthur, 28–9
Schjelderup-Ebbe, Thorleif, 103
Schumpeter, Joseph, 95–6
Seko, Mobutu Sese, 92
Selassie, Haile, 44–5
selectorates, 171–2
semi-presidentialism, 81
separation of powers, 57–8, 76
Service, Elman, 112
service-for-prestige, 104
Shinawatra, Thaksin, 46
Simmel, Georg, 42
Simon, Herbert, 184–5, 202
Sirleaf, Ellen Johnson, 246

situational leadership model, 158–9
Skowronek, Stephen, 166–70
social contract, 52, 99, 120
Spencer, Herbert, 156
Stalin, Joseph, 65
Stogdill, Ralph, 3, 109–10, 145, 158
Stone, Deborah, 184
Strachey, Lytton, 131
Suetonius, 130
Suharto, 18–19

T
tacit consent, 41
Taleb, Nicholas Nassim, 231–2
Thatcher, Margaret, 17, 28–9, 109, 124, 195
theocracy *see* autocracies
Thompson, Dennis, 69–70
Tolstoy, Leo, 156
totalitarianism, 61, 78–9
trait approach, 144–5
transactional leadership, 113, 148
transformational leadership, 148
Truman, Harry, 72–3, 178, 182
Trump, Donald, 1, 5, 132, 148–9, 217–18, 233, 235
Tsebelis, George, 83, 86
Tsipras, Alexis, 33–4
Tsvangirai, Morgan, 239–40
Turnbull, Malcolm, 94
Tusk, Donald, 86
tyranny, 57, 59, 74, 76, 108

U
übermensch, 60
utilitarianism, 50–1, 65–6

V
Valerian, 38
Van Rompuy, Herman, 86
Van Zuydam, Sabine, 39
veto players, 83, 85, 86, 93, 94, 173
Vetter, Lisa Pace, 120
virtue *see* ethics

W
Waldron, Jeremy, 51
Wallas, Graham, 133
Walzer, Michael, 67–9
Wałęsa, Lech, 162–3
Weber, Max, 30, 31, 34, 39, 196
Westminster system, 80, 83, 192–3
wicked problems, 199
Wilberforce, William, 210
Wildavsky, Aaron, 132, 199
Willhoite, Fred, 104
Wilson, Edward O., 102
Wilson, James Q., 210
Wilson, Woodrow, 137, 144
Winter, David, 138–9, 153
Wolff, Robert Paul, 50
Wovoka, 105

X
Xiaoping, Deng, 172–3

Z
Zedong, Mao, 218
zero-sum game, 222–3
Ziyang, Zhao, 137
zone of possible agreement, 222, 239
Zuma, Jacob, 71